John Wyclif was the fourteenth-century English thinker responsible for the first English Bible, and for the Lollard movement which was widely persecuted for its attempts to reform the church through empowerment of the laity. His political thought was framed in terms of *dominium*, a term which had developed theological papalist connotations, yet which in Wyclif's *Summa Theologie* involved a decidedly anti-papal programme for the English church in which the king's responsibility to God entailed divestment of ecclesiastical secular authority.

Many twentieth-century scholars argued that Wyclif had appropriated his *dominium* discourse to advance further his reformative programme, assuming that the philosophical treatises produced by Wyclif during his Oxford years have no causal bearing upon the *dominium* treatises of the *Summa Theologie*. This book argues that Wyclif's *dominium* relies upon his realist metaphysics, and that his programme of reform follows upon his relation of the universal divine *dominium* to all instances of just created *dominium*. This offers a new approach to Wyclif's career, in which his turn from theoretical to practical issues coheres with the philosophically rich theological vision of his earlier works, including the major treatises of the *Summa de Ente*.

STEPHEN E. LAHEY is Assistant Professor of Philosophy, Le Moyne College, Syracuse, New York

Cambridge Studies in Medieval Life and Thought

PHILOSOPHY AND POLITICS
IN THE THOUGHT OF JOHN WYCLIF

Cambridge Studies in Medieval Life and Thought
Fourth Series

General Editor:

D.E. LUSCOMBE

Research Professor of Medieval History, University of Sheffield

Advisory Editors:

CHRISTINE CARPENTER

Reader in Medieval English History, University of Cambridge, and Fellow of New Hall

ROSAMOND MCKITTERICK

Professor of Medieval History, University of Cambridge, and Fellow of
Newnham College

The series Cambridge Studies in Medieval Life and Thought was inaugurated by G. G. Coulton in 1921; Professor D. E. Luscombe now acts as General Editor of the Fourth Series, with Dr Christine Carpenter and Professor Rosamond McKitterick as Advisory Editors. The series brings together outstanding work by medieval scholars over a wide range of human endeavour extending from political economy to the history of ideas.

For a list of titles in the series, see end of book.

PHILOSOPHY AND POLITICS IN THE THOUGHT OF JOHN WYCLIF

STEPHEN E. LAHEY

CAMBRIDGE
UNIVERSITY PRESS

PUBLISHED BY THE PRESS SYNDICATE OF THE UNIVERSITY OF CAMBRIDGE
The Pitt Building, Trumpington Street, Cambridge, United Kingdom

CAMBRIDGE UNIVERSITY PRESS
The Edinburgh Building, Cambridge, CB2 2RU, UK
40 West 20th Street, New York, NY 10011-4211, USA
477 Williamstown Road, Port Melbourne, VIC 3207, Australia
Ruiz de Alarcón 13, 28014 Madrid, Spain
Dock House, The Waterfront, Cape Town 8001, South Africa

http://www.cambridge.org

First published 2003

Printed in the United Kingdom at the University Press, Cambridge

Typeface Bembo 11/12 pt   *System* LATEX 2$_\varepsilon$ [TB]

A catalogue record for this book is available from the British Library

ISBN 0 521 63346 X

CONTENTS

vii

ACKNOWLEDGEMENTS

It is a pleasure to express my gratitude to all who have contributed to what began as a dissertation and has evolved into this study of a crucial aspect of Wyclif's thought from 1369 to 1379. The University of Connecticut's Graduate School, Philosophy Department, and Medieval Studies Program each generously provided funds during the first stage of this work, and LeMoyne College's Research and Development Committee did the same for the final stage. I am grateful to the Dean of the Graduate School at the University of Nebraska for providing me with a Visiting Assistant Professorship for the academic year 1998–99, which allowed me to continue during the final stage. I am also indebted to the staffs at the Homer Babbidge Library, and the Noreen Reale Falcone Library for their patience and assistance with numerous Interlibrary Loans.

Many have listened carefully and patiently to my thoughts and questions about John Wyclif, and I am grateful for all the wisdom they have offered. If I have succeeded in making sense of Wyclif's thought, it is thanks to their guidance, insight, and support. Among my teachers and colleagues in philosophy, I would like especially to thank the Philosophy faculties at the University of Connecticut, and at LeMoyne College, especially Crawford Elder, Samuel Wheeler, Don Baxter, Charles Kelly, Mario Saenz, Robert Flower, Michael Kagan, Bill Day, and Karmen MacKendrick. I am deeply indebted to the University of Connecticut's Medieval Studies faculty and graduate students as well, particularly to Robert Hasenfratz, Sherri Olson, C. David Benson, Fred Cazel, and the late Charles Owen. Andrew Beedle, Matthew Berry, and Rob Hirschfeld have also helped me immeasurably over the years I have spent on this project. I have regularly given talks on Wyclif's thought at several annual conferences, at Villanova University, and at the Medieval Institute's International Congress at Western Michigan University, where many medievalists have offered truly valuable assistance. I am grateful to Cary J. Nederman, Takashi Shogimen, The Lollard Society, Christopher Fee, Bonnie Kent, Stephen Brown, Calvin Normore, and Marcia Colish, among many others.

Acknowledgements

The fraternity of Wyclif scholars has been especially supportive of my research, and I owe a great debt to Anne Hudson, Sir Anthony Kenny, Christina Van Nolcken, Ian Levy, Alessandro Conti, Paul Spade, and the late Norman Kretzman for their interest in, and suggestions for, my work. I am especially indebted to the late Michael Wilks, whose letters containing ideas, observations, and insight into Wyclif's political thought contributed importantly to this project. I would like also to thank Paul A. Streveler, who introduced me to the study of medieval philosophy at West Chester University, and Fiona Somerset, whose understanding of Wycliffite texts helped me to avoid considerable embarassment in this work's Conclusion.

Two scholars have devoted time, energy, and their considerable talents to the maturation and completion of this study, and to them I owe a debt of gratitude greater than any other. Arthur Stephen McGrade introduced me to John Wyclif, and guided me through the labyrinth of late medieval philosophical and theological dialogue as he helped me to turn what was initially a fuzzy idea into a full-fledged doctoral dissertation. David Luscombe's sensitivity to historical and textual accuracy, patience with translations, and unflagging willingness to assist in uncovering Wyclif's thought has made him an editor greater than which I cannot imagine. I am indebted to both for their encouragement, learning, and warm guidance; what is valuable in this work is their doing, and the shortcomings are mine. Finally, my dedication of this book to her is the most modest evidence of my gratitude for the constant support of my friend and partner, Julia McQuillan.

ABBREVIATIONS

CCSL	Corpus Christianorum Series Latina
DCD	*De Civili Dominio*
DCH	*De Composicione Hominis*
DD	*De Dominio Divino*
DEP	*De Ente Predicamentali*
DOR	*De Officio Regis*
EETS	Early English Text Society
OS	(Original Series)
ES	(Extra Series)
JEH	*Journal of Ecclesiastical History*
Parma	*Sancti Thomae Aquinatis Doctoris Angelici Ordinis Predicatorum Opera omnia*, 25 vols., Parma, 1852–72; rpt. 25 New York, 1948–50
PL	*Patrologiae: Cursus Completus Latina*, ed. J. P. Migne, Paris, 1844–73
SCH	*Studies in Church History*
TDU	*Tractatus De Universalibus*

Chapter 1

THE HISTORIOGRAPHY OF WYCLIF'S
DOMINIUM THOUGHT

In 1377, John Wyclif had need of powerful political support. He had been summoned to Saint Paul's by Archbishop Sudbury to account for heretical arguments threatening to the foundations of the church in England. So on February 19, Wyclif appeared at the arraignment with John of Gaunt, Duke of Lancaster and arguably the most powerful man in the kingdom. Wyclif, once an Oxford metaphysician, had become an associate of John of Gaunt two years earlier, and had begun arguing for the reduction of the church's political influence and her material wealth shortly thereafter. Gaunt was, and still is, widely believed to be eager to supplement his political power at the expense of the church, and Thomas Walsingham encourages us to believe that Gaunt's support of Wyclif that February afternoon was that of a patron for his valued servant.[1]

Had Gaunt been self-interestedly using Wyclif as his polemicist, he had made an odd choice. Wyclif's arguments for the absolute power of the king were framed neither in the theocratic kingship language of the Anglo-Saxon and Anglo-Norman tradition, nor were they couched in the more contemporary Aristotelian terms favored by other champions of secular authority.[2] On the contrary, Wyclif used language that had, until then, usually been employed by papally sponsored churchmen. His arguments were framed in terms of Grace-founded *dominium*, redolent of Archbishop Richard Fitzralph's defense of ecclesiastical property-ownership.[3] Talk of Grace as the true source of earthly justice was part of an established Augustinian tradition in England that had its immediate foundation in

---

[1] Thomas Walsingham, *Chronicon Angliae*, ed. E. M. Thompson, Rolls Series 64 (London, 1874), p. 115; Walsingham, *Historia Anglicana*, ed. H. T. Riley, 20, Rerum Britannicarum Medii Aevi Scriptores R S 28 (London, 1862), vol. 1, pp. 324–5. See also Herbert Workman, *John Wyclif: A Study of the English Medieval Church* (Oxford, 1926), vol. 1, pp. 284 –93; and Joseph Dahmus, *The Prosecution of John Wyclyf* (New Haven, 1952), pp. 7–34.

[2] For the earlier, Christ-founded English tradition, see E. Kantorowicz, *The King's Two Bodies* (Princeton, 1957), pp. 42–61; and Janet Nelson, "Kingship and Empire," in *The Cambridge History of Medieval Political Thought 350–1450*, ed. J. H. Burns (Cambridge, 1988), pp. 239–42.

[3] See Katherine Walsh, *A Fourteenth-Century Scholar and Primate: Richard Fitzralph in Oxford, Avignon and Armagh* (Oxford, 1981).

the papal hierocratic thought of Giles of Rome.[4] While Wyclif's clerical opponents might have labored to refute Aristotelian arguments similar to those of John of Paris or Marsilius of Padua, dealing with terms that most English churchmen held dear to their hearts would not be difficult. Wyclif made it easier by using *dominium* to refer both to *proprietas*, which had been its chief reference in Fitzralph's thought, as well as to *iurisdictio*, which canonists had long since ceased to see as necessarily dominative.

Joseph Dahmus effectively argues that Gaunt was doing nothing more than providing support for a loyal servant of the Crown, suggesting that contemporary chroniclers' and more recent scholars' antipathy for Gaunt motivates the popular impression that Wyclif constructed his arguments on the duke's behalf.[5] What remains unresolved is why Oxford's most eminent philosopher would suddenly turn away from metaphysics and risk all by putting forth dangerous, possibly heretical, arguments about the present state of the church. Recent scholarship has suggested that Wyclif's motives were political, or that they were theologically founded, as was the Mertonian Bradwardine's anti-Pelagian *De Causa Dei* a generation earlier.[6] Wyclif's own account is not terribly helpful, for his only explicit reference to the shift of his attention is to note that he felt it was time to introduce practically applicable issues to his theoretical pursuits.[7]

One way to understand Wyclif's interest in practical matters is to discover why *dominium* had captured his attention, for he makes occasional reference to it in his *Tractatus de Universalibus*, the last of his expressly metaphysical treatises. Why Wyclif used *dominium* as the concept central to his political writing has not been addressed. Given the English Augustinian tradition's century-old association with Grace-founded *dominium*, it is sensible to wonder what prompted Wyclif to appropriate it for his own, apparently unorthodox, purposes. If there were significant grounds for Wyclif's use of the concept in his earlier, more traditionally scholastic thought, we might be able to understand better the place of *dominium* in his political thought.

If the goal is to see why Wyclif appropriated Grace-founded *dominium* as the concept to wield in his political writings, it is tempting to suppose

---

[4] A. Gwynn, *The English Austin Friars in the Time of Wyclif* (Oxford, 1940); W. A. Pantin, *The English Church in the Fourteenth Century* (Cambridge, 1955).

[5] Dahmus, *The Prosecution of John Wyclyf*, p. 19. For a discussion of John of Gaunt's tendency to lend his support to those in his service in need of it, see Simon Walker, *The Lancastrian Affinity 1361–1399* (Oxford, 1990), pp. 94–116.

[6] For discussion of recent scholarship, see below, pp. 10–23. See Thomas Bradwardine, *De Causa Dei contra Pelagium et De Virtute Causarum*, ed. H. Saville (London, 1618), I.35.308C.

[7] "[T]empus est mihi per totum residuum vite mee tam speculative quam practice, secundum mensuram quam Deus donaverit, inniti virtutibus, ut sic salubrius discam mori." *De Dominio Divino*, ed. R. L. Poole (London, 1890), Incipit, 1.6–8.

that his aim was to hoist the papacy and its supporters with their own petard. But this raises more problems than it answers, for it suggests that Wyclif, a priest and theologian, would subvert his theology by using it for mundane ends, namely the glorification of secular power. This casts a doubtful aura on all of his later works, which were devoted to expressly theological issues. Secondly, this answer avoids the difficulty of the question of how *dominium* can involve both *proprietas* and *iurisdictio* by explaining it all as so much cynical political maneuvering. This is unsettling, because Wyclif's use of the term *dominium* is recognizably in line with, and to a degree founded in, Fitzralph's in *De Pauperie Salvatoris*. Fitzralph's position is a mixture of Augustinian theology, hierocratic papal theory, canon law, and Aristotelian political thought designed to show that the Franciscans could not rightly claim to practice apostolic poverty without relying on the church's material *dominium*. Are we to suppose that an accomplished metaphysician and theologian took this position and used it to his own private ends, without paying serious attention to the philosophical consequences of doing so? And if he did this, why did Wyclif devote such care to the relationship of Creator to Creation in *De Dominio Divino*, going so far as to make his metaphysical realism, as it appears in the *Tractatus de Universalibus*, consonant with it?

To understand why Wyclif characterized his union of theological and political thought in terms of a *dominium* that combined both *proprietas* and *iurisdictio*, we must do several things. First, we should ask whether other philosophers before him had done this. We have already mentioned that Fitzralph framed his thought in these terms; tracing the development of the tendency to frame political discourse in this specific theological language will better prepare us to argue that Wyclif was doing more than trying to make a name for himself among monarchists. Second, we should look carefully at the substance and argument of both *De Dominio Divino* and *De Civili Dominio*. What aspects of each of these works unite the two, and what aspects refer back to his metaphysics? Can we use Wyclif's metaphysical and theological language to explain his political thought as a coherent realization of his philosophical program?

Wyclif was a confirmed realist about universals, believing that individual created beings have their reality by virtue of the prior being of universals. He wrote the *dominium* treatises shortly after having finished writing *Tractatus de Universalibus*, his clearest explanation of the reality of universals. Are there sufficient grounds for holding that he believed the divine *dominium* relation functions as a universal, from which individual instances of just human *dominium* derive their reality? If sufficient grounds for this argument exist, it is reasonable to suppose that Wyclif would have been aware of the possibility of his educated readers recognizing

3

this structure, and understanding the argument of *De Civili Dominio* as a practical articulation of his realism. This would mean that his radical conclusions, including the need for a strong, Grace-favored civil lord or king to reduce the office-holders of the church to Christ-like poverty, were evident as wholly consistent with a realism evocative of Augustine's own thought.

To show this, we must look at *dominium* as Wyclif does, as the relation between Creator and Creation most expressive of the on-going governance and maintenance God provides for his creatures. We will examine the definition of *dominium* Wyclif provides in *De Dominio Divino* as founded in his metaphysics, and as it plays out in his thought on how men ought to live together. Next, we shall look at the *dominium* described in *De Civili Dominio* as a concept entailing both private ownership and political jurisdiction. If these two issues are explicable as articulations of Wyclif's realism by contributing to the conception of *dominium* as a clear causal connection between divine and just human *dominium*, it is difficult to avoid concluding that his conception of just human *dominium* is related to God's *dominium* as is a particular to a universal. This will show how unfounded are the charges that Wyclif's political writings are philosophically unrelated to his metaphysics, that they are monarchist apologetics, motivated primarily by events that occurred in his life. It will also provide a framework with which to approach the texts themselves. Philosophers will be able to understand how the last of the great English schoolmen viewed the relation of *theoria* to *praxis*, and will have the opportunity to see how holding a unique metaphysical realism about universals can lead to social conclusions not usually associated with metaphysics. Medievalists of all stripes will thus be able to understand the intellectual tenor of Oxford's last great light of the age, and they will be free to interpret Lollardy and the Hussite movement in the terms set and defined by the two movements' progenitor.

Some efforts to explain Wyclif's thought on *dominium* as it is expressed in *De Dominio Divino* and *De Civili Dominio* have been colored by desires to have it cohere with his later, more explicitly polemical writing. Rather than study these works to see how they fit in the body of Wyclif's work, this study will examine them for their philosophical content and reliance on his earlier metaphysics. While it will show that these two works are founded in Wyclif's realism as it appears in the *Tractatus de Universalibus*, this study is not meant to suggest that the *dominium* treatises make up a part of the broader, theological program established in the *Summa Theologie*.[8]

---

[8] Wyclif's two chief Latin works are the *Summa de Ente* and the *Summa Theologie*. The *Summa de Ente* includes most of his metaphysical works, including the *Tractatus de Universalibus*, and was

Peter Brown has suggested, regarding Augustine's thought on religious coercion, that we cease looking for one set doctrine, and instead be open to the shifts and developments in positions characteristic of an active thinker.[9] This might prove a more useful way of handling Wyclif's thought on *dominium* with regard to the bulk of his writings, for it figures as something more than what we now consider to be political theory, while more practically orientated than straight theology.

This chapter will serve as an overture in which we briefly survey the scholarship relating to Wyclif's political thought, beginning with analysis of the scholars responsible for introducing him to twentieth-century eyes. As the study of the history of medieval philosophy has grown more philosophically sophisticated, some thinkers like Wyclif have received less attention than the complexity and theological innovation of their work deserve. The reasons for this vary, ranging from a vested institutional interest in more theologically orthodox thinkers to the relative absence of edited versions of later fourteenth-century philosophical texts. Most twentieth-century scholars of Wyclif's thought have concluded that his metaphysics has no bearing on his *dominium* treatises. It will be best if we lay out their conclusions and their reasoning, not only to give us a starting point for our own discussion, but also to show how contemporary historians of thought have approached Wyclif's philosophy.

Following this introduction, we will assess the influence of several figures whose ideas were influential on Wyclif's realism, or on his political thought, or on both, including Augustine, Thomas Aquinas, Giles of Rome, and Archbishop Richard Fitzralph. This discussion will outline Wyclif's place in the philosophical dialogue, and provide a perspective from which to understand specific aspects of Wyclif's theory. In the third chapter we will recount the argument of *De Dominio Divino*, both as a carefully articulated piece of philosophy in its own right, as it is related to the earlier *Tractatus de Universalibus*, and as it will relate to *De Civili Dominio*. Here we will examine how the realism articulated in *De Universalibus* is borne out in Wyclif's conception of God's *dominium* over Creation and its relation to just *dominium* in Creation. Understanding how the determinist metaphysics of *De Universalibus* relates theologically and

written while Wyclif was in Oxford, between 1365 and 1372. Williel Thomson describes the *Summa Theologie* as an "extended dissection of the leading religious and political problems of his day, seen through the lens of an Augustinian realist." *De Civili Dominio* and related ecclesiastical and social writings comprise the early treatises of this *Summa*, which was written between 1375 and 1381. While *De Dominio Divino* is not included in the *Summa Theologie*, having been written just after Wyclif completed the *Summa de Ente*, it serves as the beginning point for this *Summa's* arguments. See Williel Thomson, *The Latin Writings of John Wyclyf* (Toronto, 1983), pp. 18–88.

[9] Peter Brown, "St. Augustine's Attitude to Religious Coercion," *Journal of Roman Studies*, 54 (1964), p. 107.

philosophically to his *dominium* thought is also important, for at least one scholar has argued that Wyclif's political agenda is unrealizable because of it.[10] Accordingly, we will examine both the foundation of Wyclif's determinism and its implications for his thought on *dominium*. Finally, we will look at other treatises of Wyclif's *Summa Theologie* contemporary with the two *dominium* treatises, notably *De Statu Innocencie* and *De Mandatis Divinis*, insofar as they are useful in helping us to unravel the arguments of the two principal works in question.

At this point, we will be set to explore Wyclif's thought regarding just human *dominium* as expressed in *De Civili Dominio* and also in the related work *De Officio Regis*. We will look first, in a fourth chapter, at what Wyclif says about the institution of private ownership in postlapsarian society, for this topic directs his thought on kingship as such. Wyclif devotes half of *De Civili Dominio* to explaining his thought about the evils of private ownership for members of Christ's body on earth, and the other half to explaining why it is important that just civil lords, owners of large amounts of property, should be Grace-favored, and how they should relieve the church of its material burdens. Wyclif believes Grace should function as a precondition of just private ownership, and that private ownership is a sin-stained perversion of the communal state of Eden, and resolving this apparent contradiction is necessary to a complete understanding of his thought on *dominium*. Further, Wyclif's concept of private ownership has direct bearing on our understanding of his later works, most importantly *De Ecclesia*, which was to be particularly influential in the Hussite movement.

This done, we will be ready to analyze in a fifth chapter Wyclif's picture of the duties and nature of civil *dominium*, which is functionally equivalent to kingship. His description of a monarch who must serve and protect his realm as well as the church therein has all the trappings of monarchic absolutism. But Wyclif's picture of kingship has Christian *caritas* as its chief characteristic; we will see how this is related to his thought on Grace as a precondition for just civil *dominium*. Consequently, it will be evident that this conception of the lord–subject relation is indicative of his view of the way that just human *dominium* functions as an instantiation of divine *dominium*. Thus, we will have discussed civil *dominium* in terms of *proprietas* and *iurisdictio*, and we will see how Wyclif believed these two concepts to be necessarily connected.

In a final chapter we will be set to conclude by showing how Wyclif's joint conception of private ownership and political power in just civil *dominium* depends upon his thought on divine *dominium*, which, in turn,

---

[10] Gordon Leff, *Heresy in the Later Middle Ages* (New York, 1967).

is explicable only in terms of his metaphysical realism. This will allow us to characterize the status of divine *dominium* as being a universal in which all instances of just human *dominium* participate as instantiations in terms fully compatible with Wyclif's definitions. Many students of England in the later Middle Ages have had to come to grips with the phenomenon of Lollardy. A careful examination of Wyclif's *dominium* treatises will allow us to make some headway in two important aspects of the study of this unique heresy. First, we shall be able to analyze the validity of the following hypothetical syllogism:

(a) If one adheres to a Wycliffite realist metaphysics, one can coherently adhere to the social/political conclusions of the *dominium* treatises.
(b) If one coherently adheres to the social/political conclusions of the *dominium* treatises, one can consistently embrace the political notions of early Lollardy.

Therefore, if one adheres to a Wycliffite realist metaphysics, one can coherently embrace the political notions of early Lollardy.

This does not mean that all Lollards were metaphysical realists, nor that all Lollards had read the *dominium* treatises. But it does point to a potential causal relationship between metaphysics and a *praxis*-oriented movement that would imply that modern scholars have been premature in their assessments of the relevance of Wyclif's metaphysics to his later thought.

MEDIEVAL POLITICAL THEORY'S RELATION TO SCHOLASTIC METAPHYSICS

An important element in the scholarship concerning medieval political thought has been the understanding of its relation to medieval metaphysics. Martin Grabmann's 1934 characterization of the relation of a philosopher's respective Augustinianism or Aristotelianism to his respective papalism or monarchism served as a landmark in this study.[11] He argued that political philosophers who advocated the supremacy of faith tended towards papalism, and those who desired to strike a balance between faith and reason generally favored a Thomistic Aristotelian compromise between monarchy and papacy, while those who saw reason as autonomous supported a lay monarchy founded on the consent of the governed. Grabmann divided philosophers who wrote on recognizably political issues into Augustinian hierocratic theorists, Thomistic

[11] Martin Grabmann, *Studien über den Einfluss der aristotelischen Philosophie auf die mittelalterlichen Theorien über das Verhältnis von Kirche und Staat*, Sitzungsberichte der bayrischen Akademie der wissenschaften, Phil.-Hist. Abteilung, Heft 2 (Munich, 1934).

Aristotelians, and Averroist Aristotelians. In the first group he includes Guido Vernani, Ptolemy of Lucca, Augustinus Triumphus, Giles of Rome, and James of Viterbo.[12] In the next, he includes Aquinas and John of Paris.[13] And in the group advocating reason's autonomy he includes Marsilius of Padua and William Ockham.[14] It is not hard to see a certain tendency: the Aristotelians tend towards monarchism, while the Augustinians tend towards papalism.

The most fully developed response to Grabmann's approach appeared in Alan Gewirth's "Philosophy and Political Thought in the Fourteenth Century."[15] He argues that it is simplistic to line up realists with extreme papal sovereignty and hierocratic theory, and nominalists with monarchism, and moderate realists with a "two spheres" argument.[16] Gewirth agrees that Wyclif belongs in the Augustinian political tradition, and recognizes his reliance on Giles' hierocratic thinking, but points out that Wyclif's conclusions are an equally Augustinian species of anti-hierocratic reasoning. Gewirth is not arguing that no connection exists between philosophy and practical politics, only that agreement in practical politics does not necessarily entail a correlative agreement in metaphysics. He suggests that Wyclif and Marsilius of Padua, though certainly in agreement regarding several desired political outcomes, can by no means be said to share the same values.[17] Gewirth argues that historical conditions warrant careful consideration in any attempt to relate philosophical doctrine with political program, and that one cannot suppose either metaphysics or political theory to be so open to correlativity as to allow adherence to one sort of belief to dictate adherence to another. In some thinkers, theoretical and practical philosophy were arguably correlative, while in others such an argument is bound to involve stretching the truth to the breaking point. It is best, Gewirth suggests, to take it on a case-by-case basis.

Michael Wilks' *The Problem of Sovereignty in the Later Middle Ages* effectively supports Grabmann's thesis that a tendency towards metaphysical realism was directly proportional to a tendency towards the papal hierocratic position.[18] Wilks suggests that Grabmann's approach is useful in illustrating how medieval positions on universals had real political implications, leading one to recognize the social import of the scholastic metaphysical disputes. Adherence to realism means recognizing that the

---

[12] *Ibid.*, pp. 61–129.   [13] *Ibid.*, pp. 8–40.   [14] *Ibid.*, pp. 41–60.

[15] Alan Gewirth, "Philosophy and Political Thought in the Fourteenth Century," in *The Forward Movement of the Fourteenth Century*, ed. F. L. Utley (Columbus, OH, 1961), pp. 125–64.

[16] *Ibid.*, p. 134.   [17] *Ibid.*, p. 141.

[18] Michael Wilks, *The Problem of Sovereignty in the Later Middle Ages* (Cambridge, 1963), p. 17, also p. 84.

church is an Augustinian whole more important than its members.[19] Accordingly, we would assume that Wyclif's political thought and his earlier metaphysics were either unconnected, or that one of the two projects was not in earnest, for Wyclif is at once a realist about universals and an anti-hierocratic, ecclesiastically reforming monarchist. B. Wilkinson refers to Wyclif as an extremist in matters of religious reform while a political moderate; can one reconcile this with his earlier, hearty realism about universals?[20] Wilks believed that one could, and set about addressing this problem. In so doing he set the tone for further discussion of the relation of Wyclif's Oxford metaphysics of the *Summa de Ente* to the political and reformist thought of the *Summa Theologie*.

Charles Zuckerman rightly points out that regarding the church as a universal of some sort is not commensurate with the medieval view of the church's nature.[21] Zuckerman suggests that Wilks' intuition, based on Grabmann and Otto von Gierke, is not wholly ill-founded; many of the important positions regarding the place of the church in the world were formulated by philosophers who had well-developed metaphysical standpoints, and it would be natural to look for some sort of connection. Better, though, to look to other possible explanations for the political opinions of these philosophers, for it is as likely that they formulated their ecclesiological thought for political reasons as for ontological ones.[22] Wyclif's case will allow for at least one instance of such a connection, but the universal in question is not the church, but divine *dominium* itself.[23]

A CENTURY OF WYCLIF SCHOLARSHIP

An outline of the chronology of Wyclif's Latin works will be useful in gaining fuller appreciation of the assessments of Wyclif scholars of the relations between the treatises. We are aware of ten expressly philosophical treatises that Wyclif wrote between 1360 and 1372, including three logical works (*De Logica, Logice Continuacio,* and *De Logica Tractatus Tercius*) and

---

[19] *Ibid.*, p. 21.
[20] Cited in L. J. Daly's "Wyclif's Political Theory: A Century of Study," *Medievalia et Humanistica*, 4 (1973), p. 183; see B. Wilkinson, *Constitutional History of England 1216–1399*, 3 vols. (London, 1948–58), vol. 3, pp. 92–4.
[21] Charles Zuckerman, "The Relationship of Theories of Universals to Theories of Church Government in the Middle Ages: A Critique of Previous Views," *Journal of the History of Ideas*, 35 (1975), pp. 579–94, here pp. 591–2.
[22] *Ibid.*, p. 594.
[23] Zuckerman notes Wilks' argument that Wyclif's monarchism is evidence of the possibility of his conversion from realism to nominalism (which I will examine below), and pays little attention to Wyclif thereafter. cf. *ibid.*, p. 585, n. 12.

seven metaphysical works, which include the massive *Summa de Ente* and the *Tractatus de Universalibus*.[24] In 1373 he wrote *De Dominio Divino*, which served as the beginning point for the *Summa Theologie*, which he began in 1375 and ceased work on in 1381. In this latter *Summa* are his politically and ecclesiastically reformative works, as well as treatises on scriptural interpretation and the Eucharist. We will examine the earlier works of the *Summa Theologie*, including *De Mandatis Divinis* (early 1376), *De Statu Innocencie* (mid-1376), *De Civili Dominio* (1375–76), *De Ecclesia* (1378–79), and *De Officio Regis* (mid-1379).[25]

The end of the nineteenth century saw a rebirth in interest in Wyclif's thought, and most of the Latin works now available were edited by the now-defunct Wyclif Society. The first important piece of modern Wyclif scholarship was G. V. Lechler's *Johann Wyclif und die Vorgeschichte der Reformation*, which contributed most in its biographical sketch of Wyclif.[26] R. L. Poole, later the editor of *De Divino Dominio* and of several volumes of *De Civili Dominio*, laid the groundwork for the Grace-founded *dominium* reading of Wyclif's political thought in two works, *Illustrations of the History of Medieval Thought and Learning*, and *Wycliffe and Movements for Reform*.[27] In neither does Poole consider there to be an important connection between Wyclif's metaphysics and his political thought; Poole's contribution is his understanding of the relation of Fitzralph's *De Pauperie Salvatoris* to Wyclif's thought, and of the importance of *dominium* in Wyclif's *Summa Theologie*. Johann Loserth's "The Beginnings of Wyclif's Activity in Ecclesiastical Politics" did much to found the contemporary belief among Wyclif scholars that ecclesiastically reformative concerns were absent from Wyclif's mind before 1376.[28] Another contribution to the general scholarly attitude towards Wyclif's political thought was made in C. H. McIlwain's *Growth of Political Thought in the West*. Perhaps following Poole's lead, McIlwain dismisses Wyclif's originality and relevance

---

[24] See Thomson, *The Latin Writings of John Wyclyf*, pp. 1–39, for dating, manuscript description, and bibliographical information.

[25] See Thomson, *The Latin Writings of John Wyclyf*, pp. 39–62.

[26] G. V. Lechler, *Johann Wyclif und die Vorgeschichte der Reformation*, 2 Vols. (Leipzig, 1873); translated and abridged by Peter Loruner as *John Wycliffe and his English Precursors* (London, 1873). Lechler's characterization of Wyclif's philosophy is heavily reliant on *Trialogus*, evidence of the need for the editions provided by the Wyclif Society. See also Daly, "Wyclif's Political Theory: A Century of Study," pp. 177–87. John Lewis' earlier *The History of the Life and Sufferings of the Reverend and Learned John Wiclif, D.D.* (Oxford, 1820) was meant to counter then-current Roman Catholic partisan histories in which Wyclif was dismissed, along with Hus and Jerome of Prague, as a "pretended Reformer."

[27] R. L. Poole, *Illustrations of the History of Medieval Thought and Learning* (London, 1884), and *Wycliffe and Movements for Reform* (London, 1902).

[28] Johann Loserth, "The Beginnings of Wyclif's Activity in Ecclesiastical Politics," *English Historical Review*, 11 (April 1896); cf. L. J. Daly, *The Political Theory of John Wyclif* (Chicago, 1962), pp. 177–8.

in understanding the developments of late fourteenth-century political thought.[29]

Wyclif's chief biographer is H. B. Workman, who believed that his thought on *dominium* as expressed in *De Dominio Divino* and *De Civili Dominio* was the culmination of several years of thinking, the formulation of which led naturally to closer attention to ecclesiastical matters.[30] He warns that one should avoid supposing Wyclif to have written political theory to provide "programmes of actual reconstruction," advising us to read him as we might read Plato or More. Did Wyclif seriously suppose his works would involve a radical up-turning of social order? Workman thinks not, believing the metaphysics undergirding *De Civili Dominio* to be what really interested its writer.[31] Workman's assessment of Wyclif's *dominium* treatises is colored by his belief that much of *De Dominio Divino* has been lost, and his picture of civil *dominium* is brief, serving only to show why Wyclif's ecclesiastical audience reacted the way they did. His discussion of *De Officio Regis* follows directly on a recounting of the major points of *De Ecclesia*, and neglects the ties linking the former to the works specifically about *dominium*.

Although a sustained review of the scholarship concerning Wyclif's metaphysics is not within the immediate scope of this discussion, it will be useful to note the most influential works for their insight into Wyclif's *dominium* thought.[32] S. Harrison Thomson's "The Philosophical Basis of Wyclif's Theology" describes Wyclif's thought as a continuous whole, ranging from the first books of the *Summa de Ente* through the last tractates of the *Summa Theologie*, and beyond (though perhaps not inclusive of Wyclif's polemical tracts). Although not a developed topical analysis of any of the issues important to Wyclif's metaphysics, Thomson refers to the connections between his theory of universals and his later reformative goals as evident to any careful reader of Wyclif's work.[33] Thomson's goal is to show how certain of Wyclif's metaphysical presuppositions,

---

[29] C. H. McIlwain, *The Growth of Political Thought in the West* (New York, 1932), pp. 315–17.

[30] Herbert B. Workman, *John Wyclif: A Study of the English Medieval Church* (Oxford, 1926), vol. 2, p. 3; for a summary of Wyclif's thought as it appears in *De Dominio Divino* and *De Civili Dominio*, see *ibid.*, vol. 1, pp. 257–66; for *De Officio Regis*, see *ibid.*, vol. 2, pp. 20–30.

[31] *Ibid.*, vol. 1, p. 259.

[32] See J. A. Robson's *Wyclif and the Oxford Schools* (Cambridge, 1961). Anthony Kenny's *Wyclif in his Times* (Oxford, 1986) contains several useful articles; his "The Realism of the *Tractatus de Universalibus*" is an abridgement of his descriptive *Wyclif* (Oxford, 1985). See also Norman Kretzman's "Continua, Indivisibles, and Change in Wyclif's Logic of Scripture," in Kenny's *Wyclif in his Times*, pp. 31–67; P. V. Spade's introduction to Kenny's translation of *Tractatus de Universalibus* (*On Universals* [Oxford, 1985]), and Alessandro Conti, "Analogy and Formal Distinction: The Logical Basis of Wyclif's Metaphysics," *Medieval Philosophy and Theology*, 6 (1997), pp. 133–65.

[33] S. Harrison Thomson, "The Philosophical Basis of Wyclif's Theology," *Journal of Religion*, 11 (1931), pp. 86–116, here p. 89.

primarily his realism regarding universals, drove him to the conclusions about God's unmediated power over Creation. Thomson also makes note of Wyclif's spatio-temporal atomism, which he argues led to a rejection of transubstantiation, and of Wyclif's views on modal notions of possibility and necessity, which tied into his belief that only the Elect could hope for Grace. Thomson does little more than mention these subjects, though, as premises to sustain his conclusion that Wyclif's thought is consistent throughout.

The landmark work on Wyclif's overall philosophical approach is J. A. Robson's *Wyclif and the Oxford Schools*.[34] Robson shows Wyclif's indebtedness to the thought of Thomas Buckingham's anti-Pelagian Augustinianism and to Archbishop Richard Fitzralph's authority regarding the general nature of the relation of God to humanity. The complexity of the *Summa de Ente* calls for some picture of what Wyclif had in mind when composing the individual treatises, and Robson's survey of the *Summa*'s structure provides a philosophically tenable one. Robson's assessment is that Wyclif's metaphysics indicate "a cautious and conservative Oxford don," someone more interested in affirming orthodoxy than in reforming it. Robson notes that his desire to gain an overview of Wyclif's metaphysics has caused him to stop just short of the really interesting part of Wyclif's thought, namely the "interweaving of Wyclif's polemics with his scholasticism . . . the fascinating psychology of the don in politics . . ."[35] He steadfastly avoids discussing the teachings of the *Summa Theologie*, and leaves the reader with the sense that so fully developed a philosophical mind as Wyclif's was sure to bring into its consideration of extra-metaphysical matters its rigorous approach, if nothing else.

Michael Wilks' study of John Wyclif's political thought is the only instance of an analysis that is careful to include as much of Wyclif's thought as possible while interpreting the political theory as a serious enterprise. Two main directions in which Wilks has developed his analysis deserve our attention, namely, his argument that Wyclif's political thought is in fact a valid pro-monarchic position, and his assessment of the relation of Wyclif's earlier metaphysics to that political stance. Wilks began his study of Wyclif by showing that Wyclif really does want readers of the *Summa Theologie* to carry out his radical advice.[36] Shortly before his death, Wilks published a discussion of Wyclif's influence as a prophet in the Joachimite

---

[34] See n. 32, above.   [35] *Wyclif and the Oxford Schools*, p. 218.

[36] Michael Wilks, "Predestination, Property, and Power: Wyclif's Theory of Dominion and Grace," in *SCH*, 2 (London, 1965), pp. 220–36. See also Anne Hudson, ed., *Wyclif: Political Ideas and Practice, Papers by Michael Wilks* (Oxford, 2000), pp. 16–32.

tradition, further emphasizing Wyclif's dedication to social reform as a product of his broader theological and philosophical system.[37]

What are we to make of a social theory that "seems to be justifying something not far short of anarchy?"[38] Wyclif has been accused of providing an unoriginal rehash of the established principle that divine *iustitia* should be behind all human rule.[39] He has also been accused of being unclear about how to distinguish between the Grace-favored Elect and the Damned, and of having devised his thesis in order to support the expropriation of the clergy by the laity, just as Fitzralph had used it against the Friars Minor, with neither author having shown how a connection was to be made between the righteous and the expropriators.[40] These are practical questions about the applicability of Wyclif's thought that certainly needed to be addressed, and Wilks effectively addressed them by showing that Wyclif's critics underestimate his shrewdness and perspicacity. He argued that Wyclif was not really concerned with distinguishing between the Elect and the Damned, that he was content to leave such distinctions to God. He attributed to Wyclif the position that "human life *secundum praesentem iustitiam* bore little relationship to the realities of the divine world; that there were two levels of truth, human and divine, coexistent but contradictory; that, in effect, human life could be considered with but small reference to God."[41] While Augustinian in its approach, this implies that God participates minimally in the ongoing drama of secular political life. Wilks downplayed the import of Wyclif's thought on ownership, arguing that his condemnation of ecclesiastical private ownership is really a *de facto* endorsement of the superior public right of the king's power as both prince and priest.[42] But he dismissed Wyclif's

---

37 Michael Wilks, "Wyclif and the Great Persecution," *Prophecy and Eschatology*, ed. Wilks, SCH Subsidia 10, (London, 1994), pp. 39–63. See also Anne Hudson, ed., *Wyclif: Political Ideas and Practice*, pp. 179–204.

38 Wilks, "Predestination, Property and Power," p. 223.

39 Wilks refers to W. A. Dunning, *History of Political Theories: Ancient and Medieval* (New York, 1905), p. 264; McIlwain, *The Growth of Political Thought*, and R. W. and A. J. Carlyle, *A History of Political Thought in the West* (New York, 1932), vol. 5, pp. 51–63; accusations that Wyclif's thought is Utopian at best, anarchic at worst are evident throughout the literature on Wyclif, as we will briefly discuss below.

40 See Gwynn, *The English Austin Friars in the Time of Wyclif*, pp. 59–73, 234–6; and Knowles, *The Religious Orders in England*, vol. 2, pp. 61–8.

41 Wilks, "Predestination, Property and Power," p. 229. "The result was to leave man – at least within the limits of this mortal life – as the virtual master of his own world."

42 *Ibid.*, pp. 234–5. "What he [Wyclif] deplored was the notion that private property rights were immutable – that there was a perpetual *civile dominium* inherent in ecclesiastical tenure – which would effectively deny the superior public right – the divine lordship – of the king's grace . . . the very familiar features of an ecclesiastical polity over which the prince stands supreme as king and priest."

theological justifications for his condemnation of the institution of private ownership as a smoke-screen enabling him to resurrect the old model of a theocratic monarchy, or, Wilks suspects, to presage a Tudor-style absolutism.[43]

The fullest of Wilks' explications of the mechanics of Wyclif's civil *dominium* theory is his 1972 discussion of Wyclif as proto-reformer.[44] This is also the most radical of Wilks' interpretations of Wyclif as the advocate of a Tudor-like reform of the English church. Here Wilks emphasizes the differences between Wyclif's recognizably Augustinian attitudes towards obviously theological issues, and his less recognizably Augustinian and more Aristotelian endorsement of the civil lord's holding of absolute temporal power over all subjects, ecclesiastical and secular.[45] Wilks argues that the reform that Wyclif calls for is largely a political reorganization of power, with doctrinal reform being little more than an after-effect of the king's actions. In this argument, Wyclif's ecclesiology serves as a means to political ends, in which the king is regarded as final temporal authority in all venues, sacred and secular.[46] Seen in this light, Wyclif is less a political philosopher than a revolutionary, heralding a top-down revolution to be undertaken by a *junta* of theologians who enjoy the complete trust of the civil lord.[47]

In 1969 Wilks addressed the possibility that Wyclif had formulated definite political ideas while still at Oxford, in the early 1370s. Following Grabmann's dictum that papalists are realists while monarchists are nominalists, Wilks argued that Wyclif had renounced the ontological realism of the *Summa de Ente* by the time he had come to write the *dominium* treatises. He begins his arguments referring to those occasional passages in Wyclif's later works wherein he laments his earlier, youthful digressions; in the past scholars have taken this to imply that Wyclif had earlier been swayed by Ockhamist metaphysics.[48] Indeed, Wyclif admits

---

[43] *Ibid.*, p. 235; see also "Royal Patronage and Anti-Papalism," in *From Ockham to Wyclif*, ed. A. Hudson and M. Wilks, *SCH* Subsidia 5 (London, 1987), pp. 135–63. See also Hudson, ed., *Wyclif: Political Ideas and Practice*, pp. 117–46.

[44] "*Reformatio Regni*: Wyclif and Hus as Leaders of Religious Protest Movements," *SCH*, 9 (London, 1972), pp. 109–30. See also Hudson, ed., *Wyclif: Political Ideas and Practice*, pp. 63–84.

[45] "*Reformatio Regni*," p. 116. Note the implicit reliance on Grabmann's misleading polarization of "Aristotelianism" and "Augustinianism."

[46] *Ibid.*, pp. 118–19.   [47] *Ibid.*, p. 124.

[48] Wilks, "The Early Oxford Wyclif: Papalist or Nominalist?" *SCH*, 5 (London, 1969), pp. 69–98. Wilks refers to M. H. Dziewicki, "An Essay on Wyclif's Philosophical System," *Johannis Wyclif Miscellanea Philosophica*, 2 vols. (London, 1902), vol. 1, pp. v–xxvii, and to numerous other scholarly comments on this philosophical turn, all of whom took Wyclif to have been referring to Ockhamist metaphysics. See also Hudson, ed., *Wyclif: Political Ideas and Practice*, pp. 33–62.

to having been mistaken about universals,[49] hylomorphism, theory of time,[50] and predestination,[51] among other topics.[52] Wilks suggests that Wyclif's errors in his youth were not metaphysical ones in the Ockhamist camp, but those of excessive realism about universals, and that as he abandoned his ill-fitting realism, he also abandoned his hierarchic papalism. After all, Wyclif reports himself as being, in his early days, an advocate of a hard-line interpretation of God's omnipotence, which is consonant with the papal hierocratic argument of papal sovereignty. Is it but coincidental that, as Wyclif embraced a more royalist program, he veered away from the idea that God's will directs all human and, indeed, all created action? This is consonant with Wilks' argument regarding God's relative non-interference in secular politics, suggesting a tendency to view Wyclif's theological justifications for the king having absolute material power as being subordinated to Wyclif's more material, political opinions. Given the utility of Aristotelian methods in resolving problems that Wyclif claims to have bedeviled him in his youth, and given Wyclif's occasional admission of the utility of these methods, Wilks finds it reasonable to assume that a kind of Thomistic compromise concerning a host of philosophical issues germinated in Wyclif's mind, along with which came monarchist sympathies, like a stow-away.[53] Wilks' argument relied heavily on the assumption that only an Aristotelian, and an Ockhamist at that, could argue as fervently as Wyclif does in favor of secular monarchy. Wilks did not entertain the possibility that Gewirth was right to deny a causative connection between ontological nominalism and monarchism, leaving him free to argue what he recognized to be a difficult position, given the lack of evidence for ontological nominalism in Wyclif's *dominium* treatises.[54]

In "Wyclif and the Great Persecution," Wilks explored the possibilities that Wyclif's theology is genuine, that his political theory is an outgrowth of his theological conclusions, and that his metaphysics is not nominalist. Here he argued that Wyclif's most important thought came directly after the *dominium* treatises, particularly *De Veritate Sacrae Scripturae*. In these works, Wilks suggests, Wyclif's debt to chiliastic Joachimite theology translates into a reformative vision in which no mortal power is able

---

[49] *Tractatus de Universalibus*, ed. Ivan J. Mueller (Oxford, 1985), 10: "Et sic quando fui iunior involvebam ignoranter universalia sicut forte faciunt multi hodie qui pertinaciter universalia detestantur...."; also cited in Thomson, "Philosophical Basis," p. 89; Robson, *Wyclif and the Oxford Schools*, p. 145.

[50] *De Scientia Dei*, as discussed by Robson, *Wyclif and the Oxford Schools*, p. 180.

[51] *Trialogus*, ed. G. V. Lechler (Oxford, 1869) IV, xiii, 289–90.

[52] See Wilks, "The Early Oxford Wyclif," p. 74.   [53] *Ibid.*, p. 84.   [54] *Ibid.*, p. 73, n. 5.

to cleanse Christ's church in the way it needs. He argues that Wyclif saw himself as a kind of combination of an Apocalyptic John the Baptist, a prophet of the coming age of Purification, and of a latter-day Jerome, who alone was able to interpret Scripture to guide Christians into harmony with *lex Christi*. By this reading, Wilks suggests that the *dominium* texts are comprehensible as the aspect of Wyclif's vision applicable to contemporary mundane political affairs.[55] This approach allows us see the *dominium* treatises as fitting into a much wider, theological program. But that program is so apocalyptically orientated as to detract from the value of *De Civili Dominio* and *De Officio Regis* as articulated expressions of a dialogue running back through Fitzralph, Giles of Rome, Aquinas, and finally to *De Civitate Dei*. If true, the Grace-founded *dominium* notion is still philosophically vestigial. If Wyclif had woken up one morning in 1376 and found envoys from the pope, the archbishop of Canterbury, and the king, all of whom indicated their agreement in accord with *De Civili Dominio*, would he have been satisfied? According to Wilks, he would not have been, and nothing short of the Second Coming would suffice. This may have been the case after 1379, but until then it is possible that Wyclif might have been more conciliatory. To interpret Wyclif as having been primarily a Joachimite chiliast before 1379 is to discount the possibility that a philosophical consistency unites the *Summa de Ente* and the first books of the *Summa Theologie*.

Wilks' approach changed with the edition and publication of the *Tractatus de Universalibus* in 1985. In his 1994 entry on Wyclif in the *Dictionnaire de Spiritualité*, he placed a much greater emphasis on Wyclif's debt to Aristotelian reasoning than most scholars have recognized heretofore. He explained that Wyclif's guiding philosophical principle was recognition of the importance of striking an Aristotelian mean between truly Platonic realism and excessive materialism.[56] This principle, Wilks continued, is first expressed in Wyclif's earliest writing, namely in his Commentaries on the *Physics* (*c.* 1366). Wilks envisaged this playing out in Wyclif's rejection of God's perfect knowledge being deterministic in *De Dominio*

---

[55] Wilks, "Wyclif and the Great Persecution," pp. 51–2.

[56] Michael Wilks, "Wyclif (Jean)," *Dictionnaire de Spiritualité*, 106–7 (Paris, 1994), pp. 1501–1512. "Wyclif utilisait aussi les commentaires sur la Physique de Robert Grosseteste et de saint Thomas, ainsi que divers commentateurs arabes. Il en venait par là à l'argumentation suivante; tout objet d'étude doit être considéré à partir de deux points de vue opposés, avant que ces deux points de vue soient harmonisés (un peu comme dans la célèbre gradation hégélien thèse-antithèse-synthèse). Wyclif renforçait ainsi les vues d'Aristote sur la nécessité de trouver un moyen terme entre la 'théologie' du réalisme platonicien et le matérialisme des Sophistes. Tout comme le soleil produit à la fois le jour et la nuit, ou qu'une colonne peut être élancée ou épaisse, tout dépend essentiellement du point de vue selon lequel on regarde" (p. 1505). See also Hudson, ed., *Wyclif: Political Ideas and Practice*, pp. 1–15.

Divino, and in his call in *De Civili Dominio* and in *De Officio Regis* for the civil and sacerdotal lords to be responsible for elements specific to their spheres of influence.[57]

Several scholars have attempted to provide fuller pictures of Wyclif's thought on the correct ordering of postlapsarian human society. The fullest published attempt has been L. J. Daly's *The Political Theory of John Wyclif,* although its utility is decreased by Daly's tendency to miss the forest for the trees.[58] That is, Daly has carefully described the main points of the practical aspects of *De Civili Dominio* and *De Officio Regis,* paying attention to the conventional subjects of medieval monarchic theory, such as the two swords argument, the relation of king to law, hereditary succession, and so forth, all the while overlooking the fundamental theological purpose of these two works.[59] Most notable is Daly's relative inattention to the concept of *dominium* as a relation between God and Creation, and between men. He begins his discussion with the cursory definition of *dominium* of *De Dominio Divino,* I, i, which is not Wyclif's formal definition, but a working version which he used to elucidate the relation in much greater detail in the rest of the work.[60] Absent is reference to the thirteen acts of *dominium* to which Wyclif refers at the beginning of the third book, from which we can understand the first two books of *De Dominio Divino* as having covered the first three acts (*gubernacio, sustentare, creare*), and the third book as elucidating the second three (*donare, accipere, prestare*).[61] These acts correspond to Wyclif's description of human *dominium* in *De Civili Dominio.* Daly acknowledges that divine *dominium* is indeed something different from that enjoyed by humans, but he passes over the richly developed ties between private ownership and *dominium* that Wyclif uses to show this difference with the briefest glance at its importance.[62] Instead, *dominium* is described in almost exclusively jurisdictional terms, as a political relation allowing one

---

[57] *Ibid.,* p. 1507: "Les réalistes voudraient faire que toute chose soit fondamentalement divine, en déniant la rationalité au monde naturel; les ockhamistes voudraient renier la Bible en accordant l'existence aux seuls êtres matériels, si bien que la matière elle-même serait un principe éternel; mais les uns et les autres doivent être condamnés et corrigés."

[58] See n. 28, above.

[59] The best place to get a cursory understanding of this fundamental theological purpose is in W. R. Thomson's *The Latin Writings of John Wyclif,* a catalog begun by S. Harrison Thomson in 1925 and published by his son and collaborator. Daly (*The Political Theory*) lists the relevant works of S. Harrison Thomson in print in 1962 in his bibliography.

[60] Daly, *The Political Theory,* refers to *DD,* I, i, 4.7–9.   [61] *DD,* III, i, 199.4–14.

[62] Daly, *The Political Theory,* pp. 67–8: "Hence it is that God is not lord through a regiment of hierarchically subservient vassals, but he governs immediately and directly sustains and holds all that he has. His rule therefore is not like that of other kings.... When one speaks of human lordship, then, it is really only a stewardship held from the supreme Lord; for no creature serves another except insofar as he serves his God."

person to exercise social authority over another. Daly makes no reference to the Poverty Controversy, and pays little attention to the extensive analysis of private ownership Wyclif presents in Book III of *De Civili Dominio*, save to recognize Wyclif's desire to divest the Roman church of its private property. In short, Daly focuses almost exclusively on the *iurisdictio* in Wyclif's *dominium*, viewing *proprietas* as a topic only accidentally related to the concept.

This deficiency is most evident when Daly discusses the later chapters of *De Officio Regis*. In his relation of Wyclif's portrait of the nature of monarchy, he maneuvers around the lengthy discussions of the primary royal duty of ecclesiastical reform, touching on the more conventional political topics of protection of material goods, the relation of the king to law, and the place of clerics in royal service. He refers not at all to the summary Wyclif gradually gives of the primary royal duties towards the end of the work, which include regulation of the episcopal council, of the appointment of priests, and the fostering of theological doctors, which list strays far from the conventional boundaries of monarchical theory.[63] Why did Wyclif end the one work in which he had set out to describe the mechanics of civil rule with a prolonged argument about the royal responsibilities to guiding the clergy? Not only does Daly not approach this question, one would not imagine that such a question might arise, given his discussion.[64] Daly does recognize the importance of examining the thought of Giles of Rome, Ockham, and Fitzralph, and refutes the standing accusations that Wyclif had done little more than crib from *De Pauperie Salvatoris*.[65] Further, he argues against the idea that Wyclif's pen was guided primarily by his association with John of Gaunt, which argument has been fostered by K. B. McFarlane in *John Wycliffe and the Beginnings of English Nonconformity*.[66]

Edith Comfort Tatnall's 1964 doctoral thesis "Church and State According to John Wyclif" strives to show the place of Wyclif's doctrine of political and ecclesiastical reform in light of his theology, and so exceeds the scope of Daly's work. Tatnall's thesis is comprehensive, including historical consideration of the problem of church–state relations in England through the fourteenth century, consideration of formative influences on Wyclif's theory of human *dominium*, and a careful exposition of the

---

[63] See *De Officio Regis*, ed. A. W. Pollard and C. Sayle (London, 1887), IX–XII, especially 280.22–281.16.

[64] Daly does notice that something is not quite right in *De Officio Regis*, for he says, "In speaking of the duties of the king as a ruler of his kingdom Wyclif is, unfortunately, much briefer than one would wish." Sadly, Daly does not pursue this any further.

[65] Daly, *The Political Theory*, pp. 89–96.

[66] Cf. K. B. McFarlane, *John Wycliffe and the Beginnings of English Nonconformity* (Aylesbury, 1952). This idea is strongly hinted at in Chapter 3, "Wycliffe in Politics, 1371–8," pp. 58–89.

proper motives and methods of a just civil lord. Her special strength is in showing how Wyclif's social thought is firmly based in Augustine's, and she has appended a useful collection of especially relevant selections from *De Civitate Dei* to that end. She is generous in her attention to other influences, including canon law and Aristotelian political theory, but devotes little attention to the development of the concept of *dominium* in the thought of Wyclif's more immediate predecessors. She examines the connection of civil to divine *dominium*, and the connections between *De Dominio Divino* and *De Civili Dominio* at the outset of her discussion of the nature of civil *dominium*. Although brief, this section points to the causal force that divine *dominium* has on all instances of created *dominium*, and refers to Wyclif's idea that it serves as a standard or measure for all lesser instances. Tatnall's aim is not to explicate *dominium* as such, so she devotes relatively little space to divine *dominium* outside of the direct bearing it has on civil *dominium*. As a result, she only makes note of the possibility of a universal–particular relationship holding between divine and civil *dominium*.[67] Perhaps Tatnall's only weak point is her failure to explore the ties linking the development of the concept of *proprietas* during the Poverty Controversy to Wyclif's political thought. One would think that every theorist of *dominium* would devote half of his space to an examination of private ownership, and the other half to secular jurisdictive concerns. This is not at all the way things were; for many political theorists of an Aristotelian bent, *dominium* was primarily a concept referring to ownership, and not immediately conceived to be synonymous with civil jurisdictional authority.[68] John of Paris, for instance, whose political theory has much in common with Wyclif regarding ideal end-results, views *dominium* as something wholly unrelated to *iurisdictio*.[69]

William Farr's *John Wyclif as Legal Reformer* is an attempt to illustrate W. R. Thomson's thesis that Wyclif's theology is the underpinning uniting his earlier philosophical realism and his later political ideals.[70] As such, Farr refers to Wyclif's metaphysics as contributing more of a philosophical style to the later *dominium* thought than a substantial foundation. Wyclif's fascination with the atemporal ideal of the church, a kind of universal in

---

[67] *Ibid.*, pp. 145–6.

[68] Cf., for example, Marsilius of Padua, *Defensor Pacis*, trans. Alan Gewirth (Columbia, OH, 1956), XII, xiii–xv. Here he defines *dominium* as synonymous with ownership, and refers not at all to civil government. For more on the anomalous fusion of ownership and jurisdiction in Wyclif's use of the term *dominium*, see Chapter 2.

[69] Arthur P. Monahan, *John of Paris on Royal and Papal Power* (New York, 1974), p. xxx: "The distinction between having dominion and having jurisdiction is as follows: to have dominion is to have possession or property rights; to have jurisdiction is to have the right of determining what is just and unjust." See *De Potestate Regia*, Chapter 6, pp. 22–7, in Monahan's edition.

[70] William Farr, *John Wyclif as Legal Reformer* (Leiden, 1974).

which the earthly church might be cast, is what Farr believes to be at the root of Wyclif's writings on *dominium*.[71] Farr's argument is that Wyclif's programmatic attempt to strengthen the royal position was well founded in an understanding of contemporary legal precedent, and that he used these precedents to implement his theological ends to improve their utility without perverting their original purpose. Unfortunately, Wyclif's approach was hampered by a too-complete reliance on the contemporary; Farr suggests that Wyclif's transvaluation of legal structure to accomplish his reformative ends lent itself too easily to becoming outdated by the evolution of English law.[72] This meant that when reform did come to England, Wyclif's program was of no real use through its having become badly outdated, although Wyclif's means, using secular law to effect ecclesiastical reform, had become an established principle.

In his influential *Heresy in the Later Middle Ages*, Gordon Leff has argued strenuously that the doctrine of Grace-founded *dominium* is little more than a red-herring in Wyclif's works.[73] Leff argues that Wyclif believed every priest to have been ineligible for civil jurisdiction on biblical and metaphysical grounds, with Grace-founded *dominium* being but a decorative appendage. He explains that Wyclif did little more than recapitulate Fitzralph and Giles of Rome in his articulation of Grace-founded *dominium* in the first section of Book I of *De Civili Dominio*, and, having dispensed with theory, turned to more pressing matters.[74] Rather than direct his attention to Fitzralph's interest in private ownership, Wyclif is held to have conceived of *dominium* as primarily connected with the justice involved with civil jurisdiction. Leff believes that Wyclif reduced the power of Fitzralph's contention that Grace alone makes for true, divinely sanctioned human *dominium* by making God's justice the means by which human *dominium* is sanctioned.[75] This is a curious argument, for it is unclear whether Leff means that Wyclif has shifted the justifying element from Grace to divine justice, or whether he is contending that Wyclif wrongly conflates the two. Leff's claim that Wyclif's emphasis on

---

[71] *Ibid.*, p. 22.   [72] *Ibid.*, pp. 172–3.

[73] Leff refers to *De Domnio Divino* as "an early work, which has little relevance to Wyclif's subsequent ecclesiological thinking"; Gordon Leff, *Heresy in the Later Middle Ages*, vol.2, p. 521, n. 3.

[74] *Ibid.*, p. 547: "Where Giles had emphasized the dependence of all laymen – kings included – upon the church Fitzralph developed this equation of justice with authority to make dominion exclusively from God. It was a gift which in turn pre-supposed the gift of justice and grace. Only if a man was first justified by God with grace would he rule on God's behalf. Accordingly there could be no dominion without grace as its formal cause; and conversely mortal sin in destroying grace destroyed dominion. These two propositions together with their elaboration said everything which Wyclif was to say and said it more cogently." No distinction is made between natural, evangelical, or civil *dominium* here, nor does Leff discuss divine *dominium* as having a bearing on the issue.

[75] *Ibid.*, p. 548.

the civil lord's need to make human law consistent with divine law in order to govern with true *iustitia* excludes Grace as a factor in the civil lord's *dominium*. But Wyclif stipulates that such consistency is only possible for the Grace-favored. True human justice is an effect of Grace; it is not a substitution for it.

Leff's criticism of Wyclif has two approaches, first, that people cannot know who has been saved and who has been damned, and second, that Wyclif as good as exempted secular rulers from his Grace-founded *dominium* theory. Leff suggests that because Wyclif believes the subjugation of the just to tyrannous rule can be a tool whereby God castigates or instructs, he must be arguing that God sanctions tyranny, thus nullifying the Grace-founded *dominium* doctrine. Wyclif recognized that he could be interpreted in this way, and his arguments against the equation of Grace-founded just human *dominium* with God's use of unjust human *dominium* as a means to divine ends are clear.[76] Leff says in effect that Wyclif was unable to account for any sort of difference between the justice of Solomon's rule, a case of a just individual with temporal power, and the justice that develops out of Nebuchadnezzar's rule, where the just individual lacks temporal power.

Leff's contempt for Wyclif's originality and consistency regarding Grace and *dominium* is surpassed by the contempt he holds for Wyclif as a philosopher. At virtually every turn in *Heresy in the Later Middle Ages*, Leff aims a dart at Wyclif for taking the structurally lovely concepts of his predecessors and making them wholly unserviceable, echoing R. L. Poole who dismissed the worth of Wyclif's philosophy as having the "spurious qualities of Holcot or Strode."[77] An instance of this is Wyclif's arguments that require distinguishing the Elect from the Damned; throughout his

---

[76] See my discussion of Wyclif on tyranny in Chapter 6, pp. 189–97.

[77] For example, Leff, *Heresy in the Later Middle Ages*, p. 499. See Poole's introduction to *De Dominio Divino*, p. xxi. It is easy to be baffled by Poole's attitude, given the care with which he edited Wyclif's works. He as much as relegates the work to the museum of useless ideas. "I have run very briefly through the contents of this portion of the *De Dominio Divino*, because they are of a character in which all but professed students of the history of philosophy have long ceased to take an interest. Indeed, so far as I am aware, hardly a single work of this description has passed into print for near three centuries: in order to find its models one has to seek among the black-letter quartos of the fifteenth and early sixteenth centuries. Wycliffe's work is of the spuriously technical type of Holcot or Strode; it has not the true philosophical spirit which, in spite of all his over-refinement, impresses one with admiration in Duns Scotus." Poole overlooks the attentions of John Lewis (1675–1747), who wrote *The History of the Life and Sufferings of the Reverend and Learned John Wiclif, D.D* (Oxford, 1820). Lewis appears to have begun the campaign to re-examine Wyclif's works, and included extensive (if occasionally unrelated) selections of Wyclif's Latin works in his biography. Lewis begins his work, "It is the usual practice of the men of this world, who hate the light, and will not come unto it, to defame the persons and blacken the characters of those who tell them the truth." One wonders what he would have made of Poole's opinions.

works, he holds that only the Elect can hold just *dominium*, implying that those who exercise *dominium* are among the Damned. Leff devotes considerable space to showing why this doctrine was so unsettling theologically, and refers later to it as a good reason why Wyclif probably was not serious about Grace and just *dominium*. Wyclif's realism made it impossible to deny that God knows all potential instantiations of every universal before the instantiations were actualized. Thus, God knows eternally who will be among the Elect, so he could not escape the conclusion that God knows who comprise the true church. Had Wyclif not bothered to address the thorny issue of the relation of God's knowledge to created action, Leff's criticisms would be understandable. But Wyclif's earlier philosophical works feature a complex metaphysics of necessity and possibility, and a carefully constructed account of the relation of God's eternal knowing to created action. It is hard to avoid concluding that these treatises deserve attention in an account of Wyclif's theory of just *dominium*.

Leff admitted to having jumped the gun in accusing Wyclif of philosophical sloppiness in his "The Place of Metaphysics in Wyclif's Theology," but fails to correct his misrepresentation of the place of Grace-founded *dominium*. He explains this shift in his view by referring to the recent appearance of the until then unedited *Tractatus de Universalibus*, and rightly recognizes the importance of this work in the corpus of Wyclif's metaphysical works as the classical statement of his realism. But again, Leff holds that Wyclif's doctrine that only the Elect can receive Grace means that nobody can recognize whether a civil lord is damned or not, which means that Wyclif somehow sacrificed the metaphysical consistency of his theory of Grace and *dominium* for political practicability in holding that the civil lord must be the ultimate temporal authority.[78] He argues here that Wyclif might have been serious about Grace and *dominium* when he began *De Civili Dominio*, but that as his program of ecclesiastical reform grew in importance in his mind, he sacrificed it in favor of royal absolutism in *De Officio Regis*.

Most notable is the extent to which other historians of medieval thought have followed Leff's approach. An instance of this is Malcolm Lambert's *Medieval Heresy*, in which Leff's view is championed; here Wyclif is viewed as an anti-authoritarian determinist strangely addicted to royal absolutism.[79] He accuses Wyclif of having held in *De Officio Regis* that secular lords need not rely on Grace for the justice of their temporal

[78] Gordon Leff, "The Place of Metaphysics in Wyclif's Theology," *From Ockham to Wyclif*, ed. A. Hudson and M. Wilks, *SCH* Subsidia 5 (London, 1987), pp. 217–32.

[79] Malcolm Lambert, *Medieval Heresy: Popular Movements from the Gregorian Reform to the Reformation*, 2nd edn (London, 1992), pp. 225–42.

dominium, thus defusing the Grace-*dominium* doctrine.[80] At least Lambert follows the later Leff in recognizing the force of the Grace-founded *dominium* idea in *De Civili Dominio*. The best that can be said of this dismissal of Grace-founded *dominium* from the essence of Wyclif's social and political thought is that it shows how important Wyclif's theology and metaphysics are to his political theory, for without it Wyclif sounds like a political hack sardonically employing theological justifications wherever the mood strikes him. The place of Wyclif's realist metaphysics and his Augustinian reformative theology in *De Civili Dominio* and *De Officio Regis* will become increasingly evident as we explore his characterization of *dominium* as a portmanteau concept including *proprietas* and *iurisdictio*.

In his recent survey of Wyclif and Wycliffism at Oxford in the late fourteenth century J. I. Catto has argued that Wyclif's metaphysical realism was importantly directive of his thought on *dominium*.[81] Like S. H. Thomson, Catto suggests that Wyclif's argument that universals have a reality superior to their physical instantiations sparked an interest in theological issues like the nature of the Trinity, interpretation of Scripture, and the Incarnation. Catto notes that Wyclif's first discussion of *dominium* appears in *De Composicione Hominis* (1372), a treatise on the relation of form and matter in the Incarnation, suggesting that the vigorous counter-arguments Wyclif encountered from William Woodford and others in response to this treatise planted the seed that germinated in the *dominium* treatises.[82] Most importantly, Catto recognizes Wyclif's belief that created *dominium* has God's *dominium* as its exemplar, its universal, although he does not refer to the explicit articulation of this principle in Chapter 10 of *De Universalibus*.[83] The connection perceived by Thomson and Catto will direct our examination of the *De Universalibus* and its connection to the first books of the *Summa Theologie*.

---

[80] *Ibid.*, p. 237. He continues in n. 52, "I follow Leff, *Heresy*, pp. 546–9. He differs from M. J. Wilks, "Predestination, property and power: Wyclif's theory of dominion and grace" . . . yet both dethrone the doctrine of dominion from its former position within the totality of Wyclif's beliefs."

[81] J. I. Catto, "Wyclif and Wycliffism at Oxford 1356–1430," *The History of the University of Oxford*, vol. 2: *Late Medieval Oxford* (Oxford, 1992), pp. 175–261. See also his "John Wyclif," *Routledge Encyclopedia of Philosophy*, ed. Edward Craig (London, 1998), vol. 9 pp. 802–5.

[82] See Thomson, *The Latin Writings of John Wyclyf*, pp. 36–7; *De Composicione Hominis*, ed. R. Beer (London, 1884), I, 2.21–7; Catto, "Wyclif and Wycliffism," p. 194.

[83] Catto, "Wyclif and Wycliffism," pp. 200–01; *Tractatus de Universalibus*, X, 236.680.

Chapter 2

WHY *DOMINIUM*?

By the mid-twelfth century the revival of Roman law and canon law allowed philosophers to define rulership in terms of "power," "authority," "imperium," and "jurisdiction" without addressing problems about use and possession of private property.[1] Similarly, Roman law had long provided civil and canon lawyers with careful distinctions about ownership issues, to which the term *dominium* had usually applied. Why unite ownership and jurisdiction, making *dominium* into a portmanteau concept? Janet Coleman argues that the term's use in reference to *proprietas* and *iurisdictio* was attributable to two factors.[2] First, economic conditions were moving from traditional feudal modes in which credit and other techniques of payment were of less import to conditions which favored an increasing reliance on hard currency. As the accumulation of large amounts of money became possible, so did a revulsion to avarice, she argues, and so the thirteenth century saw the growth not only of the merchant class, but of the theological glorification of the life of poverty. Secondly, this emergence of a currency-based economy complicated the issue of church holdings. The canon-law tradition had long held that natural law permitted communal ownership of property, and it developed the view that while a priest can own property, he is not an owner of the church property which he administered. Innocent IV asserted that the mystical body of Christ owned church property with coercive authority. From this it was but a step to Boniface VIII claiming that the papacy has universal coercive power and that *imperium* depends upon the church.[3] Declaring the church a property-owner gave it considerable power in an economy in which property entailed political power. If the pope is the church's steward, his political power outweighs all others thanks to his

---

[1] Brian Tierney, *Religion, Law, and the Growth of Constitutional Thought 1150–1650* (Cambridge, 1982), pp. 29–53.
[2] Janet Coleman, "Property and Poverty," in *The Cambridge History of Medieval Political Thought*, ed. J. Burns (Cambridge, 1988), p. 612. See also Ewart Lewis, *Medieval Political Ideas* (New York, 1954), vol. 1, pp. 88–139.
[3] Coleman, "Property and Poverty," p. 621.

exalted position. Property-ownership and political authority thus were united.

J. H. Burns suggests that another explanation for the unification of the two concepts might be found by looking at the two strands of thought that led to Boniface's pronouncement and the struggle that was to follow. He advises that we follow both the juristic line of thinking about *dominium*, which emphasized the mechanical aspects of property-ownership, and the theological line, which framed all talk of human dominative relations in terms of God's relation to Creation.[4] He cites Aquinas as a philosopher for whom *dominium* was an important concept, encompassing both owner-ship and jurisdictive issues in its scope, but not allowing for a confusion of these issues. For Aquinas, a civil lord who supposed that his *iurisdictio* arose from his *proprietas* and not from a constitution was a tyrant.[5] Coleman, Tierney, and Burns place the point of convergence, in which *dominium* entails necessarily both *iurisdictio* and *proprietas*, in the thought of Giles of Rome. Giles wrote *De Ecclesiastica Potestate* on behalf of the papacy in the struggle that arose from Philip IV's reaction to Boniface VIII, and argued that both jurisdictive and proprietative concerns center on and are subordinate to papal authority.[6]

As Boniface and Giles were advocating the ultimate superiority of the church over all earthly institutions, political and otherwise, another voice within the church arose articulating what sounded like the opposite sentiment. In 1279 Peter Olivi had argued in his *Quaestio an usus pauper* that *usus pauper*, a restricted use of goods, was essential to the Franciscan life.[7] Olivi's arguments were ecclesiastically dangerous because he saw the church to be entering a stage of transition, shifting from its present state of papal government to a new, purer one in which only those faithful to the original Franciscan ideal would be comfortable. Eventually Olivi's position became the rallying point of the Spiritual Franciscans, most notably of Ubertino da Casale, who so volubly challenged the papacy that John XXII condemned Olivi's apocalyptic commentary on the Book of Revelation in 1328.[8]

John XXII had embarked on a campaign to refute the Franciscans' claim to apostolic poverty. It culminated in 1328 with *Quia vir reprobus*. John's argument was that any just use of material things was a species of

[4] J. H. Burns, *Lordship, Kingship, and Empire* (Oxford, 1992), pp. 17–18.
[5] *Ibid.*, p. 24; see also *Summa Theologiae* (Rome, 1948), 1a2ae, 56, 5; 58, 2.
[6] Burns, *Lordship, Kingship, and Empire*, p. 25. See Coleman, "Property and Poverty," pp. 637–40; Tierney, *Religion, Law, and the Growth of Constitutional Thought*, p. 32.
[7] David Burr, *Olivi and Franciscan Poverty: The Origins of the Usus Pauper Controversy* (Philadelphia, 1989).
[8] David Burr, *The Persecution of Peter Olivi*, Transactions of the American Philosophical Society, 66, 5 (1976), pp. 81–3.

usus, along with *usufructus, ius utendi,* and *simplex usus facti,* that implied a right to their use. In things like food and clothing that were consumed or used up in the act of use, the right involved was that of ownership. This made it heretical to claim that Christ and the Apostles owned nothing either privately or in common, and allowed John to argue "that perfection was now commensurate with possessory rights because without rights there could be no justice."[9] The Franciscan response to this was presented in William Ockham's *Opus Nonaginta Dierum,* in which appear careful definitions for all the above-mentioned sorts of use, and for *possessio, proprietas,* and *dominium.*

The next important volley in this controversy about *dominium* came in 1356, with the appearance of Archbishop Richard Fitzralph's *De Pauperie Salvatoris.* Fitzralph argued that all *dominium,* civil and ecclesiastical, flows from the church, and is divinely sanctioned by Grace. What the Franciscans had in mind was certainly laudable, Fitzralph suggests, but was hardly a model for today's world, nor was it a re-creation of Christ's perfect *dominium.* Fitzralph's position was to be central to Wyclif's argument, and in it we see the union of *iurisdictio* and *proprietas* in Grace-founded *dominium.*

J. A. Robson commented that it is hard to think of any century more soaked in Augustinianism than the fourteenth.[10] Prominent figures including Thomas Bradwardine, Gregory of Rimini, and Walter Burley are famous for emphasizing the need to return to Augustinianism in the face of the ontological revisionism of the *Moderni.* This Augustinian revival was also notable in political discourse; as we shall see, Wyclif's *dominium* writings are based in the Augustinianism of Giles of Rome's papalism. Thus, it will be useful to turn first to Augustine to be certain of our philosophical foundation, before proceeding to later medieval thinkers.

Augustine is well known for having formulated a division between two cities in which a man might claim citizenship. Citizens of the earthly city are motivated by love of self, and their wills are turned from God and from true justice, while citizens of the heavenly city are characterized by their love of God and their contempt for self. Yet Augustine did not believe that citizens of the heavenly city had to wait for their death to claim their citizenship; one's citizenship is defined by one's presiding love.[11] The City of God sojourns in the lives of residents of the City of Man, who ultimately will reign eternally with God.[12] It is easy to assume that the

[9] Coleman, "Property and Poverty," p. 642.

[10] J. A. Robson, *Wyclif and the Oxford Schools* (Cambridge, 1961), p. 25.

[11] Augustine *De Genesi ad Litteram Libri Duodecim,* Corpus Scriptorum Ecclesiaticorum Latinorum, vol. 28 (Prague, 1894), XI, xv, 19–20.

[12] *De Civitate Dei* CCSL, vol. 48 (Turnhout, 1955), XV, i.

division between the two cities indicates two separable groups of people, but this division is readily evident only to the divine mind. For us, the two cities are inextricably interwoven, "mingled together from the beginning down to the end."[13] Because of this mixture, citizens of the heavenly city must live peacefully and abide by the laws of the earthly city, which are largely directed towards the goods of this life. If we assume, as did most of his medieval readers, that the citizens of the heavenly city corresponded to members of the church, we are faced with the problem of whether Augustine is here advising the church to submit itself to the laws of the state, or whether he is only telling its members not to disobey such laws as do not fly in the face of scriptural authority.[14]

Augustine occasionally uses *dominium* to refer to a relation between men, and in most instances he means to denigrate the relation as one following upon sin. Regarding the famous biblical account of God having given *dominium* to people, Augustine is adamant. "He did not intend that His rational creature, who was made in His image, should have dominion over [*dominari*] anything but the irrational creation – not man over man, but man over the beasts."[15] One might object that the Bible speaks of many instances of one man holding mastery over another. Did not Jacob subject himself to Laban's mastery? There are two sorts of master–subject relations, Augustine explains; the artificial one, founded in sin, involves one man dominating another, while the natural one, based in mutual love, lacks that dominative tone. "But those who are true fathers of their households desire and endeavor that all the members of their household, equally with their own children, should worship and win God, and should come to that heavenly home in which the duty of ruling men is no longer necessary, because the duty of caring for their everlasting happiness has also ceased; but until they reach that home, masters ought to feel their position of authority a greater burden than servants their service."[16] The true Lord (*dominus*) is God; no man can aspire to that degree of authority over his fellows. Before the Fall, people were given such *dominium* as was needed for their own sustenance, that they might live obediently under

[13] *Ibid.*, XVIII, liv: "... sit duarum civitatum, caelestis atque terrenae, ab initio usque in finem permixtarum mortalis excursus ..." See R. A. Markus, *Saeculum: History and Society in the Theology of St. Augustine* (Cambridge, 1970), p. 102.

[14] Richard McKeon, "The Development of the Concept of Property in Political Philosophy: A Study of the Background of the Constitution," *Ethics*, 48 (1938), pp. 297–366.

[15] *De Civitate Dei*, XIX, xv, 4–5: "Rationalem factum ad imaginem suam noluit nisi inrationalibus dominari; non hominem homini, sed hominem pecori."

[16] *Ibid.*, XIX, xvi, 8–15: "Qui autem ueri patres familias sunt, omnibus in familia sua tamquam filiis ad colendum et promerendum Deum consulunt, desiderantes atque optantes uenire ad caelestem domum, ubi necessarium non sit officium imperandi mortalibus, quia necessarium non erit officium consulendi iam in illa inmortalitate felicibus; quo donec ueniatur, magis debent patres quod dominantur, quam serui tolerare quod seruiunt."

divine *dominium*. Man could take what he needed, save where it was forbidden.[17]

Augustine makes occasional reference to the argument that just as the soul rules over the body so should the many be ruled by few or one, suggesting the natural subjection of one man to another.[18] This, Augustine explains, is what Cicero taught in *De Re Publica*. One could read Augustine as obliquely approving of this argument, but R. A. Markus denies the plausibility of doing so, suggesting that Augustine shows profound reserve about this throughout his works.[19] The argument that was to have such weight in the Middle Ages, that of kingship's natural basis, lacks real foundation in Augustine's thought. This is not to say that Augustine has nothing to say to define or improve monarchy but only that he did not mean to equate it with the natural domestic subjection of child to father.

If it is unnatural to dominate a man, is it unnatural to dominate anything else? We have already noted that Augustine felt *dominium* over beasts to be natural; did he equate this with private property-ownership? It is possible to emphasize Augustine's references to need-based use and to communal ownership, and to make him sound as if he would eliminate private property if he could; yet Augustine allowed a Christian to possess private property, if it could not be avoided.[20]

Augustine was known to have said that all things belong to the just; it was this statement that led Fitzralph and Wyclif to connect Grace and *dominium*. But only God can really claim to possess, for God alone created everything. Man's claims of possession by law or right are really infringements upon the only just claim of possession. If God's possession is wholly different from human possession, it is logical to ask in what sense human possession can be just. How does the ownership of the just participate in God's justice?

God's justice is apparent in many actions in Creation, even in actions governed by civil laws. In fact, just civil laws regulating possession can indicate God's will by participating in divine justice. Augustine suggests that God's justice is served by a clerical intercessor in civil courts seeking just restitution of goods in cases of the abrogation of civil property law. By uniting just possession of property with rightful use, Augustine can hold that since rightful use is only possible with a properly directed will, consonant with the divine will, true justice implies that only those

[17] *De Genesi ad Litteram*, VIII, xi, 24.
[18] *De Civitate Dei*, XIX, xxi, 2.   [19] Markus, *Saeculum*, p. 208.
[20] *De Moribus Ecclesiae Catholicae*, Corpus Scriptorum Ecclesiasticorum Latinorum, vol. 90 (Vindobonae, 1992), I, l xxviii.

who are just in God's eyes truly possess.[21] Elsewhere, Augustine implies that some instances of just civil possession are commensurate with divine justice. "[E]arthly goods are not rightly possessed by anyone except by divine law, by which the just possess all things, or by human law, which is in the power of all earthly kings . . ."[22] He foreshadows Wyclif, by continuing to argue that anyone holding alms for the poor or the church's buildings in the church's name but in their own interest does so unjustly. Augustine did not forbid ecclesiastical private property-holding, just ecclesiastical avarice. His position regarding private property boils down to this: "One should abstain from the possession of private things, or, if one cannot abstain from possession, then from the love of property."[23] He suggests that the final state for citizens of the heavenly kingdom will be communal ownership under Christ's perfect Lordship, but does not suppose that this is a feasible goal for those subject to the conditions of this life.[24]

Augustine's belief that divine justice appears in secular affairs implies that it is possible for a king to rule in accord with God's will. Since all citizens of the heavenly city must serve God before themselves, regardless of their place in the earthly city, a ruler's first duty is to God, which increases the likelihood of just rule of the realm. "But we say that they are happy if they rule justly . . . if they make their power the handmaid of His majesty by using it for the greatest possible extension of His worship; if they fear, love, worship God; if more than their own they love that kingdom in which they are not afraid to have partners . . ."[25] Augustine never discusses a secular ruler as the embodiment of a monarchic or imperial concept; he always frames his advice for rulers in terms of their salvation and spiritual reward rather than material well-being. This provided a degree of freedom for a Christian king to do God's bidding as His servant, even when it came to the coercion of errant priests. When Augustine approves the ruler's use of his supreme secular power to deal with errant church members, it is always with reference to the ruler as a Christian, and never as a secular political entity. It would be as wrong to say that Augustine's view of secular authority uniformly allows for

---

[21] *Epistola CLIII* (*PL*, vol. 33), VI, xxvi.

[22] *Epistola XCIII*, xii, 50: "Et quamvis res quaeque terrena non recte a quoquam possideri possit, nisi vel jure divino, quo cuncta justorum sunt, vel jure humano, quod in potestate regum est terrae." *PL* 33, col. 345.

[23] *Enarratio in Psalmum CXXXI*, v–vi: "Abstineamus ergo nos, fratres, a possessione rei privatae; aut ab amore, si non possumus a possessione; et facimus locum Domino." *PL* 37, col. 1718.

[24] *Enarratio in Psalmum CV*, xxxiv.

[25] *De Civitate Dei*, V, xxiv, 10–25: "Sed felices eos dicimus, si iuste imperant . . . si suam potestatem ad Dei cultum maxime dilatandum maiestati eius famulam faciunt; si Deum timent diligunt colunt."

secular coercion of the clergy as to say that his view forbids such an action because his reasoning is predicated not on the classical view of the functions of secular office, but on the Christian view of people as members of the church in the world.

Just as Augustine's description of the ideal master–subject relation involves the master feeling the responsibility of his mastery more than the subject feels his subjection, so it is with secular rule. With any just man who has the burden of rule, a love of power should be foreign, and a hunger for God's justice and mercy, should be foremost in his mind.[26] For the master of a household, this means putting the respective good of those dependent upon him before his personal good, and given that a citizen of the heavenly city can be a ruler, it would mean putting the good of his subjects before his own. But we cannot do this easily; the will is naturally pulled towards seeking its own good rather than that of others. It is only through vigilant faith that anyone will properly, and Grace must assist their every action. "But, owing to the liability of the human mind to fall into mistakes, this very pursuit of knowledge [of just action] may be a snare to him unless he has a divine Master, whom he may obey without misgiving, and who may at the same time give him such help as to preserve his own freedom."[27] This shows the consonance of Augustine's position on private property with his position on the optimal use of authority; in both cases justice is only possible when the individual involved is committed to God's will, and open to Grace. Thus Grace is necessary for just possession of property, and for the actions of a ruler to coincide with the divine will.

We have made mention of a duty the king has to eradicate practices contrary to God's will; this entails a royal duty to stamp out heresy. Augustine suggests that "the institution of the power of kings, the death penalty of the judge, the barbed hooks of the executioner, the weapons of the soldier, the right of punishment of the overlord, even the severity of the good father" serve as useful means of restraining the wicked and maintaining order in society, and advises the secular ruler to remember that his power is a means, not an end.[28] Therefore Augustine sees the office of king as generally being useful in preventing sin, and beneficial

---

[26] *Ibid.*, XIX, xiv, 51–5.

[27] *Ibid.*, XIX, xiv, 24–6: "Sed ne ipso studio cognitionis propter humanae mentis infirmitatem in pestem alicuius erroris incurrat, opus habet magisterio diuino, cui certus obtemperet, et adiutorio, ut liber obtemperet."

[28] *Epistola CLIII*, vi, 16: "Nec ideo sane frustra instituta sunt potestas regis, jus gladii cognitoris, ungulae carnificis, arma militis, disciplina dominantis, severitas etiam boni patris." *PL* 33, col. 660. Translation from Augustine, *Letters*, vol. 3 (131–64) trans. S. W. Parsons, The Fathers of the Church 20 (Washington, 1953), p. 293. See also Peter Brown, "St. Augustine's Attitude to Religious Coercion," *Journal of Roman Studies*, 54 (1964), pp. 107–16.

to the church when held by the Grace-favored. Furthermore, artificial human justice, while not a "natural" development of God's will, is still able to provide support for the citizen of the heavenly city desirous of right living.

Wyclif's thought on the proper relation of man both to God, to other men, and to things, is more grounded in Augustine's thought, than in any other philosophical or theological source, perhaps including Scripture. There are several key concepts of Augustine's that serve Wyclif, of which the most important is the centrality of the relation of the individual Christian to God, the true Lord. This dictates Augustine's rejection of conventional Aristotelian and Ciceronian views of the state as the vehicle by which the citizen could attain his natural end, as well as Wyclif's refusal to pay respectful notice of the established norms of political theory. Wyclif occasionally nods to Aristotelian convention, but only when it underscores the need for unrestrained relations between the just Christian and God. Because the emphasis on the just civil lord's need to strive for divine justice in earthly affairs, political authority is a tool used on behalf of God's worship. For Wyclif this led to a particularly heavy emphasis on the king's responsibility for the well-being of the church. While Augustine advises the ruler to be watchful of the development of heresy in his kingdom, Wyclif concludes in *De Officio Regis* that this is but one aspect of the royal responsibility for ecclesiastical reform. Both also view reciprocal relations as important; princes and subjects must serve one another in *caritas* as a means to realizing divine justice on earth.

Augustine and Wyclif are slightly less similar regarding the proprietorial sense of *dominium*. While Wyclif cites Augustine as the main source for his doctrine of Grace-justified civil ownership, he views the civil *dominium* as a means to the end of the restoration of communal *dominium* among church members, which Augustine does not believe attainable in this life. Still, Wyclif's overall attitude to private property is largely Augustinian in its emphasis on the will of the civil owner, rather than on the function of the individual owner in an economic state.

Wyclif's thought is best understood as an attempt to update Augustine's general approach to meet late fourteenth-century English needs. The doctrine of Grace-founded *dominium* is rooted in the notion that the relation of the individual will to the divine is the most fundamental possible relation in Creation. From this idea comes the notion that only the just can hope rightfully to possess anything. Schools of thought that emphasize mundane ownership and political power are founded on the misunderstanding of the nature of property resultant from an improperly directed will, and must be abandoned. In an important sense, the rest of this chapter and the next will be an explication of the development of these Augustinian tendencies against the backdrop of revived Aristotelianism.

DOMINIUM, PROPERTY AND KINGSHIP IN AQUINAS

While *dominium* does not systematically encompass *proprietas* and *iurisdictio* in Aquinas' thought, it is relevant here because his thought functioned as the starting point for much later analysis from a Christian Aristotelian standpoint.[29] Thus it gives us a general point of departure for an understanding of Wyclif's more immediate predecessors. Aquinas, following Ambrose, sees *dominium* as connotative of *potestas*.[30] When we refer to another man as a lord, we are implicitly referring to some kind of power which he exercises. When we set our sights on divine *dominium*, we are hampered by the strictures of negative theology: if *dominium* connotes power, we cannot meaningfully refer to God's *dominium* because His essence, the seat of His power, is unknowable.[31] Aquinas suggests that while some relative terms refer directly to a relationship, others signify only that through which a relationship exists; in the case of "Lord," the term signifies a characteristic, *potestas*, by virtue of which one has a certain relationship to his surroundings.

Aquinas contrasts "Lord" with "Savior" and "Creator," which refer directly to an action of God, and signify something through which He has a relationship. The term "Lord" follows on God's act of Creation, which is an expression of His *potestas*, itself an expression of a divine quality through which God relates to Creation. *Dominus* is predicated of God because the term "Creator" is predicable of Him. It is predicated temporally insofar as the predication conveys the relation that holds between creatures and God, but the term "Lord" does not imply anything temporal in the divine essence. Unlike "Creator," *Dominus* connotes not only God's creative power, but also His governance of what He has created.[32]

Aquinas explains that the name "lord" includes three things in its meaning; the power of coercing subjects, the ordering of the subjects that follows from that coercive power, and finally the achievement of that ordering under a lord.[33] In God, the first sense follows from divine

---

[29] See James Blythe, *Ideal Government and the Mixed Constitution in the Middle Ages* (Princeton, 1992); Quentin Skinner, *The Foundations of Modern Political Thought* (Cambridge, 1978), vol. 2, pp. 135–73.

[30] *Summa Theologiae*, 2a2ae, Q.66, a.1.   [31] *Ibid.*, 1a, Q.13, a.7, ad.1.

[32] See *De Regno Ad Regem Cypri*, in *Parma*, vol. , I, xiii, 97; also *Comm. Sent.* IV, D.47, Q.1, a.2.

[33] *Quaestiones Disputatae de Potentia*, in *Parma*, vol. 8, Q.VII, a.10; also *Summa Theologiae*, 2a2ae, Q.66, a.2.

omnipotence, and the third sense follows if we take the end to mean the goal of the lord's ordering activity. But the second sense cannot follow from using God's lordship, because God's relation to His subjects is not part of the divine essence. After all, in most relation statements, xRy, when we say that x is related to y, we usually presume there to be a commensurate yRx, by virtue of which y is, in turn, related to x. But while the temporal use of the term *Dominus* in a *dominium*-relation implies a power relation that holds from subject to lord, and from lord to subject, when we use the name to refer to God, we cannot refer to the power relation that holds between lord and subject, because of the ineffability of the divine essence. Thus, says Aquinas, we are not talking about a real relation of God to creatures; all we can talk about is a real relation between creatures and God, in which creatures rely on God's supreme *potestas* for their creation, and for their governance and sustenance.[34]

The most significant aspect of Aquinas' thought on God's power over Creation is his explication of God's governance of Creation. The purpose of God's governance is a universal, transcendent Good, identical to the divine nature, given that God's goodness is perfect and universal in His essence.[35] God's governance applies to all things in Creation, and not only because God is the primary cause of all created being. One could imagine that God's primary causality is sufficient for His universal governance. While His *dominium* does follow from His *potestas*, and is consequent on His creative act, which makes His act necessary for His rule, it does not then follow that God's rule is universal and immediate. One need only call to mind Enlightenment deism to mind to bear this out. Since the purpose of divine government is the transcendent Good, and since all individual created beings exist and move towards their own respective goods, it follows that God's governance over Creation must be universal.[36] We can see that the transcendent Good emerges from immediate effects of God's governing. First, every created being moves towards its individual good, realizing its respective goal; its movement is a similitude of the absolute Good towards which God directs all created being. While the effects of God's governance transcend a detailed accounting, we can understand the effect of God's governance: God sustains things in the good and moves them towards the good.[37] This is echoed in Aquinas' list of the general duties of a king in his *De Regno Ad Regem Cypri*: the ruler must sustain things in the good, by ensuring that the offices of public duty are filled well and by protecting the community from external threat, and he must

---

[34] *Quodlibet IX*, in *Parma*, vols. 8–9, Q.2, a.4.
[35] See *Summa Theologiae*, 1a, Q.13, a.11, r.3, and 1a, Q.103, a.2.
[36] *Ibid.*, 1a, Q.103, a.5.　　[37] *Ibid.*, 1a, Q.103, a.4.

move his subjects towards the good, by instituting and enforcing a just system of laws.[38]

As we proceed from divine to human *dominium*, we should explore more than just postlapsarian human lord–subject relations. Did Adam have the sort of mastery that political *dominium* involves, and did his mastery entail private property-ownership? People indeed had mastery over other animals in Eden by virtue of their relative perfection. "For the imperfect are for the use of the perfect; plants make use of the earth for their nourishment, animals make use of plants, and man makes use of both plants and animals."[39] While *dominium* over lesser creatures is natural, *dominium* over our fellows is less so. Aquinas avoids wholly denying the possibility of such *dominium* by making a distinction. If by *dominium* we mean the sense in which it involves servitude, it would not have existed in Eden. But if we mean the sense in which "*dominium* is referred in a general way to any kind of subject, even he who has the office of governing and directing free men can be called a *dominus*," such authority would have been permissible before the Fall.[40] This distinction is important because it indicates the disparity between a nurturing, directive relation joining two individuals meeting the mutual needs and desires of both, and an authoritarian, non-nurturing relation whereby one individual coercively subjects another to his will. Only the latter entails evil. How does this distinction relate to postlapsarian economic and political relations? And if the nurturing species of *dominium* can occur in the postlapsarian world, where is it possible? Aquinas' views on this are especially focused upon the topics of property and kingship.

Men appear designed to live in groups which allow individuals to furnish themselves with what is required for their survival from a communal reservoir of resources.[41] Aquinas notices that private possession of objects is more useful than communal possession; he observes, following Aristotle, that people tend to take better care of things that are their sole responsibility than of objects that are held in common. Human affairs tend to be more effectively organized when each individual has a responsibility to discharge; and when most are happy with their individual responsibilities, social cohesion is greater. All of this suggests that society functions best with private *possessio*, and implies that communal *possessio*

---

[38] *De Regno Ad Regem Cypri*, I, xv, 120.
[39] *Summa Theologiae*, 1a, Q.97, a.1: "Sicut enim in generatione rerum intelligitur quidam ordo quo preceditur de imperfecto ad perfectum, nam materia est propter formam, et forma imperfectior propter perfectiorem, ita etiam est in usu rerum naturalium: nam imperfectiora cedunt in usum perfectorum."
[40] *Ibid.*, 1a, Q.96, a.4.   [41] *De Regno Ad Regem Cypri*, I, i, 5–6.

tends towards less social cohesion.[42] But private ownership is not natural, because the difference between the possession of goods, and the distribution of possessed goods is the difference between natural and human law. While it is biologically necessary for people to have claims on objects required for their survival, and for them to use reason to manipulate these objects, this biological imperative does not require that people distribute them in any particular way. While private property is most likely to result in social order, it does not follow that private property is part of the natural order of things. Human law, in its most basic manifestation of the *ius gentium*, seems to be the basis for private property. Thus individual private *possessio* is a human addition to natural law, arising from the rational recognition of the usefulness of the institution in promoting overall political and social stability.[43] So taking human law as an outgrowth of natural law, we can conclude that human *dominium* generally involves private *possessio*.

But does the call to sell one's material possessions in Matthew 19:21 mean that man's institution of private property is superseded by the divine injunction to poverty? Poverty certainly removes obstacles to charity, such as love of wealth, pride, and excessive self-interest, but it should only be sought to facilitate charity in the soul. Spiritual perfection is not ruled out by a wealth of private possessions. "Indeed, the highest perfection is possible amid great wealth, for Abraham, to whom it was said, 'Walk before me and be perfect,' is said to have been a rich man."[44] Wealth of possessions allows cultivation of the merit of stewardship, and the generous man ill serves himself in giving away so much that he cannot support himself. Aquinas is careful to point out that sacred office does not preclude private possession; for the ecclesiastical hierarchy, no vow is specifically made renouncing personal possessions, and the pastoral office does not require such a renunciation.[45] But as a Dominican friar, he was sensitive to mendicancy's spiritual benefits. In *Contra Impugnantes Dei Cultum et Religionem*, a tract he wrote in response to William of St. Amour's attack on the friars in 1255, Aquinas explains that poverty is neither necessary nor sufficient for spiritual purity, but it is conducive to a life consecrated to God. A preacher of the Word is entitled to alms because his labor, like that of any laborer, warrants recompense and is beneficial

---

[42] *Summa Theologiae*, 2a2ae, Q.66, a.2; *Comm. Politicorum*, II.i–iv.

[43] *Ibid.*, 2a2ae, Q.57, a.3; Q.66, a.2.

[44] *Ibid.*, 2a2ae, Q.185, a.6, r.1: "Quinimmo potest esse summa perfectio cum magna opulentia; nam Abraham, cui dictum est, Ambula coram me et esto perfectus, legitur dives fuisse." See also *Summa Theologiae*, 2a2ae, Q.117, a.1, r.1.

[45] *Ibid.*, 2a2ae, Q.188, a.7.

to the community. That a preacher has a right to claim recompense for his ministrations suggests that those preachers who forgo it set examples of humility. These, he concludes, are the most admirable preachers.[46]

Scripture provides a useful system of property law in the judicial precepts of the Old Testament. While the New Law of the Gospels is the best expression of the Divine Law, the Old Law differs from it only a little; "the Old Law is a tutor for the young, as Paul says," preparing man for the truth of the Christian Gospels.[47] The Old Law regulates individual possession by demanding equitable distribution, forbidding permanent alienation, and instituting inheritance. Further, it establishes where one person may have claims on the possessions of another, as when providing assistance in emergencies. Finally, the Old Law regulates the transference of goods in buying and selling, borrowing and hiring, loaning, and so forth. Aquinas notes that the Old Law and Aristotle agree in suggesting that the state should strictly regulate the sale of property. "For should property be sold without restriction, it could happen that it all came into the hands of few men, and so the state or district become denuded of inhabitants."[48]

While man appears to have *dominium* over the rest of Creation by virtue of his rational powers, kings are not necessarily kings by virtue of a more fully developed rational capacity. Human political authority is different from God's because no king creates that over which he exercises authority. Further, we predicate the word "Lord" of God only by analogy, so a firm connection between divine and human *dominium* is difficult to establish. Human *dominium* is accidental, and the authority a lord has is not his by virtue of some essential property separating him from all other men.[49] In *De Regno Ad Regem Cypri* Aquinas implies that the best use of the term *Dominus* is with respect to only one unique relationship, that between men and the Son of Man. Christ's *dominium* is His not through His humanity, but through His divinity. Aquinas explains that Christ is not *homo dominicus* because men bear the title "*dominus*" only by analogy.[50] Christ's *dominium* is over all mankind, but in different degrees. Christ is primarily *dominus* of those who are predestined to be saved and who are united through lives characterized by *caritas*.[51] Bishops, including the Supreme Pontiff, must live in a manner strictly commensurate

---

[46] *Contra Impugnantes Dei Cultum et Religionem*, in *Parma*, vol. 15, 26.

[47] *Summa Theologiae*, 1a2ae, Q.107, a.1: "Alio modo lex nova est alia a lege veteri, quia lex vetus est quasi paedagogus puerorum, ut Apostolous dicit, ad Gal., lex autem nova est lex perfectionis, quia est lex caritatis."

[48] *Ibid.*, 1a2ae, Q.105, a.2.   [49] *Summa Contra Gentiles*, III,.119, n. 10.

[50] *Summa Theologiae*, 3, Q.16, a.3.

[51] *Ibid.*, 2a2ae, Q.184, a.5: "Dicendum quod, sicut dictum est, ad statum perfectionis requiritur obligatio perpetua ad ea quae sunt perfectionis, cum aliqua solemnitate. Utrumque autem horum

with Christ's *dominium*, for they occupy the place of the Apostles in the church.

The duties of the king are likewise reproductions of the duties of the ruler of the physical body, and the ruler of the created Universe.[52] In fact, Aquinas describes divine government's relation to human government as being analogous to the relation of macrocosm to microcosm. As corporeal creatures and spiritual powers are governed by God, so the parts of our body and the powers of the soul are governed by our reason. "Since, however, man is by nature a social animal living in a multitude, as we have pointed out above, the analogy with the divine government is found in him not only in that one man governs himself by reason, but also in that the multitude of men is governed by the reason of one man."[53] This is important because Aquinas explains that the relation of kingship to God's government of Creation is predicated on *potestas*. This gives us a basis for our understanding of the relation of the two sorts of rule; human governing is related to divine governing as a particular is related to its universal. And human reason, the *potestas* that allows for human *dominium*, is to man as God is to the world, for both reason and God are the source of man's, and the world's, power respectively.

Is Aquinas' kingship absolutism, a limited monarchy, a republicanism, or some kind of a mixed constitutionalism? Much depends upon our understanding of the context in which this kingship is meant to figure, for reading Aquinas as an advocate of absolutist monarchy might cast his king in a more theocratic light than a reading more disposed to republicanism or mixed constitutionalism. James Blythe suggests that Aquinas turned away from either absolutist or limited monarchy because of Thomas' generally negative attitude towards non-sacred *dominium*.[54] In governing, the king's purpose is to guide the governed to their appointed end, which for Aristotle, is earthly happiness. Since the moral virtues are the means by which earthly happiness is attained, the king must sustain the exercise of virtue. Since the final object of human life is enjoyment of God,

---

competit et religosis et episcopis . . . Similiter etiam et episcopi obligant se ad ea quae sunt perfectionis, pastorale assumentes officium."

[52] *De Regno Ad Regem Cypri*, I, ii, 19, and I, xii, 95: "Hoc igitur officium rex suscepisse cognoscat, ut sit in regno sicut in corpore anima, et sicut Deus in mundo." All translations from *De Regno* are from St Thomas Aquinas, *On Kingship*, trans. Gerald B. Phelan (Toronto, 1949), here p. 352.

[53] *Ibid.*, I, xii, 95: "Sed quia, sicut ostendimus, homo est animal naturaliter sociale, in multitudine vivens; similitudo divini regiminis invenitur in homine non solum quantum ad hoc quod per rationem regitur unus homo, sed etiam quantum ad hoc quod per rationem unius hominis regitur multitudo."

[54] See Blythe, *Ideal Government and the Mixed Constitution in the Middle Ages*, p. 45. Further evidence of the disutility of *dominium* as a term in Aquinas' political theory lies in his readiness to apply it to the most general sense of having "the upper hand" in social relations. See *In Libros Politicorum*, in *Parma*, vol. 21, 2.7.245.

for which Aristotle's virtues are not sufficient, the king must foster the theological virtues. The monarch best able to do this is the founder of the Law that facilitates these virtues specifically, namely Jesus Christ.[55] This leads us to ask how Christ's government is realized on earth in the answer to the ministry of the church and its relation to kingship.

Just as the body is subject to the soul, so ultimately the secular power is subordinate to the spiritual. This means that spiritual "interference" in secular affairs is licit on occasions when the secular authority oversteps its bounds.[56] Further, and bolder, evidence for outright subjection of secular to sacred authority appears in *De Regno Ad Regem Cypri*, when Aquinas explains that the theological virtues take precedence over the human virtues in their enforcement:

Thus in order that spiritual things might be distinguished from earthly things, the ministry of this kingdom has been entrusted not to earthly kings but to priests, and most of all to the chief priest, the successor of St. Peter, the Vicar of Christ, the Roman Pontiff. To him all the kings of the Christian people are to be subject as to our Lord Jesus Christ Himself. For those to whom pertains the care of intermediate ends should be subject to him to whom pertains the care of the ultimate end, and be directed by his rule.[57]

Given this, the earlier mention of the authority that invests the king with his power is made clearer: the pope, who speaks for Christ, has the authority to invest secular lords with power over the subordinate ends of life, and when he judges that such power has been perverted to their personal ends, he can divest them of their power. Aquinas' under-emphasized tendencies to hierarchic thought contributed to Giles of Rome's position that all just human *potestas* is ultimately reliant on the church for its just foundation because of the church's special capacity to channel Grace. Giles' position, in turn, was the point of departure for Richard Fitzralph's *De Pauperie Salvatoris*, from which Wyclif derived the elements of Grace-founded *dominium*.

Wyclif's *dominium* thought is rooted securely in the Augustinian papalism of the early fourteenth century, of which the foremost exponents were the Augustinian friars, who formed a movement suspicious of the philosophical innovations of the Ockhamists and of what they perceived as unrestrained Aristotelian rationalism running rampant in the schools. Giles of Rome, an Augustinian friar and a disciple of Aquinas, formulated

---

[55] *De Regno Ad Regem Cypri*, I, xiv, 106.   [56] *Summa Theologiae*, 2a2ae, Q.60, a.6, r.3.

[57] *De Regno Ad Regem Cypri*, I, xiv, 110: "Huius ergo regni ministerium, ut a terrenis essent spritualia distincta, non terrenis regibus, sed sacerdotibus est commissum, et praecipue Summo Sacerdoti, successori Petri, Christi Vicario, Romano Pontifici, cui omnes reges populi christiani oportet esse subditos, sicut ipsi Dominio Jesu Christo. Sic enim ei, ad quem finis ultimi cura pertinet, subdi debent illi, ad quos pertinet cura antecedentium finium, et eius imperio dirigi."

an argument for the papacy as the source of all earthly *potestas* in his *De Ecclesiastica Potestate*. For him, Grace is the necessary precondition for all just exercise of jurisdictive authority and for all property-ownership. This is unattainable without submission to God, and more specifically, to the church, the ordered reproduction of the celestial hierarchy on earth. And because the pope is at the apex of the ecclesiastical hierarchy, no temporal *potestas* can be just without its holder's submission to papal authority.

Giles' approach proved to be more extreme than his followers in the Augustinian order could accept, and so was tempered in the thought of James of Viterbo and Augustinus Triumphus, both of whom argued for papalism in a more moderately Aristotelian vein. But the stir that Marsilius' *Defensor Pacis* created in the 1320s caused the Augustinians to feel the need for a return to the Aegidian hard line. William of Cremona's *Refutatio Errorum* (1325) represents the Order's reformulation of a strict Grace-founded *potestas* position, and established William's authority at Avignon. Most importantly, Cardinal Pierre Roger, later Clement VI, adopted William's anti-Marsilianism as the official papal position on the growing "two truths" movement among the Aristotelians.

In the early 1340s, an Ulsterman of recognized preaching abilities and proven administrative talent had come to serve in the papal court at Avignon. Richard Fitzralph, later Archbishop of Armagh and a significant voice in mediating between the Franciscans and the papacy, developed a theory of just property-ownership founded in Grace that was rooted securely in the Augustinian Order's Aegidianism. It is likely that Fitzralph first learned of this from William of Cremona at Avignon, for it appears in *Summa de Quaestionibus Armenorum* Lib. X, written shortly after his experiences in the papal court.[58] Fitzralph's *De Pauperie Salvatoris* (1356) is the fullest formulation of his argument that *dominium* requires Grace as necessary precondition, although his position is not as clearly papalist as were those of Giles and his disciples. In fact, a reader inclined against papalism might easily interpret Fitzralph's position as suggesting that the spiritual authority of the ecclesiastical hierarchy could conceivably lack Grace in some cases.[59] Fitzralph's treatise caused a stir among Oxford's friars in the 1350s, sufficient to warrant a formal response from the Augustinian Geoffrey Hardeby in his *De Vita Evangelica* (c. 1357). By this time, Wyclif was an active scholar, alive to the debates that characterized Oxford in mid-century. That he read Fitzralph early in his career is likely, and that he adopted Fitzralph's theory of Grace-founded *dominium* is undeniable.

[58] Aubrey Gwynn, *The English Austin Friars in the Time of Wyclif* (Oxford, 1940), p. 67. See also Katherine Walsh, *A Fourteenth-Century Scholar and Primate: Richard Fitzralph at Oxford, Avignon and Armagh* (Oxford, 1981), pp. 129–81.

[59] Gwynn, *The English Austin Friars in the Time of Wyclif*, pp. 68–71.

But unlike its other iterations, the theory of Grace-founded *dominium* has in Wyclif a decidedly metaphysical foundation. A brief survey of its evolution from Giles and through Fitzralph will show how significant an influence Wyclif's metaphysics was to have on his version of the theory.

DOMINIUM IN GILES OF ROME

Giles of Rome wrote two works devoted exclusively to political matters, *De Regimine Principum* (*c.* 1285) and *De Ecclesiastica Potestate* (1301). The first, written for the instruction of the young Prince Philip of France (later Philip IV, the Fair), is an Aristotelian treatment of ethics and politics and is not relevant to analysis of Giles and *dominium*. In the latter work Giles abandons the Aristotelian approach for a Neoplatonic, hierocratic endorsement of the papacy. One cannot help but wonder how things would have turned out had Giles written *De Ecclesiastica Potestate* for the young prince instead. In it, his guiding principle is that *dominium* is a gift of God founded upon divine justice, and hence ultimately reliant upon Grace. Already in *De Regimine Principum* Giles speaks of *dominium* in tones notably different from Aquinas' thought. Giles abandons Aquinas' mixed constitutionalist approach in favor of strong monarchism, founded in an hierarchical power distribution that would characterize the later *De Ecclesiastica Potestate* as well. Blythe notes that Giles, more than any other Aristotelian political theorist, maintains a sensitivity to hierocratic cosmology underlying political philosophy, in *De Regimine Principum* as a monarchist and in *De Ecclesiastica Potestate* as a papalist.[60] Consonant with this metaphysical stance is a more favorable view of the lord–subject relationship; gone is the Thomistic reticence about a man exercising mastery over fellow-men.

In *De Ecclesiastica Potestate*, Giles explains that all earthly power, temporal and ecclesiastical, is rooted in the power and authority of the papacy. The image of which he is most fond is that of a papal river from which smaller, temporal streams and tributaries snake out, which streams themselves branch out into brooks and rivulets. Carrying the analogy further, this river's source is the sea, which is God, for "God is a kind of fount and a kind of sea of force and power, from which sea all forces and all powers are derived like streams."[61] Thus the authority of all earthly power flows

---

[60] *De Regimine Principium Libri III* (Frankfurt, 1968) 2.1.14.154v. See Blythe, *Ideal Government and the Mixed Constitution in the Middle Ages*, p. 74.

[61] Giles of Rome, *On Ecclesiastical Power: The De Ecclesiastica Potestate of Aegidius Romanus*, ed. and trans. R. W. Dyson (Drew, NH, 1986), III, ii, 4; Aegidius Romanus, *De Ecclesiastica Potestate*, ed. R. Scholz [1929] (Stuttgart, 1961): "Sic et Deus est quidam fons et quoddam mare virtutis et

from the papacy. Earlier, regarding property-ownership, Giles had said, "[N]o one is worthy of a paternal inheritance or of any other possession or of any other principality or lordship unless he is the servant and son of the church . . . we must acknowledge that we hold all that we possess from the church and through the church, by whose sacraments, which are the vessels of Grace, we receive the divine Grace and are made the sons and heirs of God."[62] On the face of it, *iurisdictio* is not necessarily united to this possession, but Giles believes it to be; these two references show that he sees both earthly power and private ownership to be based on the authority of the church.

Giles does not equate *dominium* with *potestas*; in *De Ecclesiastica Potestate* the subject is *potestas*, of which the major temporal manifestation is *dominium*. Yet Giles' use of the term *potestas* reveals an assumption that private ownership of property is intrinsically related to political juris-diction, which union is referred to sometimes as *potestas*, sometimes as *dominium*. What is important is that Giles linked private ownership and *iurisdictio* with Grace as a necessary precondition; that he did not explicitly unite the two concepts under the term *dominium* is less so.

Giles is a founding father in the emergence of "*dominium*" as a term for understanding the created order. The exercise of political power and possession of material goods are only possible through Grace, available only through the offices of the church. How Grace is a prerequisite for power and how the church as administrator thus has a hand in all mundane power and possession is the issue that lies at the heart of *De Ecclesiastica Potestate*. Giles was an important *auctoritas* for the Augustinian friars, and his work provided an intellectual medium for much of what was to take place in academic circles regarding *potestas*, *proprietas*, and *dominium* in fourteenth-century England.[63] His *De Ecclesiastica Potestate* was to influence James of Viterbo, Augustinus Triumphus, William of Cremona, and much of the papal platform from which Wyclif would be condemned.

R. W. Dyson suggests that three general ideas lie at the heart of *De Ecclesiastica Potestate*.[64] The first and most familiar is the distinction be-tween the spiritual and the material swords. For Giles, the church possesses both and has delegated to temporal lords the responsibility of wielding

---

potencie, a quo mari omnes virtutes et omnes potencie quasi quidam rivuli derivantur." Giles' fame as a theorist will never be overtaken by his fame as a geographer.

[62] *De Ecclesiastica Potestate*, II, viii, 15: "Igitur non sunt digni hereditate paterna nec re alia qui non sunt servi Dei. . . . omnia que habemus ab ecclesia et per ecclesiam debemus recognoscere, per cuius sacramenta, que sunt vasa gracie, suscipimus divinam graciam et fimus filii et heredes Dei."

[63] Gwynn, *The English Austin Friars in the Time of Wyclif*, pp. 35–45.

[64] Dyson (ed.), *On Ecclesiastical Power*, p. xiv.

the material sword. But why should the church possess both swords? The answer lies in the second of the three general ideas: material being is distinct from, and subservient to, spiritual being, which has authority over all matters corporeal. For Giles this dualism, seen in the proper hierarchical perspective, incontestably demonstrates supreme papal *potestas* in all earthly *dominium*. Two entities seem to have been conflated in the past few sentences; if the church possesses both swords, how is it that one man – the pope – has supreme *potestas*? Are the church and the pope the same individual, as were Louis XIV and the state? This is the third, and most significant, general idea; for Giles, ecclesiastical power is synonymous with papal power. Giles only refers to lesser clerical power in his comparison of papal and divine *dominium*, where the angelic hierarchy is to God as the ecclesiastical one is to the pope.[65] Giles tellingly never gives an explicit definition of the church. The church as repository and dispenser of Grace-causing sacraments is an hierarchic structure directed to fulfilling the requirements of the pope. But the church as Body of Christ on earth, as the Community of Believers, or as the temporal means of effecting Christ's will, is ignored. For Giles, the church as an administrative and functional entity is nothing more than the pope.

In Giles' Neoplatonic cosmology, everything functions best by serving that which is set directly above it on the great ladder of Being. In material creation, material goods are only well-ordered in the service of spiritual ends.[66] In a human being, the body only acts properly in the service of the soul, the chief end of which is, of course, salvation. Accordingly, the material sword, or the power over temporal, material goods, must be subject to the spiritual sword, which holds power over affairs central to the soul's well-being.[67] Giles is usually content to make sweeping generalizations about the rigidly hierarchic structure of the Universe, but he also refers to the participative relation of particulars to universals in explaining how temporal power relies on spiritual, ecclesiastical power.[68]

Giles uses scriptural precedent to establish ecclesiastical sovereignty over all temporal authority. A kingdom without justice is a "great band of robbers," and justice is only possible when spiritual power institutes material power, as is clear in the cosmological hierarchy.[69] So priestly institution is a prerequisite for just civil authority. When we turn to the Bible, we might easily lose sight of this. While Moses sets the precedent for a spiritual authority who bears both material and spiritual swords,

---

[65] *De Ecclesiastica Potestate*, II, xiii, 33–40.   [66] *Ibid.*, II, iv, 6.   [67] *Ibid.*, I, iv, 3, also I, v, 9.
[68] *Ibid.*, II, xii, 3: "quod ecclesia in temporalibus habet dominium universale, ceteri vero particulare. Quia ergo particularia sub universalibus continentur, satis ostensum esse videtur, quod ecclesia habeat dominium superius ceteri vero inferius."
[69] *Ibid.*, I, v, 5; see *De Civitate Dei*, IV, 4, 1–2.

there were earlier kings who, though just, seem to have lacked priestly institution. Melchizidek was God's priest as well as king of Salem. But this sort of kingship was anomalous, and those of Giles' day are more like the kingship of Saul, who was instituted on Samuel's priestly authority, and only ruled as long as he obeyed Samuel. This presents a useful distinction; command over a power is superior to the actual use of a power, for command is a function of a spiritual nature, while use is a function of a corporeal one.[70] Might the church itself wield temporal power? A superior power can certainly do anything that an inferior power can, even if the inferior power acts in a different manner, because the superior power is the source of the inferior power.[71] But power brings with it anxieties for the bearer, and the church should not be burdened down by the pesky worries of the material world.[72]

Giles equates power over material objects with possession. All claims that anyone can have on any material object can only be justified by spiritual needs. "And since temporal goods are never well-ordered unless they are ordered to spiritual ends ... when a prince or any man possesses temporal things, those temporal possessions are not goods for him unless he orders them for spiritual ends."[73] No one can realize and act on his spiritual needs without the guidance of the church, whose lord is the pope, so the pope has the only true *dominium* of all temporal things. But why should the church have the final say in the paternal–filial relation of inheritance, which Giles refers to as the most widespread basis for material possession? And while the pope may have claim on the direction of material property to spiritual ends, does this entail plenipotentiary papal lordship over all material property?

We can begin with a glance back to Giles' hierarchic universe. By accepting the subordination of the material to the spiritual, we can draw up an earthly *dominium* stratification schema. If priestly power has priority – literally *dominium* – over royal power, as is suggested in Scripture, and if royal power is appointed to have material lordship over our physical selves, which is the domain of civil authority, and if we have *dominium* (of whatever iteration) through possession of temporal goods, it follows that priestly power has *dominium* over temporal goods. Why does Giles use the term *dominium* to mean both just *possessio* and authority? Following Aquinas, he explains that the gift of *dominium* to Adam arose because

[70] *De Ecclesiastica Potestate*, I, ix, 4.
[71] *Ibid.*, II, x, 3; xiii, 6–47; III, ix, 2.   [72] *Ibid.*, II, i, 6; II, v, 17.
[73] *Ibid.*, II, iv, 6: "et quia numquam temporalia sunt bene ordinata, nisi ordinentur ad spiritualia, quia universa natura corporalis ordinatur ad spiritualem ... consequens est, quod princeps vel quicumque homo habens temporalia, nisi ordinet ea ad spiritualia, illa temporalia non sunt bona sibi, quia non sunt ei ad salutem, sed ad damnacionem anime."

man was made in God's image. But Giles is more willing than Aquinas to subvert one human to the mastery of another because of his unwavering faith in the hierarchical superiority of spiritual to royal authority.[74] Giles' account of familial inheritance is a good example of the hierarchically arranged connection of ownership and jurisdictive authority. An heir receives his inheritance through more than civil justice because in the cosmological hierarchy men are under God's *dominium*, so justice demands more for material possession than mere human assent.[75] Just inheritance is only possible for those properly acting under divine *dominium*. Initially, this was instinctive, because God instilled in Adam an "original justice," but Original Sin changed all that. If someone who turns away from his rightful lord's *dominium* has committed an act of *laesa maiestas* punishable by death, "it is manifestly clear that he who is not subject to God loses deservedly and unjustly possesses that which he holds from God."[76] The only alternative to this is to receive the sacraments of baptism and penance, the chief vessels of Grace, making us God's true heirs, and providing a just foundation to postlapsarian inheritance. And since the church has the power of excommunication, precluding an excommunicate from receiving Grace and so justly inheriting, Giles' case is made. The church alone has final jurisdiction over temporal inheritance, because it alone administers the sacraments that justify the institution.[77]

Giles notes that Hugh of St. Victor distinguishes between *dominium* of use and *dominium* of power in *De Sacramentis Fidei Christianae*.

He calls a lordship of use one which bears fruit, but that which he calls a lordship of power is jurisdictional, and to it belongs the execution of justice. And we say that the church has a universal temporal lordship in both these senses.[78]

So Giles must prove that the church has complete *dominium* in enjoyment and in power, while keeping the two separate. As it turns out, Giles appropriated Hugh's distinction to develop his own thesis that ecclesiastical *dominium* has fullness of power, without consideration as to the relation between use, enjoyment, and jurisdictive power. Giles invites us to consider the three things at stake in ecclesiastical *dominium*, namely, the human soul, the human body, and material possessions. One would imagine, he says, that three swords should correspond to these three spheres.[79]

---

[74] *Ibid.*, II, iv, 15.   [75] *Ibid.*, II, vii, 10.

[76] *Ibid.*, II, viii, 9: "[Q]ui non est subiectus Deo, digne perdit et iniuste possidet omne illud quod habet a Deo."

[77] *Ibid.*, II, xii, 21–2.

[78] *Ibid.*, II, x, 2: "Appellat autem dominium utile illud quod est fructiferum, dominium autem potestativum vocat illud quod est iurisdiccionale, ad quod spectat iusticiam exercere. Hugh of St. Victor, *De Sacramentis Fidei Christianae*, II, ii, 7 (*PL* 176, col. 420B).

[79] *De Ecclesiastica Potestate*, II, x, 3.

But because a superior power can do whatever an inferior can, the sword that rules bodies can better accomplish what the lesser sword can. Furthermore, the spiritual faculties can better accomplish what the two lesser swords can in their own inferior way; in human affairs, the intellective powers hold sway over the highest objects of enquiry, allowing for clearer, speculative judgment. And since the spiritual ends are those for which all material objects are directed, a speculative judgment exercised by the spiritual sword has complete jurisdictive power. "Therefore, since the spiritual sword can judge all temporal matters, it has a universal lordship of jurisdiction and power over temporal things; and since it can also reap all temporal things, it has a universal lordship of use and enjoyment."[80]

Might not proper judgmental abilities arise from healthy use or enjoyment of material goods? Given Giles' rigid dualism, this is unlikely, but aside from a few shop-worn exempla that beg the hierocratic question, Giles does little to explore this question. It is in discussions like this, the blood and bones of a theory of *dominium*, that Giles shows the importance of his hierocratic cosmology. Without a general familiarity and agreement with the principal assumptions about how inferior powers exist solely as material means to the spiritual ends of superior powers, the argument lacks purchase.

If the pope has full jurisdictive and usufructive powers over all the material world, does he "own" everything? If we think of *dominium* as full usufructive power, in which the lord has the claim of use and enjoyment of whatever is in his purview, ownership would appear to be a *fait accompli*. But ownership and use were to become very different concepts in later thought, particularly because of the Poverty Controversy. Possession of a thing leads to its use and enjoyment, but possession without good judgment damages the soul, which is the responsibility of the church. So Giles views possession or ownership (his equation of these two was not retained by later thinkers) as the middle term between use and jurisdiction. If the pope has absolute jurisdictive and usufructive powers, ownership seems to follow as well. But possession as such carries with it all the anxieties the clergy must avoid. And because all that we own comes from God, and must, finally, return to Him, the laity should generously contribute offerings to the church, "in recognition of due servitude."[81] This "tribute" shows our appreciation of God's loan of material objects for our enjoyment, and the church receives it, because through it that we can receive the sacraments. And if we refer back to one of his first

---

[80] *Ibid.*, II, x, 10: "Quia ergo spiritualis gladius potest de omnibus temporalibus iudicare, habet super temporalibus universale dominium iurisdiccionale et potestativum; quia vero potest de omnibus temporalibus metere, habet universale dominium utile et fructiferum."

[81] *Ibid.*, II, xi, 4.

injunctions as to the superiority of priestly to temporal powers – that it is far better to command than it is to use – we see that the pope does not need to "own" everything to hold absolute *dominium* over all the world.

It is still difficult to determine whether the pope is the highest member of the church, or whether he is the church. To unravel this, we need a good definition of the church, but Giles only describes the ecclesiastical hierarchy's similarity to the celestial hierarchy. The celestial hierarchy was created by God, Whom it was meant to serve, and is divisible into three sections: counselors, architects, and workers.[82] He then characterizes the ecclesiastical hierarchy in the same way, serving the pope just as angels serve God. If the celestial hierarchy's structure is understandable only in terms of the divisions among the servants of a mundane king, the ecclesiastical offices, mirroring the celestial ones, must be similarly organized. But civil *dominium* is just only under the aegis of the church's *dominium*; in fact, Giles repeatedly characterizes the relation of the many instances of civil *dominium* to the church's papal *dominium* as the same sort of relation as what holds between particulars and their universal. "[T]he church has a universal, and others only a particular, lordship in temporal things; since, therefore particulars are contained within universals, this seems to be enough to show that the church has a superior lordship and others only an inferior."[83]

In the celestial hierarchy, God is the source of all order and structure in Creation, celestial and temporal. Giles likens God to the ocean, as already noted, or to the Sun, for God sends His rays of goodness throughout the universe, preserving and directing everything according to a common law, a universal agent through which His causal power acts. And just as God is the instigator and source of His "common" law, so is the pope the source of all temporal law, canon and civil.[84] Further, papal *dominium* is a liberating force, providing all human action with a proper foundation. Without it, we would be in bondage to the physical world, the corporeal would not be directed by the spiritual, and the cosmological order would be upset. But with it, we are given the spiritual guidance we need, and our law codes, canon and civil, have a just foundation. Within the church, Giles explains that a special branch of law specifically ordered to ecclesiastical matters is necessary, in which the pope has supreme jurisdictive powers.[85] And in imitation of God, who can abrogate His common law as He sees fit, the pope can step beyond the dictates of canon law, using what amounts to absolute papal power.

---

[82] *Ibid.*, II, xiii, 33.   [83] *Ibid.*, II, xii, 3.
[84] *Ibid.*, III, ii, 19.   [85] *Ibid.*, III, i, 16; III, ix, 10.

Appointment to the papal office invests its holder with the office's supreme power of jurisdiction and use, elevating him above the judgment of his fellow-man. This is not the same as spiritual purity. Indeed, Giles explicitly distinguishes between purity of conscience and the plenipotentiary eminence of the papal throne. The first sort is that elevation of the soul enabling one to judge the evil of worldly men, and to live a morally exemplary life. Presumably Giles has figures like Aquinas, Francis of Assisi, or Peter Damian in mind. But the second sort of spiritual perfection is holiness according to status, "and especially according to the status of the prelate ... elevated in respect of jurisdiction and fullness of power."[86] If the pope has this absolute power, how can civil lords have granted temporal possessions to the church, if all temporal possession is only made possible by the church? God allows the user of the material sword some due power, Giles explains, and if Caesar should allow some of that power to be directed to the church, so much the better for all. This might appear contradictory, given Giles' earlier claim that the pope has supreme right of use, but the use Caesar makes of his possessions is, while perhaps more widespread, baser than papal use. Papal absolute power is not at all decreased by temporal power, and can be augmented by the gifts of temporal princes. "Therefore the church can have such fullness of power, yet will nonetheless possess temporal things by the pious devotion of the faithful, and by the gifts of the princes if the faithful themselves give to the church the right which they have in temporal things, and if the princes themselves bestow temporal rights upon churches."[87]

The general nature of Giles' vision of papal *dominium* is clear enough. Without the justice and Grace available only to the pope, no civil lord can rule. Further, enjoyment and ownership of property would be impossible without papal *dominium*. And without the pope, the church would be as directionless and impotent as all of Creation would be without its Lord; Creation would cease to be, and so would the church. Two important notions unite Giles and Wyclif: the idea that Grace and just human *dominium* are necessarily connected, and the centrality of metaphysics to recognizably "political" concerns. Wyclif's metaphysics rejects the hierarchic structure in favor of emphasis upon the more ontologically general universal–particular relationship, but we will see in the next several chapters that, as with Giles, one cannot ignore these matters in Wyclif

---

[86] *Ibid.*, I, ii, 6: "Sed qui est perfectus et sanctus et spiritualis secundum statum et potissime secundum statum prelacionis, ille est elevatus secundum iurisdiccionem et secundum plenitudinem potencie."

[87] *Ibid.*, III, xi, 17: "Potest ergo ecclesia habere talem plenitudinem potestatis, et tamen possidebit res temporales pia devocione fidelium et largicione principum, si ipsi fideles dent ecclesie ius quod habent in temporalibus, et si ipsi principes iura temporalium ecclesiis largiantur."

when attempting to understand divine and human *dominium*. Wyclif's emphasis on universal–particular relations frees him from reliance on a "most sovereign institution" within Creation, as Giles views the church in his scheme. Any real created *dominium*, for Wyclif, is an instantiation of the divine *dominium*, the truly sovereign universal outside of Creation. Thus, Wyclif is at liberty to define "church" in a notably anti-hierocratic fashion, although we should not suppose Wyclif's definition to be founded in a complete rejection of Aegidian hierarchy.[88] Nevertheless, with the re-definition of the church as the Body of the Elect, the papal office becomes one of spiritual, though not nominal, significance for Wyclif, leaving the burden of material *iurisdictio* on the individual temporal participant in the universal divine *dominium*, the civil lord. This shift from pope to civil lord would be difficult to account for without Wyclif's reliance on Grace-founded *dominium*, as we will consider in Chapters 4 and 5.

Giles lacks Wyclif's antipathy to private ownership, and views the institution's justice as primarily ecclesiastically based, the opposite of Wyclif's view. Wyclif's disagreement with Giles arises from his rejection of the church's claim to authority in temporal affairs, which follows on his redefinition of the nature and purpose of the church *vis-à-vis* Christ's restoration of private ownership-free Natural *dominium*. One could be forgiven for assuming Wyclif to be the functional opposite of Giles, arguing the monarchic position in place of the papal one. After all, both make reference to the biblical priest-king Melchizedek as importantly relevant to their arguments. Giles views him as an anomaly, the sort of king no longer possible, while Wyclif sees him as a paradigm for just civil lordship. But the difference is not based on conflicting political sympathies; Giles and Wyclif differ on ontological issues. Giles embraces a mediatory hierarchy that Wyclif's realism effectively eliminates, with the result that mediation between God and man is central to Giles' argument and impossible in Wyclif's. And because of the superiority of the spiritual to the material, Giles cannot imagine a secular lord with mediative powers that surpass spiritual authority, making the likes of Melchizidek virtually impossible. Wyclif's dismissal of the need for mediation between God and man eliminates this restriction.

JOHN XXII: DIVINE AND HUMAN *DOMINIUM*

John XXII's position warrants mentioning because his conception of human *dominium* as ultimately reliant upon divine *dominium* became a

---

[88] David Luscombe, "Wyclif and Hierarchy," in *From Ockham to Wyclif*, ed. A. Hudson and M. Wilks, *SCH*, Subsidia 5 (London, 1987), pp. 233–44. Luscombe views Wyclif as having been generally inclined to hierarchical arrangements of authority, consonant with Grosseteste.

central element in a quarrel that was to lead through Fitzralph into Wyclif's position.[89] In 1329 John wrote *Quia vir reprobus*, the last of four bulls concerned with evangelical poverty, in response to Michael of Cesena's contention that the friars could justly claim to follow Christ and the Apostles in a life wholly lacking in *dominium*. John was particularly angered by the Franciscan contention that private ownership, the assignment of terms such as "mine" and "thine," was foreign to prelapsarian humanity. This is completely false, says John, for human *dominium* is not a result of Original Sin; indeed, it existed in paradise. "And if it is asked whether [Adam's] *dominium* was private or common, it seems that before the formation of Eve, Adam's *dominium* was private, not common."[90] Individual *dominium* has existed as a divine dispensation since before the Fall; private possession was divinely instituted for all humanity after the Fall. The opprobrium associated with the institution is misguided, and claims that Christ owned nothing are groundless. Indeed, Christ's temporal *dominium* is well documented, and did not impede His saving mission. John explains that we should not err with the Franciscans, by assuming that private ownership originates in the law of human rulers, for it existed long before there were such rulers.

The other important notion in *Quia vir reprobus* is John's contention that the institution of human *dominium* is reliant upon divine *dominium*. Divine *dominium* is eternally the prime governing force in Creation. The only way anyone can give anything is on divine authority; no human authority alone will suffice. This is because God created *ex nihilo*. No one can claim such powers, so no one can have as true a claim to *dominium* as God can. Thus divine *dominium* must be the necessary condition for the institution of human *dominium*. No kind of law is just without God's sustenance, and it is only His will that provides for the power of all lesser sorts of right.[91]

DOMINIUM IN FITZRALPH

Assessments of Wyclif's reliance on Richard Fitzralph's *De Pauperie Salvatoris* have emphasized the similarities, practically equating the two

---

[89] See James Doyne Dawson, "Richard Fitzralph and the Fourteenth-Century Poverty Controversies," *JEH*, 34 (1983), p. 324. For a fuller overview of John XXII's position, see Malcolm Lambert, *Franciscan Poverty* (St. Bonaventure, NY, 1998), pp. 221–69.

[90] John XXII, *Quia vir reprobus*, *Bullarium Franciscanum* 6 (Rome 1902), 422b: "Et si quaeritur, utrum illud dominium proprium fuit vel commune . . . videtur quod ante formationem Evae, dominium temporalium Adae proprium fuit, non commune."

[91] *Ibid.*, 440b–441a.

thinkers' *dominium* theories.[92] This leads one to believe that Wyclif had cribbed much of his political thought from Fitzralph, implying that his doctrine of civil *dominium* is an afterthought, possibly cobbled together for less than honorable purposes. While Wyclif was strongly influenced by Fitzralph's thought, the two are as similar as Karl Marx is to Adam Smith. Both agree about certain fundamental value assignments, but they disagree about what sorts of conclusions follow.

Fitzralph and Wyclif agree that power and property are subordinate to *dominium*-relations, and that just *dominium* is only possible with Grace. Yet this hardly makes for complete harmony. Fitzralph wrote to shore up the papal position in the poverty controversy, holding that the friars could not lay claim to "evangelical poverty." Katherine Walsh describes Fitzralph's attitude towards the friars as antipathetic, emphasizing his stance that evangelical poverty entailed complete abdication of civil lordship. Since the friars had agreed to papal reservation of lordship in respect of their temporal goods, thereby restricting non-papal agents from access to what they had surrendered, Fitzralph reasoned that they could not realize their evangelical ideal. Walsh sees Fitzralph as having concluded that the friars' enterprise was doomed by illegality and, ultimately, by sin.[93] James Dawson, on the other hand, interprets Fitzralph's position as being more consonant with the original Franciscan spirit. On Dawson's reading, Fitzralph accepts the friars' claim to apostolic poverty but uses it to restrict their preaching privileges. Here, Fitzralph's disagreement with the friars about ownership is less a denial of Franciscan poverty and more an argument that church property-ownership partakes in original lordship.[94] For both interpretations, though, the attention is on the relation of the friars to the rest of the church.

Wyclif, on the other hand, strove to renew the apostolic purity of the church, to cleanse it of any ties to mundane goods, and to strengthen the monarchy, effectively weakening the papacy. Thus, while the doctrine that just temporal *dominium* requires Grace underlies both thinkers' positions on divine and human *dominium*-relations, one uses it to strengthen the papal stance in the face of Franciscan controversy, while the other uses

---

[92] See McFarlane, *John Wycliffe and the Beginnings of English Nonconformity* (Aylesbury, 1952), pp. 30, 61; Leff, *Heresy in the Later Middle Ages* (New York, 1967), vol. 2, pp. 546–8; Lambert, *Medieval Heresy: Popular Movements from the Gregorian Reform to the Reformation* (London, 1992), p. 236; R. L. Poole in *De Dominio Divino*, pp. xlvii–xlix, esp. p. xlviii.

[93] Walsh, *A Fourteenth-Century Scholar and Primate*, p. 404.

[94] Dawson, "Richard Fitzralph and the Fourteenth-Century Poverty Controversies," pp. 333–4; see also L. L. Hammerich, "The Beginning of the Strife Between Richard Fitzralph and the Mendicants," *Det Kgl. Danske Videnskabernes Selskab., Historisk-filologiske Meddelelser*, 36.3 (1938).

it to undermine the conventional ecclesiastical structure. This discussion can only glance at *De Pauperie Salvatoris*, but we can sketch out enough of Fitzralph's position to see just how Wyclif departed from it.[95]

Fitzralph's critique of the friars was that they sinned on two counts: first, through lack of humility by claiming the right to hear confessions, and second, by pretending to just use of goods after having surrendered possession of their goods to the pope. This was just pushing the problem of civil ownership back a degree, Fitzralph argued, since evangelical poverty must involve no truck with possession whatever. As we will see, Wyclif claimed that the civil lord had the burden of owning what those in apostolic poverty used, instead of the church. This is not the same as what Fitzralph was attacking in the friars, but it introduces a problem that it will be useful to bear in mind. If the apostolic pauper is to live on alms given by a just holder of civil *dominium*, whose own holdings are held through Grace, why is apostolic poverty somehow better than Grace-founded *dominium*? Fitzralph is not convinced that it is on all counts. If it is, why is it licit for the apostolically pure to rely on the alms of one living a less praiseworthy life?

The most basic problem of the first five books of *De Pauperie Salvatoris* is the relation between *dominium* and property, and Fitzralph addresses this by showing the differences and relations between property, possession, and right of use, all of which fall under the generic category of "property notions." Both Fitzralph and Wyclif describe the general types of *dominium*, including God's *dominium* of Creation, and human *dominium*, which includes man's original, prelapsarian *dominium*, and artificial, political *dominium*. Unlike Wyclif, Fitzralph alludes to the *dominium* of the angels, which is less than God's *dominium*, but more than human *dominium*. Furthermore, Fitzralph begins by emphasizing the relation between holding property and *dominium*, even before he discusses the nature of God's *dominium* of Creation. He explains that property is etymologically founded in *proprie* or *prope*, referring to a relation of proximity. "Thus it follows that ownership of an ownable thing is unmediated and complete *dominium* of that thing."[96]

---

[95] A complete edition of *De Pauperie Salvatoris* does not yet exist: R. L. Poole appended an edition of its first four books to *De Dominio Divino* in 1890, and Richard Brock edited the latter five books in his unpublished Ph.D. dissertation, "An Edition of Richard Fitzralph's 'De Pauperie Salvatoris,' Books V, VI, and VII" (University of Colorado, 1954).

[96] *De Pauperie Salvatoris*, I, ii, 280.13–17: "Proprietas enim a proprie, et proprie a prope descendit; quoniam quod uni est proprium est sibi prope, quia ad votum eius reponitur, sive iuxta, vel prope voluntatem ipsius, ad similitudinem rei iuxta vel prope quamquam in loco reposite: unde consequitur quod proprietas rerum ditancium est dominium immediatum et integrum rerum ipsarum."

All instances of holding property are instances of *dominium*, but not all instances of *dominium* involve holding property.[97] Right of use is also different from *dominium*; while all *dominium* involves the right of use, a lord can concede the right of use to another without then abdicating his *dominium*. One who has the right of use has "leasing and service and the [immediate] value of what they have the right of using, but they do not have *dominium* over that thing."[98] How is this different from property? Does not the holder of property have the right of using? Yes, but the holder of property might further allocate the right of use to another; the baron might grant right of use of several hides of his baronetcy to a subordinate without abdicating his claim to holding the property. In a structural sense this is just a further iteration of *dominium*, and it is difficult to see why Fitzralph did not just say that *dominium* was almost infinitely hierarchically divisible. But it is difficult only until the distinction between original and artificial, political *dominium* is made clear.

But we must add another ball to be juggled: possession is different from property and right of use, and from *dominium*. Possession is "the immediate effect of *dominium*, the medium between the *dominium* of a thing and its use. Whereas no one having *dominium* can have use of his *dominium* unless he has prior possession of what he dominates... hence possession and *dominium* should be distinguished."[99] So if a lord can only have right of use of his *dominium* if he has direct possession, how is possession different from property? Possession is not peculiar to *dominium*, while property only results from a *dominium*-relation. Thus *dominium* and *possessio* are accidentally relatable; just *dominium* is the basis of just *possessio*, while unjust *possessio* implies absence of just *dominium*. Unjust *dominium* is an oxymoron; *dominium* lacking the Grace that makes justice possible is not *dominium* at all.[100]

A preliminary fictional example may help to clarify. Bear in mind that the example involves civil *dominium*, which we have not yet thoroughly explained. Let us say that the king has *dominium* over all of England, from Cornwall to the Scottish borders. He gives a gift of an estate to a certain baron, who now has the estate as his property, and so exercises *dominium* over it. The king still has (primary) *dominium* over the estate, but has granted its property to the baron, who in turn, allows his best

---

[97] *Ibid.*, I, ii, 279.3–6; see also IV, i, 437.3–15.
[98] *Ibid.*, I, ii, 281.17–25: "[H]abent enim locatarii et commodatarii et licenciati rebus sibi locatis et commodatis ab aliis ius utendi, et tamen non habent in illis rebus dominium."
[99] *Ibid.*, I, ii, 281.29–34: "Possessio est immediatus fructus seu effectus dominii, medius inter dominium rei et usum ipsius; quoniam nemo habens dominium potest uti suo dominio nisi prius rem dominatam possideat... unde constat quod ipsa possessio a dominio suo distinguitur."
[100] See *Ibid.*, IV, iv, 441; II, vi, 344–8.

knight the right of use of a fertile valley in the far western sector of the baronetcy. The knight can profit from the rich crops and plentiful ore in this valley, so long as he is true in his fealty to the baron, his liege. But a native of the valley claims that he is its true lord, robbed of his regal heritage by the king. The native kills the knight and lays claim to the valley, thereby possessing it. The rebel certainly does not have right of use, as far as the king is concerned, for that can only come from the source of *dominium*. Full-scale war is averted when a bishop journeys to the valley and convinces the native that the king has *dominium* through God's Grace, and that his rebellion shows his own lack of Grace.

This story only illustrates the mechanics of property notions and *dominium*; as we proceed, we will discover the singular place of our fictional bishop. It is significant that Fitzralph makes these distinctions about how someone can lay claim to material goods before he describes God's *dominium*, while Wyclif devotes all of *De Dominio Divino* to God's *dominium* before he addresses the nature of human property in *De Civili Dominio*. This shows a real difference in purpose between the two thinkers. Fitzralph aims to solve a problem besetting the contemporary church with a thorough philosophical analysis of the fundamental point of disagreement. Wyclif, on the other hand, redefines the church, showing that the problem with Fitzralph's argument lies not in its workings, but in its assumptions about the created order and the church's place in this.

Not only are Fitzralph's motives for formulating a *dominium* theory more materially-based, but his assumptions about the importance of property in *dominium* are different from Wyclif's. We see a more complex explanation of property notions in *De Pauperie Salvatoris*, but Fitzralph says little to differentiate ecclesiastical from secular property holding, and he largely ignores the evils of property. Property notions are the commodity of *dominium* for Fitzralph; they are what *dominium* is all about. For Wyclif, on the other hand, property notions are a necessary evil, best relegated to the hands of one central, secular power. True *dominium* is not about earthly property at all, as we will see. With this in mind, we can begin discovering Fitzralph's characterization of *dominium*, divine, original, and civil.

God's *dominium*-relation began when time began; "in the first instant of the origin of the world He began to be lord, nor was He lord beforehand."[101] The chief cause of God's non-eternal *dominium* is His Creation, and so His governance, conservation, and direction of Creation follow from this. "Likewise, just as, when your will produces within itself

---

[101] *Ibid.*, I, iii, 283.30: "Et est fixum quod diximus, scilicet, quod Deus in primo instanti originis mundi incepit esse dominus, nec dominus ante fuit."

a freely willed action, it is immediately lord following this production, and before it conserves the action; so the cause or reason of the first dominium of God is the very creation of things, not their conservation, government, or direction."[102] In fact, God's governance and conservation are properly His use and possession of creation, not His *dominium*:

> It seems to me that all things are said to be continually made by God through His conservation, as light in the air or in water is continually supported by the Sun, thus the divine conservation of things is more appropriately named possession rather than *dominium*.... The use of lordship and possession are more properly called governance in God's case than *dominium*; likewise among temporal lords known to us, the ... conservation of things is known as possession, and their governance ... is properly called the use of lordship and of possession, not *dominium*.[103]

Fitzralph can now explain how one individual or institution can have just *dominium* over something while allowing its conservation or governance to be the duty of another. This provides for a hierarchical political theory, and is at odds with the ideal that Wyclif was to espouse, namely, that a single instance of just civil *dominium* inescapably and immediately involves possession, right of use, and property.

By this time, something remarkable about Fitzralph's thought should be apparent: he has nothing to say about *iurisdictio*, aside from the occasional recognition of this accompanying just *dominium*. Governance, which has generally involved *iurisdictio* and *iustitia*, is the use of *dominium*; it is an effect, and not really a necessary part of its definition. When Fitzralph does discuss civil law, for example, it is never to explain how it can become just, or participate in divine *iustitia*, but only insofar as it has a part in just civil property transactions.[104] A higher law is needed to make human law just, but Fitzralph does not elaborate.[105]

Angelic *dominium* provides further evidence of Fitzralph's hierarchically disposed mindset. Although God might have had proprietary *dominium*

---

[102] *Ibid.*, I, v, 285.1–7: "Unde videtur quod dominium ita immediate consequitur ad creacionem quod conservacio rei create nequaquam causaliter ipsum precedit. Pariter, sicut cum voluntas tua actum suum liberum intra se producit, domina est ipsius ex ipsa produccione immediate, prius origine quam actum conservet, sic quod causa primi dominii Dei seu racio est ipsa rerum creacio; non conservatio, neque gubernacio sive direccio."

[103] *Ibid.*, I, v, 286.18–35: "Mihi enim videtur quod per hanc conservacionem res omnes continue verius fieri a Deo dicuntur, quam lux in aere vel in aqua continue a sole fieri affirmatur, sicut dixisti; sic quod conservacio rerum a Deo Dei possessio proprie appellatur, non ita proprie Dei dominium.... Gubernacio insuper magis proprie in Deo dici potest usus dominii et possessionis, quam dominium; sicuti in dominis temporalibus nobis notis rerum detencio sive conservacio ipsarum possessio, et earum gubernacio possidentibus accomoda effectus sive usus dominii et possessionis, non dominia proprie appellantur."

[104] *Ibid.*, IV, xv, 459.24–40. [105] *Ibid.*, IV, vi, 444.6–14.

at the instant of Creation, the angels, as the movers of the spheres and instigators of heavenly motion, have a claim to governance. This is a murky discussion, and Fitzralph is loathe to ascribe precise possession, use or distinct proprietary claims in angelic *dominium*.[106] As to the heavenly spheres, "since the forms moving the spheres were then somehow natural to them, and consequently created with them simultaneously [for *dominium*-purposes]."[107] Finally, he admonishes against too much speculation about angelic *dominium*, and says that it should suffice for us to realize that God maintains true *dominium* for Himself, yet distributes it communicatively in His goodness.[108]

Divine *dominium* is certainly the principal *dominium*-relation, the basis for God's proper possession of all creatures, and the source of God's use. In God's sustenance or conservation of all things He is their true possessor "in each of their primary origins" and in God's governance lies His intrinsic use of all things.[109] As to extrinsic use, though, when any creature acts apart from God, that is that creature's own use. Through the next books, Fitzralph makes reference to divine *dominium* as the source of all true proprietary, possessive, and usufructive relations, although this theme is not as emphatically stressed by Fitzralph as it is by Wyclif. This is because original human *dominium*, which is the closest, natural imitation of divine *dominium*, is not a directly relevant factor in postlapsarian affairs, having been irretrievably lost, while civil *dominium* is but a shadowy counterfeit of divine *dominium*.

The program for the rest of Fitzralph's definitory project requires that he (1) relate each sort of property-notion to divine *dominium*, (2) explain each property-notion as regards man's prelapsarian "original *dominium*," and (3) describe the place of each property-notion in civil *dominium*. First Fitzralph clears up doubts about angelic governance. Since governance is properly the use of *dominium*, and not *dominium* itself, angels have use of Creation as it is. They cannot cause alteration of the natural order; they have the right of use of Creation as created by God. Angels have rulership (*principatus*), not real *dominium*, but this power of governance comes directly from God, and cannot be assumed by any power in Creation. This hierarchical digression on angels may seem theologically fanciful, and only remotely relevant, but there is more here than meets the eye. Fitzralph is describing an emanative *principatus* impervious to created action, a ruling power apart from any created, human *dominium*-relation.

---

[106] *Ibid.*, I, vi, 287.10–16.
[107] See *Ibid.*, I, vi, 288.16–18: "[Q]uoniam tunc forme moventes orbes eis quoquo modo fuerant naturales, et per consequens simul cum eis create."
[108] *Ibid.*, I, vi, 288.37–289.3.   [109] *Ibid.*, I, vii, 289.12–33.

This unites angelic principality and the ecclesiastical hierarchy, "So neither the angels nor the human prelates are lords of their human subjects by reason of their prelacy."[110] Fitzralph's subsequent description of the angelic acceptance of their rule as *officium* further calls the ecclesiastical offices to mind. "Whence these celestial spirits who accept from God the office of rule over this lower world receive authority, not simply a ministry or a charge to rule."[111] "A ruling ministry" is a signal phrase, which is developed later in discussion of Moses' guidance of the Hebrews. Fitzralph is, quite simply, making clerics *de facto* heirs to an angelic authority. Although little more is said of angelic *dominium* in the books appended to Poole's edition of *De Dominio Divino*, Fitzralph will make notable use of this groundwork for ecclesiastical authority in the later books directly concerned with the improper pastoral claims made by the friars.

God's *dominium*-relation properly involves His "giving," which is a communicative act. That is, God loans that over which He holds *dominium* to His rational creatures, while retaining full dominative power over the loan. "Adam's *dominium*, and still more all subsequent human *dominium*, can and should truly be called a loan and not real *dominium* . . . for God gave it to him because He communicates His goods in His giving . . . so all human *dominium* is truly a divine loan [*commodacio*]."[112] The notion of natural, original human *dominium* as a loan is important to the discussion, but is not as immediately crucial to the argument as it is in Wyclif's later use of the idea.

Another important aspect of Fitzralph's thinking appears in his discussion of the extent of what is communicated in God's giving *dominium* to Adam. Fitzralph never explicitly broaches ontological problems, but here he shows his assumptions about the nature of universals. In communicating *dominium*, does God communicate *dominium* of the species, the individual, or both to Adam? Only immediate, or particular, substances can be subject to an act of *dominium*. A species is not immediate, but mediated; that is, members of a species, or particulars, are substantially

---

[110] *Ibid.*, I, x, 294.35–7: "Unde, sicut nec angeli, ita nec prelati racione prelacionis sue sunt domini hominum subditorum: nunquid autem prelati aut angeli rerum aliarum domini sint dicendi, inferius suo loco, si libet valebis inquirere."

[111] *Ibid.*, I, xi, 295.21–4: "Unde spiritus hii celestes qui officium regiminis huius mundi inferioris a Deo accipiunt, quia auctoritatem accipiunt ut possint, ultra nudum ministerium sive nudam preposituram regendi."

[112] *Ibid.*, I, xxiv, 315.19–25: "[Q]uoniam dominium Ade, et quanto magis dominium cuiuscunque hominis subsequentis, vere dici potest, et debet dici, commodacio, non vere dominium . . . Deus sibi bona sua donando communicavit illi suum divinum dominium, Deus ea veraciter sibi dedit . . . unde omne dominium hominis commodacio quoad Deum veraciter (ut ibi dixi) existit."

subject to *dominium*, but a species *qua* species has existence only through its members, and so requires the members as media for its universal existence. "Species cannot be immediate, but supposit medially or in singular individuals, and only then can fall under *dominium* or use."[113] Furthermore, species were not created as such, for they presuppose supposits or individuals in which they are instantiable. Species are neither governed nor conserved as such by God, but only mediately in individual beings, as an effect of God's governance and conservation of particulars. This is not to say that species do not exist as ideas in God's mind, but God's *dominium* applies to creatures as a result of His act of creation, and so is not eternal, which the divine ideas must be. This is quite different from Wyclif's conception of the primacy of God's *dominium* over universals before His *dominium* over particulars.

Fitzralph further delineates aspects of divine *dominium*, most of which he handles almost cursorily, as he weaves human *dominium* into his discussion. God's giving and His loaning imply no change in the divine essence, and entail no abdication of His *dominium*. God's *dominium* follows upon His Creation and subsequent sustenance of all things, and so the *dominium* God has lent man is not a relation of this high caliber, but a pale ghost of true *dominium* that threatens divine *dominium* not a whit. Human *dominium* is only a temporary *dominium*, a loaned enjoyment for humanity's welfare.[114] The original *dominium* granted man was "the right of a rational mortal creature, or the authority of original, natural possession of things naturally subject to his own nature through a rational conformity, as well as the full use and holding of these things."[115] This original *dominium* resulted from God's instillation of Grace in Adam, and Adam's *caritas* following thereon. "From [the reasoning given], it seems to me, one can infer that *caritas* or Grace was concentrated in the origin of the first man as the prior cause of his dominion, and of all the acts of his dominion."[116] The authority of original *dominium* is dispersed to all of Adam's descendants, although the Fall altered this authority. Original *dominium* should be concomitant with each new instantiation of human nature, but original sin blots this natural authority out.

---

[113] *Ibid.*, I, xxi, 311.26–8: "[S]pecies vero nulla potest immediate, set mediante supposito sive individuo singulari, subire dominii quemvis actum seu usum."

[114] *Ibid.*, II, i, 335.21–3.

[115] *Ibid.*, II, ii, 335.40–4: "Videtur ita posse describi, quod Ade dominium fuit racionalis creature mortale ius sive auctoritas originalis possidendi naturaliter res sibi natura subiectas conformiter racioni, et eis plene utendi sive eas tractandi."

[116] *Ibid.*, II, viii, 348.25–7: "Ex hiis (ut michi videtur) racionaliter potes inferre quod caritas sive gracia primo homini in origine sua sibi collata fuit previa causa dominii et causa cuiusque, actus huius dominii." Fitzralph makes little mention here of the causal relationship between receiving Grace and subsequent exhibition of *caritas*.

The nature of man's action in this original *dominium* was characterized by *caritas*, the hallmark of Grace. Is there a connection between *caritas* and Grace, and property? If Fitzralph argues that proprietary just *dominium* in the postlapsarian world requires Grace, does he believe there to be private ownership before the Fall? If not, can it be made into a worthwhile institution? As we will see, Fitzralph holds that possession before the Fall was mostly communal. But he does not equate the institution of private property with Original Sin, as Wyclif would, intimating that private property could conceivably have been instituted had Adam and Eve remained without sin.[117] What is of interest here is not that Fitzralph is suggesting that private ownership as it exists now is necessarily beneficial to people, but that he, like John XXII, allows that something like it might have been practicable before the Fall.

Still, everyone has the opportunity of eternal life, and so is qualified to regain *dominium* through Grace. Fitzralph is not clear whether this regained original *dominium* is political *dominium*, or just a purer way of living within Creation. Given the dim view he takes of human institutions of law and government, the latter alternative is likely. Furthermore, Fitzralph describes the *dominium* lost at the Fall as more a loss of innocence, of virtues and of purity of spirit without reference to the benefits of communal ownership.[118] What can be gained is purity of spirit through faith in Christ and repentance, but Fitzralph makes no mention of social matters such as whether the renewed faithful retain just private ownership or not. For Fitzralph, this appears not to matter. Christ's redemption has allowed the reattainment of *dominium* through Grace, but where Wyclif directs the argument towards a community of the elect as the true church with Christ as its head, Fitzralph proceeds with distinguishing between original *dominium* and human law; no stirring ecclesiology appears here.

Positive human law, and artificial, political *dominium*, are both necessities because of sin's stain on human corporeal nature, and they allow a social peace. Yet political *dominium* is not necessary in a state of innocence. In fact, there are postlapsarian instances of God's allowing people to dispense with civil *dominium*'s demands. "God primarily governed His people through Moses, not through a lord, and Moses ministered to his people even as God, who was their lord, would have."[119] Fitzralph is

---

[117] *Ibid.*, III, ix, 395.6–10.   [118] *Ibid.*, II, xii, 353.21–30.

[119] *Ibid.*, II, xxvii, 371.1–3: "Item, constat hunc populum Dei per Moysem primitus gubernatum, non tanquam per dominum, set per eum tanquam per Dei, qui eorum dominus erat, ministrum."
    It was only when the people clamored for a king that civil *dominium* took hold among the Jews. This is noteworthy; while this accounting of civil *dominium* arising after the Fall as a way for people to live peaceably is the same as Wyclif's account, Fitzralph's comment about Moses is

likely to be providing a basis for priestly claims of precedence in civil *dominium*-relations; Moses' guidance is a ministry, a giving to his charges as God would give, unlike what would come with the rule of kings. Indeed, Fitzralph allows a place for counselors in a state of innocence. Original *dominium* would be undifferentiated among prelapsarian men, but some human authority might still have made itself felt.

Fitzralph's dim view of the power of civil law is the foundation for his belief that all property notions rooted in political *dominium* are little more than pantomimes. Only property notions based in original *dominium* have real weight in human society, and original *dominium* is only open to those favored by Grace. While just political *dominium* requires Grace as well, it seems little more than a shabby afterthought, with its easily twisted laws and the inevitable miscarriages of justice that result.[120] One effect of this is that the church's possessions and rights of use are beyond the reach of civil law, and the friars err in supposing the church to be bound by the same strictures that bind human *dominium*, thereby justifying papal control of their orders. Another result is that Wyclif's thought, while beginning with the same assumptions, turns out to be opposed to the effects of Fitzralph's argument. In *De Civili Dominio*, civil *dominium* justified by Grace has primacy over the mundane church, and particularly over its access to property, because original *dominium* was lost with the Fall. For Wyclif, anything coming close to original *dominium* involves communal property sharing, and no individual possession. For Fitzralph, communal possession and communal use arise from common *dominium*, which was available only in the original, prelapsarian state of innocence. Had Adam and his progeny retained innocence, individual possession would have been unnecessary though, as we have already noted, possible. Any sort of *dominium* originating after the Fall would not allow for communal property notions, and so human society seems bereft of any opportunity for communal property or use.[121]

While it seems that property should have pride of place in this discussion, original *dominium* does not involve earthly property, which arises from civil *dominium*. As created, people have original *dominium* only by God's loan (*commodacio*), and if property is involved in the natural order of things, God alone has all of Creation as property. Correctly understood, property does not arise from anything natural to man, but is an acquired *dominium* called either civil or political.[122] If we recognize that original *dominium*, which would be the only structure that might have allowed

---

different. For Wyclif, the ideal biblical civil lord was Melchizedek, and he makes little mention of Moses' role as leader.

[120] Dawson, "Richard Fitzralph and the Fourteenth-Century Poverty Controversies" p. 337.
[121] See *De Pauperie Salvatoris*, III, xi–xiii.   [122] *Ibid.*, IV, ii, 438.41–439.3.

human property, largely replaces it with communal ownership, mundane property seems a will o' the wisp.[123]

So we can tie up a loose end and answer the question whether right of use is but a further iteration of property. If we could find a reason for there to be any grounds for claiming property in original *dominium*, aside from God's loan of communal possession to all descendants of Adam, which is not real property anyway, we might allow that right of use is just an iteration of property. But in original *dominium*, people had no real property, while maintaining a common possession and right of use. In postlapsarian human affairs, God may sanction invented property, and the subsequent possession and use that follow in a Grace-infused political *dominium*-relation, but because the initial property is an invention, and not Natural *dominium*, it is hard to say of *dominium per se* that right of use is an iteration of property. We can now return to Fitzralph's statement that "all property is *dominium*, but not all *dominium* is property." The only natural property seems to be God's property of all Creation, which is the chief characteristic of divine *dominium*. Invented property necessarily carries civil *dominium* along with it, but civil *dominium* can conceivably lack property in two ways: first, through loans of property made by kings to barons, dukes, etc., and second, if we assume property to refer to the natural, not the invented, sort. This is not to say that civil *dominium* is without divine sanction; it only underscores the difference between divine and political lordship. Possession and use are certainly results of natural and civil *dominium*. Man is charged in Genesis with the governance and sustenance of all creatures subject to his *dominium*, so possession and use must come into play. Natural and civil possession, which corresponds to conservation and sustenance, give nothing to justify the possessor's unrestricted, unlimited hold on a subject. Both are only titles deriving from extrinsic claims. Human possession resulting from original *dominium* is a title given by the true holder of property in Creation, God, and in civil *dominium*, possession is an artificial title based on the invented property of human law.

In each case, just possession is an effect of *dominium*, "indeed, only when anything can have *dominium* can it come into possession."[124] The possession resulting from natural, original *dominium*, is truly conservation or sustenance, but because of original sin, man's title to the sustenance of Creation is abdicable.[125] This follows from the postlapsarian loss of un-aided, species-wide original *dominium* of man; if our original *dominium*

---

[123] *Ibid.*, IV, iii, 440.10–14.
[124] *Ibid.*, III, iv, 387.1–2: "[U]nde, nisi in eos qui possunt habere dominium, cadere non potest possessio."
[125] *Ibid.*, III, xvii, and III, v, 388.34–389.2.

is in any sense able to be decreased, what follows from original *dominium* certainly must be as well. Civil possession must be even less real than natural possession. "Just as natural possession is . . . the voluntary detention of things subject to human use from the sole authority of original *dominium*, so it seems to me that civil or political possession is . . . the voluntary detention of things subject to human use through positive, political, or civil law."[126]

Use, commensurate to governance, is the end product of *dominium*, but the rational capacity of the holder of right of use must be considered as well. Human beings only have *dominium* so that they can enjoy use, and if use were not necessary for their continued survival, their *dominium* over other creatures would end.[127] Use is not unrestrained; the very word entails the rational or useful treatment of things. Fitzralph devotes considerable energy to showing how just use in *dominium* does not involve the used thing's total consumption. He gives particularly earthy observations about the further right use of what remains after any instance of just use, as with use of the dung consequent on use of comestibles.[128] The unbridled will might strive for frivolous application, but with right reason in control, the holder of just *dominium* can be expected to exercise sensible use.

Fitzralph has little more to say about property notions in civil *dominium*. In short, although God did not institute civil *dominium*, He did allow it for people so that they could fulfill their debt to God.[129] This debt was incurred with original sin, with the loss of original *dominium*, and as has already been suggested, is honored rather shabbily with the institution of human, civil *dominium*. While Fitzralph occasionally makes reference to the civil lord's need for Grace, he does little in the way of explaining the mechanics of *caritas* in human lordship. He does emphasize the connection of *caritas* and original *dominium*, and explain that human moral purity was what allowed the just original *dominium*, which purity was then lost. Fitzralph does not investigate the connections between just civil *dominium* and *caritas* that was to be so important to Wyclif.

So we can conclude that Fitzralph's *dominium* theory views property notions as the sole commodity of lordship as such. Civil lordship, to be just, must be sanctioned by God and infused with Grace, but it can never truly emulate divine *dominium* because it is artificial. Original *dominium* is more reflective of its paradigm divine *dominium*, but it is unavailable

---

[126] *Ibid.*, IV, xi, 453.5–10: "Sicud possessio naturalis est occupacio sive detencio voluntaria rerum usualium homini subiectarum ex sola auctoritate previa originalis dominii, sic michi videtur civilis sive politica possessio (si puritatem sequamur grammatice) esse occupacio sive detencio voluntaria rerum usualium homini subiectarum ex iure positivo sive politico seu civili."

[127] *Ibid.*, III, xix, 408.29–35.   [128] *Ibid.*, III, xx, 411.21–41.

[129] *Ibid.*, III, xxxi, 424.30; IV, iv, 441.30.

to most, and those to whom it is available seem unable to enjoy its natural fruits, i.e., communal possession and use, given the realities of civil *dominium*. Fitzralph's theory is disappointing, since it neither inspires one with confidence in the possibility of successfully attaining apostolic poverty, nor does it conclusively establish the unwavering justice of the property-holding of the church. It exhibits neither the papalist hierarchic claims of the earlier Augustinian friars nor the revolutionary spirit of its immediate successor.[130]

De Pauperie Salvatoris is a work designed more to justify a return to ecclesiastical *status quo ante fratres* than anything else; Fitzralph is writing about just possession as such. Wyclif, on the other hand, has a complete overhaul of the church in mind, and writes about just possession and governance. Fitzralph displays no concern for *iurisdictio*, for connections between divine and human justice, or for human rule imitative of divine rule.

An example of this difference is found in the lists of the acts of *dominium* the two thinkers give. Wyclif's list obviously derives from Fitzralph's, but Fitzralph's lacks an emphasis on *iurisdictio*; indeed, he interprets the two characteristics that Wyclif believes to be central to *iurisdictio* as really proprietarial:

Fitzralph[131]	Wyclif[132]
gubernare = usus	*creare*
conservare = possidere	*sustentare*
dare	*gubernare*
commodare	*donare*
vendere	*accipere*
emere	*prestare*
recipere	*repetere*
acquirere	*vendere*
	emere
	locare
	conducere
	accommodare
	mutuare
	promittere
	fideiubere
	deponere

---

[130] Dawson views *De Pauperie Salvatoris* as a failure. Dawson, "Richard Fitzralph and the Fourteenth-Century Poverty Controversies," p. 341.

[131] *De Pauperie Salvatoris*, I, xx–xxxiv. [132] *DD*, III, i.

Wyclif treats only the first six in a serious manner in his works; the first three he discusses in terms that associate just civil *iurisdictio* with divine *iurisdictio*, and the second three he discusses so as to equate just civil ownership with God's "ownership" of Creation. This division is absent in Fitzralph's discussion. Fitzralph does not include Creation among the acts of *dominium*, as Wyclif does, despite holding, as Wyclif does, that it is the necessary precondition for the relation. It is possible that the reason for this is founded in a difference of approach between the two thinkers. While both believed God's perfect knowledge to be prior to the act of Creation, for Wyclif God's *dominium* over the Intelligibles is prior to God's *dominium* over Creation, while Fitzralph's ontology implicitly denies this priority. In Wyclif's scheme, then, Creation would play an important role among the acts of *dominium*, for God's prior *dominium* would be complete before the act of Creation took place. This means either that the act of Creation would have to be included among the acts of divine *dominium* over Creation, or that the act of Creation, alone among all acts, was not an act of God's *dominium*. The latter possibility is unlikely, suggesting that Creation happened without control. So *creare* must be included among the acts of God's *dominium* over Creation, to accommodate the divine *dominium* over the Intelligibles prior to Creation. This underscores the comparative importance of metaphysics in Wyclif's picture of divine *dominium*; as we will see, *De Dominio Divino* is firmly grounded in the realism of the *Tractatus de Universalibus*.

Wyclif's metaphysical realism is a subtler difference. Fitzralph assumes an Aristotelian ontology, and sees little need to elaborate on the importance of universals in *dominium*, while Wyclif believes a right understanding of universals to be crucial to the articulation of a political theory. Finally, Fitzralph disavows any likelihood of postlapsarian communal possession or use, while Wyclif rhapsodizes about the instances of truly just civil *dominium*, such as the brotherhood of the Apostles, and the community of the early church, claiming that communal property-holding was their *sine qua non*. Finally Fitzralph does not see the whole church's achievable goal as being the surrender of all private ownership, while for Wyclif the facilitation of this is the chief responsibility of the civil lord.

MARSILIUS OF PADUA AND WYCLIF

Wyclif's *dominium* writings have long been compared to Marsilius of Padua's antipapalist *Defensor Pacis*. Gregory XI's May 1377 bulls condemning *De Civili Dominio* decry Wyclif's ideas: "despite the altering of certain terms, they appear to express the perverse opinions and unlearned doctrine of Marsilius of Padua and John of Jandun of accursed memory."[133] Wyclif's apparent debt to Marsilius is most evident in *De Officio Regis* Chapter XI, in the midst of a discussion of the relation of just warfare and civil government. "But in speech restricted to the political community, it seems to me that reason dictates that each [people] make for itself a head . . . that any people make for itself a simple head, as we English have one worthy king."[134] Taken out of context, it appears that Wyclif here echoes Marsilius' famous claim that consent of the governed is the necessary condition for just legislation. This would confirm the validity of Gregory's claim, for *De Officio Regis* appeared in 1379, almost two years after the condemnatory bulls. But the context in which this statement appears suggests that Wyclif's sympathies lie elsewhere. His argument is that unaided human reason might suppose consent-based governance to be the source of justice, but that Scripture suggests an intrinsic unity of the species necessitating divine selection of a ruler. If God's will is to produce such a ruler by some sort of election, well enough, but Wyclif does not mean us to conclude that all elections are thereby just.[135] Indeed, Wyclif's discussion here suggests the likelihood of a race of divinely selected rulers, defined not by heredity but moral superiority.

Twentieth-century scholars, eager to elucidate the contemporary context in which to describe Wyclif's anti-papalist monarchism, find it difficult to avoid mentioning his similarity with Marsilius. But this has led to some confusion. H. B. Workman, K. B. McFarlane, Janet Coleman, and Quentin Skinner describe aspects of Wyclif's political thought as echoes of elements in Marsilius, though each stops far short of suggesting a causal relation. Michael Wilks once intimated that a connection may be demonstrable, but more recently has dismissed its import. Dom David Knowles declared that Wyclif is as perverse and confusing as Marsilius, and likely as innovative; L. Daly assumes some link between the two to have been likely, while Gordon Leff suggests that Wyclif used *Defensor Pacis* as a source for his antipapal reformative arguments.[136] Leff argues that Wyclif had tacitly adopted Marsilius' tactic of appealing directly to

---

[133] Dahmus, *The Prosecution of John Wyclyf*, p. 39; see also Thomas Walsingham, *Historia Anglicana*, p. 346: "licet quibusdam mutatis terminis, sentire videntur perversas opiniones et doctrinam indoctam damnatae memoriae Marcilii de Padua et Johannis de Ganduno."

[134] *DOR*, XI, 249.23–8: "Sed limitate loquendo de communitate politica videtur mihi quod racio dictat ut ipsi faciant sibi caput . . . quod quilibet populus appropriet sibi simplex caput, ut nos Anglici habemus unum regem benedictum."

[135] See *DCD*, I, xxxix, 20–3; I, xviii, 130.6–14. That Wyclif held human elections in opprobrium well into the 1380s is evident in *Trialogus*, III.ii.166: "[E]lectiones hominum ut plurimum sunt injustae . . . in electionibus humanis et privatis religionibus, communiter contenditur contra Deum."

[136] Workman, *John Wyclif: A Study of the English Medieval Church* (Oxford, 1926), vol. 2, pp. 6, 27, 86; McFarlane, *John Wycliffe and the Beginnings of English Nonconformity*, pp. 49, 71, 78;

Scripture in his denial that one man can confer spiritual power on another, and in his indictment of the Petrine commission arguments in favor of papal primacy. Prior to Leff, E. Emerton had made a similar attribution in his work on Marsilius, wondering why no one else had noticed the relation.[137] Workman suggested that any similarities between Wyclif and Marsilius were coincidental, and Alan Gewirth warns against supposing there to be anything more to the resemblance between the two. Williel Thomson's assessment is guarded: some link might be demonstrable on close analysis of *Defensor Pacis* and *De Civili Dominio* I, but unlikely. Indeed, it is doubtful that copies of *Defensor Pacis* had even been available in England in the late fourteenth century. Edith Tatnall specifically denies any sort of connection.[138] More recently, Margaret Harvey has assigned the connection between Marsilius and Wyclif in Gregory's 1377 condemnations to the misinterpretation of Adam Easton, whose reading of the first book of *De Civili Dominio* is likely to have been influential in conflating the two positions for the pope. Easton had had access to *Defensor Pacis* in Avignon in 1368–9, was a familiar of Gregory XI, and appears to have interpreted Wyclif's position in Marsilian terms in his *Defensorium Ecclesiastice Potestatis* shortly after the 1377 condemnation.[139]

Defensor Pacis (1324) was certainly a landmark in fourteenth-century political discourse. Its vigorously reasoned condemnations of ecclesiastical use of coercive temporal power and clerical abuse of temporal goods and extra-scriptural *auctoritas* drew the immediate angry attention of papal theorists, and Marsilius' confident truculence guaranteed its swift adoption by anticlerical voices throughout the church. Further, many of Marsilius' arguments do correspond to Wyclif's arguments. Both argue that the purpose of the priesthood is to instruct in evangelical law, which is impossible when coercion with temporal authority is employed. They agree that priests are ultimately punishable by the secular arm, that

---

Coleman, "Property and Poverty," pp. 644–7; Skinner, *The Foundations of Modern Political Thought* (Cambridge, 1978), vol. 2, p. 39; Wilks, "The Early Oxford Wyclif: Papalist or Nominalist," *SCH*, 5 (1969), p. 88, n. 4; Wilks, "Wyclif and the Great Persecution," in *Prophecy and Eschatology*, ed. Wilks *SCH* Subsidia 10 (Oxford, 1994), p. 43; D. Knowles, *The Religious Orders in England* (Cambridge, 1953), vol. 2, p. 98, n. 3; Daly, *The Political Theory of John Wyclif* (Chicago, 1962), pp. 20–3; Leff, *Heresy in the Later Middle Ages*, vol. 2, pp. 532–4; Leff, "Wyclif and Huss: A Doctrinal Comparison," in *Wyclif in his Times*, ed. A Kenny (Oxford, 1986), pp. 105, 113.

[137] E. Emerton, *The Defensor Pacis of Marsiglio of Padua* (Cambridge, 1920), pp. 78–80, cited in H. Kaminsky, "Wyclifism as Ideology of Revolution," *Church History*, 32 (1963), n. 15.

[138] Workman, *John Wyclif*, vol. 1, pp. 132–4; Alan Gewirth, "Philosophy and Political Thought in the Fourteenth Century," in *The Forward Movement of the Fourteenth Century*, ed. F. L. Utley (Columbus, OH, 1961), p. 154; W. R. Thomson, *The Latin Writings of John Wyclyf* (Toronto, 1983), p. 53, n. 31; Pantin, *The English Church in the Fourteenth Century* (Cambridge, 1955), p. 122; Tatnall, "John Wyclif and *Ecclesia Anglicana*," *Journal of Theological History*, 20 (1969), p. 29.

[139] Margaret Harvey, "Adam Easton and the Condemnation of John Wyclif, 1377," *English Historical Review* (April 1998), pp. 321–34.

civil *dominium* is antithetical to the priestly office, that private property-ownership should be foreign to any clergyman, and that every church member, without respect to his spiritual authority, must obey any command of his temporal lord that is not contrary to the law of eternal salvation.[140] Further, both reject heredity as a basis for selecting a temporal ruler, and argue forcefully for the temporal lord's maintaining absolute control over all temporal goods used by the church.[141] Finally, both agree that all Christians should be called "churchmen," not just the clergy, and that papal power is really a human invention, with no basis whatever in scriptural authority.[142] On the face of it, Marsilius and Wyclif appear remarkably similar.

But these similarities are illusory. As has been mentioned, Marsilius advocated rule in accord with the will of the people, arguing that God used human wills as the medium through which He establishes government.[143] The idea that God would make use of any sort of mediate cause to effect His will is foreign to Wyclif's philosophy. Marsilius denies any realist philosophical foundation for establishing just government, specifically rejecting a conception of unity in a state or body as based in a numerical form of organic unity inhering in all beings.[144] This, as we will discover, is precisely what Wyclif advocated. Again, the sufficiency of the evangelical law of the Gospels for measuring the morality of all human acts, central to Wyclif's argument, is rejected in *Defensor Pacis.*[145]

These fundamental disagreements imply significant differences separating apparently similar prescriptions. Both argue that the king must divest the church of its property for the betterment of its members. But Marsilius' argument is based on his principle of consent-based government. The king is justified only by the consent of the church members in his jurisdiction; while divine law supports his action, it by no means compels it without this consent.[146] For Wyclif, no human law is just unless it participates in divine law, which demands that the just civil lord protect the poverty of the church without regard to popular opinion. Both argue that priests must never be allowed to use coercive temporal power to enforce their spiritual guidance. But Marsilius' argument relies on the assumption that this power is only given by human law for mundane ends, and is never meant to facilitate eternal salvation. Marsilius allows secular persecution of heretics, but only to prevent social disorder, not

---

[140] *Defensor Pacis*, I, vi, 8 and II, v, 6; II, viii, 7; II, i, 4; II, xiii, 22–36; II, v, 7.
[141] *Ibid.*, I, xv–xvi; I, xv, 10, II, xvii, 16, xxi, 14.
[142] *Ibid.*, II, ii, 3; I, xix, 6–8.   [143] *Ibid.*, I, viii, 2–3; ix, 5–9.
[144] *Ibid.*, I, xvii, 11.   [145] *Ibid.*, II, ix, 12.   [146] *Ibid.*, II, xvii, 11.

because they flout divine law.[147] Wyclif's is the old Augustinian claim that God has given this coercive power to the secular arm to balance the spiritual authority held by priests. For Wyclif's king, crushing heresy is foremost among his God-given responsibilities for protecting the church. Both hold that Scripture alone is the true authority in ecclesiastical disputes, and use this position to argue against the papal monarchy. But Marsilius believes that correct scriptural interpretation is only possible when made by priests and educated laity in council, contributing to a conciliarist theory that was to be influential in the coming centuries.[148] Wyclif, on the other hand, was to argue that Grace alone is needed to ensure true interpretation of Scriptures; Wycliffite *Sola Scriptura* theology was the first ideology to be condemned when the conciliarists began their work at Constance.

The differences separating the two lines of thought sufficiently outweigh the superficial similarities to permit us to dismiss as insignificant the possibility that Wyclif relied on Marsilius' arguments. Were we to accept the separation of Wyclif's theological philosophy from his later political writings as legitimate, or to believe that Wyclif had forgotten his arguments for Grace-founded *dominium* in *De Civili Dominio* I so completely in Books II and III and in *De Officio Regis*, we would have a reason for entertaining the possibility that he had used Marsilius' arguments in these latter works. But we would not thereby have an argument; all of the differences indicated in the preceding paragraph are based in these slightly later texts, as we will see in coming chapters.

---

[147] *Ibid.*, II, x, 8.   [148] *Ibid.*, II, xix, 3.

Chapter 3

WYCLIF'S REALISM AND DIVINE
DOMINIUM

Wyclif's most definitive treatment of *dominium* is in the second treatise of the *Summa Theologie, De Dominio Divino*,[1] with a general definition of the term in the first book, and a list of the actions associated with *dominium*-relations in the third. Wyclif describes God's relation to Creation exclusively in terms of *dominium*, using the relation as a foundation for many of his theological and philosophical innovations. This is because Wyclif believes that God's absolute transcendence entails no real relation is possible between God and Creation. Only a relation following from some act of God in Creation can make the connection. And since God's *dominium* follows necessarily and immediately from the act of creating, *dominium* best defines God's continued participation in Creation. Wyclif defines divine *dominium* as "the standard prior to and the presupposition of all other *dominium*; if a creature has *dominium* over anything God already has *dominium* over it, so any created *dominium* follows upon divine *dominium*."[2]

Wyclif was a metaphysical realist about universals, and to those sensitive to late fourteenth-century Oxford philosophical dialogue, this description suggests a universal–particular relation holding between divine and human *dominium*-relations. If we are to understand Wyclif's thought on *dominium* as a theme uniting his earlier and his later writings and as a concept central to his philosophy, we will need to explore his thought on universals to see if divine *dominium* functions as one. Accordingly, we should survey Wyclif's realism, particularly as it appears in the *Tractatus de Universalibus*, to show how divine *dominium* is a universal by causality for all human *dominium*-relations.[3]

---

[1] John Wyclif, *De Dominio Divino*, ed. R. L. Poole (London, 1890).

[2] *DD*, I, iii, 16.18–22: "[D]ominium Dei mensurat, ut prius et presuppositum, omnia alia assignanda: si enim creatura habet dominium super quidquam, Deus prius habet dominium super idem; ideo ad quodlibet creature dominium sequitur dominium divinum, et non econtra."

[3] John Wyclif, *Tractatus De Universalibus*, ed. Ivan Mueller (Oxford, 1985); translated as *On Universals*, by Anthony Kenny, with introduction by Paul V. Spade (Oxford, 1985).

Wyclif's realism and divine dominium

We can then turn to *De Dominio Divino*, ready to understand how divine *dominium* serves as a measure or standard for all other *dominium*-relations in Creation. The only critical assessment of *De Dominio Divino* is that of its editor, R. L. Poole, whose withering introduction to the edition diminishes its philosophical worth, organization, originality, and content.[4] With an understanding of Wyclif's realism the injustice of this is evident, for *De Dominio Divino*, and consequently *De Civili Dominio*, are recognizably works firmly founded in a sophisticated ontology.

UNIVERSALS IN WYCLIF'S METAPHYSICS

While Wyclif's metaphysical realism is apparent in all of the treatises that he wrote at Oxford, three, written between 1360 and 1368, are particularly rich sources for an understanding of how *dominium* functions as a universal in his later works.[5] These are *De Logica*, his earliest edited philosophical work, *Purgans Errores Circa Universalia in Communi*, his 1366 response to *Moderni* criticism of his realism, and the *Tractatus de Universalibus*, his most complete summation of his metaphysics.[6] The first two of these works highlight Wyclif's particular philosophic strengths and weaknesses, for in them he patiently lays out his opponent's objections to his realism, responding with arguments that likely struck his opponents as question-begging. In the *Tractatus de Universalibus* Wyclif strikes out on his own, explaining the mechanics of his realism with meticulous care.[7]

---

[4] "Wycliffe's work is of the spuriously technical type of Holcot or Strode; it has not the true philosophical spirit which, in spite of its over-refinement, impresses one with admiration in Duns Scotus. *DD*, preface, p. xxi. Poole appended Fitzralph's *De Pauperie Salvatoris* to *De Dominio Divino* in order to show Wyclif's dependence on Armachanus.

[5] It is difficult to be certain in dating Wyclif's works, for no original manuscripts have survived. The earliest datable copies come from the 1390s, and many come from the first two decades of the fifteenth century. Most scholars rely on Harrison Thomson's estimates in "The Order of Writing of Wyclif's Philosophical Works," *Ceskou Minulosti* (Prague, 1929), pp. 146–65, and on Williel R. Thomson, *The Latin Writings of John Wyclyf* (Toronto, 1983). See also J. A. Robson, *Wyclif and the Oxford Schools* (Cambridge, 1961), pp. 115–40. H. B. Workman's speculations regarding the order and dating of Wyclif's philosophical works are based on an assessment of the development of Wyclif's philosophy insensitive both to the subject matter and to the Oxford context in which Wyclif thought and wrote. See Workman, *John Wyclif: A Study of the English Medieval Church* (Oxford, 1986), vol. 1, appendix D, pp. 332–5.

[6] *Tractatus de Logica*, ed. Michael H. Dziewicki (London, 1893), vol. 1, p. 8; *Tractatus Tertius* (London, 1896), vol. 2, pp. 33–54. *Purgans Errores Circa Universalia in Communi*, published in *De Ente Librorum Duorum* as *Tractatus Quartus*, ed. Michael H. Dziewicki (London, 1909), pp. 29–48. The *Tractatus de Universalibus* appearing in *Miscellanea Philosophica* II (London, 1905) is the work of the Czech Wycliffite Stanislav Znojmo, as noted in Thomson, *The Latin Writings of John Wyclyf*, p. 21.

[7] See Anthony Kenny, "The Realism of the *De Universalibus*," in *Wyclif in his Times* (Oxford, 1986), pp. 17–30; Norman Kretzman, "Continua, Indivisibles, and Change in Wyclif's Logic of Scripture," in *ibid.*, pp. 31–66; P. V. Spade, *On Universals*, Introduction.

Robson characterizes Wyclif's philosophy as "ultra-realist," and, in concert with many other scholars, portrays Wyclif as a lone Augustinian hold-out in an academic world given over to Ockhamism.[8] This is understandable, given Wyclif's resounding indictment of "doctors of signs" in *De Universalibus*, and his conclusion that Ockhamist error about universals is at the bottom of all that is wrong in the world.[9] But how accurate is it to claim that Wyclif's metaphysics is an important departure from the Ockhamist *Moderni* approach in mid-fourteenth-century Oxford? William Courtenay has shown that Ockhamism was far from prevalent in Oxford from the 1340s on; indeed, Ockhamism was never a "school" like that of the Thomists or the Scotists, but a movement whose adherents agreed more in philosophical approach than particular ontological commitments.[10] Further, the term *"Modern"* was only used to distinguish Ockhamist thought from Wycliffism (and eventually, Scotism and Thomism) after Wyclif's works were condemned at Constance, suggesting that Wyclif and his followers were sufficiently active in the *Moderni* dialogue to warrant the term's modification.[11]

While it remains a commonplace to speak of Oxford after the Black Death as but a shadow of its former self, making Wyclif a lonely beacon of philosophical innovation, scholarship suggests otherwise. Courtenay's survey of logical and theological work from 1350 to 1365 suggests a level of productivity only slightly less than the 1320s and 1330s. Figures like Richard Brinkley, O.F.M., Nicholas Aston, and Uthred of Bolden typify a period in which philosophical attention centered on analysis of propositions and argument while the problems of divine determinism (sparked by Bradwardine's *De Causa Dei* thirty years before), future contingents, and

---

[8] Robson, *Wyclif and the Oxford Schools*, pp. 145–61. Robson's reference to Wyclif's ontology as Platonist on p. 152 and his portrayal of Wyclif as anti-Ockhamist exemplify the standard portrayal of Wyclif's thought as a radical divergence from prevalent Oxford tendencies.

[9] *Tractatus de Universalibus*, III, 145–75: "Sic igitur indubie error intellectus et affectus circa universalia est causa totius peccati regnantis in saeculo." See Anselm of Canterbury, *De Incarnatione Verbi*, I, *Sancti Anselmi Opera Omnia*, II Tomus I, vol. ed. F. S. Schmitt (Stuttgart, 1968), 9:22–10:13.

[10] William J. Courtenay, *Schools and Scholars in Fourteenth-Century England* (Princeton, 1987), pp. 190–218. See also Katherine Tachau, *Vision and Certitude in the Age of Ockham* (Toronto, 1988).

[11] For the utility of considering Wyclif as participating to an extent within the Ockhamist dialogue, see Spade, *On Universals*, Introduction. Neal Ward Gilbert has illuminated the relation of Wyclif to the *Moderni* explaining that, until the early fifteenth century, the term "Modern" was applicable to anyone who was a contemporary philosopher; see Gilbert, "Ockham, Wyclif, and the 'Via Moderna'," in *Antiqui und Moderni: Traditionsbewußtsein im späten Mittelalter*, Miscellanea Mediaevalia Band 9 (Berlin, 1974), pp. 85–125. He argues that the emphasis on the distinction between the *ars vetus* and the *ars nova* only became important when Wyclif's philosophical views became significantly dangerous. See also Heiko Oberman, *"Via Antiqua* and *Via Moderna*: Late Medieval Prolegomena to Early Reformation Thought," in *From Ockham to Wyclif*, ed. Anne Hudson and Michael Wilks, SCH Subsidia 5 (London, 1987), pp. 445–64.

merit and justification occupied the attention of theologians.[12] Wyclif's vigorous introduction of the problem of universals appears curious in its return to ontological issues that had been put aside for decades, but his philosophical and theological concerns are very much those of his day. Why did Wyclif believe that confusion about universals was the root of much that was wrong at Oxford?

It appears that few if any Oxford scholars were much interested in championing an anti-realist ontology. Courtenay notes that most of the logicians of the 1350s and 1360s had assumed a generally realist ontology, understanding simple *suppositio* to stand for common natures and affirming the real existence of all of the Aristotelian categories, not just substance and quality, as Ockham had taught. Richard Brinkley provides a good example, accepting as valid the reality of universals with relatively few qualms.[13] Brinkley and others were concerned to combat a rising nominalist challenge to Ockhamism, however; as early as the 1320s, Hugh of Lawton, O.P. had attacked Ockham for holding that mental propositions had validity beyond their vocal or written expression.[14] This opened the door for later critics, particularly in Paris, to argue that logical analysis of propositions should be according to the meanings of vocal or written words, not of mental concepts. For them, mental intention is completely subordinated to the literal applicability of the vocal or written proposition. Brinkley's reaction was to argue that scientific truth was thereby limited to how words functioned without regard to things in the world.[15]

If Brinkley's anti-nominalist efforts are representative of Oxford logical tendencies in the 1350s and 1360s, which is likely, then Wyclif's realism is understandable. What better way to refute Lawton's Parisian descendants than to formulate an ontological program surpassing Burley's earlier refutation of Ockham in its arguments for the existence of extra-mental universals? The esteem in which he was held by his fellows in the 1360s suggests that Wyclif's efforts met with some success. A full understanding of the foundations of Wyclif's realism, then, will only be possible with an analysis of his *Tractatus de Logica*, both as it relates to the logical work of his contemporaries and to his later, metaphysical treatises.[16] Our purposes

---

[12] Courtenay, *Schools and Scholars in Fourteenth-Century England*, pp. 327–55.

[13] *Ibid.*, pp. 336–7. See also Michael Fitzgerald's introduction to his edition of *Richard Brinkley's Theory of Sentential Reference* (Leiden, 1987), pp. 1–33; Gideon Gál and Rega Wood, "Richard Brinkley and his *Summa Logicae*," *Franciscan Studies*, 40 (1980), pp. 59–102.

[14] Hester Gelber, "I Cannot Tell a Lie: Hugh of Lawton's Critique of William of Ockham on Mental Language," *Franciscan Studies*, 44 (1984), pp. 141–80.

[15] William Courtenay, "Force of Words and Figures of Speech: The Crisis over *Virtus Sermonis* in the Fourteenth Century," *Franciscan Studies*, 44 (1984), pp. 107–28.

[16] See Fitzgerald, *Richard Brinkley's Theory of Sentential Reference*, p. 6; Courtenay, *Schools and Scholars in Fourteenth-Century England*, pp. 348–55; Robson, *Wyclif and the Oxford Schools*, p. 163. If Wyclif

will be served by taking certain elements of his ontology as axiomatic
and proceeding from there to his thought on *dominium*.

WYCLIF ON WHAT THERE IS

Wyclif obviously enjoyed toying with his readers, and presumably with
his audience at lectures. It is not at all uncommon for him to end up
proving the opposite of what he appears to have set out to demonstrate.[17]
This playfulness is evident in his account of the kinds of universals. At the
opening of the *Tractatus*, he says that there are three kinds of universals
in general: universals by causality, universals by community, and universals by representation.[18] In the second chapter, he describes five different
sorts of universals.[19] Later in the treatise, he suggests that coming up
with definitive lists of the kinds of universals is impossible, since "things
counted vary in accordance with the size of the units chosen...."[20]
The list he presents in the second chapter has captured the attention
of scholars, perhaps because here Wyclif invokes the authority of Robert
Grosseteste:

The first and foremost kind is the eternal notion or exemplar idea in God.
The second kind is the common created notion in the superior causes, like the
intelligences and the heavenly spheres. The third kind of universal is the common
form rooted in the individuals. This, says Grosseteste, is what Aristotle's genera
and species are. Fourthly, there is the universal which is the common form in its
accidents, apprehended by the lowest form of intellect. There is a fifth kind of
universal – signs and mental acts – which Grosseteste sets aside as irrelevant to
his concerns.[21]

is defending contemporary Oxford logicians' implicit realism in response to Parisian critics who
had rejected Ockhamism for its emphasis on concepts, one can then read his criticisms of Ockham
not as those of an opponent, but of a colleague concerned to right the mistakes that follow from
a too-eager application of the principle of parsimony.

[17] See Michael Wilks, "Predestination, Property and Power: Wyclif's Theory of Dominion and
Grace," *SCH*, 2 (London, 1965), p. 228. Elsewhere, Wilks refers to this as "Wyclif's tendency to
play cat-and-mouse with his readers."

[18] *TDU*, 1, 15.6–16.16.

[19] Also *TDU*, 2, 59.165–78. See also *Tractatus de Logica*, III, ii, 32.14–39; Wyclif here uses Grosseteste's
commentary, *In Aristotelis Posteriorum Analyticorum Libros* (Venice, 1514; Frankfurt, 1966), I, vii,
GPos 8va–b, as noted in *TDU*, ed. Mueller, p. 59, n. 166.

[20] *TDU*, 9, 400–05: "Hic dicitur quod tantum quinque sunt universalia et tantum decem et in
quocumque numero volueris sunt universalia, quia numeri, pro rebus numeratis, coincidunt in
grossando vel subtiliando partes." Unfortunately, in *Trialogus* Wyclif makes no reference to the
number of types of universals, see *Trialogus*, ed. G. V. Lechler (Oxford, 1869), I, vii–ix, 58–65.

[21] *On Universals*, ed. Kenny, 13.165–78. See *TDU*, 2, 59.165–78: "Primum et supremum genus est
ratio vel idea exemplaris aeterna in Deo. Secundum genus est ratio communis creata in causis/
superioribus, ut intelligentiis et orbibus caelestibus. Tertium genus universalium est forma communis fundata in suis individuis. Et illa, inquit Lincolniensis, sunt genera et species de quibus

What are we to make of these varying lists of types of universals? Anthony Kenny has opted for the longer list, holding that the three listed at the opening of the treatise are a sub-set of the five in the list taken from Grosseteste.[22] Kenny explains that God serves as the first universal, the universal in causation in respect of the eternal ideas in His mind, and that secondary universals by causality, the "common created notions in the superior causes" are superlunary universals somehow related to the divine ideas. In each list, genera and species are accounted for by universals by community, although Grosseteste distinguishes between substantial and accidental forms. Finally, in both lists, universals by representation, or signs, are mentioned, but do not play a large role. Kenny believes that this alignment corresponds to the different levels of being Wyclif describes in *De Universalibus* Chapter 7. There Wyclif distinguishes between (1) eternal mental being in God; (2) being in universal causes; (3) being in particular cause; (4) particular being; and (5) being predicated.[23] We can align these, Kenny argues, with each of the types of univerals in Grosseteste's list.

This discussion can only indicate the need for sustained analysis of Wyclif's classification of the kinds of universals. Our analysis of Wyclif's realism will begin with a brief discussion of his universals by community, which correspond to the familiar Boethian genus and species. At that point, we can examine Wyclif's conception of universals by causality as they may relate to the *dominium* relation. Universals by signification need not concern us, for Wyclif holds them to be human artifices, universal only analogously; they are the terms that "doctors of signs" believe to be the only kind of universal.[24]

Spade interprets Wyclif as referring to the familiar genus and species with his term "universal by community."[25] Wyclif described a universal by community as a thing shared by many supposits, giving general ("animal") and specific ("human") natures as his examples. It is reasonable to conclude that this corresponds to the third sort of universal described in the list of five attributed to Grosseteste, the "common universals rooted in individuals," for the same examples of general and specific natures appear

loquitur Aristoteles. Quarto: forma communis in suis accidentibus, apprehensa/ab intellectu infimo, est universale. Sed quintum modum universalium – pro signis vel actibus intelligendi – dimittit Lincolniensis ut sibi impertinens."

[22] See Kenny, *Wyclif in his Times*, pp. 17–30; Robson, *Wyclif and the Oxford Schools*, p. 148.

[23] *TDU*, 7, 126.35–127.58.

[24] I am grateful to Sir Anthony Kenny for his lucid explanation of his conception of the relation of Grosseteste's list of five universals to Wyclif's list of three.

[25] Spade, *On Universals*, p. xviii. See also Marilyn McCord Adams, "Universals in the Fourteenth Century," in *The Cambridge History of Later Medieval Philosophy*, ed. J. H. Burns (Cambridge, 1982), pp. 411–39.

here as well. In fact, Wyclif presents Grosseteste's list in his description of universals by community, using it to illustrate the compatibility of the Aristotelian rejection of Platonic forms with arguments in favor of extramental universals. His use of Grosseteste is to affirm that universals by community have reality insofar as animals share a common nature, the genus "animal," which is founded not merely in a name, as the Ockhamists insist, but extramentally.

Earlier metaphysicians, notably Albert and Thomas, Wyclif explains, have argued that genus and species are the products of the human intellect's actualization of potential commonalities of common forms.[26] In arguing that genus and species do not have extramental reality, insofar as there is some disembodied being "animality" existing in a world of Forms, can they believe that the genus "animal" has no extramental reality? A creature is an animal, Wyclif believes, because something in its essential nature is the same as something in the essential nature of other, similar creatures, and that is the universal "animal" existing in each while remaining unchanging, unaffected by the individuals' births and deaths.

But this is precisely the sticking point. How can a thing exist separately in several other things without being divided up between them? Wyclif believed that he had resolved the issue not by emphasizing the commonality of form, as had Aquinas and others, but by distinguishing between first- and second-intention universals. Briefly, a first-intention term is a concept derived from a real thing; for example, when holding a white rock, I formulate an idea of this rock's whiteness. A second-intention term is a concept derived from first-intentional meanings: I formulate a second-intention idea of the whiteness of rocks in general from first-intention ideas of white rocks I've encountered. Universals by community have two kinds of being, primarily as objects of God's knowledge, and secondarily, as the being of things. If we consider them as we encounter them, we must recognize the universal "animal" as it exists in the individual essential nature of this animal as a universal of first intention. This serves as the basis for our understanding of universal's primary being, as a universal of the second intention existing in God's mind. Why, then, would second-intention universals have ontological primacy? In the example already given, second-intention concepts are reliant on the collections of first-intention ideas. Does this not mean that God's knowledge of creatures' essential natures is dependent on creatures?

It is easy to confuse logical priority with metaphysical priority here. The description of the relation of essential natures in creatures to God's knowledge answers the question of how one thing can be in several places

---

[26] *TDU*, I, 191–206.

without being itself changed. Logically, the answer lies in the relation of created natures to God's knowledge as first intention to second intention. Metaphysically, though, the relation is entirely dependent on the divine nature; the universal "animal," as it exists known by God, is the foundation of all instances of created animals. The being of "animal" in a given creature is not something different from the being of the given animal; rather, it is only formally distinct from the individual creature's being.[27] Put another way, the universal "Man" is each of its particulars, but with differing supposits, or different individual referents.[28] Yet it is nothing more than its particulars, and cannot exist without them.[29] Citing the consonance of his approach with Avicenna's, he suggests that Walter Burley's otherwise extravagant realism might be improved upon by making use of it. Thus, Wyclif sees himself as championing a *via media* between Burley and Platonism, on the one hand, and Thomists, Scotists, and Ockhamists, on the other.[30]

If universals by commonality were all Wyclif described, his ontology could be classified as a traditional response to Ockhamism grounded in Walter Burley. But Wyclif introduces universals by causality, holding that "every creature which was at any time to be, is said to be in its particular causes, at the beginning of the world."[31] These have their existence in the way that the most universal cause is God, after Whom created universal things are ordered as they proceed from the divine being. The whole human race was in Adam, then, and all sinned when Adam sinned. To argue that one's animal and human nature is in itself explicative of the causal relation between the first human and one's self is, Wyclif argues, to miss half of the metaphysical picture.[32] A universal by community explains what a thing is, but it does not explain how a thing came to be that way. A universal by causality is the reason by which I have been caused by my father, by Adam, and ultimately, by which I have been caused by God, for God's causal knowledge is the most primary sort of universal by causality.[33]

The ultimate effect of a universal by causality is to decrease the need for secondary causes, for if I have being in Adam at the beginning of Creation, the causal relation holding between my father and me is but an

---

[27] *Ibid.*, 4, 174–95. [28] *De Logica*, III, ii, 35.11–33.

[29] *Purgans Errores*, in *Johannis Wyclif De Ente: Librorum Duorum Excerpta*, ed. M. H. Dziewicki (London, 1909), 4, 41.14–30.

[30] *TDU*, 4, 56–60. See Elizabeth Karger, "Walter Burley's Realism," *Vivarium*, 37 (1999), pp. 24–40.

[31] *TDU*, 7, 48–9: "In causis qutem particularibus dicitur creatura quantumcumque futura esse in mundi principio."

[32] *Ibid.*, 7, 204–24.

[33] *Ibid.*, 1, 15.7–10: "Primum est universale causatione, ut Deus est causa universalissima et post eum res universales creatae secundum ordinem, quo originantur a Deo."

occasion realizing what was causally determined in Adam. But if God's causal knowledge is the primary universal by causality, it follows that Adam's causal relation to me is also an occasion realizing what was causally determined in the divine mind. Scholars universally recognize Thomas Bradwardine's influence on Wyclif's thought, referring to the influence of *De Causa Dei* on *De Dominio Divino* and *De Civili Dominio*.[34] The determinism that follows from Wyclif's conception of universals by causality gives evidence of Bradwardine's doctrine of God's universal, unmediated causal activity, although Wyclif himself takes pains to explain that Bradwardine's position is not as restrictive as it appears.[35] Wyclif continues in his description of universals by causality by holding that every relation that has reality is similarly reliant on this species of universal.[36] He explains that the relations described in the predication of Aristotle's ten categories are founded in universals by causality, and have a formal reality apart from the *relata* about which the predication is made.

RELATIONAL REALISM, PREDICATING UNIVERSALS, AND THE SOUL

The key to Wyclif's relational realism lies in his thought on real predication. The linguistic predication discussed by the "doctors of signs" is but a pale copy of this fundamental, ontological predication relation holding between beings. This holds between species and individuals, when discussing substantially founded universals, as in "Socrates is a man," as well as between *relata*, when discussing universals by causality. But what does it mean to say that universals by causality are related to their particulars with the same degree of reality that species universals are related to their particulars?

Wyclif explains that real predication involves Socrates' "saying," his specific nature, or his universal "Man" by which he is speciated, simply by having being. That is, Socrates predicates "Man" simply by existing as a man. In fact, not only does Socrates say his specific nature, but he appears to say his *per se* cause as well.[37] Wyclif contrasts predication *per se* with predication *per accidens*, suggesting that this real predication is about essential natures. Regarding the cause of Socrates' essential nature,

---

[34] McFarlane, *John Wycliffe and the Beginnings of English Nonconformity* (Aylesbury, 1952), pp. 18, 78–9; Workman, *John Wyclif*, vol. 1, pp. 119–25; Robson, *Wyclif and the Oxford Schools*, pp. 176–83, 210–15. For considered analysis of the extent of Bradwardine's theological determinism, see Heiko Oberman, *Thomas Bradwardine: A Fourteenth-Century Augustinian* (Utrecht, 1957). See also Gordon Leff, *Bradwardine and the Pelagians* (Cambridge, 1957).

[35] Thomas Bradwardine, *De Causa Dei*, I, 3, 171D–E; *TDU*, 14, 305–400.

[36] *TDU*, 7, 439–43.   [37] *Ibid.*, 1, 18.40–55.

Wyclif says that "whatever is required for the being of another is a cause of it, because every truth mentioned later in the series is a cause of the former."[38] Adam is at the beginning of the species' causal chain, as was God's creative act before Adam, and the Eternal Exemplar of "Man" before the creative act. One might imagine Socrates "saying" his first ancestor in his very being, but must one then recognize that this "saying" is the predication of a universal? Wyclif is somewhat vague about this. There is no doubt that he means that every created being "says" its Eternal Exemplar, but once we leave the divine mind, real predication of universals by causality becomes murky. If every created thing "says" its essential (*per se*) cause, which is indicative of a universal–particular relationship, it would appear that actions and relations, whether apart from or along with the agents and *relata*, might also be candidates for universals by causality.

This idea that the reality of a relation is based in a universal by causality relation is satisfying because of its resonance with the rest of Wyclif's teachings on the relation of divine *dominium*. If God is responsible for all of Creation's sustenance and governance by virtue of His divine *dominium*, would not divine *dominium* be as much a universal by causality for Creation as Adam is for the essential nature of every human being? If divine *dominium* follows upon the creative act, and is the signal relation between God and Creation in which God governs and sustains the essence of all that is within Creation, it follows that any created being would "say" its subject-relation to its divine Lord in its essence. If God's *dominium* were a universal by causality for all creatures, then every creature's existence "says" God's *dominium*.[39] This is the sense of Wyclif's description of Creation as the expression of divine *dominium*, as we will discuss below.

In explaining the cause of the ten Aristotelian categories, maintaining that "all the categories have also a principle which is a more immediate cause of all the things which are *per se* in that genus," Wyclif holds that God's *dominium* is the immediate cause of true possession, that every true instance of possession predicates *per se*, or "says" divine *dominium*. If every instance of just human *dominium* requires God's Grace and *dominium* for its true being, it follows that each instance "says" God's *dominium* as its causal instantiation.[40] This means that every instance of possession has

---

[38] *Ibid.*, 7, 133.210–213: "Omne tale est causa alterius quod requiritur ad suum esse, quod omnis veritas posterius nominata sit causa prioris."

[39] The idea here is similar to Anselm's in *De Veritate*, VII (*Opera Omnia*, Tomus I, vol. 1, ed. F. S. Schmitt [Stuttgart, 1968]) wherein every created essence is a predication of divine Truth.

[40] *TDU*, 10, 235.653–236.680: "Tertio notant philosophi ex dicto Aristotelis X Metaphysicae, quomodo in omni genere est unum principium quod est metrum et mensura omnium aliorum. Quod

as its universal by causality divine *dominium*. As we will discuss later, the notion that all just possession requires Grace is fundamental to Wyclif's teachings on civil *dominium*, which results in something similar to what this conclusion about universals by causality does, namely, that all instances of just possession are based in and fundamentally caused by God's *dominium*.[41] This is borne out in *De Universalibus* Chapter 7, where Wyclif argues that every relation must have a respective term which, to refer adequately, must be a universal. He does not explain whether he means a universal by causality here, but the other possibility, universals by signification, seems unlikely because he has restricted these to the terms people have invented to refer to true universals. His discussion here suggests an impressive relational realism for universals by causality:

How, I ask, could there be such a thing as man naturally prior to there being this man, unless natural priority were there to be signified? And how could that priority exist unless we postulate a truth as a basis for that ordering? That truth is the common thing we are seeking; because even if all artificial signs were destroyed, that priority would nonetheless exist. . . . We must say the same thing about acts of knowledge, and about acts of the soul and other relationships . . .[42]

So far we have argued that Wyclif believes that *dominium*, a relation that follows on the act of Creation, serves as a universal by causality. But if all just ownership requires Grace, and if God's *dominium* serves as causal universal for all just ownership, does Grace necessarily accompany all created causality? One might argue that the just ownership of property is one thing, but more ontologically basic predications are something quite different. For instance, does the fact that God's uncreated one-ness serves as the principle of the entire genus of quantity mean that the

non solum intelligitur de supremo illius generis omnia alia mensurantis, sed de rationibus exemplaribus in Deo, quae sunt principia sui generis. Sed et omnia praedicamenta habent principium causans propinquius omnia per se in illo genere. . . . Dominiumque Dei extra genus, secundum quod dominatur universitati creatae, est principium ultimi generis." Note that the final category to which Wyclif refers in Aristotle is "having," see *Categories*, 15.b26.

[41] All types of possession, real or apparent, just or unjust, are reliant on the causal universal of God's *dominium* for their predicability. Two directions of argument are possible at this point. First, one can say that whether an instance of possession is just or unjust is not dependent on the causal universality of God's *dominium*, but upon its consonance with God's *iustitia*; we will pursue this thread in Chapter 4 when we examine Wyclif's notion of *ius*. Second, one can say that apparent and unjust instances of possession are only "so-called possession," and really instances of robbery. This approach would make "just possession" and "possession" synonymous, and is the sense Wyclif means us to understand *dominium* to refer to in *De Civili Dominio* when arguing that priests claim to have civil *dominium*, but in fact do not.

[42] *TDU*, 7, 144.444–55: "Quomodo, rogo, foret prius naturaliter quod homo est quam quod iste homo est, nisi signanda fuerit prioritas naturalia? Et quomodo foret illa prioritas, nisi signanda fuerit veritas/fundana illum ordinem? Quae quidem veritas est res communis quam quaerimus, nam destructis quibuscumque signis artificialibus non eo minus foret talis prioritas cum non posset esse prius sine prioritate. . . . Et eodem modo dicitur de scientia, de actibus animae."

only true quantity predications of a substance rely somehow on Grace? That is, is the truth of the statement "Henry weighs 170 pounds" reliant upon something other than Henry's being a 170-pounder, something transferred by Grace to make the statement true? In fact, this is exactly Wyclif's idea in *De Universalibus* and in *De Dominio Divino*: a thing is the way it is because the exemplar ideas in God provide the basis for it to be; if God did not know it to be so, the thing would not be the way it is.[43]

In Chapter 10 of *De Universalibus* Wyclif is more interested in showing how God's eternal being is the principle which is the "meter and measure of all things," that each of the Aristotelian categories has this principle as the immediate cause of every possible instance of predication in it.[44] Grace comes into this in *De Dominio Divino*; in the fifth chapter of the third book, Wyclif's distinction between uncreated Grace and created Grace points to the notion that God's willing is necessary for every instance of a creature realizing its potential.[45] In Chapters 16 through 18 of the first book Wyclif recognizes that God's will is dependent on His knowing, and that what God wills, and thus causes to occur through Grace, must first be known by God. We shall see that Wyclif carefully outlines the causal powers of God's knowing and willing, attempting to strike a balance between the determinism inherent in arguing that all that occurs does so because God knew it to be so and the implied threats to divine perfection consequent on many anti-determinist arguments. Could one object that maintaining no created action to be possible without Grace makes *all* possession Grace-founded? Yes, the fact that the pope owns extensive properties is a truth reliant on the causal universal of God's *dominium*, but this is not to say that divine *dominium's* causal universality makes the pope's ownership just as such.

Another element of Wyclif's speculative philosophy relevant to his *dominium* writings is his conception of the soul. On the face of it, the vigorous debate on the plurality of the soul appears to have little to do with a conception of *dominium*, yet Wyclif himself tells us that it does. At the beginning of *De Composicione Hominis* he holds that one cannot understand how a man can both be lord and servant at the same time until one sees how two distinct natures can exist in one soul.[46] This brief treatise is easily overlooked, but its placement is important to an understanding of the relation of Wyclif's earlier metaphysical thought to his *dominium* treatises, for he wrote it upon finishing *De Universalibus* and

[43] *Ibid.*, 7, 146.486–149.574; *DD*, I, 10, 74.5; ff. *DD*, I, 16, 142.14–146.13.
[44] *TDU*, 10, 234.630–236.684.   [45] *DD*, III, 5, 240.25–241.5.
[46] *De Composicione Hominis*, ed. R. Beer (London, 1884), 1, 2.19–27.

just before embarking on *De Dominio Divino*.[47] Robson's assessment of
De Composicione Hominis is that it may be a primer for Wyclif's philosophy,
and should not be included among the treatises of *Summa de Ente*.[48] This
is inaccurate: Wyclif intended the treatise to be a resolution of the dispute
on the numerous appetitive and vegetative souls subordinate to the rational soul between John Peckham and Richard Kilwardby.[49] Peckham was
distressed at the possibility that Saints' bodies might not retain venera-
bility after death if their corporeity did not remain. However dangerous,
this prospect arises from the Thomistic contention that a plurality of substantial forms in a given composite substance is impossible.[50] This would
have meant that the veneration of relics was mistaken. Peckham's 1286
condemnation of this position gave rise to a host of "pluralist" positions, explanations of how a variety of distinct substantial and accidental
forms were possible in a given composite. One might expect Ockham's
position to be similar to Aquinas', given his ontologically parsimonious
reputation. But Ockham believed a given substance to be a composite of
at least four, really distinct things: prime matter, the form of corporeity,
sensory soul, and the intellectual soul.[51] Further, Ockham did not believe
intellectual soul to be restricted to one part of the body; rather, it exists
whole in the composite and whole in every part, in each arm, finger,
leg, etc.[52] Thus, Wyclif has sufficient precedent for his arguments that
distinct real natures can exist simultaneously in a given composite. But
Wyclif's position is decidedly less restrained than Ockham's.

Wyclif begins his description of the union of many kinds of soul
in one substance by referring his reader to his discussion of the
universal–particular relation in *De Universalibus*. As the nature of the universal is each of its singulars which are united in its being, so the same
singular thing is itself greatly disparate, for many elements or forms are
united in its substantial being. Wyclif describes several ways in which
the diverse multiplicity of the unified soul can be understood: corporeity
and incorporeity combine within the soul to define man's physical and
spiritual natures; moreover, memory, will, and understanding make up
the elements of the rational soul.[53] But Wyclif has no wish to dwell on

[47] Thomson, *The Latin Writings of John Wyclyf*, pp. 36–7.
[48] Robson, *Wyclif and the Oxford Schools*, p. 139.
[49] *DCH*, 4, 74.14–75.9. The text's reference is to "Wilvarby et Pechani." See Leland Wilshire,
"Were the Oxford Condemnations of 1277 Directed Against Aquinas?" *New Scholasticism*, 48
(1974), pp. 125–32.
[50] *Summa Theologiae* (Rome, 1948), I, Q.76, a.3.
[51] William Ockham, *Quodlibet* II, Q.11 (*Quodlibeta Septem*, ed. J. C. Wey [St. Bonaventure, NY.,
1980]); see Marilyn Adams, *William Ockham* (Notre Dame, 1985), pp. 647–69.
[52] William Ockham, *Quodlibet* I, Q.12.   [53] *DCH*, 1, 11.2–18.

these truisms; his desire is to prove that any quantitative living being in a man's body has its own soul, giving it its own quiddity. That is, my hand contains within it not only my appetitive and rational soul, as Ockham had argued, but also a quiddity for "my hand."[54] The same is true of my thumb, and of my thumbnail, and so on. But Wyclif's philosophical atomism is apparent in his warning that the number of substantial quiddities that comprise substantial forms is limited to what is distinctly sensible.[55] Wyclif's examples giving evidence of this multiplicity of forms include the writhings of a bisected worm, which would be impossible were there but one substantial form in the worm. Similarly inexplicable would be the continued life apparent in many parts of dead plants and animals, notably decapitated chickens and the bleeding of murder victims after death.[56] Wyclif's obvious delight in such detailed examples suggests the vigorous enthusiasm for his subject that must have contributed to his reputation as a preacher and lecturer.

A plenitude of souls can only exist in a substance depending on a primary soul. In the case of man, the composite consists of a primary soul, "humanity" and the finite sets of souls of the body's parts. The composite resulting is itself really indivisible. This suggests a sense in which the soul of the thumb, while grounding the thumb's being, is contained in every other part of the body as well.[57] And while each of the members' souls govern the nature of that member, this individual governance is "insensible" or unconscious; the intellect alone has "sensible" knowledge of all operations, binding together the individual acts of governance in a unitive act of absolute government of the whole.[58]

While Wyclif's conception of the soul's make-up and functions warrants further investigation as an entertaining and daring piece of philosophy, we make reference to it in light of his *dominium* theory. The probable intent behind Wyclif's opening announcement that understanding of the soul is central to his work on human *dominium* was to show how one could be at once fully servant and fully lord. But the conceptual structure itself shows a universal–particular mechanism at work within a given system. In the microcosm of man's individual substance, the universal "humanity" provides the foundation for the government of the soul of each individual part of the body which participates in this humanity. While it is not likely that Wyclif was consciously constructing a macrocosm/microcosm schema for use in his *dominium* treatises, the structure of his conception of the soul certainly prefigures that of his conception of *dominium*.

[54] *Ibid.*, 4, 57.8–25.   [55] *Ibid.*, 4, 64.16–65.30.
[56] *Ibid.*, 4, 65.14–67.16; 4, 70.16–75.8   [57] *Ibid.*, 5, 76.13–77.11.   [58] *Ibid.*, 5, 88.13–89.15.

WHY ADOPT THIS REALISM?

Wyclif's arguments for his ontology range from justifications framed exclusively in scholastic metaphysical terms to others that are startlingly
relevant to political thought. Of these, the latter group of justifications
will receive attention, particularly Wyclif's equation of being right on universals and being on the benefits of common ownership. This equation
runs through his metaphysical works as well as through the first several
tractates of the *Summa Theologie*, leading us to conclude that Wyclif's
moral-theological insight into the higher value of community is of a
piece with his metaphysical commitment to the higher reality of universals. To say that one is 'of a piece' with the other may seem to beg the
important question of which position is more fundamental, the moral or
the metaphysical. In terms of Wyclif's biography, the metaphysics came
first. But it is likely that he would want us to evaluate his metaphysics on
the basis of its moral fruits.

Augustine, Anselm, and Grosseteste figure importantly as authorities in
Wyclif's realism. Interestingly, though, Aristotle is an important authority
for his doctrine of the reality of universals by commonality. Wyclif reads
Aristotle as a confirmed realist, and rejects as obfuscation the Ockhamist
desire to understand Aristotle as having abandoned Plato's realism.[59] How
could there have been such a long, reliable tradition of realism without
Aristotle having bequeathed universals to us?[60] The first and best authority for realism, though, is Christian theology.[61] While Augustine's
philosophical doctrine of Eternal Ideas is the formal source of Wyclif's
doctrine, Augustine's theological reasoning regarding the primacy of universals is directive of Wyclif's as well. Wyclif refers to Augustine's *De Vera
Religione* for theological justification for realism about universals, relating
Augustine's advice that we love common things before we love individual
or private ones.[62]

Universals must be prior to their particulars in God's knowing, and
also in His willing, for God's will is for the greatest good, and a universal
must be a greater good than its particular. Likewise, human willing should
be directed towards universals prior to particulars. If the will prefers the
greater, universal good, it will avoid sin. "From all this it is clear – I think –
that all envy or actual sin is caused by the lack of an ordered love of
universals . . . because every such sin consists in a will preferring a lesser
good to a greater good, whereas in general the more universal goods

[59] *DCH*, 4, 52.4, see 2a14–15, 3b.15–16; *DCH*, 4, 53.25–30, see 1017b23–26, 1034b16–18 and
39–46.
[60] *DCH*, 4, 55.81–83.   [61] This remained Wyclif's belief into the 1380s; see *Trialogus*, I, 9, 65.
[62] *TDU*, 3, 75.111–76.129.

are better."[63] If only people would strive to direct their wills away from private goods, and towards the common or better ones, much of the sin of the world could be erased. Private goods entail private property, and if private property could be eradicated, the benefits of general concern for the commonwealth would be evident to all.[64] This is a common theme in Wyclif's justifications for his realism; before addressing Ockhamist ontological objections in *Purgans Errores*, he suggests that his opponents' intellects have been poisoned by materialist desires. This, he explains, is the same sort of thing that has caused the degradation of Christian society in general; a love of material goods has led to a turning away from God's will.[65]

It is not uncommon for Wyclif, a skilled preacher, to repeat himself again and again throughout a work. It is therefore particularly significant that in both *Purgans Errores* and the *Tractatus de Universalibus* Wyclif says the same thing about those who deny universals and about the correspondent social ills their denial entails. More significant is Wyclif's equation of the denial of universals with a tendency to care for private possessions, and the associated equation of realism with recognition of the beneficial nature of communal ownership. He makes no effort in either of these works to pursue this equation, presenting it instead as an example of the importance of being right in one's ontology. Elsewhere in *De Universalibus* Wyclif indicates his awareness of the peculiarity of his mission, noting that, "though for a time truth has fainted in the street, God will always provide for himself some enlightened zealots for this truth, since truth is victorious above all."[66] One gets the sense on reading the *Tractatus de Universalibus* that by the late 1360s Wyclif had already formulated the kernel of what he was to say in the first books of the *Summa Theologie*.

Evidence of this also appears in the 1369 treatise *De Ente Praedicamentali*, which is primarily about the Aristotelian categories and their relations both to one another and to predications about them. In his discussion of relations, he explains that care is needed in discussing relations between *relata* that have their being in different ways. Some relations are aggregates of many individual relations, he explains, as with that between a lord and his servants. There are three classes of these *dominium*-relations, he

---

[63] *Ibid.*, 77.145–9: "Et istis patet – ut estimo – quod omnis invidia vel actuale peccatum causatur ex defectu ordinatae dilectionis universalium, ut docet Augustinus, Epistola 22, nam omne tale peccatum consistit in voluntate praeponente minus bonum magis bone. Sed generaliter bona universaliora sunt meliora." For evidence of this sentiment's constancy in Wyclif's thought, see *Trialogus*, I, 8–9, 61–9.

[64] *TDU*, 77.152–62.   [65] *Purgans Errores Circa Universalia In Communi*, 1, 29.17–24.

[66] *TDU*, 11, 241.83–5: "Sed quamvis ad tempus veritas corruit in plateis, Deus tamen/semper providet sibi aliquos illuminatos et zelantes pro huiusmodi veritate, cum super omnia vincit veritas."

explains, divine, intellectual, and civil. Regarding the first, "it is right that all rational creatures serve God, either by acting as they should or by refraining as they should . . ."[67] This and intellectual *dominium* (the relation whereby the master has authority by virtue of superior rational powers) are natural relations, while the civil variety is artificial, founded on conquest or some other human institution.[68] Further evidence of Wyclif's interest in such matters is his frequent use of the relation of kingship or divine *dominium* as an example for whatever he is discussing.[69] These instances of Wyclif mentioning *dominium* in a metaphysical context, or referring to the importance of a proper understanding of universals in terms which he was to link together in his later thought on *dominium* are not explicit justifications for Wyclif's realism. They are, rather, implicit justifications, arguments Wyclif makes in passing for his realism by linking his thought on universals with his thought on *dominium*.

DOMINIUM IN DE DIVINO DOMINIO

De Dominio Divino is the point of departure for Wyclif's *Summa Theologie*, a turning point in his writings from the speculative to the practical. This, at any rate, is Wyclif's assessment, for he comments in the beginning of this work that the time has come for him to devote his energies to practical issues.[70] According to Thomson, Wyclif wrote the work between 1373 and 1374; directly after finishing it, he began the works that comprise the *Summa*, first among them *De Mandatis Divinis*, *De Statu Innocencie*, and *De Civili Dominio*.[71]

De Dominio Divino is divided into three books, of which the first is a general discussion of the nature of *dominium*, the second is an examination of the nature and extent of divine *dominium*, and the third is a careful investigation of three aspects of divine *dominium*, namely, giving,

---

[67] *De Ente Predicamentali*, ed. R. Beer (London, 1901), VII, 66.17–19: "cum oportet omnem racionalem creaturam servire Deo, vel agendo ut debet, vel paciendo quod debet."

[68] *DEP*, VII, 67.9–14; Intellectual *dominium* plays no part at all in the *dominium* treatises, and because of the lack of reference to proprietative issues, is not importantly analogous to the natural *dominium* of *DCD*.

[69] *De Logica* II, 3, 5–15; II, 8, 208.33–209.24; *De Logica* III, 10, 135.11–38; III, 10, 148.14–21; III, 10, 152.9–16; on bearing up under tyranny, see *De Ente Libri Secundi, Tractatus Tertius* (*Librorum Duorum Excerpta*, ed. M. H. Dziewicki [London, 1909]) 16, 268.39–269.32. Regarding other references to divine *dominium* (none of which diverges from *De Divino Dominio*), see *De Ente II:III*, 5, 169.10–33; *De Logica* I, 14, 198.35–199.19, regarding antecedent nature of divine being to divine lordship. Wyclif makes practically no direct reference to kingship as an example in the *De Universalibus*, although he does make passing reference to the need for prudence in the governance of the commonwealth; see *TDU*, 11, 310–13.

[70] *DD*, I, 1, 1.6: "[T]empus est mihi per totum residuum vite mee tam speculative quam practice, secundum mensuram quam Deus donaverit."

[71] Thomson, *The Latin Writings of John Wyclyf*, pp. 39–48.

receiving, and lending. At the beginning of the third book Wyclif gives a list of sixteen acts of *dominium*, which clarifies the discussion of the second book, uniting it with that of the third, making the entire work a consideration of the universal relation of *dominium*. He explains that the first three acts of *dominium* are Creation, sustenance, and governance, which describe the nature and extent of the divine *dominium*. He lists the second three acts of *dominium* as giving, receiving, and lending.[72] Wyclif says nothing about the remaining ten acts in *De Dominio Divino*, which has led to the hypothesis that much of the work has been lost.[73] I think that Wyclif realized that these six acts of *dominium* were sufficient to illustrate the ties between divine and human *dominium*, and abandoned the remaining ten as superfluous.[74]

The first book is an examination of the nature of *dominium* as such, a relation or a condition of rational being.[75] And because all beings must serve their Creator, rational created beings who enjoy *dominium* only can do so as servants of God. *Dominium* involves service (*servicium*), but not necessarily servitude (*servitus*), he explains, for service is a condition (*habitudo*) of the blessed, while servitude is a consequence of sin.[76] Further, we should not equate *dominium* with use or power, nor can we hold it to be an essential part of the divine nature, for it is an effect following Creation.[77] This makes the necessary precondition for having *dominium* to be creating, and leads Wyclif to hold that divine *dominium* is the standard or measure upon which all instances of created *dominium* are founded.[78] Wyclif discusses the permanence of the divine *dominium*-relation, and that of the service owed the divine Lord by all created subjects, and examines God's perfect use of His *dominium*, which is best served

---

[72] *DD*, III, 1, 198.9.

[73] See Gotthard Lechler, *John Wycliffe and his English Precursors*, trans. P. Lorimer (London, 1884), pp. 259–60.

[74] *DD*, III, 1, 198.6–12: "[D]eclarandis quod sedecim sunt actus quos contingit famosius circa dominium exerceri: scilicet, creare, sustentare, et gubernare, quos oportet necessario appropriate Deo competere; et tredecim alii, scilicet donare accipere, prestare, repetere, vendere, emere, locare, conducere, accommodare, mutuare, promittere, fideiubere, et deponere: de quorum differenciis et speciebus patet posterius in processu." Included in Wyclif's discussion of lending he describes *prestare, accommodare, et mutuare*; this, strictly speaking, leaves eight acts of *dominium* unexplored. The abruptness with which Wyclif dismisses the relevance of *accommodare* [*sic*] *et mutuare* from the discussion in III, 4 supports my hypothesis that the unexplored acts of *dominium* were never a serious part of his agenda.

[75] *DD*, I, 1, 4.7–6.11: "Dominium est habitudo nature racionalis secundum quam denominatur suo prefici servienti." See also *De Ente*, I, 3, i, 4.22–35; *DEP*, 7, 66.15–67.19 for earlier references to *dominium*.

[76] *DD*, I, 1, 7.4–8.21.   [77] *Ibid.*, I, 2 See also *De Ente*, III, 1, 4.22–9.

[78] *DD*, I, 3, 16.18–22: "Ex quo sequitur quod dominium Dei mensurat, ut prius et presuppositum, omnia alia assignanda: si enim creature habet dominium super quidquam, Deus prius habet dominium super idem; ideo ad quodlibet creature dominium sequitur dominium divinum, et non econtra."

when every part of Creation acts in accord with its directive universal cause.[79] This line of thought will appear again in the beginning of the second book in Wyclif's idea that God's *dominium* over universals is prior to His *dominium* over particulars. That Wyclif means us to recognize divine *dominium* as a universal–particular relation is further suggested by his later (mid-1381) comment that in any given genus there is one primary act that serves as the measure of all others.[80] While Wyclif does not explicitly say that God's *dominium* is the universal *Dominium* in which all created instances of *dominium* participate, one cannot help but make this conclusion from the argument of Book 1, Chapters 5–10. In Chapter 8, for example, Wyclif explains how Fitzralph's denial of the ordering of divine *dominium* from universal to particular is misplaced, arguing that a universal has its particular in itself, so *dominium* will have successive *dominium*-relations within it.[81]

The second book is about the acts of governance, sustenance, and creation of God's *dominium*-relation to Creation. Again, Wyclif argues that God's *dominium* is first over universals, for it is these that God knows before particulars. God's knowing-relation to them directs His governance and sustenance. God not only knows, but creates, sustains and governs all things in their universal causes before they come to be in their particular instantiations.[82] The third book of *De Divino Dominio* describes the acts of giving, receiving, and lending associated with the God's *dominium*. Here he explains how God alone can give, because as Creator, He alone can truly be said to have anything. When God gives of what He has, He does not truly surrender that which is given, for all that God has is reliant upon God for continued existence.[83] Nor does God's receiving involve any real enrichment of the divine nature, as acts of receiving enrich a lesser receiver. All that we receive is from God, and so Wyclif's doctrine that God's giving, or Grace, is a necessary prerequisite for just temporal *dominium* is founded in his description of the divine *dominium*. By the end of *De Dominio Divino* it is clear that Wyclif is ready to approach the nature of human *dominium* as a relation wholly dependent upon Grace and just only insofar as it participates in the universal divine *dominium*.

---

[79] *Ibid.*, I, 5.

[80] *De Blasphemia*, fol. 126, c.2: "In omni genere est unum primum quod est metrum et mensura omnium aliorum." Cited in Lechler, *John Wycliffe and his English Precursors*, p. 236, n. 2.

[81] *DD*, I, 8, 50–2.

[82] *Ibid.*, II, 2, 184.14–19: "Deus prius dominatur universali quam alicui singulari signabili, videtur exinde capere veritatem quod Deus dominatur creaturis secundum ordinem quo ipse adinvicem habent esse; cum ergo omne universale sit prius naturaliter suo singulari, videtur quod correspondenter de Dei dominio debet dici."

[83] *Ibid.*, III, 1–2.

THE DIVINE *DOMINIUM*-RELATION

What sort of relation is God's *dominium*? Wyclif addresses this by explaining that it is like the relation of paternity:

Every particular paternity whatever of Adam in relation to a particular child is therefore the common [i.e. universal] paternity in relation to its object, and yet it is distinguished in concept, just as the universal is distinguished from its supposits, and correspondingly the same is said of having *dominium*. For there exists one common paternal adoption, which every adoption of God is.[84]

God alone is able to create, and does so through the exemplary reasons. Further, it is impossible for any creature to produce anything without God having produced it in His eternal, exemplary reasons.[85] This means that the necessary conditions for created motion or act lie primarily in God's eternal principles, and that the apparent temporal factors enabling his act are of lesser import. Wyclif's arguments here for the relation between God's eternal principles and created actions offer a notably un-Aristotelian view of causality; Wyclif's source is the pseudo-Aristotelian, neoplatonic *De Mundo*.[86]

Wyclif was not alone among scholastic philosophers in arguing that God is immediately causally involved in every created action, but his emphasis on creatures having primary being in the eternal principles takes the place of the more recognizably Aristotelian attention to the secondary causes found in earlier thinkers like Aquinas and Scotus. He explains that other philosophers err by positing intermediate causes through which God moves, and he distinguishes between two sorts of agency. There is mediated instrumental agency, through which inferior agents act, as when created beings use other created beings to produce effects, and there is unmediated causal agency, through which God acts without reliance on other beings. And because God's being is the primary cause of all mediated instrumental agency, as well as of all unmediated causal agency, it is better to focus on unmediated divine causation than on secondary causes.[87]

---

[84] *Ibid.*, I, 9, 55.8–11: "Communis ergo paternitas ad obiectum est quelibet singularis paternitas ipsius Adam ad filium singularem; et tamen secundum racionem distinguitur, sicut universale distinguitur a suo supposito:et correspondenter de habitudinibus domini est dicendum. Est enim una communis adopcio paternalis que est omnis Dei adopcio."

[85] *Ibid.*, I, 10, 72.29–73.5.

[86] Poole refers the reader to 399a: "For at a signal given on high from Him who may well be called their chorus leader, the stars and the whole heavens always move . . . when therefore the ruler and parent of all, invisible save to the eye of the mind, gives the word to all nature that moves betwixt heaven and earth, the whole revolves unceasingly on its own circuits . . . revealing and again hiding diverse manners of things from one and the same course." *De Mundo*, ed. E. S. Forster (London, 1914), included in *The Works of Aristotle* ed. W. D. Ross (London, 1931).

[87] See Wyclif's discussion of this in *DD*, I, 10, 74.5–75.32 and ff.

Wyclif veers towards occasionalism by arguing that God is the true primary cause of all created action, making it difficult to avoid concluding that creatures do not really act autonomously. Archbishop Thomas Bradwardine had made a similar argument earlier in the century in his *De Causa Dei*, formulated to counter the perceived Pelagianism of Ockham and his followers. Wyclif's debt to Bradwardine is evident throughout *De Universalibus* and *De Dominio Divino*, for he frequently mentions the *Doctor Profundus* as having been one of the few recent thinkers to have seen the proper relation of theology to philosophy. Bradwardine recognizes that his position, in which all created being is unmediatedly caused by God, risks occasionalism, and attempts to head it off by arguing for the co-efficiency of divine and human action in human willing.[88]

It is likely that Wyclif's reliance on Bradwardine is primarily as a source for theological arguments supporting the necessity of Grace for any good (or just) created action, and for an anti-Ockhamist picture of the relation of God to Creation. Bradwardine nowhere describes *dominium* as the primary relation between God and Creation, nor does he make the slightest reference to the place of universals in the relation.[89] But Wyclif admired Bradwardine for abandoning the distinction between absolute and ordained power that had long been used to describe the relation; Bradwardine appears to have identified it as a tool by which Pelagians detract from divine omnipotence, and Wyclif loyally follows suit. In his attempt to ameliorate Bradwardine's position, Wyclif emphasizes the Eternal Exemplars as the organizing principles through which God knows and wills Creation, no doubt believing that his realism would serve as a reliable replacement for talk of absolute and ordained power. An important effect of Wyclif's emphasis on God's unmediated causality of all action was his rejection of the Aegidian hierocratic structure of ecclesiastical office and its concomitant political authority. David Luscombe suggests that Wyclif's rejection of papal-hierocratic reasoning is replaced by a hierarchically structured monarchism based in Grosseteste's worldview. While the structure of the political scheme is perceivably hierarchic, the reasoning for it as it appears in *De Dominio Divino* is presented

---

[88] Thomas Bradwardine, *De Causa Dei*, ed. H. Saville (London, 1618), II, 20, 542E. See Heiko Oberman, *Thomas Bradwardine: A Fourteenth-Century Augustinian* (Utrecht, 1957), pp. 105–22. Bradwardine's earlier *De Futuris Contingentibus* is a philosophically rigorous argument against Ockham's position on future contingents lacking the theological majesty of *De Causa Dei*.

[89] *De Causa Dei*, I, 6; Bradwardine's discussion of God's knowledge, refers not at all to universals. It is probable that Bradwardine's earlier extensive work at Merton college in Aristotelian physics disposed him against ontological issues. See also Edith Wilks Dolnikowski, *Thomas Bradwardine: A View of Time and a Vision of Eternity in Fourteenth-Century Thought* (Leiden, 1995).

in terms stressing the unmediated nature of God's *dominium*.[90] Thus God is the most basic, immediate and proper cause of all action, and creatures do nothing unless previously mediated through and aided by God's movement.[91] This is important because if all created movement relies directly upon God, all acts of power are realized only through God's unmediated direction. One creature may give another power to act, or hold *dominium* over others, but all created action relies directly on the act of Creation, the basis of God's *dominium*-relation. If there is truly an instance of one individual having authority over another, it is because God, not some artificed hierarchical order, ordained it.

One could object in the face of this gloomy view of human autonomy that reasoning does nothing but sully faith or, as Gregory the Great put it, "that faith has no merit which human reason proves through experiment."[92] This may seem trifling, given the standard Anselmian "faith seeking understanding" response that Wyclif gives, but many of his opponents took a doctrinal approach to their defense of the hierocratic model, which Wyclif could not overlook. Thus if he could found his own approach on the likes of Anselm, he could escape accusation of heresy. His firm endorsement of the illumination theory of understanding is accompanied by a sly dig at the *Moderni*, who put too much emphasis on the natural capacity of intuitive cognition.[93] By framing the issue this way, Wyclif champions an illumination theory of understanding in line with traditional Augustinian thought, thereby reinforcing his position that no created action is possible without God's unmediated direction. Thus he uses this potential objection to bolster his rejection of any sort of hierarchic structure in God's *dominium*.

IS DIVINE *DOMINIUM* DETERMINIST?

Wyclif's reputation for determinism is understandable, given his contention that God's *dominium* is so all-pervasive and unmediated as to be the cause of all created acts. While this makes inarguable the thesis that

[90] See David Luscombe, "Wyclif and Hierarchy," in *From Ockham to Wyclif*, ed. A. Hudson and M. Wilks, *SCH* Subsidia 5 (London, 1987), pp. 233–44.
[91] *DD*, I, 10, 74.5–12: "Et patet quod Deus principalissime, immediatissime, et propriissime efficit omne opus; principalissime, cum sit dux et archomotor in toto opere; immediatissime, quia pro mensura sua creat effectum sine adminiculo se iuvantis, sed creatura nichil facit, nisis mediante previa Dei movencia se iuvantis; et propriissime, cum agere proprius ascribitur supremo et principalissimo Agenti, quod tot agenciis et movenciis agit, quam suo postero instrumento."
[92] *Ibid.*, I, 11, 76.4: "Fides non habet meritum, cui humana racio prebet experimentum." The reference is to Gregory, *Hom. in Evang.*, II, 26, no. 1, Op.1, 1552 D.
[93] *DD* I, 11, 85.13–21.

all just human *dominium* is immediately based on God's *dominium*, and allows for the two being related as particular to universal by causality, two problems arise. First, would not unjust human *dominium*-relations be equally attributable to God's *dominium*, if all created acts are primarily caused by that relation? Wyclif's response to this would be that the will's subservience to sin, not God, is the immediate cause of unjust human *dominium*, but this only pushes the question back. What impels the will to enslave itself to sin? Surely this is a created act; if God is the unmediated cause of all created acts, is not God responsible for human sin? The problem to resolve will be the classically Augustinian one of human freedom of choice. Wyclif must find a way to explain human sinning, and hence unjust human *dominium*, while upholding God's unmediated *dominium*. Without human freedom, God's *dominium* seems an archetype for tyranny as well as for just rule. Wyclif's solution involves some fairly involved theological reasoning, for he believes it necessary to explain first how God's willing is not compelled by His perfect knowing. This requires a careful exposition of the relation of divine intellection, willing, and act, as separate operations within the divine unity, which when shown to be not compelled by any sort of restrictive necessity, allows for an argument that created wills' actions are not restrictively necessitated by divine willing. This, in turn, will assist in showing how God's *dominium* involves governance as well as sustenance and creation. If we are to show that Wyclif's idea of governance is the same in divine *dominium* as in the civil variety, we should account for interaction between governor and governed, or be content with an empty species of *gubernare*.

At the heart of Wyclif's argument is his distinction between two different sorts of necessity: absolute necessity, truths which cannot not be, and necessity *ex suppositione*, truths having an eternal cause from which their temporal being flows formally.[94] Suppositional necessity is identical to Wyclif's hypothetical necessity as described in *Tractatus de Universalibus* and is consistent with the supreme contingency of the Eternal Exemplary ideas.[95] Say Eternal Exemplary idea A causes event B to occur at Tn. While the truth about the connection of A and B is absolutely necessary, the causal antecedent is contingent in itself. That A is the case is not temporally contingent, but eternally so. Wyclif envisages eternal contingency as the counterweight to hypothetical necessity.

---

[94] *Ibid.*, I, 14, 116.2–26.
[95] *TDU*, 14. See Simo Knuuttila's "Modal Logic," in *The Cambridge History of Later Medieval Philosophy*, ed. A. Kenny, N. Kretzmann, and J. Pinborg (Cambridge, 1982), pp. 342–57, for an introductory discussion of the gradations of necessity in later medieval thought. See also Bartholomew R. De La Torre, O. P., *Thomas Buckingham and the Contingency of Futures* (Notre Dame, 1987), pp. 41–103.

Again, with the knowledge of any given creature, God's knowledge is eternal, irresistible, and contingent on the existence of the creature.[96] If the creature did not exist, God would not know of its existence. Does this mean that a temporal creature's act has causal power over divine knowledge? In fact it does, but this does not implicate a reduction in God's power, because as eternal knower God is prior ontologically to Creation. Further, since God primarily knows created beings through divine Ideas, Eternal Exemplars, the being of the creature's act is dependent upon the Exemplar's being.[97] In short, Wyclif's arguments for divine knowledge's dependence on created act relies heavily on his belief in the priority of the order of Being over the order of Knowing.

Undergirding this eternal contingency is God's will.[98] Here Wyclif differs from Bradwardine, whose position he deems excessive.[99] There is a sense in which the divine will is "caused" by human willing. While God is the immediate cause of all created acts, He is not the immediate cause of sinful ones. The evil in a sinful act lies in the will of the agent, and is accidental to the act. "[F]ree choice lies not in the corporeal matter [involved in the act], but only in the intellectual nature which is indivisibly able to turn away from [the performance of] the act by virtue of the [directive] willing beyond it."[100] Could God have prohibited the will from sinning? Not without compromising the will's freedom. But this freedom is not boundless. While God cannot will me to choose anything that I would not want myself, if I choose to act with an evil intent, that is my doing, but if I choose to act for the good, the good can only come with the assent of the divine will. "It is not possible for a created essence to be good unless God is pleased that it be so; thus, if any creature does good, it is in conformity with God's pleasure."[101] So far, this is in agreement with Bradwardine and the Augustinian tradition. God is causally accountable for the act and its goodness; only the act's evil comes from the agent's will alone. It sounds as if men are only free to act sinfully; since the act itself is value-neutral, if I act with a good will, the goodness of the act comes from God, not my willing, while if I act with evil intent, the evil of the act comes from a defect within me.

---

[96] *DD*, I, 16, 142–44.　　[97] *Ibid.*, I, 18, 164.

[98] *TDU*, 14, 335.116–21: "Et patet ulterius quod fons primae necessitatis et primae contingentiae est in Deo, nam nihil creatum est necessarium nisi de quanto ipse necessitat ipsum ad esse, nec aliqua creatura potest contingenter esse vel non esse ad utrumlibet nisi de quanto Deus potest aeque velle ipsum libere/vel non velle."

[99] *DD*, I, 17.

[100] *Ibid.*, I, 14, 117.21–3: "cum libertas arbitrii non primo residet in natura corporea, sed solum in natura intellectuali que potest indivisibiliter super se voluntarie reflectere actum suum."

[101] *Ibid.*, I, 17, 150.22–5: "quod non hoc possibile create essencie bene esse nisi quod Deus complacet ita esse; ergo, si aliqui creature bene fuerit, illa congruencia Dei beneplacito est conformis."

To avoid coming to such a premature conclusion, we should be careful defining "freedom." An act does not need to be free because it depends on God. That we have freedom of willing God knows and wills with absolute necessity, but how we will is only hypothetically necessary. Human willing is caused insofar as individual men are instantiations of the contingent Eternal Exemplar "Man," but self-caused regarding the direction it takes in each act of willing. Given eternal contingent truth A, that we have free will, A causes an individual to will an event B to occur in time. While the truth about the connection of A and B is absolutely necessary, the causal antecedent A is itself eternally contingent, since God could as easily have known ~A. B is only causally necessitated by A, which dictates that B occur as the result of an act of free willing.

We must remember that Wyclif is addressing *gubernare* as well as *creare* and *sustentare* in this discussion, and that his desire is only to refer to his more fully articulated position in *De Universalibus*. If God is to "govern" in any sense, this would involve His subjects carrying out God's will. We have considered how God knows with purely hypothetical necessity the actions of His subjects. Can we then say that our actions carry out God's will? We are free to will for good or evil. If we will the evil, this action does not carry out God's will, because God only wills the good. But if we will the good, what we will is only good with God's Grace-ful confirmation. Just as what God knows is contingent, but that God knows it is necessary, Wyclif believes that what God wills is contingent, but that God wills it is necessary. The modality of divine willing is no different from the modality of divine knowing. So when we will the good, it is good by God willing it along with us, and that God wills it is absolutely necessary. But we might have willed evil, against God's will, so it would have been absolutely necessary that God's will runs counter to our action. Here Wyclif departs from Bradwardine, who would not countenance any sense in which God's will runs counter to created action.[102] The aim throughout is to show that there is a degree of interaction in the divine *dominium*-relation with Creation. That God's will brings about Creation is not in question; for the relation to involve governance as well as sustenance and Creation, the created will should carry out the divine will in some way. Indeed, Wyclif embraces the sense in which a creature's acts "cause" God's knowing and willing, just as subjects' acts "cause" governance.[103] This comes from the freedom of

---

[102] *Ibid.*, I, 18, is primarily a response to the objection Wyclif knows Bradwardine would make.

[103] A passing but foreshadowing suggestion of precisely this is in *TDU* 14, 373–5: "Sicut ergo dominatio causatur in Deo a creatura sibi serviente – et quantumlibet posterius causat prioritatem praecedentem tam tempore quam natura."

the human will, which is made possible by the concept of hypothetical necessity.

DIVINE *DOMINIUM* OVER UNIVERSALS AND PARTICULARS

The importance of Wyclif's realism to his thought on *dominium* is apparent in his discussion of the relation of divine being to the being of universals, and consequently to their particulars. Most of the second book of *DD* is concerned with this problem. Wyclif begins characterizing the extent of divine *dominium* with the most general instance of the relation, that between divine being and the most common genus, created being or "Being-as-such." The divine *dominium*-relation follows upon the act of Creation, so that created Being-as-such, created first of all, is that over which God has the most primary *dominium*. "Just as Being is created first of all, so *dominium* directed to created analogous Being is the first *dominium* possible for our Lord, not only first in nature, but first in time, and indeed in dignity."[104]

From our discussion on Wyclif's thought on the types of universals, we can classify this "Being" as the most primary of universals by community. Wyclif believes that God's *dominium* over "Being" is necessary for any successive divine *dominium* over more speciated universals by community. If divine *dominium* is a universal by causality for human *dominium*, we must first address the most primary of all of the divine *dominium*-relations. It seems as if *dominium*, a universal by causality, follows upon the creation of Being, a universal by community. From this Wyclif arrives at three conclusions: first, universals exist distinct from material things; second, the genus "Being" is the first possible universal; third, God has *dominium* over universals before having it over any singulars included in the universal.[105]

The first conclusion does not deny the position of *De Universalibus*; universals do not exist apart from their particulars. Rather, we are meant to remember that while universals by community are formally distinct from their *supposita*, they are still numerically identical with them. It is the most general universal by community, the genus "Being" that provides for all further individuation of lesser universals by community.

---

[104] *DD*, II, 1, 173.9–16: "ut, sicut primo omnium creatur esse, sic dominium terminatum ad esse creatum analogum est primum dominium possibile Deo nostro; nedum primum primitate nature, sed et temporis, et eciam dignitatis."

[105] *Ibid.*, II, 1, 173. 22–8: "Sed pro primitate nature oportet tria supponere: primo, quod sint universalia ex parte rei (ut alias diffusius declaravi); secundo, quod ens analogum sit primum universale possibile; et tercio, quod Deus prius dominatur universali quam alicui singulari signabili. Ex quibus patet assignati dominii divini primitas naturalis."

"[A]nd while all priority presupposes ordering, just as all comparatives presuppose something positive, it follows that an ordering has been given between God's *dominium* and simple creatures, which order is presupposed prior to the *dominium* directed over this individual creature."[106] Without the structure provided by the supreme genus, all further general and specific ordering would be impossible, and God would have *dominium* over nothing in particular.

Dominium implicitly requires there to be a prior order established in the dominated; in this case, the first created universal by community provides this order, and the kind of order needed prior to earthly *dominium* is given a precedent. Wyclif goes on to stress the commonality of all things when viewed as instantiations of the genus "Being," providing evidence for understanding the extent and nature of *gubernare et sustentare* in divine *dominium*. "God can give or promise the creature as much good as evil without anything being specified to any individual creature, in which case it is clear that the things which are sent forth are sent forth commonly, thus the community of creatures is not denied."[107] This will resonate clearly and distinctly when we discuss God's giving- and lending-relations to Creation, and again when we articulate Wyclif's position on the superiority of communal *dominium* over private ownership. Even at this most abstract level of discussion of the relation of God to Creation, the superiority of the common to the particular is clear.

But this brings a troubling notion to mind. In Wyclif, order of presentation is of great importance, and in his list of the classes of universals, universals by causality precede universals by community. Yet our reasoning here suggests that the universal by causality that is God's *dominium* would follow from the existence of the most general universal by community, the genus "Being." Does the universal by causality precede or follow the universal by community? Two answers come to mind, each based in Wyclif's discussion of determinism. First, God's knowing-relation to the Eternal Exemplars precedes the existence of the genus "Being," and that relation must surely be a universal by causality for the existence of the genus "Being," for we have already described the Eternal Exemplars as being comprehensible only as universals by causality. Another approach to this problem would lie in remembering the difference between the Order

---

[106] *Ibid.*, II, 1, 174.20–5: "[E]t cum omnis prioritas presupponit aliquod positivum, sicut omne comparativum presupponit aliquod positivum, sequitur quod est dare ordinem inter dominium Dei et creaturam simpliciter, qui quidem ordo presupponitur tanquam prior ad dominium hanc individuam creaturam terminans."

[107] *Ibid.*, II, 1, 175.7–11: "Deus potest dare vel promittere creature tam bonum quam malum signabile sine hoc quod ipsum specificetur ad aliquod singulare; in quo casu oportet quod res que promittitur sit communis; ergo non est neganda communitas creature."

of Being and the Order of Knowing. To understand God's *dominium*, we must first understand there to be an order pre-existing in the dominables. But this does not mean that God's *dominium* is somehow less primary than the universal by community, "Being." After all, any *dominium*-relation can be knowable either through its subject, or through its object, and in this case, knowing it through the subject, God, is impossible because of the incomprehensibility of the divine unity. And because we can only know the objects, the dominables, as particulars under the genus "Being," we must assert that the genus "Being" is prior to God's *dominium* in the Order of Knowing, though not necessarily in the Order of Being. That is, it is only comprehensible to us that the universal by causality that is divine *dominium* would follow upon the universal by community, "Being"; but that does not mean that it truly is that way.

The second conclusion of Book II, Chapter 1, that the genus "Being" is first among universals by community, follows from the first. Wyclif explains this briefly, saying, "No universal is able now to be more common and at another time to be less common, but analogous being is able to be as common as anything else that is significable can be, so this is as common as anything can be."[108] The third conclusion, that God has *dominium* over universals before He has it over particulars is not as thorny as might first appear. We remember that universals by community must exist in particulars, and it seems that God has *dominium* over something inhering in Peter before having it over Peter. This does not sit well; it seems that divine *dominium* should first be over Peter, then over whatever follows from Peter's existing. But this is not the way universals are related to particulars, *Moderni* protestations to the contrary. We should remember that God knows universals prior to their particulars, which relation directs the divine *dominium*-relation, "for God posits to be true eternally and intrinsically whatever follows formally and posteriorly."[109]

Another problem arises regarding this genus "Being." If God's essence is pure being, as Wyclif notes it must be, would not God's *dominium* over the most primary sort of being be over His own essence, rather than over created "Being?" It would, Wyclif responds, if we suppose "being" to be univocally predicable of God and creatures. That is, if we can say that God has being in the same way as we say that creatures have it, we would be forced to conclude that God's *dominium* is eternal, and hence

---

[108] *DD*, II, 2, 179.21–4: "quod nullum universale potest nunc esse communius et alias minus commune; sed ens analogum potest esse ita commune sicut aliquod signabile potest esse; ergo est ista commune sicut aliquid potest esse."

[109] *Ibid.*, II, 2, 183.11–12: "cum Deo posito cum suis eternis intrinsecis sequitur formaliter quodlibet posterum verum esse."

not a consequence of the act of Creation. This would spoil everything, because there would be no way to characterize divine *dominium* as having the acts of *creare, sustentare, et gubernare*, nor any of the others, if it were not something that held between God and creatures in time. This is why Wyclif refers to the genus "Being" as *ens analogum* throughout his discussion; we predicate "being" of creatures and of God only analogously, thus allowing for the necessary being of God and the contingent being of creatures. Wyclif's discussion here is consonant with the Thomistic doctrine of predication by analogy; he broaches the subject largely to fend off unnecessary objections from critics.[110]

These two problems, the determinism issue and the primacy of universals in the divine *dominium*-relation, illustrate what Wyclif believes to be central to *creare, sustentare, et gubernare*. As we have already equated this set of acts with *iurisdictio*, we can now come to conclusions about what Wyclif believed to be important about divine *iurisdictio*, remembering that these same issues should be important in his thought on human *dominium*, if the human and divine varieties are related as particular to universal.

First, human subjects can carry out the divine will, thereby causing God's will to be realized in Creation. Then again, we can flout God's will by freely willing evil. The governor's responsibility for the actions of all of the governed is total, so when the potential for sin arises, it is in the governor's interest to check that potential before sin occurs. When sin does occur, it is the governor's task to identify its occurrence and to punish the sinner. In either case, the governor sustains the well-being of the realm, and nurtures and serves it. As we will discuss below, reciprocity is central to Wyclif's notion of human *dominium*; a just lord is at once master and servant of his subjects, while a subject is in the service of, and has mastery over, his lord. In divine *dominium*, God's *caritas*-based *dominium* can be interpreted as both perfect mastery over Creation and loving, and nurturing of each of its members. This is not to say that God's *dominium* involves any sort of compulsory duties being placed upon God. In *De Civili Dominio* I, xv, Wyclif explains that the *caritas* of divine *dominium* involves God necessarily loving and caring for Creation, without a duty on God's part to act against His will. As supreme lord, God has all His laws in the vault of His heart, but willingly conforms to them. "Among others there is one law, that if a rational creature loves God, God anticipatively returns that love . . . [but] it would be impertinence to assert

---

[110] *Ibid.*, II, 2–4. For earlier fourteenth-century thought on univocal predication, see Matthew Menges, O.F.M., *The Concept of Univocity Regarding the Predication of God and Creature According to William Ockham* (St. Bonaventure, N.Y., 1952).

some negativity in God because of this duty."[111] This comes in the midst of Wyclif's explanation of the centrality of *caritas* to just human *dominium*, preceding his observation that such *caritas* is very difficult in a world rife with material hindrances to it.[112] As we will see, Wyclif presents similar arguments for kings obeying their own laws in *De Officio Regis* III.

Second, that which is common is purer through being undifferentiated, and should therefore be first in the mind of the governor/sustenance provider, before worrying about matters involving individuated aspects of that which comes from what is common. An instance of this in civil *dominium* would be Wyclif's advice that the king not shrink from pulling down the church buildings to make a tower or a wall in the event of the kingdom's invasion; the well-being of the whole of the kingdom should outweigh not the needs of the church, but certainly the convenience of some of its members.[113]

DIVINE GIVING, RECEIVING, LENDING, AND GRACE

Wyclif's treatment of the second set of acts of God's *dominium*, namely *donare, accipere, prestare*, or giving, receiving, and lending correspond to his thought on *proprietas*, the second aspect of the *dominium*-relation. The third book of *De Dominio Divino* is a unified disquisition on the place of Grace, the giving of the divine essence to Creation, in God's *dominium*. Only God's giving is true giving, for God gives of Himself through Himself, while we can only give what God wills us to give. This much follows from God's unmediated primary causality. The same is true in divine receiving; God truly receives only from Himself through His giving. Thus all that God gives of and through Himself, He receives in the same way. God surrenders nothing in His giving, and acquires nothing in His receiving, as opposed to creatures, who gain everything in receiving from God, and lose everything in giving back to God what they received from Him. The crucial action in God's *dominium* is lending, for here sustained interaction takes place between Lord and subjects. The vehicle of God's lending is Grace; all that man can claim to hold by God's authority is held by Grace. Wyclif's belief that just civil *dominium* requires Grace, the central idea of *De Civili Dominio* I, is founded in the ideas he examines in this section of *De Dominio Divino*.[114]

---

[111] *DCD*, I, 15, 104.28–105.3: "Deus sit imperator supra leges, habens omnes leges in scrinio cordis sui, vult tamen propriis legibus conformari. Inter alias autem hec est una, quod si creatura racionalis Deum diligit, Deus eam prevenit reamando [*sic*] . . . Inpertinens enim fuisset Deitatem asserere istam negativam de debito."

[112] *Ibid.*, I, 16, 111–18.   [113] See *DOR*, 6, 185.

[114] Evidence for this appears in his frequent references to his work on "human *dominium*" in this section. See *DD*, III, 3, 223.24; III, 6, 250.25; III, 6, 255.15.

There are three important aspects of God's giving. First, God's giving does not entail alienation or abdication of His *dominium*. Proprietative giving, on the other hand, involves surrender of the owner's power over the gift. Because God does not participate in any relation like that of private ownership, this surrender never occurs. Every creature depends upon God's power for existence, and the idea that God's giving a creature being would involve some sort of subtraction from God's essence would be nonsensical. Further, bearing in mind that God's *dominium* is a standard for all created *dominium*-relations, earthly giving must be measurable according to God's giving.[115] If we were to assume that God somehow surrenders *dominium* over what He has created when He gives, the standard would be less than perfect, and created giving would be impossible. That God's *dominium* is not decreased, Wyclif implies, is what allows created giving to occur.[116]

At this point we should take note of Wyclif's distinction between communicative and translative giving. Translative giving entails spoliation, misuse, and the potential for perversion of the will; it is a surrender of the gift. Thus it requires that the giver lose *dominium* over the gift, and in any proprietary relation, such giving leads to discord.[117] Communicative giving, on the other hand, does not involve surrender, but enriches the giver, as happens in acts of charity. This is how Grace is given, in a communication between Giver and receiver.[118] The evil of private ownership lies in its indisposition to being given communicatively. Wyclif envisages a correspondence to the difference between the common and the particular here; the more common the gift, the more the giver and the receiver are mutually enriched, while the more particular the gift, the more the giver loses. As a rule, he equates the more common with universals, and the more particular with material individuation. Thus, any gift of a material particular involves a material loss or surrender, while a spiritual gift does not. With this distinction, Wyclif further clarifies the ideas he has developed so far regarding the superiority of the communal to the private.

Finally, although God gives perfectly and communicatively, creatures can only give imperfectly, depending upon what they have been given. Wyclif suggests an analogy with the gifts made by a royal steward. "Just as the steward distributes the gifts from his lord not of himself, but disposes of them [for his lord], so it is with the giving of any creature."[119] If the

---

[115] *De Ecclesia*, 12, 278.29.   [116] *DD*, III, 1, 200.14–201.31.
[117] *Ibid.*, III, 1, 205.24.   [118] *Ibid.*, III, 1, 205. 11–21.
[119] *Ibid.*, III, 1, 206.7–10: "Sicut ergo dispensator terreni dominii [*sic*] manualiter tradendo dominia domini donantis proprie non donat ea tam proprie, sed dispensat; sic est de donacione cuiuslibet creature."

steward were to give without his lord's authority, the giving would be an abuse of his office; likewise, if the temporal lord improperly gives, his giving (and hence his *dominium*) would be an abuse. Wyclif means to make it clear that good creaturely giving corresponds to God's giving when communicative giving takes place; creatures can only do this when giving as though the gift comes not from the creature giving, but from God. In short, good creaturely giving is an aware participation in God's giving.[120] Does this mean that I cannot give my brother a loaf of bread, since that would entail me no longer having it? Not at all; I am able to give him the loaf communicatively when I recognize that I am in possession of it thanks to God's giving, and that I never really had it at all. At base is the principle that truly just human giving requires recognizing that all that we have to give is on loan from God, and not truly ours in the first place.

What exactly does Wyclif have in mind as the gift God gives? He has already intimated that it can only be God Himself. "Primarily He gives being, insofar as being is intelligible to the creature, which being is really the divine essence."[121] This communicative giving takes place through the Holy Spirit, which is eternally given primarily to Christ, in Whom lie the Eternal Exemplars. From these Exemplars come created, material being through the Holy Spirit. Anything received by creatures given by God is through the vehicle of the Holy Spirit, particularly two gifts Wyclif believe to be inextricably related:

The Holy Spirit is the same gift for all, and a thing is possessed as much by God as by any material creature in created *dominium*. Formally speaking, it is clear that this is what it is to give *caritas* or *dominium* among created subjects, who receive and are informed as singular creatures by the Holy Spirit; the gift of *caritas* is what it means for a person to be loving, while that of *dominium* is what it means for a creature to be a lord. So it is for all supernatural gifts following upon the indwelling of the Holy Spirit; they are called plurally the gifts of God.[122]

God's gift of the Holy Spirit is charitable, in that there is no guarantee in the nature of the species that man should receive the gift, and its utility is two-fold: by permitting adhesion with delectation ending most purely

---

[120] *Ibid.*, III, 6, 255.11–20.
[121] *Ibid.*, III, 2, 207.15–17: "Nam primo omnium dat esse, in quantum esse intelligibile creature, quod est realiter divina essencia."
[122] *Ibid.*, III, 2, 210.8–17: "Spiritus sanctus est omnibus idem donum, et res possessa est tam Deo quam quotlibet creaturis idem materiale dominium. Formaliter autem loquendo, patet quod est dare caritatem, dominacionem, et cetera in creatura subiecta, qua appropriate formaliter singule creature, que illud donum recipiunt, informantur: ut caritas, que est hominem esse carum, dominacio, que est creaturam esse dominum,-et sic de aliis donis supernaturalibus, que ad inhabitacionem Spiritus sancti consecuntur-vocantur vere pluraliter dona Dei."

in God, God's gift gives enjoyment (*fruicio*), and by terminating first in creatures, then in God, God's gift provides use (*usus*) for the creature receiving it.[123] So if God gives *dominium* through the Holy Spirit to a lord, the lord may enjoy his *dominium* as a kind of direct communion with God, and he may use his gift as it places him above his subjects, but only remembering that this placement is for God's purpose, not his own.

In the same way that communicative giving among creatures is the giving of something coming from beyond the giver, just receiving among creatures entails awareness that the gift is unmerited. Receiving in God involves no change in the divine essence, for God receives nothing more than was His all along. "It is clear that whatever and however much God gives, that much He receives from Himself."[124] But what sense does it make to speak of God receiving anything? While it is no great strain for the faithful philosopher to conceive of God's gracious giving through the Holy Spirit, to imagine God receiving anything from Creation appears to require a temporality and mutability discordant with divine perfection.

God's receiving is different from creaturely receiving in that God needs to receive nothing.[125] But divine *dominium* is not co-eternal with the divine essence, and there must be some sense in which God as lord receives from His *dominium*. God as Christ receives and holds the riches of Grace on earth. If we think of Christ as Lord of Creation, Wyclif explains, we understand His *dominium* in terms of how He is at once master and subject. "[F]or He is of two natures, human and divine, of which the lesser one serves the preeminent one most regularly."[126] And as Christ serves Creation, He serves God as well. What Christ receives as lord of Creation is the service of the recipients of the gift of the Holy Spirit, or Grace. When one of the Grace-favored acts caritatively, that act is the use of the gift antecedently on other creatures, consequently in God in fulfillment of the divine will. When one of God's gifts is abused, God's will is disappointed, and Christ is frustrated by His servant's abuse.

We must not assume that God or Christ receives in the sense most familiar to property holders; God neither gives nor receives translatively. The true riches Christ receives communicatively from His subjects are the same as those that were communicatively given them by God, that is, *caritas*, *dominium*, and the enjoyments and proper use thereof. Wyclif depicts Christ's *dominium* over the predestined as the ideal operation of

---

[123] *Ibid.*, III, 2, 211.18–212.30.

[124] *Ibid.*, III, 3, 216.28: "Patet ex hoc quod in quantum donat aliquid, in tantum illud accipit a se ipso."

[125] *Ibid.*, III, 3, 219.5.

[126] *Ibid.*, III, 3, 221.32–222.4: "cum sit duarum naturarum utraque, scilicet, humanitas et deitas, quarum inferior servit regularissime preminenti."

God's receiving, in which all that Christ, in serving God, gives to His subjects is returned to God's greater power and glory.[127] Noteworthy is Wyclif's stipulation that all of these individuals enjoying Christ's *dominium* on earth have "all in common." In this way, translative giving and receiving is forestalled, and communicative giving and receiving, in which giver and recipient share equally, is facilitated.

Wyclif is vague here about whether he means this description to apply to anything before the Last Judgment, but in *De Civili Dominio* this ideal relation between Christ and His subjects is realized in the church, here and now. Christ's receiving is obstructed when His church is involved in anything other than common ownership and lacks any possibility for communicative giving and receiving between lord and subject. Christ is the servant both of God and man, giving communicatively the gifts of the Holy Spirit to the deserving. As Lord of Creation, He receives from His subjects the glory emanating from their charitable acts. God the Father receives only what He has given, but Christ as Lord receives the service of His subjects as He provides for them.

In Creation, God's giving and receiving collapse into a lending relationship.[128] God must ultimately receive back every part of what He gives, so what is really happening, in the terms of fallen, created reason, is that God lends of Himself. As with any lending relation, Wyclif notes, the lender looks for evidence that the borrower deserves the loan, and deserving becomes an important issue here. A lending relation is, on the face of it, more complex than giving or receiving because, aside from a temporary giving (and correspondent receiving) there must also be the promise of some future return which should equal or exceed the initial loan. Other acts of *dominium* are not to be confused with lending; lending is the Lord stipulating that he personally holds onto what he lends and may retrieve it when it suits him.[129] When God lends, He retains *dominium* over the loan because all that He lends comes unmediatedly from His nature. Anything that a temporal lord lends, on the other hand, comes to him from God, and not from his own nature. If the temporal lord seeks to retain *dominium* inappropriately over that which he lends, he administers God's loan poorly and unfaithfully.[130] This would be a signal demonstration of the temporal lord's not deserving to borrow the *dominium* that God has lent him. It is only when a temporal lord lends with *caritas*, recognizing that his own *dominium* has been lent to him by God, that he lends properly. Wyclif makes no mention in this discussion of the evils of simony or usury, but it is clear that his

---

[127] *Ibid.*, III, 3, 223.11–16.   [128] *Ibid.*, III, 4, 226.6–12.
[129] *Ibid.*, III, 4, 224.22–5.   [130] *Ibid.*, III, 6, 251.26–34.

condemnation of these practices would be associated with this line of thought.[131]

Wyclif is careful to explain the nature of merit, as well he might be, for we have already made note of his observation that no one deserves to receive from God as God deserves to receive from Creation. When lending takes place between a temporal lord and his subject, the subject merits the loan. A mutual agreement arises from the *dignitas* or worth of both parties. The subject's merit is condign in every instance of receiving or borrowing from a temporal lord, but man cannot merit Grace *de condigno*, because he can only do good with the help of the Holy Spirit. Condign merit is only possible among individuals who are able to expect something in return for some act, and no one can expect Grace.[132]

But man must in some sense deserve Grace. "It is the invariable law of God that nobody is awarded blessedness unless they first deserve it."[133] If there were no means by which anyone could merit God's lending, no good could be done, Christ or God would not receive from blessed subjects, and divine *dominium* would be diminished. Wyclif explains that people merit Grace through no ability of their own, for "merit requires the motion of an object, the deliberation of the mind, and finally voluntary adhesion to equity, which does not happen instantly."[134] We are able to move our wills towards the good, and from this Grace may – but need not – follow. This is merit *de congruo*, based not on any action or ability but solely on God's generosity towards a will directed in accord with the divine will. In effect, God lends merit. "Indeed God lends all merit and instruments of meriting, and preveniently excites and necessitates to meriting; He necessitates, I say, not absolutely, but *ex suppositione* [i.e. hypothetically], preserving the freedom of the will of the deserving."[135]

Why is there no congruent merit in human *dominium*? Why is all lending or giving by a civil lord based on condign merit? Would not a generous royal gift or loan to a needy, undeserving subject show that the subject at least congruently merited the gift or loan? If the gift or loan

---

[131] See Terrence McVeigh's useful introduction to his translation of *De Simonia*, in John Wyclif, *On Simony* (New York, 1992), pp. 1–28.

[132] *DD*, I, 17, 150.22. For a complete and explicative treatment of merit *de condigno*, see Heiko Oberman, *The Harvest of Medieval Theology* (Cambridge, MA, 1963), pp. 166–72.

[133] *DD*, III, 4, 229.18: "Est ergo lex Dei invariabilis quod nemo beatifice premietur nisi prius debite mereatur."

[134] *Ibid.*, III, 4, 234.24–6: "[M]eritum enim requirit mocionem obiecti, deliberacionem animi, et tercio conclusionaliter adhesionem voluntariam equitati, que non fiunt subito in instanti."

[135] *Ibid.*, III, 4, 226.9–13: "Ipse enim prestat omnino meritum et instrumentum merendi, ac preveniendo excitat et necessitat ad merendum: necessitat, dico, non necessitate absoluta sed ex supposicione, salva libertate arbitrii promerentis."

arose from the lord's *caritas*, would this be like God's giving or lending? Anything that a creature has to give has been given by another already, that is, God. A civil lord is only a steward:

Any rational creature is only improperly [called] a lord, and is rather a minister or steward of the supreme Lord. It is clear from this that every creature is a servant of God, and whatever he has to distribute, he has purely by Grace.[136]

No civil lord is able to judge the direction of a subject's will, and since all that the lord has is from God, even the most apparently generous or altruistic of giving or lending acts in temporal *dominium* are based on condign, not congruent merit.[137] So the goodness of the lord's act would be a divine gift, an act of Grace.

Grace has two aspects: divine and temporal. The former, uncreated Grace "essentially denotes the divine essence, or personally denotes the Holy Spirit, or habitudinally denotes God's good will towards creatures . . . [it is] simply coeternal as the understanding, knowing, and willing of the Lord are said to be."[138] Temporal or created Grace is supernaturally given but to many creatures as the basis for all theological and moral virtues, "and all rational creatures ought have such Grace by virtue of being caused by God, and effectually conserved, and this is prevenient to meriting."[139]

Uncreated Grace and condign merit appear to be complementary; both correspond to a quality in the subject, for the latter indicates a quality in the deserving subject, while the former indicates God's good will towards Creation. If we could have a perfect will, we might merit God's gifts *de condigno*. Created Grace and congruent merit also appear to be complementary, for both are based on something extrinsic to the recipient, namely the uncreated Grace of God's will. In fact, because created Grace is what is given or lent to us having congruent merit, and so is evidence thereof, they must both be corresponding elements of one event, God's lending. Thus we can conclude that God's lending is the temporal bestowal of created Grace on the congruently meritorious, which bestowal is based in the uncreated Grace that characterizes the Holy Spirit. Here

---

[136] *Ibid.*, III, 6, 250.25–9: "[Q]uelibet creatura racionalis sit improprie dominus, quin pocius minister vel dispensator supremi Domini. Patet ex hoc quod quelibet creatura est servus Domini habens quidquid habet ex mera gracia ut dispenset."

[137] *DCD*, II, 16.

[138] *DD*, III, 5, 236.20–6: "Increata tripliciter potest intelligi, vel essencialiter pro divina essencia, vel personaliter pro tercia Persona, vel habitudinaliter pro quacumque volicione divina qua Deus vult benefacere creature: et sic sunt nobis infinite gracie Deo intrinsice contingentes et omnes Deo simpliciter coeterne, ut dictum est de intelligenciis, scienciis, et volenciis Dei nostri."

[139] *Ibid.*, III, 5, 237.12–16: "[E]t talem graciam oportet omnem creaturam racionalem habere eo ipso quo a Deo causatur vel effectualiter conservatur: et illa gracia dicitur preveniens ad merendum."

again Wyclif diverges from Bradwardine. In *De Causa Dei* Bradwardine argues that the predestined condignly merit their salvation, thanks to the immediacy of God's causation of their good will.[140] God acts in them to such an extent that they, as divine instruments, merit their salvation *de condigno*. The extremity of this position verges on occasionalism, in which created causal efficacy is totally absent, and Wyclif's belief that human willing in a sense causes divine willing forestalls this by obviating condign merit.

What bearing does this have on issues of *proprietas* in *De Civili Dominio*? Wyclif condemns private ownership as founded in sin, while holding that just civil *dominium* requires Grace as a necessary precondition. These ideas seem to be mutually exclusive, but for Wyclif they are not. Both have some grounding in the thought expressed in this section of *De Dominio Divino*. Wyclif's dismissal of the licitness of any private property-relations stems from his view that they provide the owner with an exclusive claim to, and hold over, some material object or individual. An exclusive claim would rule out two owners, and so private property-relations conflict with divine *dominium*, for God has unmediated *dominium* over everything in Creation. If an owner condignly were to merit God's gift of a material object or individual, things might be different, but since man can only lay claim to elements in Creation through congruent merit, private property-relations are unmerited.

People who have just civil *dominium* have it through congruent merit, because their wills are in concord with the divine will. The majority enjoying that concord are entitled to more than just civil *dominium*, and as we shall also see, having just civil *dominium* is more an onerous duty than a desirable gift, but there is enough here to lay the groundwork for exploring this apparent paradox. In short, God's giving, receiving, and lending set the standards for human giving, receiving, and lending for those people with sufficiently properly directed wills. Deviations from these standards, such as translative giving and receiving, invariably lead to sin.

We cannot end a discussion of the third book of *De Dominio Divino* without taking note of Wyclif's closing admonition to civil lords. To emphasize the complete reliance of temporal *dominium*-relations upon divine *dominium*, Wyclif warns against the tendency of civil lords to pomp and self-importance. The apparent ability of civil lords to give generously or altruistically is illusory, for all that man can give comes from God. The true nature of a civil lord is to be a steward of the true Lord of Creation. Wyclif refers his readers to Philippians 2:21 and to 1 Corinthians 10:31

---

[140] *De Causa Dei*, I, 39.

saying, "If we bear these sentences in mind, then we will not be inanely glorified as if what we have comes from ourselves, but we will distribute the gifts of God with fear to the deserving only, ascribing the honor to God, and not to ourselves, who can only distribute as servants, useless in ourselves."[141]

DIVINE *DOMINIUM* AS CAUSAL UNIVERSAL

If human *dominium*-relations are related to divine *dominium* as particulars to a universal, this relation must be more than an imitative relation holding between the two kinds of *dominium*, and more than a relation in which God's *dominium* simply provides the basis for human justice. While just human *dominium* does imitate divine *dominium*, and God's *dominium* infuses true human *dominium* with its justice, neither of these explanations accounts for the whole of the relation between divine and human *dominium* as fully as a description in terms of universal and particular does.

The relation of causal universality that holds between divine and human *dominium* means that divine *dominium* (*D*) is that which makes all human *dominium* (*d*) to be real *dominium*. Without the prior existence of *D*, and without *D*'s causally creative action upon men, there would be no *d* possible. *D*'s existence causes each *d* to come about, and each *d* will have every essential characteristic of *D* only through that causation. *D* is necessary for the continued being of each individual *d*, and all that makes each *d* "*d*-like" is primarily in *D*, and can only be in each *d* through *D*'s agency. If someone were to call a relation "*dominium*" that was not brought into being by *D*'s causal action, then even if it had many of the characteristics of true *dominium* it would not be *d*. Wyclif believes that *D* causes *d* through created Grace, and that God's will, at work in Creation, carries out every act of *D*. Of these one is lending (*accommodare*) whereby God allows man to participate in *D* by being human lords. Grace is the medium through which *D* as cause brings about *d* as effect, and that Grace allows each instance of *d* to maintain its being by participating in *D*. For creatures the recognizable characteristic in individuals who are changed by Grace to be lords is *caritas*, so *caritas* is the essential characteristic of *d*, without which *d* would not be like *D*. Put differently, God acts in Creation as Lord in many ways, one of which is by lending man a

---

[141] *DD*, III, 6, 255.16–21: "Si ergo istam sentenciam haberemus pre oculis tunc non inaniter gloriaremur quasi hec haberemus ex nobis; sed cum timore distribueremus bona Domini solum dignis, ascribentes Deo honores, et non nobis, qui solum sumus dispensatores et servi sibi inutiles." Wyclif then refers his readers to "capitulum VII Librum III de humano Dominio," a discussion of the apostolic purity of evangelic poverty, evidence that the notion that the just are more servants than lords is inextricably connected to the ideal of apostolic poverty.

degree of divine authority so that he instantiates divine *dominium*. Thus describing the relation between *D* and *d* as one of causal universality does two things: it allows us to account for just human *dominia* as participants in divine *dominium*, and it allows us to explicate the actions of divine *dominium* within Creation. The universal–particular relation allows for a reciprocity between real human *dominium* and the divine *dominium* that would not be otherwise available if it did not hold.

Two alternatives to this explanation are possible, both of which are iterations of the Grace-founded *dominium* doctrine. We could interpret Wyclif as believing that human *dominium* is just insofar as it is imitative of divine *dominium* and we would not be wrong. We could also suggest that Wyclif believes divine *dominium* makes human *dominium* just by some less direct measure, say by infusing divine justice through Grace in the acts of a human lord, or by Grace-fully turning the will of the human lord so that only just acts ensue. This, too, is not inaccurate as far as it goes. But while both alternatives could result from a universal–particular relation, neither on its own would be sufficient for us to deduce the universal–particular relation.

In the first case, Grace is what allows human *dominium* successfully to imitate divine *dominium*. Where the universal–particular relation is absent, divine *dominium* would be an unattainable goal or paradigm beyond the grasp of the created being, which would be at odds with Wyclif's picture of a divine *dominium* that is directly active in all Creation. How could rational beings be continually subject to divine *dominium*, be aware of it, strive to imitate it, and yet constantly fail, and have this suffice as an explanation of how a divine lord motivated by *caritas* causes human justice to occur? Worse, an imitative basis for the relation would involve a human lord striving to be God-like, which is precisely what Wyclif wanted to avoid. It is not enough to say that human lords strive to imitate the divine Lord and are successful only insofar as God allows. This fails to allow for God's lending relation having a significant bearing on the relation between divine and human *dominium*, and also downplays significantly the reciprocity of lord and subject as well as the strong element of stewardship that runs through *De Civili Dominio*. The imitative model allows for a too-passive divine Lord.

The model in which God infuses justice in human *dominium* through Grace also does not go far enough. It assumes that there would be human *dominium*-relations in existence anyway and that God could use these by purifying them with Grace to carry out His will. But what would there be about these not-yet purified human *dominium*-relations to make them sufficiently like God's *dominium* to warrant their utility? Only God can provide justice whereby the authority of the human lord is real, and these yet-to-be justified human *dominium*-relations would not really be *dominium*; we might as easily call them anything we choose. There would have to be something already good in such a relation for God to be willing to infuse it with Grace, but this is impossible given the fallen human state. If a lord's will were inclined to goodness one might conclude that the human *dominium*-relation were good enough, but not every human *dominium*-relation characterized by a well inclined will must necessarily warrant Grace *de congruo*.

This model would have God make some human authority relation sufficiently good with Grace so that He could again use Grace to infuse it with justice. This is not as simple as the universal–particular relation, in which there are no human *dominium*-relations save those which Grace forms out of God's *dominium*. While we can say that God makes human *dominium* just, what we mean is that the only real, just human *dominium*-relation is one that participates in divine *dominium* as an instantiation participates in its prior universal.

It has become apparent that the attempt at clearly distinguishing be-tween *iurisdictio* and *proprietas* in a *dominium*-relation is fruitless in Wyclif's case. Strands of his treatment of God's knowledge of universals join up neatly with his discussion of the possibility of just human giving, receiv-ing and lending, while so much of what Wyclif says about *caritas* in the final section elucidates the unmediated, loving relation he describes early on in the work. In short, *De Dominio Divino* illustrates how Wyclif views *iurisdictio* and *proprietas* as two sides of the same coin in God's *dominium*. If we were to see them clearly distinguished in human *dominium*, we would be justified in doubting that the two relations were related as universal and particular. The following two chapters will show how the two concepts are similarly joined in Wyclif's picture of civil *dominium*.

Chapter 4

PROPRIETAS IN WYCLIF'S THEORY OF HUMAN *DOMINIUM*

De Civili Dominio is the largest of the treatises of the *Summa Theologie*, as well the most significant, for it introduces most of Wyclif's later theological recommendations for ecclesiastical reform. Wyclif wrote *De Civili Dominio* in late 1375 through 1376, directly upon completing *De Divino Dominio*, and even the most fleeting acquaintance with the earlier works shows the thematic ties between first works of the *Summa* and *De Civili Dominio*.[1] Having explained the nature of God's perfect *dominium*, a continuing, unmediated relation between Creator and Creation, Wyclif was ready to address the earthly species of lordship and its two chief characteristics, *proprietas* and *iurisdictio*. Not surprisingly, given the significance of giving, receiving, and lending to *dominium* in *De Dominio Divino*, private property-ownership lies at the center of the arguments in *De Civili Dominio* and *De Officio Regis*. So before approaching the recognizably jurisdictive, governance-related aspects of his thought, we should address Wyclif's discussion of postlapsarian ownership.

We cannot begin as Wyclif begins, for he plunges us into matters with minimal introduction. *Dominium*'s necessary ties to God's Grace are the subject of much of the first book, while the second and third are devoted to *dominium*'s political and ecclesiastical ramifications. A better introductory approach is to see why Grace-founded *dominium* seemed so radical an idea to Wyclif's contemporaries. *De Civili Dominio* was, after all, the subject of great papal ire, resoundingly declared in a bull from Gregory XI to Edward III in 1377:[2]

Recently, with great bitterness of heart we have learned from the report of very many trustworthy persons that John of Wicluffe, rector of the church of Lutterworth, of the diocese of Lincoln, a professor of holy writ – would he were not a master of errors! – has burst forth in such execrable and abominable folly, that he does not fear to maintain dogmatically in said kingdom and

---

[1] See Williel R. Thomson, *The Latin Writings of John Wyclyf* (Toronto, 1983), pp. 48–55.

[2] Papal reaction to *De Civili Dominio*, and the ensuing ecclesiastical attack on Wyclif, is best described in Joseph Dahmus, *The Prosecution of John Wyclyf* (New Haven, 1952).

publicly to preach, or rather to vomit forth from the poisonous confines of his breast, some propositions and conclusions, full of errors and containing manifest heresy, which threaten to subvert and weaken the condition of the entire church . . .[3]

Gregory included nineteen propositions specifically directed to Wyclif's heresy, several of which illustrate what appeared revolutionary in Wyclif's conception of *dominium*.

(1) The whole human race without Christ does not have the power of simply ordaining that Peter and all his successors exercise political dominion over the world.

(2) God cannot give civil dominion to man, for himself and his heirs, in perpetuity.

(4) Anyone who is in that state of Grace which finally justifies, not only has a right to, but in fact possesses, all the gifts of God.

(6) If God be, temporal lords may lawfully and with merit take from a delinquent church the blessings of fortune.

(9) It is not possible for a man to be excommunicated except that he be first and principally excommunicated by himself.

(17) It is permitted kings to deprive those ecclesiastics of their temporalities who habitually misuse them.

(19) Any ecclesiastic, indeed even the Roman pontiff, may lawfully be rebuked by those subject to him and by laymen, and even arraigned.[4]

Wyclif responded to these accusations in 1378, reiterating several of his positions. As with the papal condemnations, we will list only those conclusions directly concerned with *dominium*.

(1) Civil dominion is proprietary dominion, the act of a viator over goods according to human law.

---

[3] *Chronicon Angliae*, ed. E. M. Thompson, Rolls Series 64 (London, 1974), p. 180: "Litera missa regi ab apostolico deprecatoria ut faveat episcopis in exsecutione praescripti mandati." ". . . Sed nuper cum ingenti cordis amaritudine, plurimorum fide dignorum significatione percepimus, Johannem de Wiclyffe, rectorem ecclesiae de Litteworthe, Lincolniensis dioescesis, sacrae paginae professorem, utinam non magistrum errorum, in illam nefandam et abominabilem prorupisse dementiam, . . . quod nonnullas propositiones et conclusiones, plenas erroribus, et manifestam haeresim continentes, quae statum totius ecclesiae subvertere et enervare nituntur"; trans. Dahmus in *Prosecution of John Wyclyf*, p. 46.

[4] *Chronicon Angliae*, pp. 181–2: "Hae sunt propositiones, sive conclusiones, quas praedictus J. W. dicitur asserverasse et publice praedicasse." "Totum genus humanum, citra Christum, non habet potestatem simpliciter ordinandi ut Petrus, et omne genus suum, dominetur politice in perpetuum super mundum. Deus non potest dare homini, pro se et heredibus suis in perpetuum, civile dominium. . . . Quilibet exsistens in gratia gratificante finaliter, nedum habet jus, sed in re habet omnia dona Dei . . . Si Deus est, domini temporales possunt legitime ac meritorie auferre bona fortunae ab ecclesia delinquente . . . Licet regibus auferre temporalia a viris ecclesiasticis ipsis abutentibus habitualiter . . . ecclesiasticus, immo et Romanus pontifex, potest legitime a subditis et laicis corripi, et etiam accusari"; trans. Dahmus, *The Prosecution of John Wyclyf*, pp. 49–50. cf. also *Historia Anglicana*, pp. 353–5.

(2) No cleric may hold civil dominion without mortal sin, and by "cleric" I mean Pope, Cardinal, Bishop, Deacon, and other priests.

(4) Civil dominion, understood formally, smacks inseparably of sin.

(6) Just as God cannot act civilly, nor could any man in a state of innocence, so it is illicit for any cleric to act civilly.[5]

Why, on the one hand, is Grace necessary for any *dominium*, with sin automatically precluding it, while on the other hand, *dominium* is somehow inseparable from sin? Why does someone need Grace to have a relation that is rooted in sin? The holder of jurisdictional civil *dominium* has a responsibility according to human law, as described in the first restated conclusion, which *dominium* came about because of Original Sin. But, as we will see, if the human law is just, it is so because it presupposes divine law. So if the civil lord justly holds property, there is a real sense in which he does so according to divine law. And only those favored by Grace are trustworthy enough to act on behalf of God to protect the interests of property-holders.

THE STRUCTURE OF *DE CIVILI DOMINIO*

De Civili Dominio is chiefly about just human temporal *dominium*, and the need for a clarification of the respective purviews of secular and sacerdotal offices. Wyclif presents his arguments in three books, of which the first is a systematic explication of his prescriptions for the right-ordering of human relations in society, the second is a more careful explanation of the proper alignment of church and state, and the third is a disquisition on the place of private property-relations in the grand scheme of his argument.

Book I can stand on its own as an articulation of Wyclif's "nineteen theses" condemned by Gregory XI in 1377.[6] R. L. Poole, the work's editor, sees five general divisions in Book I, which arrangement provides a useful means for summarizing the book's major points. Chapters 1–16, beginning with the motto "Divine law is presupposed by civil law; Natural *dominium* is presupposed by civil *dominium*," contain Wyclif's introduction to the doctrine of the necessity of Grace for just human *dominium*.[7] Here the connections between *De Civili Dominio* and *De*

---

[5] *Historia Anglicana*, ed. H. T. Riley, Rerum Britannicarum Medii Aevi Scriptores 20 (London, 1962, 1964), pp. 363–4: "Dominium civile [est] dominium proprietarium, actum viatoris super bonis plene secundum leges humanas. Non stat pure clericum absque mortali peccato civiliter dominari; [et intelligit per pure clericos, Papam, Cardinales, Episcopos, Diaconos, et alios sacerdotes.] ... Dominium civile, formaliter dictum, sapit inseparabiliter peccatum ... Sicut Deus non potest exercere actus civiles, nec homo in statu innocentiae, sic illicitum est alicui pure clerico actus civiles aliquos exercere."

[6] See Dahmus, *The Prosecution of John Wyclyf*, pp. 39–50.

[7] *DCD*, I, 1, 1.5: "Ius divinum presupponitur iuri civili/Dominium naturale presupponitur dominio civili."

Dominio Divino are most evident, for Wyclif explains how God grants just civil *dominium* on the deserving in the postlapsarian world in partial recompense for the loss of natural *dominium*. Further, he explains the difference between two types of human *dominium* as characterized by the institution of private ownership; natural *dominium* entails its absence, while civil *dominium* has it at its very core. The third book is devoted to explaining the moral and political consequences of this aspect of civil *dominium*.

Chapters 17–25 of Book I introduce the relations between divine and human law, and distinguish between the artificial, but potentially just secular law, and the equally artificial but ultimately superfluous canon law. More important is the Law of the Gospel, which Wyclif also refers to as *lex Christi*, the source and measure of all earthly justice. Matters that were to be more fully developed in *De Officio Regis* are the concern of Chapters 26–34, including the nature of just accession to rule, the problems of tyranny and servitude, and the general nature of kingship. Wyclif does not yet argue, as he will in *De Officio Regis*, that the king's first duty is to church reform, but the basis for this appears here and in the next section, where he discusses the nature of human grants, and their relation to the problem of sorting out church and state squabbles about property. With the discussion of grants and giving in Chapters 35–42 appear such key ideas as the ultimately steward-like nature of just human *dominium*, the general need for non-ecclesiastical lords to regulate ecclesiastical wealth, and the redefinition of "Church" in terms of the Elect, rather than the Roman institution. Here we see the basis for ideas that will receive their fullest treatment in the later, more explicitly polemical works of the *Summa Theologie*, such as the identification of the church with the universal body of the Predestined, the need for the widespread availability of Scripture, the dissolution of the friars' orders, and so forth.

The second book is Wyclif's response to the papal condemnation framed in terms of English law and justifying the lawfulness of secular correction of sacerdotal wrongs.[8] That such a correction is necessary is obvious from Wyclif's discussions of the purviews of the two realms in I, xviii, and of the evils of private ownership in Book III. The range of Wyclif's arguments in favor of secular divestment of sacred temporalia is truly impressive, though, for it ranges from historical precedent, through a host of authoritative corroboration, both from Scripture, theological doctors, and canon law. The book ends with a brief discussion of the nature of a just war; wars arising from a want of *caritas* must forfeit claims

---

[8] For analysis of *De Civili Dominio* II as an articulation of the English legal tradition, see Edith C. Tatnall, "John Wyclif and the *Ecclesia Anglicana*," *Journal of Theological History*, 20 (1969), pp. 19–43; and William Farr, *John Wyclif as Legal Reformer* (Leiden, 1974).

on true justice. Interestingly, *De Officio Regis*'s final chapters include a similar discussion, and one cannot help thinking that Wyclif saw talk of just war as a climactic end to a prolonged argument, in a kind of "– and if it comes to this . . ." sense.

The third book is as long as the first two combined, and consists largely of a sustained attack on the institution of private ownership in general, and the ecclesiastical form of this in particular. Unlike the second book, it is not grounded in English law, but in ecclesiastical theory. Herbert Workman and Eric Doyle, among others, have argued that Wyclif had initially said what he had wanted to say in the first book, and that the second and third had been written in response to ecclesiastical criticism.[9] What we recognize as generally jurisdictive aspects, namely Creation, sustenance, and governance, have already been addressed in the first two books; the third book is devoted to a careful discussion of giving, receiving, and lending, which require an analysis of the institution of private ownership.

The third book's theme appears first in Chapter 22 of Book I, with the phrase, "to have civil goods [i.e. temporalia privately held] is onerous and dangerous."[10] Book III begins with a reverent explanation of the purity of apostolic poverty enjoyed by all Christ's followers. Civil authority, notably private ownership, is more foreign to *lex Christi* than is carnal marriage, he says, leaving one to wonder how Grace can systematically justify civil *dominium*. This he explains in Chapter 11, describing the need for some participants in the *via activa*, whom he calls *activi viatores*, to act as shepherds for the flock of the Elect. His definition of civil *dominium* here appears elsewhere in the treatise, "Civil *dominium* is the proprietary *dominium* held by the active over the goods of fortune in full accord with human law."[11]

DOMINIUM AND GRACE

Wyclif's belief is that true, just *dominium* is only attributable to the righteous, to those whom God favors unmediatedly with restorative Grace. Earlier theorists like Fitzralph believed such Grace evident in

---

[9] Workman, *John Wyclif: A Study of the English Medieval Church* (Oxford, 1926), p. 264; Eric Doyle, O.F.M., "William Woodford's *De Dominio Civili Clericorum* Against John Wyclif," *Archivum Franciscanum Historicum*, 66 (1973), pp. 49–109; Doyle, "William Woodford, O.F.M. and John Wyclif's *De Religione*," *Speculum*, 52 (1977), pp. 329–36; Doyle, "William Woodford, O.F.M.: His Life and Works," *Franciscan Studies*, 43 (1983), pp. 17–187. See also Thomson, *The Latin Writings of John Wyclyf*, p. 52, n. 19.

[10] *DCD*, I, 22, 155.18: "Divicias civiliter habere est onerosum et periculosum."

[11] *Ibid.*, III, 11, 178.10: "Civile dominium est dominium proprietarium activi viatoris super bonis fortune plene secundum leges humanas." cf. also II, 189.

the ecclesiastical hierarchy, but Wyclif rejects earthly imitation of heaven mediated by hierarchic structure. While no one can claim mundane eminence by virtue of position in an ecclesiastical hierarchy, David Luscombe has noted a lingering respect for hierarchy in Wyclif's distinction between the active and the contemplative life, and in his description of the three hierarchies necessary in a kingdom in *De Officio Regis*.[12] But he has no need for a mediative celestial or earthly hierarchy in describing divine *dominium*. All that occurs in Creation does so in accord with the unmediated divine will.[13] "Nor can the faithful doubt that the Highest Lord, by reason of His omnipotence, and the efficacy of His will, has whatever He wishes in His kingdom, and will not have whatever He does not wish; and it is clear that all just civil occupation requires that this Lord authorize, ratify, and confirm, for all that He does not approve is not just."[14] Luscombe properly distinguishes between Wyclif's rejection of hierocratic thought and his respect for hierarchy, a distinction strengthened by interpreting God's *dominium* as a universal in which human lords participate. Mundane hierarchies in civil *dominium* are licit, indeed necessary, given the heavy responsibilities of the just civil lord; as we will see, not only lesser barons and knights but also bishops and priests must serve as the civil lord's servants. What precludes hierocratic thought here is the argument that civil lords serve as instantiations of God's unmediated *dominium*; the civil lord has no real power of his own, but serves as a managerial steward in God's structure.

Civil *dominium* appears throughout *De Civili Dominio* as a grievous burden to be borne with patience. As we will see, the Grace-favored are likely to want to stay as far away from civil *proprietas* and *iurisdictio* as possible; only the most stalwart of the Grace-favored will be given the unpleasant duty of civil authority. But Wyclif does not begin with a clear indication that he believes civil *dominium* to be a burden rather than a privilege, for this would presuppose too much about ownership, the possible types of human *dominium*, and the function of just civil authority. He begins by underscoring the divide between the sinful and those favored by Grace, explaining that all actions derive their moral value from the intent of the agent. Those trapped in sin can only act wickedly, despite occasional apparent externally good acts, and those

---

[12] *Tractatus de Officio Regis*, ed. A. W. Pollard and C. Sayle (London, 1887), 3, pp. 58–59; quoted in Luscombe, "Wyclif and Hierarchy," in *From Ockham to Wyclif*, ed. A. Hudson and M. Wilks, *SCH* Subsidia 5 (London, 1987), p. 237.

[13] *DD*, I, 5, 33.8–12. See also 74.5–12.

[14] *DCD*, I, 1, 7.18–24: "Nec hoc licet catholicis dubitare, cum iste magnus Dominus, racione sue omnipotencie et eficacia sue volencie, habet in suo regno quidquid vult, et quidquid noluerit non habet; et patet quod ad omnem iustam occupacionem civilem oportet quod iste dominus auctoriset, ratificet, et confirmet, cum omne quod ipse non approbat, non est iustum."

favored by Grace tend towards virtuous acts. Thus, anyone not favored by Grace making use of anything in Creation is guilty of unjust use, for, as Augustine explains, all things belong to the just.[15] Without this connection, it would be impossible to make sense of *dominium* as an institution founded in justice, given all the relations of possessor and possessed in the world. With it, Wyclif associates all instances of just use, and of just *dominium*, with those favored by Grace.[16]

God permits the Damned to have what they have, but their possession is only apparently just; the credit goes to God for allowing them to go on surviving.[17] It is the same with the good deeds of the Damned; all good can only come from God, and so, when the Damned appear to do good, they do so by Grace, and not through any strength of their own.[18] The actions of the selfish may promote the common good, but they are improperly motivated, and cannot warrant merit. Someone who acts unselfishly, or charitably, deserves praise for acting well, but the praise is due first to God, whose Grace allows such charitably motivated action in the first place.[19] For example, both John and Judas help Peter with his nets. Judas is motivated by his desire to get Peter's favor, the better to take advantage of them. John, on the other hand, is motivated by the desire to alleviate Peter's difficulties. Both do a good deed, but only John acts well. Wyclif believes that John's charitable motivation is only possible with God's help. He explains later that it might seem better for God simply to eliminate all instances of wicked *dominium*, but that that would be too deterministic.[20]

This provides Wyclif with the opportunity to begin discussing the terms bound up with Grace-favored *proprietas*, namely *iustitia* and *habicio*. What does it mean to "have justly?" First, he explains, "having" (*habicio*) has three senses: natural, civil, and evangelical.[21] Civil *habicio* is divisible into the sort that is justified, and the sort that is a mere pretense. Natural *habicio* has already been explained by distinguishing between God's giving gifts to the blessed, and allowing the Damned their illusion of possession. The third kind of having, here called evangelical, is superior, having by communal sharing. His explanation here is abbreviated, given his

---

[15] Given the mileage this remark of Augustine's had accumulated in debates on *dominium* and *proprietas* prior to Wyclif, it is not surprising that it appears early on in his discussion. This is the first extended quotation of any authority in *DCD*, and occupies a place of pride in Wyclif's attempt to show that all ownership is rooted in Grace. See *DCD*, I, 1, 5.24–6. Wyclif explains that Grace alone is what provides this justice in I, 2, 9.18.

[16] *DCD* I, 1, 6.9–16. See also I, 7, 49.3–32.   [17] *Ibid.*, I, 2, 11.6–31.   [18] *Ibid.*, I, 2, 13.4–9.

[19] Wyclif follows Bradwardine here; see *De Causa Dei contra Pelagium et de Virtute Causarum*, ed. H. Saville (London, 1618), II, 20, 540E ff. See also H. Oberman, *Thomas Bradwardine: A Fourteenth-Century Augustinian* (Utrecht, 1957), pp. 65–186.

[20] *DCD*, I, 6, 45.26.   [21] *Ibid.*, I, 3, 17.9–16.

familiarity with Fitzralph's complete analysis of *possessio, proprietas*, etc., but introduces the reader to the distinction between natural, civil, and Christ-founded possession. Wyclif will develop this distinction, and the implications that arise with it, through the course of the work.

The initial explanation of *iustitia*, or justice with the sense of righteousness, is also cursory and explains Grace-founded *dominium* more than it proves it. At the outset, *iusticia* is divisible into the active, perfect sort, and the passive, imperfect sorts.[22] Active justice is the essence of God and of God only. But active justice is also "an accident in the genus of quality, and in this way only can rational creatures who are in a state of Grace be just."[23] The distinction between essence and accident is a further instance of Wyclif relating divine and just civil *dominium* by using the model of universals and particulars. Passive *iusticia* is possessed by all creatures, including those in mortal sin, for all rely on God for their very being. Insofar as their being is divinely ordained, the being of their actions is also, so there can be nothing in Creation essentially contrary to God's order. This would seem so weak a species of *iusticia* as to be meaningless, but Wyclif can now hold that someone actively wicked is able to have a very few basic things by virtue of his passive righteousness, which is his because of his existence in Creation.

As we have seen, Wyclif distinguishes between true and false civil *habicio*. He focuses on what transpires from the two different sorts of possession by explaining that the righteous alone truly use what they have, while the unrighteous can only misuse their possessions. Evidence for the human eye of the use or abuse of a possession is the *caritas* exhibited by the possessor. If he acts with *caritas*, his possession will result in fruitful use, indicating the just nature of the possessor. Wyclif stakes all on *iusticia* indicated by *caritas* as a prerequisite for just *habicio*, and so for just *dominium*, and devotes the rest of the work to proving it. His analogy at the end of this brief overview is colorful, "The mortal sinner does not have [true] lordship any more than the perpetual virgin has carnal paternity, because he lacks the basis upon which such a relation is founded."[24]

---

[22] Wyclif's discussion of *iusticia* in the beginning of *De Civili Dominio* develops from his explication of the relation of divine justice to the just in Creation in *De Mandatis Divinis*. Analysis of *iurisdictio* in the following chapters will provide a fuller account of *ius* and *iusticia* than appears here.

[23] *DCD*, I, 3, 18.4–11: "et hoc contingit dupliciter; vel quod ista iusticia sit essencia iusti, quomodo solus Deus potest esse iustus, vel quod ista iusticia sit accidens de genere qualitatis, et taliter sunt creature racionabiles existentes in gracia solum iuste. Secundo modo est omnis creatura iusta, cum ens iustum et bonum simpliciter convertuntur."

[24] *Ibid.*, I, 3, 22.1–4: "ideo peccans mortaliter non habet dominium pocius quam virgo perpetua habet paternitatem carnalem, quia deficit fundamentum in quo huiusmodi relacio fundaretur."

Wyclif's language verges on confusion. Is it the justice of a wicked person's possession that is illusory, or is it the possession itself that is illusory? In the first case, the possession is real, but unjust, while in the second it is inaccurate to call the relation holding between the wicked subject and the object possession. While Wyclif occasionally speaks as if the justice of the wicked person's possession is illusory, and indeed even of unjust *dominium* (largely in the case of prelates and priests who exercise civil *dominium* unjustly), early on he warns that this is not really possession or *dominium* but just an equivocation.[25] There is no possession or *dominium* which is unjust; there are only unfounded fictions taking those names unjustly.[26]

To understand the weakness of man-made *dominium* Wyclif suggests we turn to individual reputations. We all know of people with undeservedly good reputations, and readily distinguish between true and false reputations. Reputations among people are fleeting, spatially restricted, and undependable, while a truly good, lasting reputation is founded in the perfection of the Trinity, irrevocable unless the holder wills it, like virtue in that "nobody can destroy his own virtue unless he wishes to do so."[27] A good reputation depends on virtue, the only source of which is a Grace-inspired will. *Dominium*, Wyclif explains, is as reliant on God's approbation as is a truly good reputation, even suggesting that humanly justified lordship is so ill-founded as to be abdicable by those favored by Grace. When a civil lord renounces his claim in favor of Christ, "even if it seems foolish to everyone, it is still an action of the greatest prudence, because the lordship of the nay-sayers is non-existent, and such action leads to the acquisition of true universal lordship."[28] The sense seems not to be directed towards proving that civil *dominium* must be abdicated, but towards reiteration of the benefit of *caritas*, and the lack of selfishly motivated action on the part of the actively righteous. Only those favored by Grace with the ability to act virtuously, and to will in accord with the divine will, are able to possess anything, including a good reputation.

Caritas is a term with many senses, and Wyclif defines it in light of the list of its associated characteristics in I Corinthians 13. First is patience, which is indicative of human love of God despite adversity. Next is goodness, the signal characteristic of God's relation to Creation, in that

---

[25] *Ibid.*, I, 3, 19.17–20.22.

[26] It is possible that Wyclif's use of contrasts like that between just *dominium* and unjust holding in *DCD*, I, 10 is more rhetorical than philosophical. *Iustum dominium* is redundant; there are no real unjust instances of the relation.

[27] *Ibid.*, I, 8, 57.30–5.

[28] *Ibid.*, I, 8, 58.25–59.2: "renunciacio autem civilitatis propter Christum, etsi videatur multis stulticia, est tamen magna negociandi prudencia; cum, propter dominium sophisticum non existens, acquiritur verum dominium universi."

He freely adheres to the laws He set out for Creation, loving those who freely love Him. *Caritas* supports all things in their weaknesses, providing order and sustenance through the divine order.[29] The tendency to recognize the inherent superiority of the eternal to the temporal good, to hold the eternal lovingly in the mind's eye, and to mourn its absence in the world indicates *caritas*. The material universe dims God's eternal light, but our reason can penetrate this darkness to a clear understanding of the divine essence. This penetration is a Christian responsibility, demanding unquestioning love of God and a willingness to forgive injuries so that reason can pierce the shadows of corporeity.

Although Wyclif makes no mention of it here, these preconditions are impossible without Grace; unaided human power cannot possibly overcome the material universe. So man needs Grace to direct his will properly, exhibit *caritas*, and use reason to enjoy God's eternal light, all of which qualifies him for *dominium* over the material world. This is not to say that materiality obstructs Creator from Creation; rather, men are hindered through their corporeality, which can be overcome through use of their spiritual facilities. Grosseteste's influence resonates in Wyclif's discussion of *caritas*, with his references to light metaphysics as a way of understanding God's unmediated *dominium* and man's difficulty in appreciating it.[30]

Wyclif now turns to the matter of the *dominium* given humans upon their Creation, and addresses the problems stemming from the Fall. Underlying all of the argument of *De Civili Dominio* is the dichotomy between humanity's natural, prelapsarian *dominium*, and its unnatural, sin-based proprietative *dominium*. Prelapsarian *dominium* was non-exclusive. Any member of the species had an inalienable lordship, because no one had a will bent on serving itself rather than God, and no one could countenance such distinctions as "mine" and "thine." There was no private ownership in natural *dominium*. Postlapsarian, civil *dominium*, on the other hand, excludes through its formalization of "mine" and "thine" relations, must be supported and enforced by legal and physical restraints, and tends to cause people to become concerned more with themselves than with the good of their community and the will of the Creator. Wyclif defines

---

[29] *Ibid.*, I, 15, p. 109.15–30: "omnia suffert, credit, sperat, et sustinet." This description echoes I Corinthians 13:2–4: "Caritas patiens est, benigna est, caritas non aemulator . . . caritas nunquam escidit." Tyndale caused a stir by translating the Greek *agape* as love, but the translator of the 1380 Wyclif bible did not have the Greek, and so rendered it *charite*: "Charite is pacient, it is benygne; charite enuyeth not, it doth not wikidli." See *The New Testament in English*, translated by John Wyclif, revised by J. Purvey, Sexcentenary Edition, Facsimile of Oxford, Bodleian Library, Rawlinson 259 (Portland, Oregon, 1986), p. 110.

[30] *DCD*, I, 16, 111.17–24. See also 114.20: "Unde Lincolniensis, Dicto XV, declarat quod omnes eterna temporalibus postponentes dormiunt sompno gravissimo."

civil *dominium* in the second book of *De Civili Dominio* as a proprietary *dominium* enjoyed by those in the *via activa* over the goods of fortune in accord with human law.[31] Natural *dominium* is inclusive, holistic, and characterized by an outwardly directed caring for others, while civil *dominium* is exclusive, individualistic, and marked by selfishness and cupidity.[32]

Did humanity completely lose natural *dominium* with the Fall, and if so, what connection can there be between contemporary human lordship, and God's? God never deprives the *iustus* of any gift without recompense, for when someone takes away such a gift from the righteous without justification, the righteous are all the more entitled to it through their virtuous patience.[33] This patience indicates a greater deserving of Grace, hence a stronger claim to *dominium*. It seems as if the righteous have the *dominium* that was all mankind's before the Fall: "man in a state of innocence had lordship over every part of the sensible world, and the virtue of the passion of Christ is [the basis] for righteous remission of all sins and for restitution of lordship, so the temporal recipients of Grace justly have complete universal lordship."[34] Indeed, Wyclif argues that Christ's death and triumph over sin frees the members of His living body from the constraints of private ownership, owning nothing and sharing everything in apostolic community. All of this follows, given the premise that true *dominium* is consequent on Grace, for if Adam's sin is wiped away through the Redemption, those predestined to be saved must be as pure as Adam was in Eden. Wyclif's predecessors shied away from the possibility of temporally regaining prelapsarian *dominium*, even for those hierarchically elevated. This divergence needs further examination; if just civil *dominium* involves individual *proprietas*, and prelapsarian *dominium* lacked any such individuation, how can the two be similar?[35]

Rather than address this issue immediately, Wyclif suggests that just human *dominium* is even more extensive than it was in Eden because of

---

[31] *Ibid.*, II, 15, 189.8–13: "Vocavi autem alias civile dominium proprietarium activi viatoris super bonis fortune plene secundum leges humanas, quod fit quando secundum omnem speciem iuris humani ad hoc pertinens licet ipsum ipsa acquirere, defendere, et mutare et per consequens sapit coaccionem personalem . . ." Wyclif repeats this in *DCD*, III, 11, 178.11–13, without including "quod fit . . . personalem."

[32] See *DCD*, I, 18, 126.5–131.22; also *DCD*, III, 11, 183–5.

[33] *Ibid.*, I, 9, 61.3–21: While most believed that before the Fall men had supernatural powers and were immortal [e.g. Aquinas, *Summa Theologiae* I, Q.94, a.1, a.3, a.4, Q.97], and Wyclif himself was inclined to make these assumptions in his treatise on the prelapsarian state [see *De Statu Innocencie*, 2, 484.9–485.8], he subordinates such beliefs to the notion that the truest state of innocence is that of the human mind freed of sin in *De Statu Innocencie*, 1, 475.12–18.

[34] *DCD*, I, 9, 62.9–13: "homo in statu innocencie habuit dominium cuiuslibet partis mundi sensibilis (ut patet tractatu secundo capitulo –), et virtute passionis Christi est iustis plena peccatorum remissio ac dominium restitutum; ergo iam tempore gracie habet iustus plenum universitatis dominium."

[35] See also *Ibid.*, I, 9, 64.16–65.8.

the Fall. Sin makes the lordship of the just more extensive, as does the added ministry of Christ, whose final victory over evil further strengthens the *dominium* of the righteous.[36] He even suggests that the predestined are so pure, and so blessed through Grace, as to be different in species from the Damned. "The whole human race is more complete through God's mediation, and man is more redeemed than he was lost, and with this declaration I hold that the multitude of the Elect are one genus, whose beginning is the Celestial Adam [i.e. Christ]; and that all the Damned are the wickedest generation, whose father and prince is the devil."[37]

Wyclif's hyperbole is meant to underscore the import of Grace in his explication of *dominium*; he is trying to show the vast difference between those favored by God, and consequently those with a just claim to lordship in God's Creation, and those rejected by their divine Lord, lacking any sort of claim through their soiled nature. The context of the discussion does not lead one to suppose that Wyclif honestly believed there to be a species difference, for that would only be possible if the predestined had Grace essentially. As mentioned earlier, the only claimant to essential (active) *iusticia* is God; this is Wyclif expostulating from the pulpit, not reasoning from the study.

EVANGELICAL *DOMINIUM*

Wyclif is cautious in explaining the difference between just and unjust lordship. Rather than simply delineating aspects of unjust human lordship, thereby committing himself to a recognizable political approach, he makes general statements about *dominium* that will illuminate his later broadsides against instances of unjust lordship. He divides human lordship into civil and evangelical *dominium*, akin to the standing distinction between secular and sacred authority. It is different, though, in that Wyclif shifts from sacred or ecclesiastical to evangelical, and frames the distinction not in terms of *potestas* but *dominium*. He writes, with regard to the difference between civil and evangelical *dominium*, "an ecclesiastic should not dominate in the first [civil] way, but every Christian dominates, in his own way, everything, and thus the Prophets were appointed to be kings

---

[36] The effect of this is that Adam's sin was God's opportunity for improvement upon divine governance, as Wyclif appears to be suggesting in *DCD*, I, 10, 66.21–5. He says as much in *De Statu Innocencie*, 9, 521.18–23, holding that God, while not willing sin, uses it for Creation's improvement.

[37] *DCD*, I, 10, 68.29–69.2: "Secunda veritas est ista, quod totum genus humanum complecius per mediatorem Dei et hominum est redemptum quam fuit perditum: pro cuius declaracione suppono quod tota multitudo predestinatorum sit una generacio sive genus, cuius principium sit secundus Adam celestis; et totum genus prescitorum sit generacio pessima, cuius pater seu principium sit dyabolus."

by God, and Christian prelates whose law is Grace are kings of those whom they rule spiritually, and are more truly kings than secular kings, since they rule souls . . . and just as secular kings make use of civil laws in their rule, so too spiritual lords use unadulterated evangelical laws in theirs."[38]

The idea that every Christian has evangelical *dominium* is striking, for it can be read to nullify the need for an hierarchically ordered ecclesiastical institution. The qualification "in his own way" (*suo modo*) apparently blunts the statement's impact, for the majority of Christians could dominate by accepting and protecting the ministry of their ecclesiastical superiors. Again, *suo modo* could mean "according to his status," which would preserve the need for some kind of hierarchical ordering. This is certainly consonant with his reference to Prophets and the spiritual kingship of priests. The elevated status of the priesthood remains through *De Civili Dominio*, and indeed, through *De Officio Regis* as well. Thomson dates the latter treatise to mid-1379, suggesting that *De Ecclesia* was written between the two more recognizably political works.[39] The first six chapters of *De Ecclesia* contain Wyclif's argument that only the predestinate can claim rightly to be the living body of Christ, and that the only true spiritual authority is Christ.[40] But from Chapter 7 on, Wyclif proceeds as if the office of priest is central to the church. In this section, his aim was to defend John of Gaunt's interests in the Hauley–Shakyll incident, when several of the Duke's soldiers killed fugitives who had sought ecclesiastical sanctuary in August 1378.[41]

This tension between the true spiritual authority of Christ and the earthly spiritual authority of the priest runs through *De Officio Regis*, with Wyclif arguing for the subordination of the episcopacy to the king to ensure that the kingdom's priests refrain from their present abuses.[42] Loserth has argued that Wyclif's most fully developed ecclesiology begins to appear in *De Potestate Pape*, at the end of 1379, so it is likely that this

---

[38] *Ibid.*, I, 11, 73.20–74.12: "Hic oportet notare distinccionem in principio tractatus de Divino Dominio, capitulo tercio, declaratam, quod aliud est dominium divinum, aliud angelicum, et aliud humanum: ipsum autem subdividitur, cum aliud civiliter coactivum, et aliud ewangelice regimentum; primo modo non debet ecclesiasticus dominari, sed secundo modo debet quilibet Christianus modo suo dominari cuilibet; et sic prophete erant reges eorum quibus a Deo preficiebantur, et prelati tempore legis gracie sunt reges eorum quibus spiritualiter sunt prefecti, et tanto verius quam reges seculi, quo officium regendi exercent in animam . . . [E]t sicut reges gencium utuntur iuribus civilibus pro suo regimine, ita debent reges spirituales uti pro suo regimine lege ewangelica inpermixte."

[39] Cf. Thomson, *The Latin Writings of John Wyclyf*, pp. 58–62.

[40] *De Ecclesia*, ed. J. Loserth (London, 1886), 1, 7.20; 17.1–7.

[41] *De Ecclesia*, 7–15. On Wyclif's defense of John of Gaunt's position in the Hauley–Shakyll incident, see Dahmus, *The Prosecution of John Wyclyf*, pp. 74–82.

[42] *De Officio Regis*, ed. A. W. Pollard and C. Sayle (London, 1887), 7.

tension regarding the status of the priesthood lasts into the 1380s.[43] In *Trialogus*, which Thomson dates to late 1382/early 1383, the priesthood is still given responsibility for spiritual guidance of the church.[44] A working definition of Wyclif's conception of spiritual lords recognizes priests as evangelical lords because of their responsibility for the spiritual growth and welfare of their fellows without inquiring too carefully into the extent of that responsibility. This ambiguity allows Wyclif to argue for the temporal divestment of the clergy, including the removal of all secular legal authority and of most of the ecclesiastical authority accompanying the priestly office (e.g. the power of excommunication). Illustrative of this ambiguity is his remark on the optimal government of the church: "[I]t would be best for the catholic church to be ruled wholly by non-avaricious successors of the Apostles following the rule of Christ; less good would be a mixed regime with co-active secular civil powers and lords, but worst of al is when ecclesiastical prelates rule who are immersed in the worries and cares of civil lords."[45]

Wyclif discusses the superior nature of evangelical *dominium* in terms that suggest his general statements about human *dominium* at the end of *De Dominio Divino*.[46] *Dominium* properly understood involves as much an attitude of service towards those to whom one holds a *dominium*-relation as it does power over them; certainly nothing compels God to give and sustain Creation in perfect *caritas*. Among Natural lords in Eden, this role of lord and servant was clear to all, but now only the Grace-favored can exercise *dominium* charitably.[47] Thus the same absence of compulsion that characterizes divine *dominium* should also characterize human *dominium*. The civil variety of *dominium* is inferior, since it was introduced after the Fall. It involves a coercion unnatural in Creation, and even when civil *dominium* is exercised by the Grace-favored this coercive force is present,

---

[43] See Loserth's introduction to *De Potestate Pape* (London, 1907), p. i. Even in this treatise Wyclif believes the priesthood has a role to play in the church, for example, *De Potestate Pape*, 12, 356.27–32: "[N]am Christo et apostolis debebantur de lege Dei stipendia officio spiritualis ministerii necessarii et lex Dei atque suum iudicium plene excuciunt istorum iniurias, quia faciat sacerdos spirituale officium sibi debitum; et incompossible est quod desint sibi vite necessaria ad dampnum anime."

[44] *Trialogus*, ed. G. V. Lechler (Oxford, 1869), IV, 15–16; 26. See also R. Vaughan, *Tracts and Treatises of John De Wycliffe, D. D.* (London, 1845), pp. 163–72, see 184–6 for a translation of this section of *Trialogus*.

[45] DCD, I, 28, 195.24–30: "[O]ptimum esset ecclesiam katholicam regi pure per non avaros apostolorum successores secundum regulam Christi; minus bonum esset quod cum illo regimine permixta sint coactiva dominia potentatuum [sic] seculi; sed pessimum omnium est quod prelati ecclesie secundum tradiciones suas immisceant se negociis et solicitudinibus civilis dominii."

[46] DD, III, 6, 250.25: "Primo quod quelibet creatura racionalis sit improprie dominus, quin pocius minister vel dispensator supremi Domini. Patet ex hoc quod quelibet creatura est servus Domini habens quidquid habet ex mera gracia ut dispenset."

[47] *De Statu Innocencie*, 2–3, and DCD, III, 13.

albeit tempered with love.[48] Evangelical, or Christian *dominium* is more natural, more pure, because it precludes unnatural servitude of one man to another. "[T]he servant or minister, insofar as he is such, looks upon his lord relatively, but every Christian should reciprocally minister to another; therefore he is reciprocally lord and servant...it is clear that evangelical lordship and servitude are not opposites but mutually follow upon one another."[49] This natural relation among humans mirrors the balanced power and subordination in each of them; it is the reciprocity of soul and body writ large.[50]

Unnatural servitude is a fuzzy concept for Wyclif, when he argues that natural *dominium* can be restored with the assistance of Grace-favored civil *dominium*. If both are arguably "natural" by being Grace-favored, exactly what is *un*natural? Briefly, any sort of relation where the subject is coerced into contravening divine law qualifies as unnatural subjugation. So long as lord and servant are in accord with divine law, and the relation is Grace-favored, there is reciprocity:

All men, greater or lesser, are respectively servants and lords. This is based upon the fact that every man has a dual nature, each element, namely body and soul, serves itself and every just man, if [the human composite] is in a state of Grace. Accordingly, in his corporeal nature he is lower than he or his brother is in his spirit, and so he is his own lord and servant.[51]

If civil *dominium* is unnatural in its institution of large-scale subservience, and evangelical, Christian *dominium* is natural in its reciprocity, why does Wyclif excoriate the existing ecclesiastical institution, and claim that it should be under the purview of civil lords? The answers to these questions, and to those regarding the discontinuity of prelapsarian non-proprietary *dominium* and civil lordship rest to a large degree on Wyclif's conception of the nature of property. There are, Wyclif explains, two sorts of riches men can desire, temporal riches and spiritual ones. Our brief characterization of *caritas* should explain why spiritual riches are

---

[48] *DCD*, I, 11, 76.28; I, 34, 243.30–3.
[49] *Ibid.*, I, 11, 75.15–76.7: "Secundo confirmatur ex hoc quod minister vel servus, in quantum huiusmodi, respicit dominum relative; sed quilibet Christianus debet reciproce alteri ministrare, ergo et esse reciproce servus et dominus...Et patet quod dominus et servus ewangelicus non repugnant sed pocius se invicem consequuntur."
[50] See A. S. McGrade, "Somersaulting Sovereignty: A Note on Reciprocal Lordship and Servitude in Wyclif," in *The Church and Sovereignty*, ed. D. Wood *SCH* Subsidia 11 (London, 1991), pp. 261–8.
[51] *DCD*, I, 11, 77.32–78.6: "[H]omines, reciproce se maiores et minores, sint sibi invicem servi et domini. Solucio vero stat in hoc quod omnis homo cum sit duarum naturarum, utraque (scilicet corpus et anima) servit sibi ipsi et cuilibet iusto, si sit in gracia; et sic secundum naturam corpoream est inferior quam ipse vel alius frater suus est secundum spiritum, et sic est servus ac dominus sui ipsius."

superior, for they bring men closer to their divine lord, while a desire for material riches brings only separation and slavery. "For all men that are rich in God are truly, greatly, and most usefully rich themselves, while those rich in the mundane sense are falsely or supposedly rich, restricted and damnable because of it."[52] We have by now little reason to equate spiritual purity with a capacity for material *dominium*; indeed, Wyclif is disapproving towards things of this world. People who have focused their desire on temporal goods have enslaved themselves to temporal things, causing them to grow to hate that for which they strive. Those who hold temporal goods in small regard, on the other hand, exhibit mastery over them, inasmuch as they recognize the true utility of temporal goods. This tacit recognition is better called "love" than "small regard," for it is indicative of a will in accord with God's ordained created structure, in contrast to one striving to pervert God's order.[53]

There is still quite a jump from the idea that spiritual riches entitle one to material lordship to the idea that the non-proprietal natural *dominium* is restored through Christ's redemption to the Elect. In fact, the latter appears to preclude the former through elimination of all individual private possession. After all, Giles of Rome makes the same claim about temporal and spiritual riches to justify the foundation of all claims of *proprietas* on papal authority. Why should Wyclif argue that those truly qualified for *dominium* must bother with private property-relations? Why should the Grace-favored administer a state devised to protect individual ownership, a perversion of God's order? What, in short, is the connection between civil *dominium*, and private and communal *proprietas*?

Here Wyclif is guilty of slightly foggy writing, for the reader of *De Civili Dominio* can only answer these questions after completing a reading of the work. In this introductory section, Wyclif is content to condemn private property-relations as inferior to communal ones, and to explain that large groups of people could indeed live without private property-relations, despite what Aristotle says.[54] We must remember, that all goods that God gives are for the entire species, not for any one person. Ideally, all people

---

[52] *Ibid.*, I, 12, 81.4–9: "Patet autem ex dictis istorum diversitas, cum omnis dives in Deum sit vere, large, et utiliter, sibi dives; econtra autem dives in mundum sit false vel reputative dives, stricte et dampnabiliter sibi. Primum patet ex hoc quod solum dives in Deum habet verum titulum possidendi; cum, deficiente titulo illius Domini, est omnis dissimiliter occupacio usurpata."

[53] *Ibid.*, I, 12, 85.21–30: "Omnis sic odiens hec temporalia vult plene de illis conformiter, quoad predicta quatuor, ut vult Deus; sed oportet voluntatem Dei generaliter esse adimpletam, ergo et cuilibet moderate odienti hec temporalia modo dicto; et cum hoc sit servire voluntati humane, in omnibus se conformari et subici ad gaudium et profectum: et iste sensus Scripture, 'Omni habenti dabitur et habundabit', Math. XXV.29, et Prov. XII,21,'Iustum non contristabit, quidquid ei acciderit.'"

[54] *Ibid.*, I, 14, 98.7–17.

would be lords of creation, but this can only be without the institution of private property, for property-owners pretend to possess what God gives in a way other than God meant it. Underlying this assumption is Wyclif's picture of divine *dominium*; God is Lord first over universals, then over particulars. So, when God bestows a gift upon something in Creation, He gives it first to that which is universal, closest to His perfect understanding. If a particular enjoying the universal gift supposes the gift to be somehow not a universal gift, but a gift directly given to the particular, the created order is shaken, and the divine gift is cheapened through its loss of universality.[55] As it turns out, all of the arguments in favor of private property-relations overlook this truth, either through want of proper understanding, or through misguided will.

PROPRIETAS IN CIVIL DOMINIUM

Wyclif argued that Christ's redemption allowed the regaining of the prelapsarian natural *dominium* that was free of civil ownership. The church, as Christ's body on earth, can best function as Christ had intended it if its members resume living as the Apostles had, owning nothing and sharing everything. But how is this vision of a church reconcilable with the dictum that Wyclif took from Fitzralph, Giles, and ultimately Augustine, that only the just could possess anything? The papal theorists, notably but not exclusively Giles of Rome, had reconciled the ideal of apostolic poverty with Augustine's position by making all just *dominium*-relations proceed from ecclesiastical authority, arguing that a poverty of spirit was of greater import than physical want. But Wyclif was to argue that this was a cheap dodge made by theorists with wills drunk on material excess, and saw the church's divestment of all private property by secular temporal authority as the only real recourse.[56] The members of the church most needing this divestment are its pastors, whose duty it is to act as exemplars of *lex Christi*. The class of evangelical lords ideally consists of all church members, but is presently equivalent to the sacerdotal class; thus, priests must be shown the necessity of giving up civil ownership. This demonstration, Wyclif will argue, is the task of the civil lord.

The problem, then, is pinpointing the source of the civil lord's legitimacy. Is he outside the church? If so, it would be difficult to explain how he would be Grace-favored. If not, then some church members must be exempted from the apostolic poverty exemplified by Christ. This seems

---

[55] *Ibid.*, I, 14, 97.12–23, see also *DD*, II, 174.5–177.19.
[56] *DCD*, I, 22, 159.15ff. This chapter begins with the heading, *Divicias civiliter habere est onerosum et periculosum* [155.18].

an even worse position than that of Giles, evocative of an Orwellian "Some animals are more equal than others." The way to begin resolving this problem is to see where Wyclif disagrees with his predecessors about the nature of *proprietas*. The subject gets minimal treatment in the first two books of *De Civili Dominio*, but the third book (equal in length to the first two combined) makes the argument that Christ's body on earth must be free of civil ownership. Once Wyclif has established the need for the church's liberation from *proprietas*, he will be able to show how God intends to use civil *dominium* as the means of liberation.

Wyclif's thought on property-relations can be summarized in three statements about individual ownership: (1) having wealth in society is a great danger; (2) civil law is directly opposed to evangelical law; and (3) man was given universal communal ownership at Creation, which gift is attainable again in this life. Analysis of each, ending with a careful look at poverty as the evangelical ideal, will help to solve the enigma of just civil lordship.

A surfeit of material goods is injurious to the human spirit for several reasons. God's lordship requires that His subjects must be accountable for the goods He has given them; those to whom God has given a wealth of goods are all the more accountable. This is because Wyclif describes *dominium* as such, which is God's, as inabdicable in *De Dominio Divino*. To be sure, the Grace by which the human possessor of material goods has them facilitates a good account of stewardship. But such possession, even strengthened and justified by Grace, requires an attention to corporeal matters, and the accompanying degradations. Riches are truly impediments to human dignity, "for they do not foster, but rather extinguish . . . charity," and expose one to the trials of the flesh, the world, and the devil.[57] The rich man is not necessarily a bad man, for Scripture tell us of Abraham, Job, and David, but these examples instruct us as to the proper attitude of the wealthy, which should be that of the good and faithful servant of his Lord.

Civil ownership as an institution, without the benefit of Grace, serves to drive a wedge between the owner and God. Not only is the owner more likely to suffer physical harm from thieves, war, and the vicissitudes of the marketplace, but his will drifts ineluctably to selfishness and the host of sins attendant upon it. The devil, Wyclif warns, is able all the more easily to lead the property-owner into the sins of the flesh, carnal lust and luxurious indolence, and ultimately to the tyranny of inextinguishable

---

[57] *DCD*, I, 22, 160.30–5. See also Anne Hudson, "Poor Preachers, Poor Men: Views of Poverty in Wyclif and His Followers," in *Häresie und vorzeitige Reformation im Spätmittelalter*, ed. E. Müller-Luckner, Schriften des Historischen Kollegs Kolloquien 39 (Oldenbourg, 1998), pp. 41–53.

avarice. Owning anything is the first step on a slippery slope from righteousness; it intensifies all other sins by insidiously compelling one to be concerned with selfish needs. All civil ownership relations not justified by Grace involve a turning away from God's love by the perversion of the owner's will; all such turning away involves a venial sin, and so all civil ownership not justified by Grace is, at base, venial sin.[58]

THE OPPOSITION BETWEEN CIVIL AND EVANGELICAL LAW

Civil laws that protect and govern property widen man's separation from God. Priests cannot act as judicial authorities in civil law, because in many cases civil law is contrary to Christ's law. "For the law of Christ teaches about the glory of tribulations and condemns fame, prosperity, and the riches of the world, advising the relinquishment of proprietary lordship; civil law seems to command the opposites of all of these."[59] And human law is unfit as a vehicle for truly just judgment according to Grace-founded justice, since property is distributed so randomly among humans that many of the Grace-favored lack lordship, while many who are not Grace-favored wrongfully have it.

Christ's law regarding our duty to worldly goods is very different from civil law. "Christ teaches the church completely in His law how one ought to stand with regard to temporal goods."[60] Earthly riches should be distributed as alms not for human honor, but privately, to give greater glory to God. Are civil law and Christ's law are incompatible? Fitzralph points out that original sin automatically negates anyone being born with natural rights to any sort of possession, and the only factor introducing just claims is Grace.[61] But Grace is not randomly distributed; Wyclif associates it with *caritas*, which arises from obedience and willing acceptance of Christ's law. Christ's law is equivalent to the evangelical law undergirding the church, which Wyclif believes to be superior to civil law.[62] This means that instances of civil legislation that are just insofar as they are commensurate with Christ's law can only be carried out by members of the church. Thus the only real basis for any claims or titles is that Grace

---

[58] *DCD*, III, 10, 161.39–162.15.

[59] *Ibid.*, II, 16, 209.13–18: "Nam lex Christi docet suos in tribulacionibus gloriari, famam, prosperitatem et voluptatem mundi contempnere et proprietatem dominandi relinquere; omnium opposita videntur iura civilia precipere."

[60] *Ibid.*, 11, 16, 213.23–5: "Docet ergo Christus in lege sua complete ecclesiam, quomodo debet ad temporalia se habere; nam quantum ad querendum ac servandum divicias satis dictum est proximo capitulo."

[61] *De Pauperie Salvatoris*, I, 11–22.

[62] *DCD*, I, 44, 396.26: "patet primo lex Christi pure per se sufficeret pro omni statu dirigere sponsam suam."

embodied in Christ's law, so rather than undermining human law, it gives it its only possible support. "All human traditions that evangelical law does not teach us to make are superfluous and wrong."[63]

While human justice must participate in divine justice to be just, requiring human legislation to be commensurate with Christ's law, it does not follow that adherents of Christ's law should contest instances of imperfect human justice where it appears that they may suffer property loss. Wyclif explains that a Christian cannot fight for temporal goods, and should submit to temporal judges for decisions. "Similarly, since all goods of Christians should be held in common, and proprietary relations are onerous and despicable, it seems that it is not right for one Christian to fight with another over property, since it should suffice [for both] that the church possess the goods [at issue]."[64] The church here means the community of Christians, and not the existing ecclesiastical hierarchy. This is sufficient evidence for the place of property in Wyclif's vision of a just society; Grace-favored individuals should have no private property, and should leave matters concerning civil ownership up to the civil courts, which are just insofar as they are founded in divine justice.

Wyclif's later defense of John of Gaunt in the Hauley–Shakyll incident of 1378 points to the unseemly clerical striving after temporal goods that he had foreseen in De Civili Dominio II. In this case, the English clergy claimed that secular powers had no jurisdiction over the soldiers who had violated the right of ecclesiastical sanctuary that had been claimed by the unfortunate Hauley and Shakyll. But prosecuting the violators of sanctuary was a privilege that had been granted to the priests governing ecclesiastical affairs. That priests can exercise this power, Wyclif responded, is not indicative of any worldly authority they enjoy by virtue of their clerical office. It is granted them by their king. He suggests that the bishops' claims to have the civil authority to prosecute the duke's murderous soldiers reveal a corrupt and misguided clergy, who use the royally granted privilege of sanctuary as grounds for their claim. The kinds of privileges priests enjoy are spiritual goods of *lex Christi*, not the mundane political privileges of civil law.[65] Had the prelates kept *lex Christi* firmly in mind, struggling for temporal goods like right of civil punishment would never have troubled the church.

---

[63] *Ibid.*, I, 44, 399.10: "Omnes tradiciones humane quas lex ewangelica non docet facere sunt superflue et inique."

[64] *Ibid.*, II, 17, 233.33–7: "Similiter, cum omnia bona christianorum debent esse communia, et esse proprietarium sit onus atque abieccio, videtur quod non licet christiano propter proprietatem pugnare cum altero, cum sufficit quod ecclesia bona illa possideat."

[65] *De Ecclesia*, 6–11.

The system of laws regulating human commerce prompts us to look to the social differences that arise; some can claim great worldly wealth, while others suffer in want. But poverty and wealth are relative terms, better explicable by distinguishing between wealth or poverty in God, and wealth or poverty in the world, for the two are not always synonymous. "Just as that individual is wealthy in God who having Christ has all . . . so he is a pauper in God who lacking in the primary justice lacks any just title in simply possessing anything."[66] In fact, the only instance of true material wealth, founded on just, deserving ownership, is God's individual possession of His Creation. All enjoyment of Creation by creatures is really reliant on God's goodness. "It is clear that God alone is rich in Himself . . . Divine nature alone has all things from and in Itself, and so cannot really be poor; whoever is poor in Christ, then, is not poverty-stricken."[67]

Wyclif's discussion is filled with reminders of the true perspective of the nature of wealth and poverty, leading the reader to think of all material commerce as having less connection to divine justice than does the ceaseless activity of a garden ant-hill. Are there no material transactions between good men that participate in God's justice? Scripture suggests that one can be a righteous businessman; Job's riches, for example, are presumed to be a measure of God's favor. Wyclif can easily sound as if he condemns every instance of postlapsarian, private property-based commercial activity. Wyclif explains that merchants sin grievously only in striving after excessive profit, while those who buy and sell for profit only to allow for the necessities of life are not serious offenders. "It appears . . . that all civil lords or businessmen sin at least venially by living in this way, that if a merchant sells to a buyer [for what exceeds the bare necessity of living] he sins mortally, because it is against the law of nature that asks one to do unto another as another would do to you, and so [selling for profit] defrauds Christ."[68] Perhaps Wyclif's inflexibility is not complete; while any private property-based commercial exchange

---

[66] *DCD*, III, 8, 108.30–109.3: "possunt autem dives et pauper subdividi in divitem et pauperem in Deum, divitem et pauperem quoad mundum. Sicut ergo ille est dives in Deum qui habendo Christum habet omnia, ut dicit Apostolus Rom. VIII, 32, sic ille est pauper in Deum qui deficiendo a prima iusticia deficit a quocunque titulo iusto simpliciter aliquid possidendi."

[67] *Ibid.*, III, 8, 110.5–12: "Ex istis elicit Lincolniensis primo quod cum vere divicie sint naturam racionalem sine indigencia habere sibi bona; patet quod solus Deus est per se dives, sicut dicitur epistola II et III. Sola quidem natura divina ex se et per se habet omnia, sic quod inpossibile est quidquam sibi deficere; ideo non potest esse pauper formaliter; quamvis enim sit pauper, quia Christus pauperrimus, non tamen potest pauperari."

[68] *Ibid.*, III, 16, 312.30–313-8: "Videtur ergo esse sentencia huius sancti quod omnis civiliter dominans vel negocians peccat ad minimum venialiter sic vivendo; quod si vendat merces emptas preter vite necessaria propter questum peccat mortaliter, quia contra legem nature qua debet alteri facere sic racionabiliter sicut debet velle sibi fieri, defraudat per Christum."

involves the stain of individual ownership, businessmen who have properly directed wills stand a chance of being condemned only for living in a
postlapsarian society. The onus of mortal sin resulting from avarice only
threatens those addicted to profit for profit's sake.

Is Wyclif is trying to have things both ways? His argument appears
to fluctuate from condemnation of all civil ownership to condemnation
of excessive riches. This is because his primary intent is not to write
an economic treatise, but to concentrate on the salvation of postlapsarian
man in society. As with Augustine, the emphasis is on the direction of the
individual will, the receptacle of Grace. The sense of Wyclif's argument
is that the one's will is likely to be more receptive of Grace when one
lives in apostolic poverty. When occupying an ecclesiastical office, one's
duties include living an exemplary life, as did Christ, so civil ownership is
a mortal sin in this instance.[69] Since Wyclif starts off condemning riches in
particular and gradually comes to include all ownership in his indictment,
could he have allowed himself to be carried away by the force of his own
argument? No, one can conceivably maintain material wealth and remain
pure so long as Grace provides one the wherewithal, which it will not do
for the clergy. So Wyclif moves from talk of material wealth as a general
danger to men to talk of all ownership as a perversion for the clergy.

Recognizing the necessity for material transactions is an important
factor in Wyclif's analysis of property. Even before the Fall, people needed
sustenance and shelter. Given the postlapsarian necessity of the institution of private property, when owners limit themselves to a degree of
moderation the better to serve God, some degree of divine approbation
seems possible. Wyclif makes reference to Aristotelian authority, citing
the *Eudemian Ethics* to support his claim that moderate use of temporal goods, taken as a means to a higher end, is beneficial: "[Aristotle
illustrates] that temporal goods are necessary for active happiness in life,
but as a moderate occupation with temporalia is a proportionate medium
to happiness, an excessive occupation such as the rich have who are not
evangelically poor is an impediment."[70]

Wyclif provides every apparent nod in the direction of the *status quo*
with a reminder of need for the elimination of civil ownership. While

[69] *Ibid.*, III, 23, 487.14–24; 509.40–512.18; also 490.35–9: "omnis nuncupative clericus simplex vel
aggregatus approprians sibi cum illo clericatu pretensam dominacionem civilem peccat mortaliter,
sicut eciam omnis homo ex curiositate abutens bonis Domini."

[70] *Ibid.*, III, 10, 148.38–149.7: "Arguunt enim philosophi ex sentencia Aristotelis I.Ethic., 'quod
divicie necessarie sunt ad felicitatem, cum sine illis foret homo insufficiens sibi et suis et involutus
magna miseria'. Hic concludo quod temporalia sunt necessaria active felicitati pro statu vie, sed
sicut occupacia temporalium moderata est medium proporcionale huic beatitudini, sic occupacio excessiva qualem habent mundo divites qui non sunt evangelice pauperes est obstaculum
tardativum."

it is possible for owners to do good by means of their ownership, as was the case with the good rich men of the Old Testament, the sort of use most conformable with the way material things were created is the use of the apostolically poor. The virtue of men like Job lies in their good will, not in their possession of material goods. These were anomalous cases, anticipating the perfection of Christ's poverty, and do more to show us how man's state was improved with Christ's coming than to illustrate the benefits of individual ownership. A blanket condemnation of civil ownership is optimal, if for no other reason than because of the exemplary power of such a condemnation.

CIVIL AND EVANGELICAL *DOMINIUM*

Throughout the third book of *De Civili Dominio*, *dominium* is used to refer both to lordship in the governmental sense and to ownership equivocally.[71] Political duties of civil lords are not considered; as far as the contrast between private property-relations and the ideal of evangelical poverty is concerned, a civil lord is an owner. Wyclif sets the tone for this equivocation in the eleventh chapter, defining civil *dominium* in purely proprietary terms. "Civil lordship is proprietary lordship in an active way-farer over the goods of fortune fully according to human law."[72] Wyclif specifies an active path in contrast to monk's contemplative one, and 'the goods of fortune' means material goods as the things that come a person's way in daily life. Civil *dominium* necessarily involves the use of terms such as "mine" and "thine", which always ends up leading to discord among people.[73] Evangelical and natural *dominium* are free of these strictures; *proprietas*, or individual ownership and the legal strictures that invariably accompany it, are peculiar to civil *dominium*.

There are three sorts of property-relation relevant to distinguishing between civil and evangelical/natural *dominium*, namely civil *dominium* (or ownership), civil use, and the spiritual use of an object:

An example of the first is that property that the king or another secular lord has in his kingdom by *dominium*; which excludes any other sort of joint *dominium* among equals, although an emperor or other chief lord may co-dominate with him. An example of the second is property that has been hired, as with a room

---

[71] *Ibid.*, III, 13, 223.19–30.
[72] *Ibid.*, III, 11, 178.9–17: "Unde propter delectacionem (quam dixi III huius XVIII capitulo) descripsi sic (in IV huius, XV capitulo) dominium civile: Civile dominium est dominium propri-etarium activi viatoris super bonis fortune plene secundum leges humanas; dixi autem dominium proprietatum ad differenciam naturalis dominii ex titulo gracie; . . . Ideo seculare dominium voco dominium proprietarium." The reference to a previous definition is to *DCD*, II, 15, 189.8–13.
[73] *Ibid.*, III, 11, 179.19–31.

or home without the actual civil ownership of same. Such personal use is licit by civil contract but does not include the right to sell the house in any way nor fully to exercise civil acts, but nevertheless this is *dominium* by title of grace, and one can say "my house" or "my room," but it is not civil *dominium*. In the third type are uses that cannot be construed as civil which the holy may have.[74]

Here we have the basic elements of ownership sketched out; (1) actual individual ownership; (2) the use of something subject to someone else's ownership; and (3) spiritual use. The third is Wyclif's ideal for the church, wherein members of the ecclesiastical community civilly own nothing as individuals, nor as a community, but make use of material goods owned and donated by a civil lord. This distinction makes Fitzralph's *possessio* into a kind of use by bracketing all civil uses other than actual ownership as not involving the liberty to exercise the right to sell, let, or loan. The "grace" Wyclif refers to in this second type is not the divine variety, but the favor of the civil owner in allowing the use. For Wyclif's purpose, in distinguishing between evangelical or spiritual *dominium* and any of the civil species, these are sufficient.

Wyclif views civil corporate ownership as individual ownership writ large, and has as little regard for it as he does for its smaller relation. With civil communal ownership, we have something no better than civil individual ownership, because both are based on the imperfections that make civil society necessary.[75] A body of individuals in a civil ownership relation to an object or group of objects is no less morally impure because the many in the body have agreed to act as one. The ownership relation is still private. Corporate ownership can take the form of an ecclesiastical body owning according to civil law and communal lordship under evangelical or natural law. The former, of course, is anathema for Wyclif, because Christ's body should not subject itself to Caesar's law for the base

---

[74] *Ibid.*, III, 11, 180.1–20: "[E]t sic tripliciter in genere dicitur aliquis proprietatem habere in rebus fortune vel quoad civile dominium vel quoad civilem usum, vel quantum ad spiritualem usum quomodocunque aliis est communicatum [i.e. the types of having property are so-named depending upon the degree of having]. Exemplum primi est proprietas quam rex vel alius secularis dominus habet suo regno sive dominio; que excludit quemcunque alium super eodem condominari ex equo, licet imperator vel alius dominus capitalis condominetur eidem. Exemplum secundi est proprietas quam conductorius habet in domo vel camera sine civili suo dominio; licet enim dominus talis ex contractu civili habet proprium usum cui non licet sibi vendere domum huiusmodi nec plene exercere actus civiles inferius memorandos, quilibet tamen utens re aliqua est dominus eiusdem ex titulo gracie, sic quod vere posset dici domus sua, camera sua vel res sua, licet non dominetur ei civiliter. In tercio gradu sunt usus sensibiles incompossibiles quos appropriate habent sancti sine civilitate dominii vel usus."

[75] *Ibid.*, III, 20, 411.26–33: "Ex quo videtur, cum non datur sacerdotibus Christi potestas nisi as edificacionem ecclesie, quod non datur eis et specialiter religiosis claustralibus potestas ad civiliter dominandum; sive enim dominetur civiliter in communi, sivie civiliter in proprio suo, dominacio est civilis; nam dominacio civilis in communi non distrahit quin sit dominacio civilis."

reason of civil ownership. Wyclif countenances ecclesiastical submission to civil law only if the clergy surrender all civil ownership to allow the church communal lordship by evangelical, or natural law. This differs from communal lordship by civil law in that a civil corporation is based in its members' greed for benefits arising from joint ownership according to human law. The grace of Natural lordship engenders the charitable absence of private property-relations, allowing for more reciprocity between lord and subject. "Grace-endowed lordship it is not held by virtue of the quantity of the dominables but is founded in the *caritas* of lordship; such that the more *caritas*, the more the lordship . . ."[76] This *caritas* is the hallmark of all just lordship, and its manifestation in evangelical or natural communal lordship is purer than it is in any case of communal lordship founded in civil ownership.[77]

Assuming for the moment the relative equivalence of natural and evangelical lordship, Wyclif distinguishes between natural (and, by implication, evangelical) and civil lordship using the same criteria for *dominium* that he used in *De Dominio Divino*: giving (*donare, dotacione*), lending (*prestare*), buying and selling (*empcio et vendicio*), letting and hiring (*locare et conducere*), and lending and borrowing (*accommodare et mutuare*). Giving is a good place to begin. Wyclif has scant interest in gifts that arise in civil property-transactions, dismissing civil giving as dependent on individual ownership. Consequently, he vigorously rejects the legitimacy of a church's claim to own property based on a bequest of a generous layman. Transfer of civil ownership to clergy is impossible, so the layman retains his civil ownership whether he means to or not. Royal grants to clergy do not involve giving over actual civil ownership, for the grants are eleemosynary, in return for prayer, and are to the church of God, allowing only bare use of the property. Transfer of civil ownership to clergy is impossible, which would imply that the bequester retain civil lordship of his gift.[78] There is a great gulf between the giving of civil property, which can involve absolute transference of the gift to the ownership of the receiver, and endowment of the church. The latter cannot lead to further instances of civil ownership-transactions; there is no title to sell. "For the law of alms-giving is pure evangelical law, as Christ spoke, 'Sell what you possess and give alms' . . ."[79] The illegitimacy of all the church's secular

---

[76] *Ibid.*, III, 13, 232.7–12: "Correspondenter dictum est de dominio gracie, quod non solum capit suam quantitatem a dominabili sed a fundamento dominii caritate, sic quod beati ut maioris caritatis magis dominantur, et sic de viatoribus in comparicione ad se invicem et beatos."

[77] *Ibid.*, III, 13, 230.5–15; III, 11, 181.27.   [78] *Ibid.*, III, 14, 237.27–33.

[79] *Ibid.*, III, 14, 237.5–8: "Si enim pure ex titulo elemosine quis dominatur, tunc non plene secundum leges humanas et sic non civiliter. Nam lex elemosine est pure lex evangelica, dicente Christo Luce XII.33, 'Vendite que possidetis et date elemosinam' . . ."

holdings, from the smallest benefice to the Donation of Constantine, is inescapable. Any ecclesiastical property holding can only be just insofar as it exhibits the communal non-exclusivity of natural *dominium*.[80]

POVERTY AS EVANGELICAL IDEAL

The vehicle for the abolition of civil ownership is a poverty imitative of Christ's earthly life. Scripture describes the early Christian community as enjoying a lack of individual ownership, in obedience to Christ's injunction to sell one's possessions and give the proceeds to the poor.[81] Wyclif was certainly not original in his emphasis on Christ's poverty as exemplary for the church, taken variously as the ecclesiastical institution and the body of the Predestined, be rid of all civil ownership.[82] The Poverty Controversy, which split the Franciscan Order through competing interpretations of St. Francis' teachings, led to John XXII's harsh suppression of the Minorite ideal. This was foremost in Wyclif's mind as he wrote, and most of his discussion of property is in terms of strong protest against John XXII.[83] Still, Wyclif is not a Franciscan apologist, for he distinguishes between St. Francis' ideal and Christ's by pointing to the divine foundation for complete evangelical poverty. Followers of St. Francis are called Franciscans, while followers of Jesus Christ are not "Jesuans," but rather Christians, indicative of something more than an Order. In a humanly instituted Order, obedience of the rule may or may not be a necessary precondition for Grace, whereas a faithful life in Christ, a divinely endowed ideal, is needed to receive Grace. It is likely

---

[80] This resonates through Wyclif's later works; for example, *De Ecclesia*, 14, 303–8; *Supplementum Trialogi*, 2; *Dialogus*, 6–7, 17–19; any sort of lending, buying or selling presupposing individual ownership is precluded by evangelical law. That Christ "bought" the human race through His redemptive passion does not suggest any acquisition of lordship that He did not already have. See *DCD*, III, 15, 277–84.

[81] Wyclif does not use Matthew 19:21 to prove that the apostles had to have been poor, only that they were told to embrace poverty. The scriptural evidence of their poverty he finds in the Acts of the Apostles. Franciscans like Michael de Cesena held that the apostles lacked all rights of legal ownership, from private to corporate *proprietas*. Because the effect of Wyclif's position is to make the latter a species of the former, we will refrain from distinguishing between the two, save where necessary.

[82] Wyclif is ambiguous about this, for in some places he argues that the entire church ought be relieved of private ownership (see *DCD*, III, 12, 212.16–20, also *De Officio Regis*, 6, 133.20–23), while in others he argues for divestment of the private holdings of the prelacy and the priesthood (*DCD*, III, 12, 193.26–7). The problem arises from his not yet fully developed concept that all Grace-favored believers are true priests (see *DCD*, III, 13, 230.5–15 and *De Officio Regis*, 6, 133). Wyclif is arguing in *DCD* at the least for total divestment of the private holdings of the clergy, while leaning towards including the entire body of Christians (save the civil lords) in this prescription.

[83] *DCD*, III, 9, 133.11–28; *DCD*, III, 16, 304.9–28; *DCD*, III, 17; *DCD*, III, 18, 358.22–31 and 370.15–373.35; *DCD*, III, 21, 440.10–443.36.

that Wyclif's arguments with William Woodford O.F.M. in 1376 contributed to the growth of his suspicions regarding the legitimacy of the friars, for the first solid evidence of his antifraternalism appears in *De Civili Dominio* III.[84]

Wyclif saw Christ as the first man since Adam to achieve the freedom from private property equivalent to the Natural lordship lost with the Fall. Christ shared this through His exemplary life with the Apostles; no member of that community had exclusive claim to any material object in the community, and each took what they needed without waste. Because the community lived according to Christ's rule, it was not an instance of communal ownership under civil law, for Christ's authority far exceeds any artificed secular arrangement. "Christ was a true pauper, as was prophesied in the Old Testament, in that He came into the world to destroy sin, and above all the customs of human secular commerce that had developed since the state of innocence . . . which He could not have done unless He adopted the opposite state of poverty."[85] John XXII taught that Christ as universal Lord had *dominium* over temporal things, but Ockham responded that John had construed this to involve ultimate civil authority. Wyclif and the Franciscans believed that Christ's *dominium* and His law are untainted by association with property ownership, and upheld a spiritual perfection removed from material concerns.[86]

The relationship between Christ the Lord and His servants in poverty is a *dominium*-relation between evangelical *dominus* and subject. In all *dominium*-relations, the lord must serve as moral exemplar. In this case he is the moral measure by which the subjects' submission to evangelical law is evaluated. This is not to say that Christ's Lordship is imitable by an earthly evangelical lord. "The life of Christ, which is the exemplar or rule of all other [lives], should not and cannot be seen as comprising all the kinds of lives that Christians who follow Him lead themselves, because then it would mean that Christ should have married, or lived a civil life, and done everything else that is laudable in a Christian life."[87] Wyclif's implication

---

[84] *Ibid.*, III, 2, 15.5–23. See Penn Szittya, *The Antifraternal Tradition in Medieval Literature* (Princeton, 1986), pp. 152–82.

[85] *DCD*, III, 4, 51.17–24: "Quibus suppositis patet primo quod Christus fuit vere pauper, ut prophetatum est de eo in veteri testamento; nam Christus venit in mundum peccata destruere et potissime ritus gentilitatis de seculari conversacione secundum quam sunt a statu innocencie . . . [sic] quod non fecisset nisi in persona propria statum paupertatis illi oppositum observasset, ergo hoc perficit."

[86] Ockham, *Opus Nonaginta Dierum*, in *Guillelmi de Ockham: Opera Politica* I, ed. H. S. Offler (Manchester, 1950), c.93, 680.419–25.

[87] *DCD*, III, 8, 123.23–9: "Correspondenter vita Christi que est exemplar et regula cunctis aliis non oportet nec potest esse quod sit ita grosse distincta secundum partes sicut vite christianorum quas regulariter exemplat, quia tunc oportet Christum vivere vitam coniugalem, vitam civilem, et ita de omni genere vite christiane laudabilis."

is that marriage and civil ownership are perfectly laudable elements of the Christian life, despite Christ's having renounced both. The community of Apostles constituting the early church sustained Christ's ideal so long as they rejected civil ownership. Wyclif gives eight reasons why the early church should serve as the model for all religious institutions, and by extension, for society as a whole, five of which are concerned primarily with the church's communalism. Given the descriptions of poverty and property already set out, these reasons come as no surprise. First, the factor prohibiting amicable civil intercourse, namely private property, was eliminated, "for we should show more concern for the good of the body [of Christ] than for the good of property."[88] Thus, second, the resultant unification of interests leads to a greater tendency to share with one another. Third, no discord among people arises from social divisions that have been abolished with the elimination of proprietary division. Next, the disciples' act of selling their property fostered their spiritual purity, which would have been threatened had they been saddled with civil lordship. Finally, all that came into the apostolic circle from individual members was not given to the circle as a separate corporate individual, but rather was divided as was needed among the members.

Poverty is not simply a lack of temporal possessions, though; one lives sinfully in squalor by hungering after possessions, ownership, and so forth. Wyclif recalls Bonaventure's distinction between three sorts of righteous poverty – natural, evangelical or scriptural, and Grace-founded poverty.[89] Natural poverty is evocative of a state of innocence, consonant with a state of blessedness. Evangelical poverty involves renunciation of power to hold civil lordship for love of obedience to Christ's rule. When this is done with *caritas*, in submitting oneself to be a tool of God, one's actions can be founded by Grace, thus making evangelical poverty a precedent for all types of virtues. While Wyclif presents these mostly to distinguish between poverty as an economic phenomenon and poverty as the evangelical ideal, Bonaventure's distinctions are of interest for anyone seriously considering Wyclif's treatise as a rejection of earlier synthetic theology. It is not enough for Wyclif that members of the body of Christ surrender all claims to civil lordship/ownership, although this would be sufficient for mere submission to Christ's rule. Wyclif's ideal requires Grace as foundation, so the *caritas* that Bonaventure admits is not necessary in simple evangelical poverty must be evident for communal ownership according to evangelical rule. The distinction here is between submission

---

[88] *Ibid.*, III, 6, 78.20–5: "Et hinc dicit I.Cor.XII, 12 quod 'sumus membra corporis Christi' et debemus plus et principalius intendere bonum illius corporis quam bonum proprium, quia aliter non potest quis esse Christi discipulus, 'nisi sic renunciet omnibus que possidet'."
[89] *Ibid.*, III, 7, 89.25–30; the reference is to Bonaventura, *De Statu Innocentiae*, II.

to Christ's rule, and whole-hearted embrace of life in accordance to its requirements.

It is difficult to identify Wyclif's conception of poverty as such, because he appears to want to say that not everyone who does not own things is in poverty. Civil paupers are not necessarily evangelical paupers, while the evangelically poor need not all be as property-less as the civilly poor are. Temporal goods are worthwhile in their absolutely necessary sense, as daily bread is for sustenance. And insofar as the user of these goods makes use of them in doing God's work, the use is right. Consequently, poverty involves nothing more than the minimal use of temporal goods to maintain daily activity; considerations as to how temporal goods are allocated in the community are not a part of poverty as such. So evangelical poverty is not simply an economic term in the common sense. It refers to the state of one's spirit, specifically to its virtuous character, and is not only a matter of having or not having things. Evangelical poverty, he explains, is absolutely separated from the sphere of civil ownership. It is "a way of having by caring for an increase of riches which now can be augmented, or decreased, just as on the other hand, a privation of riches can be now augmented, or decreased."[90]

Wyclif seems to be trying to have his cake and eat it, but his aim is to reinforce the absolute separation of evangelical and civil matters. A definition of evangelical poverty cannot even take civil ownership concerns into consideration. Wyclif recognizes that it is easy to interpret his program as nothing more than a rejection of civil ownership for the church, a useful tenet in a laborious monarchist argument. His stipulation that evangelical poverty has nothing whatever to do with civil ownership considerations frees him from this trap, providing a purely theological basis for defining the civil and evangelical spheres as essentially different. This is a dangerous approach to take, though, because it detracts from the argument that evangelical poverty involves not having anything. While evangelical poverty in the spiritual sense is a matter not of things but of the direction of the will, in the social sense, Wyclif believes that it involves most Christians – and all priests – in not participating in civil ownership.

When one holds a thing in evangelical poverty, and not as a mere possessor, the degree of one's evangelical poverty is measurable by how concerned one is with using it for the greatest possible spiritual good.[91] While Wyclif is never so explicit as to clarify this, he employs *caritas* as the quality

---

[90] *DCD*, III, 8, 119.34–120.7: "modo habendi respiciens cum augmento diviciarum nunc augeri nunc minui potest, sicut econtra cum privacione earum potest minui nunc augeri."

[91] *Ibid.*, III, 10, 151.1–5; 153.26–31.

used to measure the having as mere ownership, or as caring poverty.[92] This appears to countenance individual ownership so long as the owner's motives are right, and Wyclif had argued elsewhere in *De Civili Dominio* that one's motives are unmeasurable by one's fellows.[93] How can we tell the difference between someone who is truly evangelically poor and someone who is an owner? Further, does this not suggest that ecclesiastics are the best qualified for custodianship, given their spiritual vocation? Wyclif is clear that evangelical poverty need not imply an absence of civil property, but that private ownership is the most onerous burden possible to those striving to live under evangelical law. Further, he is adamant that while civil poverty is not sufficient for evangelical poverty, ecclesiastics should be civil paupers. How to resolve this?

Civil lordship is made just through Grace, yet it is less perfect than evangelical poverty, itself only possible through Grace. This is a gradation of sorts, for unjust civil possession is less preferable than just civil possession, which is less preferable than evangelical absence of civil possession, which itself is divisible into the baser evangelical poverty practiced by those who live "in the world" among property-owners, and the purer evangelical poverty enjoyed by those who live the contemplative life apart from mundane affairs.[94] How can someone enjoy presumably just civil possession, while living in evangelical poverty? Just as there are degrees of Grace-founded just property-relations, there are degrees possible within these just relations. That is, it must be possible for someone to enjoy a private property-relation justly, yet without evangelical poverty. It must also be possible, conversely, for someone to lack private property, yet want evangelical poverty. Thus, it must be possible to hold civil lordship and enjoy evangelical poverty.[95]

Wyclif reasons that nobody has true evangelical poverty without humility, which requires Grace. So evangelical poverty necessarily involves Grace. Nobody is truly freed of the burdens of temporal property without evangelical poverty, which means that freedom from want requires Grace.[96] But this freedom does not entail absence of the need to use material objects, only the lack of solicitude humans enjoyed before sin. Those bound to this solicitude, whether because of civil responsibility

---

[92] *Ibid.*, I, 6, for Wyclif's explanation of the signs of having *caritas*, foremost of which is the preference of eternal good over temporal goods. See also *DCD*, I, 19, 132.14–133.26; I, 22, 158.19ff.

[93] For Wyclif's belief that men cannot judge the motives of their fellows, see *DCD*, I, 20; II, 12, 139; II, 13, and especially 16, 218–25; see also his rejection of excommunication, which rests on this tenet, for example, *DCD*, I, 38; I, 40.

[94] *Ibid.*, III, 10, 161.25–8; 168.16–22.

[95] *Ibid.*, III, 10, 162.26–163.6. See also III, 7, 89.13–19, and III, 8, 120.36–122.8.

[96] *Ibid.*, III, 7, 95.16–21.

for property, or because of a lack of availability of needed objects, do not experience the true freedom allowed by Grace.

One might be excused for suspecting that Wyclif is trying to justify civil ownership for those who can withstand its pitfalls, while denying it to everyone else. But the crucial issue is not whether or not one owns things; it is evangelical poverty, a state of the soul. If Wyclif were interested solely in declaiming against civil ownership considered as a purely economical category, one is at a loss when confronted with such passages as "it is clear that Christ's life serves as an example for many distinct Christian lives through subtle variation and for disparate reasons."[97] When it is clear that evangelical poverty is a state of the soul, one need not struggle to explain away Wyclif's apparent inconsistency. But we must then wonder why Wyclif so resoundingly equated evangelical poverty with the divestment of civil ownership in the case of the church.

ECCLESIASTICAL POVERTY

Wyclif's primary concern is not to justify the conformity of civil property-relations with evangelical law; it is to explain the need for an absolute surrender of all civil ownership relations by an institution not grounded in Christ's law. Understanding the purity of apostolic poverty makes it easier to appreciate that the responsibilities of evangelical office place greater restrictions on the possible range of actions by spiritual lords than do the responsibilities of civil lords:

[I]f the virtues of temporal lords add to their fulfillment of duties, they are more perfect thereby than their subjects, and if evil, they are more culpable than their inferiors. And since the genus of secular offices of whatever stripe is made of a lesser dignity than those of the clergy ... it is clear that if the holder of the ecclesiastical office acts well, he is more meritorious, but if evilly, the more culpable. This is a more monstrous and infectious danger ecclesiastically ... than civilly.[98]

Priests do not need temporal goods to carry out their duties, while civil lords do seem to need temporal goods and wealth in fulfilling their roles.[99]

---

[97] *Ibid.*, III, 8, 123.30–33: "patet quod eadem vite Christi secundum subtilem variacionem et racionem disparem exemplat quotlibet vitas Christianorum distinctas specifice."

[98] *Ibid.*, III, 10, 163.14–26: "quia domini temporales si virtuose presint secundum exigenciam officii sui, sunt suis subdidis plus perfecti, et si male presint, sunt suis inferioribus plus culpandi; et cum totum genus laicalis officii quantumlibet creverit est dignitate inferius quam officium clericorum ... Et per hoc patet quod ecclesiastici preposita si bene rexerint, plus merentur, si male, amplius demerentur. Maior autem monstruositas et periculum infectivum ecclesie est in oneroso preposito ecclesie quam civili, quia ubi est ex casu maius periculum, est ex perseverancia maius inmeritum."

[99] *Ibid.*, III, 9, 126.9–15. For the works of mercy that comprise the priest's duties, see III, 12, 460–1.

Wyclif is alert to instances of superfluity in all use of temporal goods, and since civil *dominium* can easily lead to superfluous use, its burden and attendant risks would be too much for individuals with sacerdotal responsibilities to bear.

One might object that this reasoning is based on a too-literal interpretation of Scripture. Christ did not *forbid* His priests to possess things, He just did not encourage them to do so. This, Wyclif counters, flies in the face of Christ's words. "Here and in all other cases I hold that Christ's advice should be observed to the letter."[100] For instance, when Christ advised against superfluous adornment, He was not advising that we do without clothing, but that we wear no more than is necessary. Clothing designed to flatter "superfluous vanity, excessive sumptuosity, or novelty of cut" should be avoided.[101] In fact Wyclif believes priests have strayed too far away from Christ with their luxurious vestments, and have come to equate the luxuries of civil *dominium* with their own office. The sort of use for which material objects were created is the use of the evangelically poor, in which there is no superfluity or waste.[102]

Wyclif imagines someone using the Donation of Constantine to justify clerical ownership by arguing that priests already enjoy Christ-like communal ownership of all that the civil authority has ceded to them, despite the cession's having been under the auspices of civil ownership. He concedes that, "to infringe on the possession of the church might implicitly destroy the Christian religion, so that it is impossible to deny priests true temporal lordship unless through [consequent] defects in observing the law of Christ."[103] But given all that has been said, true temporal *dominium* would involve the communal lordship enjoyed by the Apostles, and any deviation would transgress evangelical law, making the Donation less a political title than a political recognition of the church's peculiarity. But the church has ceased to deserve the Donation and has erred with Pharaonic greed, "perverted by temporal occupations from the title of

---

[100] *Ibid.*, III, 9, 137.27–9: "[S]ic et in aliis preceptis dicitur primo, quod omnia Christi consilia oportet observare ad literam." Wyclif distinguishes here between Christ's counsel and theologians' precepts. While all Christ's counsels should be observed to the letter, theologians' precepts should be taken in *sensus catholicos*, by which he means logically, gramatically, and metaphysically in concord with Scripture. Cases of conceptual misinterpretation are possible, but are always rectifiable through the Holy Spirit's moving assistance in spiritual judgement and understanding.

[101] *DCD*, III, 9, 139.26: "scilicet in superflua vanitate, in excessiva sumptuoisitate, et in curiosa sculpcione."

[102] *Ibid.*, III, 10, 161.7–14.

[103] *Ibid.*, III, 13, 216.19–24: "Quantum ad istud, concedi debet conclusio quod dotacio ecclesie sit licita et meritoria utrobique; conceditur eciam quod infringere possessionem ecclesie foret implicite religionem christianam destruere, eo quod impossibile est clerum deficere a vero temporalium dominio, nisi propter defectum observancie legis Christi."

caritas, more prodigal with rich ornamentation . . . more prone to richness in food, families, and clothing . . . than the laity."[104] This surrender of *caritas* indicates absence of Grace, and a turning away from the apostolic lordship of evangelical law. Thus, whatever validity the Donation might conceivably have had, the ecclesiastical hierarchy's greed has made it a document no longer pertinent to evangelical law.

The only justifiable postlapsarian use of civil *dominium* is when the civil lord, from whom the right to usufruct would emanate, is guided by a sense of utility commensurate with that accompanying evangelical poverty. It is easy to recognize the need for divine guidance here; without it, the civil lord's use might well be superfluous. Is Grace sufficient for civil *dominium* as well as necessary? No, but it is necessary and sufficient for natural *dominium*. If someone is Grace-favored, they have been redeemed by Christ, and the natural *dominium* automatically accompanying redemption is only possible through that Grace.[105] Only those Grace-favored Christian Natural lords on whom God has imposed the duty of stewardship are civil lords, so while Grace is necessary for civil *dominium*, it is not sufficient. It cannot be that all Natural lords are thereby just civil lords on the principle that God gives back to the just more than they had lost, since civil *dominium* is not an improvement on natural *dominium*.

Wyclif speaks of civil *dominium* in two senses: as the sin-founded type of *dominium* that is distinct from evangelical and natural *dominium*, and as the type that Grace allows its holders to rule and own in the interests of the evangelically poor and priests. In the first sense it is logical to distinguish between the just and the unjust civil lord, because individuals wielding civil power without Grace are worth the concern of anyone trying to show how ownership tends naturally to corrupt the owner. But in the second sense "unjust" civil *dominium* is not really possible. The only true civil *dominium* is that founded in Grace, while the supposed authority of the unworthy is a sham and not civil *dominium* at all. Illusory civil *dominium* might well be sanctioned by civil law, but without Grace true justification is absent. As we will see in the next chapter this does not mean that the just are given *carte blanche* to ignore the civil authority of even those most obviously unjustified pretenders to civil *dominium*.[106]

---

[104] *Ibid.*, III, 13, 217.24–9: "Sed in tercio digno defecerunt ut magi Pharaonis, perversi ab occupacione temporalium ex titulo caritatis, et circa civile ac seculare dominium prodigaliter sumptuosi in ornamentis, esculentis et familiis et aliis fastum seculi sapientibus eciam plus quam layci seculares."

[105] *Ibid.*, I, 13, 92–3.　　[106] *Ibid.*, III, 17, 346.9–15.

NATURAL, EVANGELICAL, AND CIVIL *DOMINIUM*

The largest part of *De Civili Dominio* is meant to prove that the church, especially its spiritual stewards, must be free of civil ownership, because Christ's redemption made possible the return of natural *dominium*. Throughout the final chapters of Book III Wyclif reviews Natural, Evangelical, and Civil *Dominium*, summarizing the main points of his ecclesiastical and social vision. Now that we have a better understanding of how Wyclif sees *proprietas*, we will be in a good position to measure the three classes of *dominium* against one another. The concept of use, or what is done with property, allows Wyclif to make clear distinctions between Natural and Civil *dominium*. Fitzralph treated *usus*, itself divisible into rightful and unrightful varieties, as a separate category under *proprietas* and *possessio*. Wyclif is not so tidy a theorist, because he assumed the necessity of some sort of *dominium* relation as antecedent to any just instance of *usus*. A supposed "lord" who abuses, or uses wastefully shows the hollowness of such a claim, and abuse is equivalent to superfluous use.[107] Exploring superfluity of use will show how Wyclif distinguishes between natural and civil *dominium* through his reliance on the necessity of a pre-existing *dominium*-relation for use.

Wyclif defines the different species of *dominium* in several places throughout *De Civili Dominio*. The clearest definition of civil *dominium* appears in II, 15, and again in III, 11: "proprietary *dominium* in this world over the goods of fortune in accord with human law."[108] In I, 18, he equates natural and evangelical *dominium*, but the fullest definition of natural *dominium* appears in III, 13. Natural *dominium* existed before the Fall, extending over the whole world, involved no anxiety on the part of the bearer, was inabdicable and identifiable with the essential nature of the bearer, and rooted in the society of one's equals. Here Wyclif effectively makes natural *dominium* equivalent to evangelical *dominium*:

For all men besides Christ coexisting in *caritas* communicate in each *dominium* those things that they possess . . . since all members of the church hold unmediatedly their *dominium* from Christ their chief lord, and this I call natural *dominium*, evangelical *dominium*, original *dominium*, or Grace-endowed *dominium* . . . which same *dominium* is held to be more basic than civil *dominium*, for in this way people originally, by nature held *dominium* by the title of Grace. After the Fall this was restored by the gospel, beyond which all *dominium* superadded by priests would be superfluous.[109]

---

[107] *Ibid.*, III, 15, 282.3.   [108] *Ibid.*, II, 15, 189.7–9; see III, 11, 178.12–16.

[109] *Ibid.*, III, 13, 230.3–15: "Nam omnes homines citra Christum coexistentes in caritate communicant in quocunque dominato quod possident, sine hoc quod unus teneat dominium illud de

God ordained that material creation be self-sustaining, and that the consumers in Creation be able to survive and reproduce without needless hardship. The consumers have no claim to superfluous use, though, and Wyclif presumes that waste would have been unknown in the prelapsarian world. Wyclif avoids the descriptions of superfluous use that make Fitzralph's definitions sparkle with clarity, and that emphasize the difference between Fitzralph's legalistic precision and Wyclif's theoretical vigor. Wyclif occasionally repudiates the waste implicit in any profit-based economy, where merchants are encouraged to acquire more goods than they can possibly use. But he is careful to allow the need for merchants in the order of things, so long as they do not profit more than absolutely necessary for subsistence.[110] Economic reform does not find a place in Wyclif's assessment of superfluity in use.

In any instance of *dominium*, just use is only possible with the consent of a holder of *dominium*, the lord. In cases of civil *dominium*, a serf might eat something without the civil lord's permission, perhaps a stolen turnip, without necessarily abusing the turnip, for "all use of comestibles presupposes natural *dominium*."[111] If the serf is starving, and needs the turnip to hold onto life, he is justified according to the laws of God's lordship, despite his breaking civil law.[112] This illustrates the eminent nature of God's *dominium* over the civil variety, but raises an interesting problem. If Adam's Fall robbed his descendants of the birthright of natural *dominium*, which was only rectified by Christ's redemption, then it seems curious that Wyclif would make reference to natural *dominium* as the basic justification for all acts of eating for survival. Why not allow only the Elect, members of Christ's body on earth, this license?

It is easy enough to distinguish between natural and civil lordship, between created and artificed relation. Why should Wyclif distinguish between natural and evangelical *dominium*, though, beyond recognizing that the former is the birthright given up with the introduction of sin, and that the latter is a Christ-given reprieve to those favored by Grace with salvation? What part does natural *dominium* play in a world in which only members of Christ's body on earth can enjoy the communal ownership

reliquo, cum omne membrum ecclesie inmediate tenet illud dominium de Christo dominio capitali; et illud voco dominium naturale, dominium evangelicum, dominium originale vel dominium gracie secundum quadruplicem disparem racionem; quod quidem dominium supponitur fundanter ad civile dominium; nam illo modo dominaretur homo ex naturali origine primo tytulo gracie; post lapsum est per evangelium restitutum, preter quod omne dominium superadditum clericis foret superfluum."

110 *Ibid.*, III, 16, 313.16–25.
111 *Ibid.*, III, 17, 340.30: "primo quia omnis usus talis vescibilis presupponit naturale dominium."
112 See *Ibid.*, III, 12 and 17. See also Thomas Aquinas, *Summa Theologiae* 2a–2ae Q.66, a.9.

once promised to all men? We have established that, for the purpose of arguing for the divestment of the sacerdotal class, the equation of natural and evangelical *dominium* is useful. Two possibilities seem likely, then: either Wyclif wants to contrast natural and civil use and lordship to emphasize the artificiality of civil *dominium*, or he thinks that there is an important postlapsarian difference between natural and evangelical *dominium*. The former seems more likely, for it contains an implicit contrast between God as divine lord of Creation and a civil lord, whose power is based on artificed human law. Instances where subjects of human law suffer want indicate the limits of human lordship. On the other hand, God's *dominium* is encompassing enough to provide for all the needs of all Creation. The second possibility is difficult to support, given Wyclif's equation of natural and evangelical *dominium* throughout the rest of the book.

Is there some sense in which we can connect natural and civil *dominium*? We have enough instances of how the two differ: one is created by God, while the other is a postlapsarian institution of man; one is characterized by communal ownership, while the other depends on the institution of civil ownership; in one, use is guided only by necessity, while in the other, superfluity of use is a constant threat. But there must be some sense in which civil and natural *dominium* are related, for just civil *dominium* requires the same Grace that made prelapsarian natural *dominium* just by definition.

Wyclif's assessment is that just civil *dominium* follows on natural *dominium* afforded by Grace insofar as civil ownership will allow a just relation. This seems to be a compromise on Wyclif's part for an institution for which there is no natural justification, likely caused by his recognition of the place of the Christian in the postlapsarian world. As he was writing *De Civili Dominio*, Wyclif had a generally favorable attitude towards mendicant friars, and argued that they had a right to consumptive use of material objects under natural law that arose from the natural *dominium* consequent on their adhesion to *lex Christi*. That is, the friars are naturally unable to recover the *dominium* that was Adam's, but through allegiance to evangelical law exhibited by living according to Christ's example, they can enjoy the sort of communal ownership practiced by the Apostles while remaining in society. This right of the friars to what they consume is not a civil right, though, despite being civil use, which can only be made civilly just by an encompassing instance of civil *dominium*. The friars seem to benefit from civil *dominium*, but only as a supporting context for their natural just use. An example might make this clearer. If Friar William eats some porridge, his use, in order to be "just" in civil terms (which do not necessarily coincide with divine justice), must be authorized by some holder of civil *dominium*. But if a tyrant has given him the porridge, Friar William's use is not thereby unjust. This is not to say that the friar needs the tyrant's permission for just use; under the friar's natural *dominium* his use is just without regard to the tyrant's permission, whether given or withheld. Friar William's *caritas* through his obedience to evangelical law, which suggests Grace, gives him a right to the porridge despite the unjust *dominium* exercised over it by the tyrant. The right to make use of the porridge was not rightfully the tyrant's to give to Friar William; Friar William's right came from his acquired natural *dominium* through his Grace-indicating *caritas*. Is Friar William's use just in the case where the tyrant robbed the porridge from some peasant to make it easier for him to provide for the church? If Friar William colludes with the tyrant and knowingly uses the ill-gotten porridge, there is no sense in which his use is just, for it is founded not in the *caritas* natural *dominium* but in tyranny. If Friar William uses the porridge without knowledge of this, the matter gets more confusing. Assuming Friar William's Grace-favored status and the tyrant's lack thereof, if the robbed peasant is not among the Grace-favored, the friar's claim is likely to be just through its foundation in restored natural *dominium*.[113] If the robbed peasant is among the Grace-favored, it is likely Wyclif would still not condemn the good friar's unwitting consumption of stolen goods, for the robbed peasant who has submitted his will to Christ's cannot suffer from a lack of worldly goods.[114]

This may sound a trifle legalistic, but the principle is clear. There are some cases of legitimate use under just civil *dominium* whose justice is founded on what Wyclif calls "right of Grace."[115] This is based on the resonance of the natural *dominium* regained by evangelical *dominium*, and allows the just to make just use of temporal things despite tyranny. Wyclif speaks as if this is only possible for the Franciscans, but the argument of *De Civili Dominio* plainly points to the entire church as potentially justified by natural *dominium* in civil society.

If such a thing as just civil *dominium* is possible, we are forced to suppose that all of this justification would be unnecessary. That is, the Grace-favored Christian, living according to evangelical law, would be able to make use of eleemosynary offerings over which the Grace-favored civil lord would exercise just *dominium*. It would make little sense to claim that the Christian had just natural use of his *temporalia* because of the justice of the civil lord's *dominium*, for that would make the natural consequent

---

[113] This is extrapolation from *DCD*, I, 3, 28 – 6, 39, and from I, 21, 150–2.
[114] See especially *Ibid.*, III, 7, 94–5.   [115] *Ibid.*, III, 17, 346.9–15.

on the artificial. But neither would it make sense to say that the Christian's civil right to make use of his *temporalia* had nothing to do with the civil lord's just *dominium*. Wyclif seems to be saying that Grace would suffice to justify the civil lord's just *dominium* as well as the Christian's just natural use. Thus it is possible to imagine instances of natural *dominium* in civil lordship.

In summary, Wyclif has shown that in the light of property, civil *dominium* cannot be exercised by evangelical lords or priests because of the risk of detracting from the purpose of the institution of which they are the spiritual stewards. Still, the evangelical poverty that precludes civil ownership among priests can be consonant with Grace-founded civil *dominium* so long as the civil lord's *caritas* affords a caring ownership. That is, just civil lords are just insofar as their ownership is commensurate with the caring owning of evangelical poverty. If they own things and enjoy their use for their own benefit, selfishly, they have surrendered their claim to evangelical poverty. But if they own things and enjoy their use to God's glory, in an unselfish spirit of *caritas*, their mode of having is akin to natural *dominium*, although the means of civil ownership differs.

This is not to say that civil *dominium* is a licit replacement for natural *dominium*, for two reasons. First, Christ's law allows Christians the opportunity to live in the church as did the Apostles, free of civil ownership. At the very least, it requires evangelical lords, priests, to do so. Thus, a viable replacement for the lost natural *dominium* exists in a life of alms gathering, along the *via contemplativa*. Second, Wyclif is tireless in pointing out how dangerous civil *dominium* is; the institution of civil ownership is so conducive to the holder's lapsing into selfish behavior that only the Grace-favored can hope to bear its burden.

Recognizing the absence of true individual ownership among post-lapsarian men is the key to understanding why civil *dominium* should be utterly foreign to evangelical lords. Only God truly "owns" anything, for He alone created everything. Wyclif's doctrine of divine *dominium* makes his position on civil *dominium* and civil ownership clearer, for the civil lord's just holding is only possible with his recognition that he is, in fact, God's steward, rather than a real lord.[116] Wyclif's position regarding the artificiality of civil ownership only makes sense theologically given his argument in *De Dominio Divino*. So long as the civil lord recognizes that his "property" is a loan from God, he will treat it with the care such a loan requires, Wyclif implies; this attitude is in the spirit of evangelical poverty. We have now to see this need for *caritas* in the adjoining

---

[116] *DD*, III, 6, 250.25–9.

operation of civil *dominium, iurisdictio.* Once we have shown how Wyclif's thought on the governing aspects of civil *dominium* is of a piece with his thought on *proprietas,* we will see just how much the civil *dominus* needs Grace. This, in its turn, will bring us nearer to being able to show the unity of Wyclif's position on divine *dominium* and his vision of civil *dominium.*

Chapter 5

IURISDICTIO IN CIVIL DOMINIUM

If Wyclif believes *proprietas* to be antithetical to the evangelical *dominium* of the priests as well as ultimately threatening to the restored Natural *dominium* of the Elect, how can he argue that a civil lord, the chief owner in society, is an instrument of God's justice? Wyclif's answer to this will show how he believes the king, the primary civil lord of the kingdom, can bring about a just society for the church and for his kingdom as a whole.[1]

IURISDICTIO IN DE CIVILI DOMINIO AND DE OFFICIO REGIS

Wyclif's views on secular earthly power, to which he refers as either kingship or civil *dominium*, appear mainly in *De Civili Dominio* (1375–76) and in *De Officio Regis* (1379), two non-consecutive treatises of his *Summa Theologie* (1375–81). His account of the more practical concerns of rule is brief; Wyclif offers no programmatic advice to rulers, no well-developed plans for class-harmony in the realm, no schemes for the increase of monarchic power in the world. If his discussion of monarchy is comprehensible only by conceiving it as an outgrowth of his theological and metaphysical assumptions, why did he treat it as a separate concern? Why not view it as an outgrowth of Wyclif's more theoretical concerns? One might also ask why Wyclif devotes two separate treatises to the subject in his *Summa*. Why has he paid such close attention to secular power, and why has he lavished so much attention to showing its superiority to ecclesiastical authority?

Wyclif's discussion of monarchy is interesting precisely because he treads the middle path between purely theological speculation and hardeyed political prescription. He wants not only to show the need for immediate purification of Christ's body on earth, but also to show its

---

[1] The term "king" is equally applicable in every instance of our use of the word "civil lord," as Wyclif believes the class of kings to be a subset of the class of civil lords.

likeliest means, without becoming tangled in associated details. Wyclif's portrayal of civil *dominium*/kingship as the means to that reformative end can be divided into four major topics, including the nature of law and *ius*, how the lord–subject relation can be just in a postlapsarian state, the nature of kingship, and the problems of royal succession and tyranny.

Wyclif's thoughts on the origin and nature of law, and the relation of civil to ecclesiastical law, as well as his conception of *ius*, or what is right, lie at the heart of his conception of civil *dominium*. The subordination of the earthly church to the king suggests that what ought to be rendered unto God ought first to be rendered unto Caesar, which apparent danger Wyclif must eventually address. To understand how he will do so, we should first examine his picture of the relation of God's justice to created justice. His discussion of the relation of *ius* to law and of the types of human law in *De Mandatis Divinis* provide a basis from which we can understand how men can justly dominate one another. This will show a further cohesion between *De Dominio Divino* and the works we are examining, for *De Mandatis Divinis* is the second treatise of the *Summa Theologie*, written just before *De Civili Dominio* and just after *De Dominio Divino*.[2] The value of Wyclif's treatments of law and *ius* lies in their evidence of Wyclif's conviction that God's *dominium* is inextricably connected to just (or real) human *dominium*. The arguments of *De Dominio Divino* are important to understanding man's attempts at justice and the systems of jurisprudence that men rely upon in the postlapsarian world. Wyclif's belief in the lack of conflict between Christ's law and truly just secular law, and his mistrust of canon law, will further show his desire that monarchy be understood as an outgrowth of divine lordship.

How can a thinker who believed that men were created to be equals, who (unlike Fitzralph) believed there to have been no distinctions between men in Eden, have advocated the secular lord–subject relation as a likely vehicle for divine justice?[3] Wyclif admits that monarchy is not the ideal state in which to live, but the Fall has made necessary, and Grace has made possible, a just lord–subject relation. Just earthly *dominium* appears to develop as Wyclif's argument develops; in some cases it seems a benign and non-intrusive relation, predicated more on seigneurial responsibility than on the lord's ability to dictate his will to his subjects, while in others its authoritative aspect is more evident. Wyclif emphasizes the doctrine of stewardship in *De Civili Dominio* in his characterization of civil

---

[2] See W. R. Thomson, *The Latin Writings of John Wyclyf* (Toronto, 1983), pp. 46–8.

[3] For Fitzralph's belief that, even before the Fall, some men would have been pre-eminent over others, see *De Pauperie Salvatoris*, in Wyclif, *De Dominio Divino*, ed. R. L. Poole (London, 1890), II, 27; I, see also Walsh, *A Fourteenth-Century Scholar and Primate: Richard Fitzralph at Oxford, Avignon and Armagh* (Oxford, 1981), p. 393.

dominium, but does not in *De Officio Regis*. Has Wyclif embraced a more absolutist strain of monarchy in the later work, or do stewardship and *caritas* remain important? Given that the human *dominium* portrayed in *De Civili Dominio* and *De Officio Regis* is, when just, instantiative of divine *dominium*, we should be able to describe the relation that encompasses both its stewardly and authoritative elements.

Wyclif's view of monarchy as the seat of final mundane *proprietas*, and of the extent of the king's *iurisdictio*, suggests principal royal duties, and how the king should carry these out. Ultimately, the king's chief duty is the governance of the church, and each topic Wyclif mentions regarding the origin and nature of monarchy is tied to this goal. The king must eradicate a host of evils in the church, and the erring clergy have thrown up a multitude of obstacles to impede him. Their chief weapon, Wyclif explains, is the doctrine of *plenitudo potestatis*, and excommunication is the means by which this weapon is wielded. Wyclif's arguments against this relate directly to his thought in *De Dominio Divino* on the impossibility of one man having more power by nature than any other. Also important is the eradication of perpetual grants and mortmain, the chief means by which the errant church has gained and held so much worldly wealth. At this point two possible stumbling blocks arise for a theory in which the king reigns through personal spiritual excellence: how to find such an individual, and what to do if something goes wrong with the office-holder's spiritual excellence. Wyclif pays particular attention to the problems of royal succession and the specter of tyranny, although his conclusions fall noticeably short of the practical standards of other fourteenth-century political thinkers like Marsilius of Padua or William Ockham.

An objection might be that Wyclif's *dominium* theory can as easily suggest an aristocracy in which a group of benevolent, Grace-favored lords rule in concord as might suggest monarchy. After all, the "lord–subject" relation defines the foundation for a generic aristocracy as much as it does monarchy. But Wyclif will reject interpreting "*dominus*" to mean an aristocrat. Natural *dominium* does indeed entail an aristocracy in which no one lord is superior to another but, as we will discuss, such a relation is impossible in postlapsarian civil society. The concord of a benevolent aristocracy was a possibility in the time of the Judges, but Wyclif believed it to be no longer possible.

Wyclif's picture of just postlapsarian secular government illustrates how his doctrine of civil *dominium* emerges from his discussion of *dominium* as such in *De Dominio Divino*, and provides a means by which Wyclif believed the needed ecclesiastical reforms could be carried out. This elucidation of the tie between the theory and practice of *dominium* will help to resolve questions about the specter of absolutism in *De Officio Regis*; if the first book of *De Civili Dominio* is a definition of civil *dominium* contingent upon the theology of *De Dominio Divino*, *De Officio Regis* is an articulation of the defined in terms of the fourteenth-century English *status quo*.

IUS AND LEX

Understanding what Wyclif thinks about *ius*, or what is right, and *lex*, the law which classifies and organizes what is right, will help in analyzing his arguments for the justice of a lord–subject relation founded in civil *dominium* and its accompanying jurisdictive duties.[4] In his thought on *ius* Wyclif shows how what God wills corresponds to *ius* in Creation, supporting the idea that his causal universal defines the relation of divine to human *dominium*. While Wyclif's description of this relation between created and divine *ius* does not explicitly express the universal-particular relation between divine and human *dominium* in *De Dominio Divino*, it certainly supports this interpretation. If Grace-founded civil *dominium* instantiates divine *dominium*, it must be an articulation of divine *dominium*. This makes it an expression of God's will, in accord with what God knows to be right. Therefore the *ius* of Grace-founded civil *dominium*, itself expressed through the civil lord's *caritas*-directed *iurisdictio*, is not merely imitative of, but a part of, uncreated *ius*. We have already discussed the difference between the active and passive species of *iustitia*, noting that the lesser active justice, a qualitative accident of Grace-ful beings, is just by participating in the perfect active justice of God. Wyclif believes justice to be founded in the creature living in accord with what is right (*ius*), so to understand justice we must first understand *ius*.[5]

Wyclif describes *ius* and *lex* in *Tractatus de Mandatis Divinis*, which Thomson believes that he wrote in late 1375, just after finishing *De*

---

4 For a general introduction to *ius* and *iustitia*, see Richard Tuck, *Natural Rights Theories: Their Origin and Development* (Cambridge, 1979), pp. 5–31; Quentin Skinner, *The Foundations of Modern Political Thought* (Cambridge, 1978), vol. 2, pp. 113–34; A. S. McGrade, "Right, Natural Rights, and the Philosophy of Law," in *The Cambridge History of Later Medieval Philosophy*, ed. A. Kenny, N. Kretzman, and J. Pinborg (Cambridge, 1982), pp. 738–56. For discussions of Wyclif's conception of right in the context of other later medieval rights theories, see Annabel S. Brett, *Liberty, Right and Nature* (Cambridge, 1997), pp. 72–6, which relies primarily on *De Civili Dominio*. James Muldoon, "John Wyclif and the Rights of Infidels," *Americas*, 3 (1980), pp. 301–16, examines the relation of Wyclif's theory of right to the conquest of the Americas, while my "Wyclif on Rights," *Journal of the History of Ideas*, 58 (1997), pp. 1–20, explicates Wyclif's theory as an instantiation of "objective" right. For Gerson's criticism of Wyclif's concept of *ius* as it relates to *dominium*, see Brian Tierney, *The Idea of Natural Rights* (Atlanta, 1997), pp. 228–35.

5 *Tractatus de Mandatis Divinis*, ed. J. Loserth and F. D. Matthew (London, 1922), I, 1.7: ". . . iusticie que est huius dominii fundamentum."

Dominio Divino.[6] While its purpose is primarily to show the obligative power of the decalogue, there is much in *De Mandatis Divinis* relevant to his description of civil *dominium*. Noting that Isidore calls *ius* a general name, used when something is just, Wyclif begins by explaining that the relation of *ius* to *iustitia* is not necessarily immediately evident.[7] To show that *iustitia* is an effect of being in accord with right, *ius*, Wyclif describes three senses of the term *ius*. First, it describes any created state of subjugation, including the use of the subject, and anything that should be so according to reason. Secondly, it is used to describe the power of a lord to use something/someone (a right of use). Finally, it is used to refer to the uncreated eternal truth paradigmatic for all (created) *iustitia*, "which some call the art of the fair and the good, and some say that it is a holy sanction, which commands the honest and forbids the opposite, but some more completely say that *ius* is the constant and perpetual will granting to each what is his own."[8]

Can this constant and perpetual will be anything other than *ius*? Here Wyclif extrapolates from Justinian's *Institutes*, where the emperor begins with the working Roman definition of *iustitia* just given.[9] It is likely that Wyclif reasons that if created *iustitia* is founded in a constant and perpetual *voluntas* in men, the uncreated and purer divine *iustitia* must be founded in the divine will. If so, and if one reads Justinian's definition "constans et perpetua voluntas ius suum cuique tribuens" as presupposing a *ius* which is each person's due, it is natural to conclude that God knows as He wills what is each person's due. This would make *ius* at least contemporaneous with divine willing, and certainly prior to *iustitia*, the perfect willing's effect.

Iustitia, Wyclif explains, is usually defined as a moral virtue, or habit, and because the divine will is essential to God's nature, not a habit,

---

[6] Thomson, *The Latin Writings of John Wyclyf*, p. 45. This may be too late a date, for Wyclif makes only a muted reference to the respective spheres of influence of sacerdotal and royal *iurisdictio*. That he does not refer to the duty of the civil lords to reform the church, an idea prominent in *DCD*, in a work reputedly written at roughly the same time, given Wyclif's propensity for lusty repetition of common themes, leaves one suspicious of the dating. Perhaps *De Mandatis Divinis* was written earlier in 1375. Nevertheless, Wyclif's doctrine that the civil lord has temporal superiority over sacerdotal power is present this early in his writing, presumably directly after the completion of *DD*. See *De Mandatis Divinis*, 26, 380.35–381.14.

[7] *De Mandatis Divinis*, 1, 8–10. See PL, vol. 82, p. 199.

[8] *Ibid.*, 1.13–2.6: "Et tercio accipitur ius pro veritate increata omnem creatam iusticiam exemplante; quam quidam vocant artem equi et boni; et quidam dicunt quod est sanccio sancta, precipiens honesta et prohibens contraria; sed quidam dicunt complecius quod ius est constans et perpetua voluntas tribuens unicuique quod est suum."

[9] Justinian, *Corpus Iuris Civilis*, vol. I, *Institutiones*, ed. Paul Krueger (Berlin, 1963), I.i.1: "Iustitia est constans et perpetua voluntas ius suum cuique tribuens. Iuris prudentia est divinarum atque humanarum rerum notitia, iusti atque iniusti scientia."

ius must be prior to and causative of *iustitia*.[10] But Wyclif eschews the Aristotelian definition of *iustitia*; the Aristotelian version of *iustitia* could possibly direct uncreated *ius*:

All created justice is a virtue of a rational creature, but it comes under the power of no creature to grant each his right, so this description does not match created justice; indeed, if it matches with any justice, it would be uncreated justice, in which the right, the just, and pure justice coincide.... This, then, is the order: from right, which is the simplest and the first rule, it is by the virtue of justice that the rational creature is formally just. And by... [this objective right] the works of men are just, thus a human work is just by justice, as justice [is just] by right.[11]

One might ask why, if in God the just, the right, and justice are identical, created justice would be causally dependent on the uncreated right and not on the uncreated justice, leaving talk of "right" out of the picture. Wyclif has made it clear that all that is just in Creation happens because God wills that it happen.[12] While *what* happens is just, *that* it happens is right, since God knows and wills that it happen, which knowing and willing is the uncreated right.[13]

It is not surprising that Wyclif argues that created standards of right are as nothing in comparison to uncreated right, given his description of the all-encompassing nature of God's *dominium* in *De Dominio Divino*. What stands out is his reference to *ius* as a just instance of subjugation of something/someone and anything that should be so according to reason, and also as the power of *dominium* or use. This suggests in one case a diversion from the traditional Aristotelian objective right as it appears, for example, in Aquinas, and in the other a potential sensitivity to the idea of the subjective *ius*, described by Marsilius as an act, power or habit.[14] Could both of these references be to Aristotelian objective *ius*? Perhaps the first sense, a created instance of just subjugation, including the subject's use as reason dictates, is in accord with Aquinas' description of *ius* or *iustum* as "commensurate with another person according to some sense

---

[10] *De Mandatis Divinis*, 2.7–16.

[11] Ibid., 2.17–3.2: "Item, omnis creata iusticia est virtus creature racionalis, sed nullius creature potestati subiacet unicuique ius suum tribuere; ergo dicta descripcio non competit create iusticie; immo si alicui iusticie conveniat, hoc erit iusticie increate, in qua ius, iustum atque iusticia mere concidunt; et per consequens dicta descripcio iuri primo convenit. Iste ergo erit ordo: a iure, quod est simplicissima ac prima regula, infunditur creature racionali virtus iusticie, qua ipsa est iusta formaliter. Et ab hiis simul dicitur denominacione extrinseca opus hominis esse iustum, sic quod opus humanum fit iustum a iusticia, sicut iusticia fit a iure."

[12] See *DD*, I, 10, 74.5ff.

[13] See *De Mandatis Divinis*, 1, 4.15–5.2. Compare Thomas Aquinas, *Summa Theologiae*, 2a2ae, 57.1.

[14] See Marsilius of Padua, *Defensor Pacis*, ed. Richard Scholz (Hannover, 1932), II, 12, 10.

of fairness."[15] But what sort of "created truth" justly exercised is important: the use of the term *servum* suggests *dominium*. Aquinas describes the *dominium*-relation as being a special kind of *ius*, detracting from the *ius* and *iustum* of the lord and the servant. The only way Wyclif's first description of *ius* can align with Aquinas' definition of objective right is if Wyclif saw *ius* as exclusively dominative, which diverges from Aquinas' theory. It makes more sense to interpret this first description as a state of affairs between the holder and those over which the relation is held that is "right" because it is exercised justly. Wyclif's reference to justice as a habit could correspond to this description; were someone to ask how the relation could be exercised justly, the response would be that *ius* came from the practice of the moral virtue of justice on the part of the holder. This would make the phrase "et quicquid racionabiliter debet esse" suggest an objective right in that the created nature or state of affairs is ordered according to some outside standard, namely reason. But Wyclif has already argued that justice is founded not in some artificial system of thought, but in the perfect justice of uncreated *ius*. The reference to justice as a habit is not his final word on the topic; in fact, Wyclif believes such a description to be inadequate for true justice. So his first description is of a rationally formulable created state of affairs commensurate with the *ius* of God's will. In short, what is truly right or just in man's affairs depends on what is divinely right or just.

The second description is different; here, *ius* is a lord's power to use. This might suggest the movements towards modern, subjective rights that Brian Tierney reports of the canonists.[16] In this case, individuals holding *dominium* are free either to use or not to use that over which they exercise *dominium*. There are no strictures; Wyclif does not add, "according to the established laws of use regulating such *dominium*," nor does he say, "in accordance with God's will." He does restrict it to people who are lords, which is no longer a universal condition but, since anyone *might* be a lord with Grace, this is no evidence against a subjective right. For now it is enough to note how the second description of *ius* implicitly refers to property-ownership, or the *proprietas* in *dominium*, and that this description could conceivably be understood as a kind of subjective right. Since Adam's Fall, Grace has been needed to have this power, and since Wyclif devotes much more attention to Grace as the primary foundation for *dominium*, we cannot conclude that he has based his *dominium* theory on the basis of subjective rights in any significant sense.

---

[15] *Summa Theologicae*, 2a2ae, 57.2: "Dicendum quod, sicut dictum est, jus sive justum est aliquod opus adaequatum alteri secundum aliquem aequalitatis modum."
[16] See Tierney, pp. 629–38.

The next step is to explain how properly to use the term *ius*, which he does in Chapter 3 of *De Mandatis Divinis* by showing that all conceptions of created right rely on uncreated right.[17] He begins by making use of the distinction between *ius in re* and *ius ad rem*, asserting the canonists' dictum that "it is impossible to have a right to a thing unless you already have a right in a thing."[18] All rational creatures as subjects of the divine will can only have things by right and title through God's willing, which is the most powerful right. "If the giving of a temporal lord makes the receiver have the right [to the gift] from the giver, how much greater is the giving of the Lord of lords."[19] This remark about a lord's giving refers to Wyclif's discussion of the directive force of God's giving, and of the reliance of all created acts of giving upon it as a necessary cause in *De Dominio* III, Chapters 1 and 2.[20] When we discussed this earlier, we noted that God's act of giving to His subjects does not detract from His own *dominium*, and is the only means by which any creature can have existence, the most fundamental of properties.[21] If this is so with existence, it must be the case with any right a creature might have to use or exercise *dominium* over another. So in order to have a right to use or *dominium*, one must first have been given this use or *dominium* by God in His eternal willing.[22] Wyclif likens this reliance of man's use and *dominium* on the divine act of giving to the relation of steward to master. "Just as the steward of a temporal lord, in distributing the *dominium* on behalf of his lord does not strictly grant anything, but dispenses it, so it is with the giving of any creature."[23]

This reference allows him easily to distinguish *ius* from *dominium* by claiming that *ius* causally precedes *dominium*; one cannot have *dominium* over something without first having a *ius in re*. What of those who object that this precludes any creature from either acquiring or destroying his right, since that he has it is eternally established in the divine will? Wyclif assumes his readers are familiar with his discussion of the

---

[17] The second chapter is a discussion of how useful this conception of the uncreated, objective right is in interpreting Scripture, and does not contribute importantly to this discussion.

[18] *De Mandatis Divinis*, 3, 15.20–3: "[L]icet ius ad rem ac ius in re tanquam antecedens et consequens distinguantur, impossibile est tamen aliquem habere ius ad rem, nisi habuerit ius in re pro suo tempore et econtra."

[19] *Ibid.*, 3, 16.1–3: "Si enim donacio domini temporalis facit ius donatorio ad donatum, quanto magis donacio domini dominorum."

[20] See especially *DD*, III, 1, 199.19: "Unde omne donum concedendum est a Deo procedere."

[21] *DD*, III, 2, 207.15–25.

[22] See my discussion in Chapter 3 of Wyclif's idea that the predication of the Aristotelian categories is reliant on the divine nature, especially the predication of having being reliant upon God's "having-relation" to creation of *Tractatus de Universalibus*, 10, 680–3.

[23] *DD*, III, 1, 206.7: "Sicut ergo dispensator terreni dominii manualiter tradendo dominia domini donantis proprie non donat ea tam proprie, sed dispensat; sic est de donacione cuiuslibet creature."

non-deterministic nature of God's perfect knowing in *De Dominio Divino*, I, Chapters 14–19.[24] There, his distinction between absolute necessity – truths which cannot not be – and necessity *ex suppositione* – truths having an eternal cause from which their temporal being flows formally – allows Wyclif to hold that God's knowing and willing are necessary *ex suppositione*, and so not fatally deterministic. Wyclif concludes that people can deserve, through Grace, just use of possessions, and power to that use, both of which differ from *dominium*.[25] Not that Wyclif is suggesting that people cannot deserve *dominium* through Grace; he is demonstrating how *ius* and *dominium* are distinct, and here he has shown that people can merit non-dominative rights to things through God's having given them rights in things.

Wyclif notes that he has used three senses of the term *ius* in the context of this discussion:

Three kinds of right are ordained essentially: the right which is divine willing, the right which is power over the usable, and the right which is use. The second of these cannot exist unless the first precedes it eternally, nor can the third exist unless the second precedes it in time or in nature.[26]

This is a reordering of the three senses of *ius* noted above; now that the applicability of these senses is clear, he appears to be saying, we can arrange them in the proper order. In this formulation Wyclif distinguishes between the ability to use or to forbear from using an object and the object's use by referring to the right which is power over the usable and the right which is use. It is possible that Wyclif did not have this distinction in mind when he listed the uses of *ius* in Chapter 1, for both of the first two senses in the first description are formulated to distinguish between potential and actual use. Still, the second sense in the earlier list looks like "power over the usable," and "use" in this section might be what Wyclif had in mind by "an instance of just subjugation." It is best to take this reformulation not as having superseded the earlier list, but as having explicated aspects of it.

Now that the causal necessity of uncreated *iura* for just law-making is clear, it remains to consider whether Wyclif believes that just legislators can create laws that would establish just, created (objective) *iura*. That is, if uncreated right is necessary for the law-makers to legislate justly, do the created, objective rights resulting from their legislation have any claim to

---

[24] See *DD*, I, 14–19.   [25] *De Mandatis Divinis*, 3, 16.20–24.

[26] *Ibid.*, 3, 16.24–8: "Patet eciam quod ista tria iura essencialiter ordinata sunt; ius quod est volicio divina, ius quod est potestas ad usibile, et ius quod est usus; sic quod secundum non potest esse, nisi primum eternaliter precesserit, nec tercium potest esse, nisi secundum precesserit tempore vel natura."

the justice of that legislation? Given that created rights based in human legislation not guided by Scripture cannot be just, can any created right be just? Wyclif addresses this in the final section of his discussion of how to use *ius* properly in political discourse.

So long as created *ius* is regulated according to uncreated *ius* it is an expression of divine will. If created *ius* is an articulation of divine will, it is because it agrees with uncreated *ius*, which is God "essentially, personally, and notionally, as is said of divine willing, [and] of divine love and Grace."[27] But if the necessary condition for justice in created *ius* is its foundation in uncreated *ius*, who may establish whether a given created *ius* is so founded? As already indicated, only the Grace-favored are capable, suggesting that a ruler's subjects who are not Grace-favored are incapable of realizing the justice of his actions, which means that government by universal consensus is out of the question.[28] But it would also suggest that anybody who is Grace-favored might assess the quality of the ruler's legislation. Wyclif suggests that the Grace-favored would likely be concerned more with spiritual perfection than with the mundane concerns of civil legislation.[29]

Created *ius* has proved to be divisible by those not aware of the priority of uncreated *ius*, and Wyclif ends his discussion of rights with a brief summary of these divisions. This summary is in concert with the medieval Aristotelian approach to the division of created civil power, and the unwary reader might presume Wyclif to be beginning his exploration of man's justice and *dominium* from an Aristotelian standpoint. This presumption is easily dispelled by bearing in mind Wyclif's low opinion of the Aristotelian view of justice as moral virtue. One might explain created *ius* in two ways, he begins; the first is by dividing the kinds of *ius* according to the different nations in which they appear. Some rights are Roman, while others are Athenian, and still others are English. But this explanation is of no use, for it is a confusion of variation and contrast.[30] More useful is a description based in the rhythms of created nature. At its most basic, created *ius* is what philosophers recognize as governing the development of life in the world. Among men, an underlying body of *ius* is recognizable, the *ius gencium*, whereby all agree that it is right for people to live virtuously, to marry for procreation, and to live socially and politically.

Less generally defined is the final species of created *ius*, whereby man's reason or the natural law provides for the regulation of estates, cities, and

---

[27] *Ibid.*, 3, 23.5: "Et sumitur tale ius nunc essencialiter, nunc personaliter, et nunc nocionaliter, ut dictum est de voluntate divina, de caritate et gracia."
[28] See *DCD*, I, 18, 130.6–14.   [29] See *De Officio Regis*, 6, 133.16–30.
[30] *De Mandatis Divinis*, 3, 23.23–7.

kingdoms in conformity with the primary right. The conclusions of this regulation are called economic, civil or political right. Politics may be aristocratic, democratic, or oligarchic, according to whether the rulers are guided by virtue or wealth, by nobility or by popular election.[31] Philosophers are capable of dividing the political laws that come from these varying methods of rule into common, or public, and private laws. Of these divisions Wyclif has nothing more to say in this discussion, referring his reader to the third book of Aristotle's *Politics*.[32] Wyclif's contempt for political thinking that does not take uncreated *ius* as necessary for created objective right is manifest. Why, then, this reference to the types of government described in the *Politics*? It is possible that he had not yet developed his monarchism when he wrote *De Mandatis Divinis*, but more likely that he felt the need to avoid framing the discussion of the decalogue that was to follow in exclusively monarchist terms, given the relatively late development of kingship in the history of the nation of Israel. Wyclif's view of rights, involves, then, a created right being wholly reliant upon the *ius* of divine will. An individual has a *ius* to *usus* or *dominium* only if God wills that the individual have the *usus* or *dominium*. Man-made systems of assignment or division of rights unfounded in God's revealed will are fictions in which true *ius* appears only accidentally.

Armed with the notion that human legislators can achieve *iustitia* only if their legislation participates in *ius* and is commensurate with divine will, we should be able to distinguish between the various types of laws for men. This will give us an idea of what civil lords have jurisdiction over, and allow us to see the more quickly how true, Grace-favored civil *dominium* is just. Wyclif makes reference to six different sorts of law: divine, natural, Christ's, evangelical, secular human, and ecclesiastical human law. Wyclif never takes the time to explain how each sort of law is related to every other, but we can construct a sufficient system of relations given in his expressed opinions to understand which sorts of laws should prevail over others, and which he believes to be without important foundation.[33] *De Civili Dominio* begins with the dictum that civil *ius* presupposes divine *ius*, and we have seen how God's *ius* serves

---

[31] *Ibid.*, 3, 24.20–3. The ordering of kinds of government and what guides their rulers is Wyclif's, not Aristotle's in *Politics* III, 7, to which Wyclif refers.

[32] Wyclif makes occasional references to these Aristotelian themes, but only to illustrate his own, non-Aristotelian ideas. For example, *DCD*, I, 27, where he discusses aristocratic polity as being ideally suited for men in a state of nature, but impracticable for post-lapsarian men; also *DCD*, III, 20, for a cursory discussion of the relation of *ius gencium* to civil law.

[33] In *DCD*, III, 13, 239, he explains that evangelical, natural, original and Grace-endowed *dominium* are synonymous, distinct according to reason only; it does not necessarily follow that the bodies of law correspondent to these types of *dominium* are likewise the same. For his initial discussion of the types of law, see *DCD*, I, 18, 124–31.

as the foundation for all that is right in Creation. Our interest here is to see how secular human law can fulfill God's justice, and our needs will be served if we can see how it can be commensurate with Christ's law.

Christ's law is characterized by its central tenet, which is *caritas*, and the nature of this law is discoverable in the teachings of Christ and the example of His earthly life.[34] Wyclif uses the term evangelical law as a synonym for *lex Christi*, usually in contrast with secular or ecclesiastical human law. The best explication of the differences between evangelical and canon law appears in *De Civili Dominio*, I, xviii, "Divine law is instituted by God alone, explained through Christ's law and actions as evangelical law."[35] Our invented laws regulating the life of church members tend to emulate civil, not evangelical law, yet perniciously assume the dressing of the latter.

The problem with canon law is that its attention to the church's material concerns distracts from theological knowledge. The clergy should obey secular human laws as part of their subordination to temporal lords, and Wyclif sees no need for a separate ecclesiastical authority in these matters. "[I]f papal [canon] law resounds against God's law, or against the just laws of a secular prince, the rest of the church must dispense with them . . . whenever a civil law, canon law, or any rite distracts or impedes *simpliciter* from theological knowledge, it should be superseded by both branches of the church [secular and sacred] together."[36] Wyclif has scant regard for the utility of canon law, since either secular human law or the evangelical law of *caritas* should supplant it; continued attention to this branch of law traps the church deeper in the mire of property-fed sin.[37]

Secular human, or civil, law can have two uses: first, it can provide a basis for secular life for all people, and secondly, there are times when it augments evangelical law.[38] All human laws should be founded in evangelical law, which functions as the directive exemplar.[39] Just civil law, like just civil *dominium*, must be not only consonant with the divine will,

---

[34] *Ibid.*, I, 15–17.

[35] *Ibid.*, I, 18, 125.2: "Ius divinium est ius a solo Deo institutum, per christum verbo et opere explanatum, ut lex ewangelica."

[36] *De Officio Regis*, 7, 191.14–31: "Secundo videtur mihi quod si lex papalis sonuerit contra legem dei, vel contra leges iustas secularium principum, per residuum ecclesie debet tolli . . . [V]idetur mihi quod ubicunque terrarum ius civile, ius canonicum, vel ritus aliquis distrahit vel impedit simpliciter a theologie noticia, ipsum est ab utroque brachio suspendendum."

[37] *De Officio Regis*, 9, 221.30–222.3; 7, 179.29–180.21; 7, 189.30: "Unde ergo racio inutiliter onerandi ecclesiam fidelium cum lege superflua?" Despite his disdain for canon law, Wyclif relied upon it heavily for precedents in his arguments for the elimination of ecclesiastical property and reform of the clergy. See William Farr, *John Wyclif as Legal Reformer* (Leiden, 1974), pp. 95–138.

[38] See *De Officio Regis*, 7, 192, for encouragement of theologians studying civil law consonant with God's will; the notion of a king justly relieving the clergy of the ownership that has encumbered the church is surely an instance of civil law augmenting evangelical law.

[39] *DCD*, I, 20, 139.1–2: "Ex istis patet quod totum corpus iuris humani debet inniti legi ewangelice tamquam regule essencialiter directive."

but actually an expression of it. "It follows then that civil or human law is the law which ordains what is best for the protection of temporal things for the welfare of the republic, to protect wills from unjust disruption of it, and for their wise administration in times of necessity."[40] It is likely that Wyclif believed the chief purpose of civil law to protect material things, for "human laws which are made because of transgressions would be impossible in the state [of innocence] because no one would transgress . . . there would be no disagreement, for all would be held in common."[41] This further indicates Wyclif's equation of *proprietas* and *iurisdictio* with civil *dominium*.

The civil lord's primary responsibility is to Christ's body on earth, and to that end, all men, church members and non-members alike, should be able to live harmoniously in a society in which the former can live under Christ's law while non-members are not so obliged. Church members can expect to enjoy the freedom to live under the perfect law, so only for them does the civil lord serve as a governmental "parent." Since no one can accurately identify the Grace-favored, it is likely that Wyclif would have the king treat all who would be numbered among the church members as members; non-members will reject apostolic poverty as too mean a life. When Wyclif speaks of the distinction between church members and non-members it is to distinguish between the Elect and the Damned. While the just, Grace-favored have things through God's gift, the Damned have them as squatters; civil law rules both the just and the unjust, without regard to their being Grace-favored.[42]

The compelling force of civil law is worth closer examination, as Wyclif shows in his discussion of the relation of the monarch to the law. Is the civil law so strong as to bind the actions of the king as well as those of his subjects? The first half of the answer will show how Wyclif distinguishes between coercive and voluntary compulsion (Wyclif's distinction between the king as an individual and as the embodiment of the law will emerge in our treatment of kingship). We must distinguish between the sense of the compelling force of law as the embodiment of reason and truth, binding all people, including Christ on earth, as well as the king, and the sense of law as contracted "through *civilitatem*," instituted by men

---

[40] *Ibid.*, I, 18, 129.4–9: "Sequitur ergo quod ius civile vel humanum . . . est ius ordinans ydoneum ad custodiam temporalium pro utilitate reipublice, ad refrenandum voluntates ipsam iniuste dirrumpere, et ad sagiciter ministrandum illa in necessitatis tempore."

[41] *De Statu Innocencie*, 4, 499.4–16: "Et quoad leges humanas que propter transgressores sunt posite, patet quod in statu cui impossibilis fuisset transgressio non fuissent . . . Ex quibus patet quod non forent placita innocentium nec quevis rebellio, nam non est possibile aliquos velle opposite, nisi alter inordinate vel in penam peccati ignorancia sit cecatus; quorum utrumque statui innocencie repugnaret."

[42] *DCD* I, 38, 282–3; I, 9, 65.

in civil *dominium*, in which sense the king is the founder of his law.[43] One can be subject to a species of law by virtue of the force of that law, or because a higher law requires obedience to that law.[44] The first is a coercive, compulsory force, while the second is voluntary. "In the first sense . . . all Christians are subject to the law of Christ, and in the second way Christ the man Himself is subject to His own law."[45] The king is subject to civil law through his obedience to the higher, divine law, and not by the binding force of the law he creates, although he is not coercively compelled by civil law through being compelled by Christ's law. Since his compulsion by Christ's law is in accord with his own will, his compulsion by civil law is wholly voluntary. Thus the monarch is the connecting agent between civil law and natural, and hence divine, *ius*.

This model makes all men equal through their universal non-voluntary obligation to obey *ius gentium*, and to obey the divine law as instituted in Scripture. As described above, all church-members are compelled by Christ's law non-voluntarily, which makes them equally bound to its dictates, from pope to lowliest convert. This underscores the superfluity of a separate canon law and the impiety of viewing the sacerdotal office as having powers for the enforcement of evangelical law beyond the powers of non-clerics. While Wyclif makes little use of the coercive-voluntary distinction in his call for ecclesiastical reform, the principle's consistency with his overall approach is unmistakable. His treatment of kingship will illustrate the ideal relation between Christ's law to civil law, and since Wyclif's thought on the just subjection of people to a lord is the foundation of his conception of just kingship, it warrants some preliminary attention.

THE LEGITIMACY AND UTILITY OF CIVIL *DOMINIUM*

Our earlier discussion of property and its evils suggests that any dominative relation in which something or someone is exclusively subject to another according to postlapsarian private ownership is morally questionable. How, then, can Wyclif envision any civil lord–subject relation

---

[43] *De Officio Regis*, 5, 93.92.

[44] W. Courtenay argues that this distinction is founded in the doctrine of *potentia absoluta et ordinata*, noting that papalists held that the pope *de potentia absoluta* is not bound by the fundamental laws of the church, but that he binds himself to them *de potentia ordinata*. Wyclif does not frame his argument with this language, although the sense of his argument is consonant with the papalist use. See W. Courtenay, "The Dialectic of Divine Omnipotence," *Covenant and Causality* (London, 1984), pp. 1–37; also his *Capacity and Volition* (Bergamo, 1990), pp. 87–103.

[45] *De Officio Regis*, 5, 94.7: "Primo modo omnis Christianus subicitur legi Cristi, et secundo modo ipse Cristus humanitus subicitur sue legi."

to be just? After all, the relation lacks the equality and mutual harmony of Natural *dominium*, and Wyclif has made an extensive case for Christ not having been a civil lord. Showing how Wyclif believed that a civilly dominative relation could be commensurate with divine law will enable us see in a later section how Wyclif's vision of kingship is an instantiation of divine *dominium*.

The dictum with which *De Civili Dominio* begins is: "Divine law is presupposed by civil law; Natural *dominium* is presupposed by civil *dominium*."[46] In both *De Civili Dominio* and in *De Statu Innocencie*, Wyclif describes divine *dominium* as directly providing men with the Natural *dominium* described in Genesis. This relation is untrammeled by private ownership, and all who participate in it have their needs fulfilled with the unrestricted use of temporal goods made possible by harmonious communal ownership. Wyclif believes this to be infinitely expandable, for "Natural *dominium* on account of its spirituality excludes no one," is inabdicable, and inalienable by its holders.[47] Its inabdicability is because Natural *dominium* is founded in Grace, which provides for the sustained maintenance of Natural *dominium* in a Natural lord who bequeaths a portion of his lordship to another. That is, if Adam wanted to share something with Eve, he could easily have done so without having to worry about having thereby surrendered his natural claim to the shared object. Grace simply makes sharing effortless. Sin makes this harmonious state impossible for people to maintain on their own, and requires the institution of civil *dominium*, which is equivalent to private ownership, and the social structure consequent upon that institution.

The Fall brought with it a change in what ideal government involves. There are two sorts of rule: first, the natural rule of an aristocracy according to the laws of God, and second, the rule of a monarch, according to the laws of men. The ideal polity of an aristocracy would be preferable, for it is most like what people enjoyed in a state of innocence, is most consonant with the laws of Christ, and is most consistent with the correct workings of the Church Triumphant (i.e. the church as it will be upon Judgment).[48] The benefits of the rule of a benevolent aristocracy, whose members would live a contemplative life, would be manifold, for

---

[46] *DCD*, I, 1, 1.5: "Ius divinum presupponitur iuri civili/ Dominium naturale presupponitur dominio civili."

[47] *Ibid.*, I, 18, 126.14: "dominium enim naturale propter sui spiritualitatem aliud non excludit." Also, *De Statu Innocencie*, 6.

[48] Perhaps in Eden, since no one was subject to anyone else, a kind of polity ruled. This is unlikely, though, because there was no human law, no disagreement, and no need for the cultivation of arts or virtues in Paradise (see *De Statu Innocencie*, 4–8). Possibly Wyclif's affection for aristocracy is due to his belief that the Elect today function as a spiritual aristocracy in the world; among themselves, they live with equanimity and harmony, as did men in paradise.

communal living would be facilitated and the likelihood of governmental corruptibility would be remote. This seems to contradict Wyclif's indictment of non-monarchical government in his arguments against the rule of the many. Why espouse kingship as the most likely of postlapsarian paths to good government when a benevolent aristocracy remains an option?

The Old Testament description of the time of Judges suggests that such a benevolent aristocracy was realizable, for the will of God was enacted by judicial enactment of divine law without the office of kingship. "[P]eople subject to temporal lordship, or a king, are more likely to put their faith in man, setting aside the worship of God taught by judges [or an aristocracy], making them irreligious and impious like the gentiles."[49] Wyclif's biblical reference may suggest that a benevolent postlapsarian aristocratic rule is possible, but he believed the rule of the Judges to have been an anticipation of the apostolic community of the church; the success of a secular aristocracy is forestalled by the incompatibility of human law and human will, as we will see.

Wyclif's most complete picture of the harmonious aristocracy of Natural *dominium* is in *De Statu Innocencie*, written in mid-1376, probably in the midst of his work on *De Civili Dominio*.[50] The state of innocence is the state of the rational nature free from sin, which is not necessarily limited to the Edenic time.[51] Christ enjoyed this state, and it was the partial state of some saints, if they lived for a period free of sin. If men had remained in this state, or if they could return to it, sin would not dog their wills, and a benevolent aristocracy might again be possible. Actually, human government would be superfluous, for no one would transgress any sort of law, and everyone would have all that they need.[52] *De Statu Innocencie* is helpful in its connection of ownership with *dominium*, for Wyclif explains in it that those who doubt that people enjoyed complete communal ownership should gain a good understanding of it, and its related topics, ownership and community.[53] It is further useful in showing the place of aristocracy in Wyclif's political thought: it is less a potentially viable option than it is a description of what the ideal human society is in the terms formulated in response to the Fall, which made the ideal effectively unattainable. From the outside looking in, the society connected with Natural *dominium* seems like an aristocracy, but because

---

[49] *DCD*, I, 27, 194.20–4: "Et causa innuitur ex hoc quod populus recognoscens terrenum dominium, sive regem, est pronior ad ponendum spem in homine, et dimissa latria docta per iudicem, fiant irreligiosi et inpii sicut gentes."
[50] *See* Thomson, *The Latin Writings of John Wyclyf*, pp. 47–8.
[51] *De Statu Innocencie*, 1, 475.12–21.   [52] *Ibid.*, 4, 499.4–9; see also 3, 491.15–18.
[53] *Ibid.*, 6, 505.9–20.

secular lordships entail coerced commoners, Natural *dominium* cannot really be an aristocracy, because there are no commoners, no coercion, and most importantly, no sin. If everyone is an aristocrat, it is hard to label the society an aristocracy. Christ's redemption makes the restoration of Natural *dominium* possible, but only for those foreknown to be worthy to enjoy it.[54] We have shown earlier that the ecclesiastical lord should be a stranger to civil *dominium*, and with a spiritual sphere of influence should aim for the cultivation of spiritual purity sufficient among those subject to it to allow them to regain Natural *dominium*.[55]

A more general element to consider is Wyclif's opinion on the sort of life men should enjoy, and what they are constrained to endure. Throughout his writings on the plight of postlapsarian humanity, Wyclif distinguishes between the contemplative and the active life. People were created to enjoy the contemplation of God in Natural *dominium*. The Fall introduced worry about the acquisition of foodstuffs and so forth, so humanity was forced to abandon its former, more intellectually satisfying lifestyle in favor of an active life. Along with Natural *dominium*'s freedom from the need to have property, Christ's redemption provided a return to the contemplative life; the present state of ecclesiastical disrepair is due to clerical participation in the active life rather than the more peaceful life for which they were meant. One cannot live as did Christ, Wyclif insists, unless one embraces the *vita contemplativa*.[56] Thus, Grace-founded civil lords in the active life should provide for the clergy so that they can regain a life free of the concerns of the mundane hurly-burly. This clerical reform, Wyclif contends, will benefit not only the clergy: the king will benefit from more clear-headed advice from the clergy on matters requiring their talents. Further, *iustitia* will be the more widespread not only because of the well-advised rule of the king, but also thanks to an absence of ecclesiastical private ownership. Finally, the congregation of the church will benefit from the clergy's improved instruction and exemplary behavior.[57]

RECIPROCITY IN *DOMINIUM*

Whenever Wyclif discusses *dominium* as such, it is always primarily in terms of having or owning; from this, talk of *iurisdictio* follows. In *Tractatus de Universalibus* Chapter 10 Wyclif identifies having as an Aristotelian

---

[54] *DCD*, I, 9, 62.9–13: "homo in statu innocencie habuit dominium cuiuslibet partis mundi sensibilis (ut patet tractatu secundo, capitulo–), et virtute passionis Christi est iustis plena peccatorum remissio ac dominium restitutum; ergo iam tempore gracie habet iustus plenum universitatis dominium." Note: *iustus* is translatable both as "just" and as "righteous."

[55] *DCD*, I, 11, 73.24–74.12.   [56] *Ibid.*, I, 23.   [57] *De Officio Regis*, 4, 73–5.

predicable fundamental to all being.[58] Wyclif explains that Aristotle is accurate in a general sense, but as a pagan unfamiliar with the truth of Scripture; his description ignores the difference between prelapsarian, communal having, and postlapsarian private ownership. The Grace-favored civil lord, who has custodial ownership for the community, enjoys the best postlapsarian civil having.[59] The civil lord must recognize that his position is artificial, and that all men are properly lords and servants of one another. This is naturally evident from the relation of body to soul, for each serves the other thereby strengthening the whole. Thus, provided the individual is in a state of Grace, Justice is maintained.[60] In the evangelical law, more reflective than human law of what is right in God's eyes, all Christians, that is, church-members, are respectively lords and ministers to one another, for all are equal before God. Thus, evangelical lordship and servitude mutually follow upon one another, just as lordship is reciprocally related to servitude in body and soul.[61] We have already indicated that civil law is just insofar as it embodies divine *ius*; so it must also be for civil *dominium*.[62] The just civil lord recognizes that he is God's steward, rather than an autonomous sovereign, as Wyclif explains in his proof that man's grants are just only insofar as they embody the divine will:

Similarly all men are simply stewards, servants, and bailiffs of God, as is clear in *De Dominio Divino*. But bailiffs, who should always act in the name of the Lord, do not bestow [*donare*] goods [on their own] which the lord himself has arranged and commanded. Likewise men cannot legitimately give [*dare*] God's gifts without God having already bestowed them, for it follows that if a creature fittingly receives a gift, God has bestowed it, entailing that God's nature as donor is prior to humanity's as stewardship.[63]

The essence of any just lord–subject relation is this reciprocal relation of stewardship; in civil *dominium*, artificed human law has made the lord God's bailiff to care for his charges as divine steward. A. S. McGrade has noted the significance of this, suggesting that Wyclif's conception of how this reciprocity is realized politically is neither conventionally egalitarian, as Aristotle suggests in 1277b13–15, nor is it a hybridized "two swords"

---

[58] 15b17–30. See also the earlier discussion of Wyclif's interpretation of this final category in *Tractatus de Universalibus*.

[59] *DCD*, I, 18, 128.28–129.8.   [60] *Ibid.*, I, 11, 78.1–5.

[61] *Ibid.*, I, 11, 75.15–76.7.   [62] *Ibid.*, I, 5, 37.9–38.1.

[63] *Ibid.*, I, 36, 259.20–9: "Similiter omnis homo est pure prestarius, accommodarius, et balivus Dei sui, ut patet de Dominio divino, capitulo – ; sed balivus non donat bona que dominus accommodat sibi et precipit in nomine suo tribuere; ergo nec homo, qui debet in nomine Domini facere quidquid facit. Similiter non est possibile hominem dare donum Dei legitime recipienti nisi Deus ipsum prius donaverit; cum sequitur, si creature digne recipit donum aliquod, tunc donat ipsum Deus, et per consequens prius natura Dei est donacio quam est creature ministracio."

argument.[64] Instead it is a relation between Christians, requiring the secular lord to be as much his subjects' servant as their master, inasmuch as all true Christians are each other's "good Samaritans." It also requires that all secular subjects are as much their lord's true masters as they are his subjects, insofar as each Christian has regained mankind's once lost Natural *dominium*.

McGrade notes that Wyclif's explicit references to this reciprocity are few, but, because Wyclif emphasizes that Christ's redemption provides Adam's birthright of communally harmonious contemplation to the Grace-favored Elect, this reciprocity is reinforced. The reader must define just *dominium* as a relation in which lord and subject are terms comprehensible only with reference to the sort of *dominium* involved. Is the lord–subject relation under discussion civil or natural? A just civil lord is responsible for and to his subjects, among whom are Christians, true Natural lords, to whom the just civil lord is an equal, as much fellow-lord as fellow-subject. Wyclif's belief that the just civil lord's primary responsibility is to the church, and especially his arguments for divestment of clerical private property, are based on this reciprocity. The church is the living body of Christ, the community in which Natural *dominium* has been re-established; in making its well-being his first priority, the civil lord is subjecting himself to the Natural lords that comprise it.

Wyclif's writings suggest little reciprocity in the secular political lord–subject relation, for he uses political language to describe relations between a lord and all his subjects, Christian and non-Christian alike. Seen as a secular lord, the just civil lord is responsible to all his subjects insofar as he is God's steward. But from an even clearer vantage point, the civil lord is truly the servant of the Natural lords, the Christians in his realm. The class of the Natural lords includes all the Grace-favored, among whom must be numbered the just civil lord. So, in a sense, the civil lord as Natural lord is his own, secular master, insofar as he is responsible for the well-being of the church, and, as secular lord, his own servant, as a member of that church.

There could be a difference between a just basis for any coercive authority and the personal justice of someone exercising that authority. Are we implicitly shifting from talk of just civil *dominium* to talk of the just civil lord, and does this conflate the two? In an earlier chapter we made reference to the possible redundancy in the phrase "just civil *dominium*"; talking about civil *dominium* as "just" suggests that unjust civil *dominium* might be a concern for Wyclif. In one sense it is important, for the

---

[64] A. S. McGrade, "Somersaulting Sovereignty: *A Note on Reciprocal Lordship and Servitude in Wyclif*," in *Church and Sovereignty*, ed. D. Wood, *SCH* Subsidia 11 (London, 1991), pp. 261–8.

Christian in society may have to deal with a civil lord who rejects *lex Christi*. A tyrant may call himself a civil lord, without being one in the true, Grace-favored sense. In these cases, as we shall see, Wyclif says that the Grace-favored in society must serve the tyrant, either by obeying him as an embodiment of God's just punishment or, interestingly, by rebellion.

In another sense, "unjust civil lord" is an oxymoron, since Grace alone founds true civil *dominium*. So "just civil *dominium*" is shorthand for "the class of human *dominium*-relations by which Grace brings about justice in the postlapsarian world." It is one thing to speak of justice in founding the general construct "civil *dominium*," but talk of whether individual holders of that *dominium* are just is something different. Are we talking about the class or about members of the class? If we are right in viewing the class as a collection of particular instantiations of God's causally universal *dominium*, there is no problem in eliding from talk of just civil *dominium* to talk of a just civil lord. When we conceive of the class of instantiations that we call "just civil lords," we mean nothing more than the collection of individual civil lords, all of whom are members of the class because they are Grace-favored. What Wyclif wants to explain about all the members of this class of just civil lords can be expressed equally well in talk of "just civil *dominium*" and "the just civil lord," for there are no unjust civil lords, and just civil lords are not just in different ways.

There are two *dominium*-relations in any instance of just civil *dominium*, each of which involves reciprocity between lord and subject. We shall call the secular just civil *dominium*-relation A, and the Natural *dominium*-relation B.

A1. The civil lord is master of his subjects, church members and non-members, and is enabled by Grace to rule justly through jurisdiction founded in *lex Christi*.

A2. The civil lord is subject to his subjects, church members and non-members alike, insofar as he must put their needs before his own, and is answerable for their welfare to God.

B1. The civil lord is master of subject church members – who are themselves also Natural lords (along with the just civil lord) – as their material protector and facilitator of their apostolic communalism.

B2. The civil lord is subject to subject church members, for, as both the civil lord and the subject church members are Natural lords, any church member is subject to a fellow Natural lord under *lex Christi*.[65]

The reciprocity of the A relation is founded in, and reliant upon, the B relation, for B is the more natural relation, and more consonant with *lex*

---

[65] *DCD*, I, 11, 75.15–78.6.

Christi, and Wyclif's guiding theory is that no human law is just unless it is founded in divine (in this case, Christ's) law.[66] If the civil lord were not both master and subject to his fellow Natural lords, he would be flouting Christ's law, which would preclude his receiving Grace. Without Grace, he could not be a just civil lord to any of his subjects.

The priority of the B relation explains Wyclif's contention that the civil lord's chief responsibility is to the welfare of the church in his realm. B1 is recognizably the foundation of Wyclif's arguments in favor of the secular divestment of the clergy, which underlies *De Civili Dominio* and *De Officio Regis* as the chief concern for the just civil lord. B's priority thus explains Wyclif's relative inattention to the more customary topics for discussion in political theory. The civil lord's reciprocal relation to the other Natural lords in his realm is the necessary condition for his just civil *dominium*, itself reciprocal, over all of his subjects. Since civil *dominium* follows upon Natural *dominium* insofar as private ownership allows of a just relation, it follows that the artificial civil *dominium*-relation, to be just, needs to be related in some way to Natural *dominium*, the natural relation. That relation is the B relation, which makes the justice of the A relation real. Our discussion of *iurisdictio* in civil *dominium*, then, must be predicated on Wyclif's vision of civil *dominium*'s connection to Natural *dominium*. This will make Wyclif's version of the secular lord–subject relation more than a delineation of secular power and authority; it is an aspect of just human *dominium* in general.

Another way to see the relation of ideal *dominium* to the civil variety is to examine Wyclif's views on the nature of the liegeman, or what it is to be a royal subject. Wyclif defines a royal liegeman as "being subject to the king's rule."[67] This includes two groups: the class of people who are from birth subject to the king's law, and the sub-class of those who hold private property subject to the king's rule. It is easy to imagine an individual subject to two kings, Wyclif says, for someone might own property in two different kingdoms.[68] This is not contradictory to the nature of subjection, for since the only true mastery is that exercised by God, the liegeman of two kings does not sin in serving both; he may serve one king in one sense, and another in a different one. So long as neither king exacts a servitude contrary to divine *ius*, the

---

[66] *Ibid.*, I, 5, 37.33ff: "[N]ullum civile dominium est iustum simpliciter, nisi in naturali dominio sit fundatum."

[67] *De Officio Regis*, 8, 198.32–199.3: "Hic videtur mihi quod homo legius regis potest dici quicumque homo regis qui subicitur legi regis, sic quod ista non consecuntur se, homo legius regis et homo a nativitate subiectus regis legibus, cum hoc regi conveniat et multi alienignene deveniunt legii regum terre, multique diffidant vel extraneant a rege suo nativo."

[68] *Ibid.*, 8, 199.5–9.

dual servitude is licit. We should note that property-holders owe service because it is on the liege-lord's authority that the property is lawfully held. It appears that Wyclif believes this authority to be equivalent to being voluntarily compelled by the law. That is, only a civil lord holding final authority in a realm by God's Grace can exact service as a liege-lord.

Regarding the kinds of servitude, Wyclif provides an example of the most extreme kinds of servitude. When a master is unfaithful to just laws, the subject still owes service, but need not follow the master into error. The service owed might be rendered by rebelliously resisting, through which the subject instructs, and thereby serves, the lord. There are even cases where the service due a tyrant is tyrannicide, but Wyclif does not pursue this, using it only as the most extreme example of the different sorts of service possible. It is difficult to believe that Wyclif means this to be taken normatively, for he uniformly counsels submission to tyranny in his more sustained discussions of the topic.[69]

Ideally all members of the clerical classes, including cardinals, foreign curates, and papal familiars, are subjects of the liege-lord in whose land they practice, for they enjoy his protection.[70] This is also true of the pope with respect to the Emperor, despite the Donation, which Wyclif rejects as a mistake which the clergy had no business accepting. "Just as Christ was liegeman of Herod and Caesar, so all His imitators must, in their poverty, be liegemen to their king."[71] Priests have some degree of *iurisdictio* in being able to imprison and punish the king's subjects for spiritual reasons, namely heresies, but they are nonetheless subject to royal authority. Elsewhere Wyclif holds that the king is responsible for rooting out heresy.[72] Who should be the "spiritual police," then, the priests or the king? So long as the priests themselves are spiritually pure, they have immediate responsibility, but in the end it falls upon the king, because the priests are his subordinates. All punishments, including spiritually motivated ones, carried out in the king's realm are the responsibility of the king, the authority for which he may delegate to servants lay or clerical, according to the duties relevant to their offices.[73] His business is to ascertain that his servants carry out their duties, just as a majordomo,

---

[69] *Ibid.*, 8, 201.3–18; see also *DCD*, I, 28, 199–201; I, 6, 43, as well as my discussion below.

[70] *De Officio Regis*, 7, 163.7–164.27; 8, 201.32–204.24. From this it follows that resident aliens are as much subjects of the lord of the realm as are the lord's subjects. "Quantum ad alienigenas, eciam cardinales, videtur mihi quod quamdiu licenciantur a rege calcare solum suum, habere vescibilia regni sui, et tenentur moderare se ne offendant in legem regis vel regnum, sunt homines legii talis regis." (8, 203.23–7.)

[71] *Ibid.*, 8, 203.3–6: "Sicut ergo Cristus fuit legius Herodiis et Cesaris, sic debent exproprietarii eius conversacionem propinquius imitantes."

[72] See *Ibid.*, 9, 229.18–21.   [73] *Ibid.*, 9, 205.14–20.

whose first responsibility is to his lord as chief steward, must oversee the lesser stewards' work.[74]

As has been shown, the only truly legitimate servitude is to God; all other types fly in the face of natural law, for "all men naturally desire freedom, which could not be unless freedom were natural law, and thus God's law."[75] Wyclif now gives a novel argument for servitude, in the light of its apparent unnaturalness. Christ's law enjoins that we love one another, and the civil lord should love his subjects accordingly. But everyone, including the civil lord, Wyclif has noticed, has a natural aversion to anything resembling servitude. Thus, Wyclif explains, Christ's law as exhibited in the *caritas* of a lord for his servant makes servitude beneficial for both lord and subject. Subjects are loved by their lord through his provision for their well-being, and the lord is loved by his subjects in return, all because Christ's law breathes *caritas* into the lord–subject relation, making the unnatural consonant with divine *ius*.

At first this makes it seem as if the Romans had been right to sneer that Christianity is the religion of slaves. But the Fall has robbed man of the capacity to act freely and correctly; unrestricted action coupled with a fallen will results in sin. Thus the Christian can gain more in servitude, especially of a just kind, than in postlapsarian liberty, for "it is the will of God that Christians be in service to temporal lords, not for their [the temporal lords'] sake but for Christ's sake, who counsels humility, patience, and obedience."[76] This implies that Christians ought ideally to serve a just lord, although Wyclif suggests that servitude of any sort is beneficial as a "bridle to pride and disobedience." The *caritas* of a civil lord makes him just, ensuring not only that subjects gain spiritually from their subjection, but that this opportunity does not vanish quickly:

[T]hus lords must love their servants as they love themselves, for there is no *caritas* without the universal love of Christ... they should not exact service from them unless this is to their benefit or brings merit to lords or others.[77]

---

[74] This is Wyclif's analogy, from *DD*, III, 6.

[75] *DCD*, I, 32, 227.14–16: "Confirmatur ex hoc quod omnis homo naturaliter appetit libertatem, quod non esset nisi libertas esset de lege nature, ergo et de lege Dei." The servitude Christians owe one another is not servitude in the same sense, because they are also equally one another's lords.

[76] *DCD*, I, 32, 230.8–10: "Ecce quod de voluntate Dei est quod Christiani serviant terrenis dominis, non finaliter gracia illorum, sed gracia Christi qui precipit humilitatem, pacienciam, et obedienciam."

[77] *Ibid.*, I, 32, 230.27–35: "Sed quoad dominos, oportet indubie quod sint in caritate, quia aliter non forent domini alicuius; et per consequens oportet secundo quod diligant servos ut se ipsos, quia sine universali dileccione christi non inest caritas... non exigerent ab eis ministerium, nisi eis utile vel ad suum vel alterius meritum."

Lest we interpret this argument as viewing *dominium* as an end in itself, Wyclif reminds us that *caritas* requires that a lord treat his servant as he would himself be treated:

The Christian lord should not desire subjects for love of dominating, but especially for the honor of God, for the correction and spiritual improvement of his subjects, and so for building up the church . . . [they] should treat them more gently than gentile lords or Old Testament fathers, unless they are forced into greater severity through obstinate rebelliousness, which is dangerous for men to gauge.[78]

Servitude is no badge of shame, but its demands should be borne with the equanimity exemplified by Christ's life. Christ's law allows men to regain the goodness of being human with which Adam was created, and since the greatest goodness is the generosity that characterized Natural *dominium*, subjection to a just civil lord seems to be the best means by which one can regain one's Edenic birthright. The real abasement of men is enslavement to the World, the Flesh, and the Devil, under which the Damned suffer.

The civil lord is a steward of God, participating in divine *dominium*.[79] In doing this, he is carrying out God's will, as a vehicle of Grace, in all jurisdictive actions. If, as we discuss the secular mechanics of civil *dominium*, we lose sight of the true place of the just civil lord actively engaging in fulfilling divine *dominium*, we might forget that the civil lord functions primarily as a facilitator of the Natural *dominium* restored through Christ's redemption, leading us to expect the wrong thing from Wyclif's discussion of civil *dominium*. If we view Wyclif as having written about civil *dominium* as an end in itself, his treatment will seem wanting. But if we succeed in viewing civil *dominium* as Wyclif envisions it, as a participation in God's caritative *dominium*, the centrality of the relation of king to church will make sense. The lord–subject relation is, for Wyclif, more than a political relation between people; it is a theological relation between people under God.

---

[78] *Ibid.*, I, 32, 231.18–33: "domini Christiani non debent appetere servitutes propter libidinem dominandi, sed specialiter propter honorem Dei, ad castigandum vel proficiendum spiritualiter servis suis, et per consequens ad edificandum ecclesiam: . . . cum domini debent racionem reddere de custodia et quacunque negligencia circa servos, et sic micius tractarent eos quam gentiles domini vel patres Veteris Testamenti; nisi forte ex rebellione obstinati plus severitatis exigerent, quod grave est homini iudicare cum fastus seculi excecat iudicium."

[79] *De Officio Regis*, 3, 58.20–27: "Deus autem omnipotenter mundum creat correspondenter ad patrem, sapienter creatum inesse conservat correspondenter ad filium, et conservatum in suo esse benivolenter in suo processu gubernat correspondenter ad spiritum sanctum. Correspondenter rex debet facere proporcionabiliter quo ad corporalia comissa suo regimini, debet enim legios suos in gradibus suius statuere, in bonis nature eos defendere, et tercio quo ad bona temporalia eos in suo iure provide gubernare". See also *De Officio Regis*, 1, 10.24.

Chapter 6

ON KINGSHIP

De Officio Regis reveals what Wyclif believed to be the place and duty of the king in the postlapsarian world, and explains some aspects of his thought that were under-developed in *De Civili Dominio*. The title *De Officio Regis* may lead one to expect Wyclif to give a more recognizably practical description of kingship in the treatise than he does, but it is no "mirror of princes." Wyclif was firmly committed to uncovering the connection between the *a priori* truth of divine justice and its created instantiations, and has scant interest in the daily mechanics of royal administration. The work follows *De Ecclesia* in Thomson's chronological ordering of the tractates of the *Summa Theologie*, and was written in mid-1379.[1]

The treatise is divided into twelve chapters, of which the first five explain Wyclif's belief that secular monarchs are ordained by God to reform and hold temporal *iurisdictio* over the church. In the first chapter, Wyclif begins with God's having ordained two vicars in His church: a king acting as vicar of God the Father with final authority in all temporal matters, and a priest acting as Christ's vicar with final authority in spiritual affairs. That the king's authority is over *temporalia*, while the priest's is over spiritual matters means that the sacerdotal dignity is of a higher nature and superior to royal dignity. But this elevated authority does not translate into a temporal authority beyond the king's; in every temporal affair, the king's authority is complete.[2] The second chapter continues in this vein, concluding that priestly tyranny's likeliest characteristic is a desire for the acquisition of temporal authority. This is more monstrous than any king's abuse of power because of the respective depth to which the priest has fallen.

The third chapter introduces the three central aspects of the king's duties: he is a private property-owner before God, *paterfamilias* of a royal household, and lord of the realm. To reign well the king must strive in each of these tasks for *iustitia* imitative of, and ideally participative in,

---

[1] W. R. Thomson, *The Latin Writings of John Wyclyf* (Toronto, 1983), pp. 60–1.
[2] See *DOR*, I, 13–17.

divine justice. In resolving possible problems with this, Wyclif explains that the compelling force of the law is different for subjects than it is for a king. While the king is not bound to obey his law, he must voluntarily observe his law as a mark of his service of the higher, divine law. To ensure success, Wyclif advises moderation in regulating commerce, a rare instance of practical political advice.

The remaining seven chapters slowly bring the argument to the chief duty of the king. As lord of the realm striving to institute divine justice in human law, the king must provide for the right operation of the church and the pastoral mission of its officers.[3] To facilitate the fulfillment of this duty the king must rely on a coterie of theologian-doctors, whose job it is to help the king to avoid allowing affronts to Christ's law in the realm. This is the only form of council Wyclif advocates; he mentions the royal household and its stewards on occasion, and parliament not at all. The reason for this lies no doubt in his vision of the nature of the power of a civil lord. God's own rule is unmediated, and since just civil *dominium* is comprehensible as an instantiation of divine *dominium*, the king's rule must also be unmediated. Wyclif does not suppose that the king can carry out every single jurisdictive duty that follows from his rule, and allows for royal stewards to act in the royal stead. This is consonant with his overall *dominium* theory, for the royal stewards are analogous to the place of civil lords in divine *dominium*.

To govern the church the king needs bishops as royal stewards. Wyclif advises that bishops form synodical councils subordinate to the king, and suggests that their first business should be the strict regulation of clerical abuses such as pluralism and absenteeism. Although excessive canonical regulation of ecclesiastical matters detracts from the church's purpose, which is to serve as a community wherein Natural *dominium* is realized, Wyclif says little about the church's purpose in *De Officio Regis*. This has been more thoroughly argued in *De Civili Dominio* and *De Ecclesia*, the work's immediate predecessors.

Wyclif then defines the liege-relation to make all priests liegemen to their king, again illustrating his rejection of an hierarchic power structure and emphasizing the universal–particular relation of divine and temporal *dominium*. A consequence of the liege service all priests owe their king arises from Wyclif's tireless references to excommunication, and the impossibility of its being used against the royal office. Because the only true act of excommunication can proceed from God, among men it can only

---

[3] *Ibid.*, 6, 121.9–14: "Nec dubium quin prinipes sunt necessariores ad defendendum ecclesiam contra inimicos eius domesticos, qui venientes ut clerus in vestimentis ovium rapiunt subdole bona pauperum, quam ad defendendum ipsam contra exteros inimicos."

be just provided that God has already performed the excommunication. The temporal authority's duty to the protection of the church is better suited for wielding this weapon than is the more nutritive sacerdotal power. By Chapter 10 it is clear that Wyclif sees that papal use of excommunication to protect clerical temporal authority is unimpeachable evidence of the need for immediate reform of the church.

By the end of the work Wyclif has formulated three conclusions for the government of a kingdom consonant with divine law. First, the king must use his bishops as a means of ecclesiastical governance. Next, the king must provide for his own good counsel by fostering the theological sciences. Finally, he must respect the theological doctors' advice to be sure he conforms to the law of the church. These are exaggeratedly focused conclusions, given the work's broad title, and they assume that the reader has realized that the chief royal duty is less to the realm than to the church in the realm. Despite appearances, Wyclif has not strayed from royal duties as such, for he has already held that just rule is only possible with Grace, and that successful participation of human justice in divine *iustitia* requires that the king protect Christ's body on earth from temporal corruption. This means that all justice in the realm depends upon the smooth functioning of the church. This has been intimated in *De Civili Dominio*, with the introduction of the idea that *lex Christi* is the sure path to true justice. The church is the only means by which *lex Christi* can be realized, so a rightly ordered church is the necessary condition for secular human justice. All of the practical matters that follow, Wyclif implies, will do so in a fashion that is self-evident, if not to the king, then certainly to his enlightened theological advisors.

WYCLIF'S VIEW OF KINGSHIP

Wyclif does not present his prescription for kingship in the fashion of Marsilius of Padua, who examines monarchy in measured Aristotelian tones. Instead, we must piece together Wyclif's picture of kingship from *De Civili Dominio* and from *De Officio Regis*, in which Grace-founded monarchy is primarily a means for the realization of the church's reformation, and secondarily for the kingdom's well-being. In the latter chapters of the first book of *De Civili Dominio*, Wyclif explains that civil society relies on a particular ordering of its participants separating inferior from superior. This ordering is reliant for its institution and maintenance upon a single power base, a king. Even if there were many people exercising *dominium*, living together in a republic, a king would still be necessary, "otherwise there would be no order in the implementation of political acts, if all had equal power."[4] Civil order is founded in the natural order, which also requires a single source of authority and direction; just as the form of the body gives order to its matter and regulates it, so it is with a king and his people. Further, a strong central authority is needed to deal with rebellion, secular and civil; for which purpose a king is ideal:

Since the king is the minister of God, according to his corresponding eminent degree of virtue, it is clear that the king should rule in accord with the divine law by which people are ordered. Since it is the part of justice to decline from evil and to do good, the king should coerce rebels against divine law and other authorities, and advance what brings about justice according to the rules of *caritas*. It is clear from this that kings have the power from God of ruling subjects as a minister. There is no regulation of men if not, so they have the power from God to do this.[5]

Thus Wyclif begins his discussion of kingship in *De Civili Dominio*. His differences with the Aristotelian tradition are obvious, for he makes no reference to the purpose of civil government's being to facilitate individual virtuous action, although this would certainly be an effect of Wyclif's monarchy. Rather, kingship is a natural institution needed to maintain social cohesion and order through law enforcement. Individuals must rely upon the king's interpretation of *iustitia* and his personal *caritas* for their own enjoyment of earthly justice.

One does not encounter the familiar Aristotelian ordering of means to ends, of justice as a function and goal of government, or of society as a medium for leading the virtuous life. Wyclif's first authority instead is Augustine, whom he reports as explaining kingship's purpose as, first, sanctioning laws consonant with divine laws, secondly, destroying laws contrary to divine law, next, compelling the people to serve God, and finally, pacifying the people by preventing internal and external threats.[6]

---

[4] *DCD*, I, 26, 186.1–5: "Si enim multi fuerint in populo dominantes, sed illis concurrentibus pro regimine reipublice, necesse est esse aliquem principalem; quia aliter non foret ordo in execucione actus politici, si omnes forent simpliciter equeparium potestatum." Wyclif says that the aristocracy of the Old Testament judges was superior to monarchy because the people were not tempted to put their faith in a man, but in the body of law (*Ibid.*, I, 27, 192.22–4; 193.8–10). But Wyclif implies that this aristocracy of the judges could not last even with God's chosen people; so, as far as secular government goes, monarchy is best at providing the necessary principle of rule in the postlapsarian world.

[5] *Ibid.*, I, 27, 188.14–24: "Cum ergo regis sit ministerium Dei, secundum eminenciam virtutis gradui correspondens, patet quod regis est regere secundum legem divinam homines regni sui; et cum partes iusticie sunt declinare a malo et facere bonum, patet quod rex debet rebelles divinis legibus et aliis subministrantibus cohercere, et factores iusticie secundum caritatis regulas promovere. Patet ex hoc quod reges habent a Deo potestatem subiectos suos ministraliter regulandi; non est regulacio hominis, si non ista: ergo habent a Deo potestatem ut illud faciant."

[6] The reference is to Augustine's *Epistola CLIII*, vi, 19.

A king can only be successful in achieving these goals, Wyclif adds, by making *caritas* the chief characteristic of his reign.

The third purpose, compelling people to serve God, requires us to extrapolate from what Wyclif wrote to address the possibility that he advocated a state in which all subjects are required to be law-abiding Christians. While he may have thought that this would be ideal, it is hard to envision him requiring all citizens to live as the Apostles did, completely obedient to Christ's law. The king serves God by obeying his own legislation, while the people are compelled to serve God through their service of the king. So long as the king's laws are consonant with *lex Christi*, the people can be said to be compelled sufficiently to serve God. There need not be a compulsion to live by Christ's law, but only to live according to a civil law that allows the Grace-founded to voluntarily subject themselves to *lex Christi* without hindrance.

In contrast with a more Aristotelian model for the justification of monarchy, which would be founded in the principle of justice, Wyclif's model for justification of monarchy is founded in the principle of divine authority. We get a more complex justification in the opening of *De Officio Regis*, but one founded in divine authority just the same, although in this case it is not based on the operation of divine law but on the verity of Scripture. God's word has been misinterpreted to justify clerical secular authority, Wyclif warns, but, because the clearest picture people can get of the truth is from this source, we must counter this tendency to misinterpretation, whether willfully or accidentally motivated.[7]

Human *dominium* rightfully exercised is sustaining and nourishing, in imitation of God's lordship; so the king is an image of God in temporal affairs, just as a bishop is Christ's image in spiritual concerns.[8] In fact, Wyclif says, because the king must rule justly in allegiance to Christ's law, the king is as much Christ's vicar as any bishop, if not more so:

It is right for God to have two vicars in His church, namely a king in temporal affairs, and a priest in spiritual. The king should strongly check rebellion as did God in the Old Testament. Priests ought to minister the precepts mildly, in a humble manner, just as Christ did, Who was at once priest and king.[9]

A difficulty is Wyclif's claim that Christ was king, for earlier he had denied that Christ was a civil lord. How could He have been king without having

---

[7] *DOR*, 1, 10.13–21.

[8] *Ibid.*, 1, 12.27; here Wyclif relies upon Augustine's *Quaestiones ex Vet. Test.* 11 (CCSL, vol. 33 [Turnhout, 1958]).

[9] *DOR*, 1, 13.2–8: "Oportet ergo deum habere in ecclesia duos vicarios, scilicet regem in temporalibus et sacerdotem in spiritualibus. Rex autem debet severe cohercere rebellem, sicut fecit deitas in veteri testamento. Sacerdos vero debet ministrare preceptum miti modo humilibus tempore legis gracie sicut fecit humanitas Cristi, qui simul fuit rex et sacerdos."

had civil *dominium*? Christ alone among postlapsarian men enjoyed true Natural *dominium*, making His *iurisdictio* free from proprietary concerns. So from the standpoint of Fallen humanity, Christ's authority as a man was describable only in terms sensible to the Fallen; since only a king exercises the sort of authority prelapsarian people enjoyed in their communal state, Christ was a king. In all other cases in which godly kingship and priesthood intersect, Wyclif says, as with Melchizedek, the individual was first king, and accidentally a priest. His authority was founded in goods of fortune, while his priesthood followed, presumably from Grace. Sacerdotal dignity is spiritually founded, so those living according to the *lex Christi*, who should be free of private ownership, have a dignity superior and foreign to the temporal version. Just as Christ was at once human and divine, the two branches of earthly authority correspond. The bishop, bearer of spiritual authority, corresponds to the humanity of the Incarnation through the gentleness of his ministrations, while the king corresponds to the Incarnation's divinity through being an image of God's lordship on earth.[10] The king is vicar of Christ the heavenly king, while priests are vicars of Jesus the man; here Wyclif is refuting the papal hierocrats by turning on its ear their chief justification for papal fullness of power, that the pope is vicar of Christ. But this is not an approach which Wyclif follows with any seriousness, aside from referring to it to underscore the need for clerical subordination to secular powers. Regarding the king's duties, Wyclif appears to have two distinct agenda in *De Officio Regis*, for in the beginning he describes them in general in terms of kingdom, people, and *res publica*, yet by the end of the work the chief duties have switched to being reformative of the church.

Wyclif begins his definition of kingship in *De Officio Regis* with a familiar patriarchal association of manhood, fatherhood, and kingship, each being an iteration of the former with a progressively wider scope.[11] That is, a man as a private owner serves his possessions, as a father his family, and as a king his domain. What Wyclif has in mind is just *dominium* in its most unadorned, unpolitical sense, a just *dominium* founded in Grace, characterized by *caritas*. To be a good king, then, one must first be a good

---

[10] *Ibid.*, 1, 13.10–12.

[11] *Ibid.*, 3, 46.8–14: "Et patet quod eius officium stat in tribus, scilicet in regendo personam propriam in quantum homo, in regendo suam privatam familiam in quantum pater familias, et in regendo suam rem publicam in quantum rex. Quantum ad omnia ista simul patet quod omnia illa reducuntur ad unum analogum quod est Deo servire commune cuilibet creature." Here Wyclif is in fundamental opposition to Aristotle, who says, "Some people think that the qualifications of a statesman, king, householder, and master are the same, and that they differ not in kind but only in the number of their subjects. . . . But all this is a mistake; for governments differ in kind . . ." (1252a7–25).

person, by obeying the evangelical law of the true church. As father the king should follow Christ's example in providing care for his family members, to include the extended family of the royal court. In this sense the king should provide firm guidance and support to all of those who serve him, both secular and spiritual members alike.[12]

Of special interest here are priests, who must assist their liege in instructing the members of his household in the laws of God by teaching and example. "It is neither sufficient nor helpful that they be the king's daily table companions, but they should prudently watch over the king and instruct his sheep and . . . if any difficult questions arise, all should be able to rely on the advice of the priests."[13] Wyclif stipulates as well that the priest should restrain the soldiery from excess. The king must oversee the priests, as a father does his children, making sure that they avoid simony and similar abuses, for a defect in a minister indicates a defect in the master. This is especially so regarding mendacity; a royal minister who lies abrogates the royal duty of promulgating divine truth, for "the king is vicar of God who cannot lie."[14]

As lord of the realm, the king must provide for the kingdom:

few and just laws, and their wise and accurate administration, and generally defend the statutes and rights of all in allegiance to him. It is right that the king live civilly not only as king, but also as ruled by law, for Aristotle says that the law is more necessary to the community than the king, for law is perpetual, inflexibly making remedies for all sorts of injury.[15]

It is noteworthy that Wyclif says that laws should be few; a superabundance of them distracts from divine law by their multiplicity. Laws generate confusion in those who must understand and obey them, requiring a special class of ministers whose sole task is this endeavor, which only clutters up governance. "God condemns the king and the kingdom who frustrates [His] rational and serious commands [by ordaining a mass of superfluous laws] which are foolish and sacrilegious to the institution

---

[12] *DOR*, 3, 51.1–4.

[13] *Ibid.*, 3, 51.23–8: "Nec oportet vel convenit quod sint secum cottidie conmensales, sed sufficit quod prudenter in regno vigilent et instruant oves regis et suas in hiis que sunt ad deum, et si quid questionis ardue in domo regis natum fuerit ad ipsos ut satrapas habeant recursum et securum secundum legem dei consilium."

[14] *Ibid.*, 3, 54.29.

[15] *Ibid.*, 3, 55.22–30: "Stat autem regimen regni in paucarum et iustarum legum institucione, in illarum sagaci et acuta execucione et generaliter in status ac iuris cuiuscunque legii sui defensione. Oportet enim regnum cum vivit civiliter non solum rege sed lege taliter regulari, in tantum quod Aristoteles videtur dicere quod lex est necessior communitati quam rex, cum lex sit perpetua inflexibilis faciens expedite generalius quibuscunque iniuriatis viris remedium." This is a curious use of Aristotle's argument for the superiority of the rule of law, for in its most powerful iteration Aristotle uses it to argue against the absolute rule of one man. See 1287a.19–25.

of divine laws."[16] Kings who bend their law for their ministers place themselves and their kingdoms in servitude to selfish chaos, the harshest opponent of God's law. The occasions when this is permissible are few, and can only be recognized by individuals of sound judgment, with God's assistance.

Throughout the first half of *De Officio Regis*, civil *dominium*'s two primary components, *proprietas* and *iurisdictio*, are apparent, though frequently undifferentiated. As bearer of absolute *proprietas* the king is chief owner in secular society; he owns his kingdom, bearing in mind that such ownership is really stewardship of a part of Creation, founded in the king's obligation to imitate God and in his worthiness by Grace to fulfill that obligation. Consequent and reliant upon that relation between God and king is the king's institution of law, which provides the legal basis for all possible instances of just ownership. While the king is truly a steward of God, from a civil standpoint, he is chief owner, from which all other ownership-relations enjoyed in his kingdom would arise.

Wyclif discusses the *proprietas* of the civil lord in this way in *De Civili Dominio*, especially in his reasoning for the reliance of the clergy on royal alms, but he is not absolutely clear about this in *De Officio Regis*. In *De Civili Dominio* he writes of the finality of the ownership of civil lords as a group, and of their responsibilities regarding the church, and in *De Officio Regis* he tirelessly speaks of the king's responsibility to the church, yet he never explicitly states that the king is the chief civil owner in the land. Perhaps we are expected to assume this, given his repeated equivocation in his use of "civil *dominium*" regarding *iurisdictio* and *proprietas*, and his contention that the king is absolutely powerful in *iurisdictio*. The closest Wyclif comes to an outright recognition of the king as chief owner is his advice about property distribution in the lower classes:

So it is right that a king institute just laws and virtuously obey them as an exemplar of the laws of God, honoring all according to the dignity of their position, as with good dukes, counts, and barons, and also knights, faithful servants.... For the body of the kingdom's health is reliant on that of its heart, which is the power of the king, and which influences as much the highest priest as the lowest of the vulgar as to the nature of the just.... Thus nothing is more destructive in the political life of a kingdom than immoderately to deprive the lower classes of the goods of fortune.[17]

---

[16] *DOR*, 3, 56.5–57.2: "Et patet prudencia quod leges ille sint pauce . . .", especially 56.35–57.2: "Deum igitur contempnit, regem et regnum, qui frustrat tam racionale solempne mandatum, cum in re dicit legem illam nedum esse superfluam sed stulte ac sacrilege institutam."

[17] *Ibid.*, 5, 96.9–27: "Oportet ergo quod rex iuste statuat iustam legem et ipsam, ad exemplar legis dei, virtuosus exequatur, quemlibet prudenter secundum dignitatem sui status et meriti honorando, ut bonos duces, comites, et barones, et milites tamquam tales, fideles operarios tamquam tales,

This passage illustrates the blending of *iurisdictio* and *proprietas* in Wyclif's thought; the kingdom is best arranged with mutual respect between higher and lower orders, which is framed in jurisdictive terms, and exemplified in proprietary ones. The best way of exercising royal *iurisdictio* is to make certain that widespread *proprietas* concerns be met.

Wyclif devotes all of *De Officio Regis* 6 to a treatment of the nature and cause of absolute *iurisdictio*. For any action a subject performs, if that action is in any sense governed or governable by human law, his lord has *iurisdictio* over that act, and is responsible for it insofar as his laws apply to it.[18] This is a broader range of authority than might at first be evident: the king must prevent abrogation of all civil law, such as theft, murder, and rape, but his power is not restricted to civil law. Any sin endangers human society, for the least transgression inevitably leads the sinner to ever greater sins. Thus, the king must castigate all sin that might lead to civil upheaval, and should expect his bishops to work actively towards this end. This makes the king responsible for all evil, spiritual or temporal, that might occur in his kingdom. The bishops have their power insofar as they are the king's men, and the king gives them the temporal goods they need solely to extirpate sin.[19]

It is easy to see how this range of royal *iurisdictio* dovetails with Wyclif's call for the divestment of church property, and Wyclif suggests that the king should begin correcting heresy by divesting heretics of property. Heresies have led to the current papal schism, Wyclif explains, and it is the king's duty as Grace-founded lord to root out these threats, by recognizing misinterpretation and infractions of *lex Christi*.[20] He cannot be expected to have the search for heresy foremost in his mind, however; this is the province of the king's theologians. Presumably the theologians would present the king with instances of heresy on a case by case basis, along with their reasons for the charges, allowing the king to recognize the consonance of their reasoning with *lex Christi*.[21]

---

et clericos procedentes debite in suis statibus tamquam tales, et demum honorando decore vindicte eos qui a statu suo degenerant, tanquam tales. Nam corpus regni tunc constat in sanitate politica quando cor eius, quod est regia potestas, influit tam superioribus clericis quam inferioribus wulgaribus quod est iustum. Et quia animal homo magis attendit ad bona temporalia, ideo sunt prudencius in temporalibus moderandi inferiores qui nutriuntur temporalibus, tanquam grossis cibariis debent librari quo ad possessionem et officium temporalium, superiores qui nutriuntur claro et leni spiritu animati debent ab amplexu sanctorum amoveri. Unde quo ad primam partem nihil potencius destruit regna, quo ad vitam politicam, quam immoderate auffere ab inferioribus bona fortune."

[18] *Ibid.*, 6, 118.30–119.7.   [19] *Ibid.*, 6, 120.2–7.
[20] As Wyclif wrote in 1379, Urban VI claimed the papacy in Rome, having been elected 8 April 1378, while Clement VII claimed the papacy in Avignon, having been elected 20 September 1378.
[21] DOR, 6, 125.14–16; DOR, 11, 256–60.

This universal *iurisdictio* does not mean that the king is the absolutely final judge of right and wrong in his kingdom. As God's servant, the king is first among equals, but he is the most responsible for what occurs in his kingdom. Wyclif explains that this is because all acts of a given genus are effectively the acts of the founder of the genus, "as Adam does what his race does."[22] As all human actions are successive ripples outwards from the first human action, so all actions in a kingdom emanate causally from the royal action of reigning. This is in keeping with his model of unmediated divine *dominium*, in which all created acts are successive ripples outwards from God's loving sustenance and governance.

The king can judge, but only as a functionary responsible to God for the actions of his charges, as the majordomo is responsible to the lord for the actions of lesser servants. If the king were not worthy to receive the Grace which makes his *caritas* possible, he could not carry out his office properly. Thus, only by Grace can the king judge the actions of his subjects. As with the royal preeminence in *proprietas*, his superior *iurisdictio* is illusory, for both are truly God's alone; that the king is granted them is a measure of his worthiness to serve God.

The king's worthiness to serve God as just civil lord is most clearly exhibited in the correspondence of his actions with divine *iustitia*, which is embodied most fully in evangelical law. Wyclif believes this is most likely to be the case when the king recognizes that his duty is "steadfastly to defend evangelical law, and attentively to observe it in his dealings."[23] Much of this lies in the king's recognition that he is more securely bound to his subjects than are they to him. This is more than the recognition of the fact that an Englishman can move to France, and become a subject of the French king, while the English king can neither move to France and become a French subject, nor can he abandon England and begin ruling France instead. "[T]he rule the king should mete out with his laws should be more precious than the service or debt which [his subjects] render to him, for the virtuous rule of a king is more acceptable to God than good fortune or temporal service".[24] Because the king is taking divine justice as the exemplar, that he gives more to his subjects than they give to him is inescapable, for the rule of God gives more to Creation than it could possibly give to Him.

---

[22] *DCD*, I, 36, 261.7.

[23] *DOR*, 4, 79.2: "quod officium dominorum temporalium et regum precipue est legem ewangelicam potestative defendere et ipsam in sua conversacione diligencius observare."

[24] *Ibid.*, 4, 79.33–80.3: "Nam regimen quod rex debet suius legiis debet esse preciosius quam ministerium vel redditus quem rependunt, cum virtuosum regnum in rege sit Deo accepcius quam bonum fortune vel ministerium corporale."

If a king cannot do as he wishes, and enjoy the fruits of his lordship at his will, why be king? Wyclif sternly responds that this heretically disregards the source and purpose of royal power. A king can only enjoy the fruits of his rule under evangelical law, for "it is not licit for people to do anything except for the honor of God and the utility of the Church Militant."[25] Thus all the acts of the king must embody *caritas*, consonant with God's loving lordship of Creation.

The first obligation of a king is to the realm's church, rather than to the realm as such, for a king cannot serve his kingdom unless his church is healthy. If peace in the kingdom is valuable, we must recognize the need for a healthy church, the primary means by which God's laws – the cornerstone of worldly peace – are promulgated.[26] Unfortunately, the precise identity of the church is not always easy to pinpoint:

[T]he most proper way of accepting "church" is as the entire body of the pre-destined, and this is called the mystical body of Christ, Christ's bride, and the kingdom of heaven. Although the Damned are in faith and Grace according to contemporary justice, and thus a part of the church in the second aspect, yet they are not a part of this church. And in this way the term "Church Militant" is understood to refer to the multitude of the living predestined, and the term "Church Triumphant" to the body of the predestined in their reign [in heaven], and now them both for the complete body of the predestinate.... [Hence] it is clear that the house of the spiritual church has for its foundation faith in Christ, its walls are a life of hope, and its roof is *caritas*.[27]

Wyclif has been criticized for advocating the reform of a church that consists entirely of people that are unidentifiable, or the predestined.[28] We cannot know who are in that number, because we cannot look into the souls of others. How seriously are we to take a treatise on monarchy that concludes that the king's first duty is to protect and defend an institution whose members are unidentifiable? The only evidence that someone may be a church member would be that they are favored by Grace, with

---

[25] *DCD*, I, 19, 136.19–21: "Probatur sic: Non licet homini quidquam facere nisi ad honorem Dei et utilitatem ecclesie militantis."

[26] *Ibid.*, I, 22, 157.3–14.

[27] *Ibid.*, I, 39, 288.7–289.18: "Tercio vero accipitur ecclesia propriissime pro universitate predesti-natorum, et ista vocatur corpus Christi misticum, sponsa Christi, et regnum celorum. Licet enim presciti sint in fide et gracia secundum presentem iusticiam, et sic pars ecclesie secundo modo dicte, non tamen sunt pars huius ecclesie...Et illo modo intelligitur quedam ecclesia militans (ut multitudo predestinatorum viancium), quedam triumphans (ut multitudo predestinatorum regnancium), et nunc utrumque pro tota universitate predestinatorum...Et istis patet quod domus spiritualis ecclesie edificata habet pro fundamento fidem Christi pro parietibus spem vite, et pro tecto caritatem." See also *De Ecclesia*, 1, ed. J. Loserth (London, 1886), 2.25–3.13.

[28] Gordon Leff, *Heresy in the Later Middle Ages* (New York, 1967), vol. 2, pp. 516–44.

caritas characterizing their actions. Those who embrace apostolic poverty are likely to be Grace-favored, while those who willingly retain private ownership are not, unless they use their worldly power to alleviate the burdens of the poor and to reform the church by being responsible for its material needs. Thus, the attitude of an individual towards property and worldly power is not a certain guide, but a reliable indicator of that individual's likely church membership.[29] It is easy to imagine a more likely answer coming from Wyclif's pen: the king is God's servant, and if the master has ordained that His servant protect and reform an institution perhaps invisible to the servant, but not to the master, the servant must obey with a good spirit and with faith in the master's ultimate ends. But this is question-begging for non-Wycliffites; are there better reasons for taking this primary responsibility seriously?

In fact, there are. First, the institution claiming to be Christ's body on earth, ripe with worldly wealth and corruption, is laid open to secular management by virtue of Wyclif's argument. From the *realpolitik* standpoint, defining the true church as the unknowable predestined deflates any argument for legitimacy put forward by the papalists, for the harder they argue in favor of retaining their mundane power and property, the more likely their absence of Grace, and by implication, the less likely it is that they are members of the church. Therefore Wyclif's argument that the king ought chiefly to shepherd the church rather than his kingdom has great utility in a world where the church is a potent political force.

A second reason lies in the theoretical structure of Wyclif's argument. The king's first duty is to a body or institution not necessarily identical to his material kingdom, the purpose of which is to provide spiritual guidance to all those willing to accept it. One need only substitute "crown" for "church," and "legal stability" for "spiritual guidance" to see the structural similarities to the model of kingship Kantorowicz described as having arisen in England. Wyclif was not alone in defining the church as the mystical body of Christ, but his equation of the truly faithful with the predestined makes the mystic body truly mysterious in practical terms. Kantorowicz argued that the crown came to be a sempiternal, corporate person to whom the king owes allegiance before any more materially recognizable demands, and that the chief reason England was fertile ground for this was that Bracton's writings had planted the seed in the thirteenth century.[30]

---

[29] See Marcia Colish, *Medieval Foundations of the Western Intellectual Tradition 400–1400* (New Haven, 1997), p. 257.

[30] See Cary Nederman, "Bracton on Kingship Revisited," *History of Political Thought*, 5 (1984), pp. 61–78.

Wyclif's thought also has a bearing on Kantorowicz's argument because he, like the Norman Anonymous of the Twelfth Century, argued that the king is image of God, while a priest is image of Christ.[31] But it is unlikely that Wyclif had any more than second-hand familiarity with the Norman Anonymous. Manuscripts of the "York" Tractates were possibly not available to English schoolmen until after Wyclif's death; the earliest substantiated evidence of their presence is in the collection of John Bale (1495–1563), from which it arrived in Cambridge, in the hands of Matthew Parker, Archbishop of Canterbury, in 1575.[32] While both Wyclif and the Norman Anonymous hold that the king has his authority through the power of Christ's Divinity and clerics have theirs through Christ's Humanity, the similarities end there. The Anonymous emphasizes coronation, a sacramental act equivalent to clerical ordination, as the source of the king's royal authority. Through coronation, the king becomes Godlike in his power to rule, to forgive sins, and to perform communion. He is not "first among equals" among the predestined, as he is with Wyclif; instead the king is holy mediator of God's rule.[33] While the Anonymous prefigures Wyclif in his insistence that priests lacking outward saintliness suggest an absence of true ordination, with occasional suggestions that all the Elect are priests, and with his distaste for the binding nature of canon law, his exalted conception of kingship outstrips even Wyclif's notion of a royal stewardship.

SOME SPECIFIC ROYAL DUTIES

Although Wyclif's advocacy of the just king's responsibility to relieve the church of its civil *dominium* flows as an undercurrent throughout the first book of *De Civili Dominio*, its first developed appearance is not until Chapter 37. "From these discussions the corollary plainly follows, that when an ecclesiastical community or person habitually abuses wealth, kings, princes, and temporal lords can legitimately take it away."[34] For any evil in the world, God has provided a means for its eradication, and for the

---

[31] E. Kantorowicz, *The King's Two Bodies: A Study in Medieval Political Theology* (Princeton, 1957), p. 161.

[32] See George H. Williams, *The Norman Anonymous of 1100 A.D.* (Cambridge, MA, 1951), pp. 2–26. Williams hypothesizes that the Anonymous was a scholar from the cathedral school of Rouen, concluding that earlier references to the "Anonymous of York" should be replaced with "Anonymous of Rouen." See also Ruth Nineham, "The So-called Anonymous of York," *JEH*, 14 (1963), pp. 31–45.

[33] G. Williams, *The Norman Anonymous of 1100 A.D.*, pp. 158–69.

[34] *DCD*, I, 37, 265.29–266.4: "Ex istis videtur correlarie plane sequi quod quacunque communitate vel persona ecclesiastica habitualiter abutente diviciis, reges, principes, et domini temporales possunt legitime et valde meritorie ipsas auferre, eciam quantumcumque tradicionibus humanis eis fuerint confirmate."

specific evil of clerical abuse of temporal goods, which abuse is implicit in equating civil ownership with Original Sin, God has instituted temporal lordship, with its chief concern being the public good. Ideally, Wyclif envisions the two branches of lordship, secular and spiritual harmoniously assisting one another. As we shall see, spiritual lords play an important part in providing counsel for the king. "But a church laden with riches should expect help in dispensing them from the secular arm, wherefore the secular arm should act in accord with the law of Christ by taking up the duties of acquiring, husbanding, and distributing the wealth."[35] As things stand with the church now, Wyclif says, immediate action appears to be necessary, although he leaves the final decision to civil lords.[36] Coming from a theologian, this is a less disingenuous hedge than it may appear, for Wyclif is conscious of his status as a priest, and must remain consistent with his doctrine.

The first, and certainly broadest, royal act that Wyclif believes will contribute to the stability of the realm (as well as the purification of the church) would be to force the bishops to attend to the state of their dioceses as the laws of the church dictate, namely, by correcting the errant and rewarding the diligent among the clergy. This is because, "the law of God is the law of the church, and the law of the king, not only because the king is Christian, but because the custody of the church is the responsibility of the holder of the royal office."[37] Wyclif suggests that the king set up and monitor strict provincial councils made up of abbots, presbyters, deacons, and clerics, to evaluate the extent to which the clergy fulfill their duties.[38] The early church, after all, provides a precedent for conciliar evaluation, although perhaps not the royally mandated variety. This practice would keep the number of clergy to a minimum, and the laity would presumably welcome such a mechanism, if only because their taxes would decrease as the fat was trimmed from the church.[39] Wyclif's reasoning is less theological and more economical: the fewer the clergy, the fewer the individuals who would be dependent upon royal alms.

[35] *Ibid.*, I, 37, 267.27–268.1: "Item quidquid ecclesiasticus debet a brachio seculari exigere iuxta legem Christi, debet brachium seculare de eadem lege perficere; sed ecclesiasticus prepeditus diviciis debet exigere a brachio seculari iuvamen in dispensando illas divicias; ergo secularis debet in tali casu de lege Christi subire officium acquirendi, custodiendi, et distrahendi divicias."

[36] *Ibid.*, I, 37, 269.12–14.

[37] *DOR*, 7, 152.16–18: "quia lex dei, et per consequens lex ecclesie, est lex regis, non solum sub racione qua christianus, sed sub racione qua in istarum legum custodia stat precipuum regimen regni sui."

[38] *Ibid.*, 7, 153.10–21. Wyclif's references here are to *Corpus Juris Canonici*, D.XXI.c.1 (St. Isidore); D.IX.c.2 (St. Augustine); D.XVIII.c.51 (Council of Pope Martin); *Decreta* C.x, Q.i.10 (Council of Toledo); and III.i.9 (Gregory VII).

[39] *DOR*, 7, 158.18–159.20.

The second royal act should be the elimination of pluralism and its attendant absenteeism. "[T]he king should ordain through his bishops that curates reside in every church who are educated and zealous in their pastoral offices ... whence it follows first that the king must not permit alien [non-liegemen] clergy to hold benefices in England, unless mandated by divine command."[40] This is a familiar lament, and Wyclif was by no means the first to articulate it. But his justification for it is consistent with his doctrine: how could a king protect his church, which is his primary task, if many, or any, of its office-holders reside outside the bounds of his realm, perhaps liege to a foreign king or enemy? This would be a foothold for a host of external threats to the kingdom, but more importantly, it prevents the church from being fully divested of its material burdens, for the foreign benefice holder's goods are property under the custody of another lord, perhaps one not as concerned with reform. The papal claim to appoint to foreign benefices vanishes when all clergy are subject to secular power.

Wyclif is willing to make one exception:

The king and the realm may, for a good reason, allow benefice holders to be absent from the kingdom, or be elsewhere therein, to the greater utility of the kingdom and the church, with sufficient sub-curates remaining, with God's approval, because otherwise a curate could not attend university, which attendance greatly profits the parish, and [otherwise] the curate would needlessly be restricted to his parish like an anchorite.[41]

This allows the growth of a class of theologian advisors, the third royal action necessary for the kingdom. Here Wyclif's philosophical program, which is predicated on the supremacy of theology among the sciences, comes into play, "for according to the other [higher] laws, it is necessary that the kingdom have theologians for the conversion into faith in Christ, and for the regulation of the faithful in their parishes."[42] Wyclif does not explicitly exclude these theologians from the provincial councils, but his description of their function suggests that they act primarily as royal

---

[40] *Ibid.*, 7, 163.7–23: "[R]ex ordinet per suos episcopos ut in cunctis suis ecclesiis parochialibus resideant curati qui sint docti et animati in officio pastorali ... Et ex isto primo sequitur quod rex non permittet alienigenam vel indigenam curatum beneficiatum in Anglia, nisi ex causa deo accepta."

[41] *Ibid.*, 7, 165.24–30: "Si itaque pro causis legitimis rex et regnum licenciant beneficiatum absentare se extra regnum vel intra ad maiorem utilitatem regni et sic ecclesie, salva sufficienti residencia procuratoria, subest causa deo accepta, quia aliter non staret curatus in scola, ubi ecclesie et parochianis suis magis proficeret, sed includeretur irracionabiliter in sua parochia tamquam anacorita."

[42] *Ibid.*, 7, 176.31–5: "Tercia lex regnum stabiliens foret dilatacio, defensio et rectificacio theologice facultatis. Nam iuxta leges priores necesse est regnum habere theologos ad conversandum in fide Cristi et ad regulandum in eadem fide suas parochias."

counselors.[43] Wyclif's references to the need for this class of scholars are relatively few, but indicate that he does not expect the king to be well schooled in the intricacies of theology, for his business is to govern, to excel in the *via activa*.

As a forceful illustration of the extent of the power the king has over the church, Wyclif makes a startling statement:

> It is permissible in a state of imminent necessity in the defense of a city to tear down the church and construct a tower from it . . . for since the stones of life are better than earthly rocks, it is better to put them to use to the members of the church, to sustain them corporeally and spiritually. . . . Those divine things that are not subject to Caesar's power are not these material goods, such as gold, vestments, or stones, but the worship of God, for which these objects provide assistance . . .[44]

He suggests this directly on his description of the three royal actions needed for fulfillment of the royal duty, which no doubt is meant to underscore the king's responsibility. In the defense of the realm, the physical church is sacrificable, and the true church will not be harmed thereby.

Thus in temporal matters, including the maintenance of the physical body of the church, the king is the final authority, for he is universally responsible for all in his realm. He may appear to have spiritual authority, but this is only because repeated clerical claims of power over material goods have acquired a spiritual patina. The duty to stamp out sin and heresy is for the benefit of the realm, to prevent divisive factionalism and discord. The council Wyclif prescribes prevents material abuse, the duty to eradicate heresy keeps material peace in the kingdom, the effective deflation of the curial machinery allows spiritual lords to do only their proper duty. All the apparent spiritual authority is only materially corrective; the only spiritual power to which the just king can lay claim is the purity of Natural *dominium* resulting from membership of the church.[45]

The king faces impediments invented by avaricious clergy, including excommunication, the doctrine of papal *plenitudo potestatis*, perpetual

---

[43] *Ibid.*, 6, 125.14–17.

[44] *Ibid.*, 7, 185.9–21: "Licet enim in casu quo immineat necessitas ad defensionem civitatis basilicam prosternere et ibi turrim construere; calices vendere vel conflare et precium militibus ministrare; quia, cum lapides vivi sunt meliores saxis terrestribus, tunc melioriatur eorum usus quando ad utilitatem ecclesie membra eius corporaliter vel spiritualiter sustentantur. Et ad istam defensionem ecclesie de bonis propriis principes seculi obligantur, spoliando si oportet avaros presbiteros a bonis ecclesie que iniuste occupant tanquam sua. Unde oportet decretistam notare quomodo res divine que non subiacent Cesaris potestati non sunt bona ista materialia, ut aurum, vestimentum vel lapides, sed cultus dei qui instrumentaliter ex eis prevenit . . ."

[45] *Ibid.*, 5, 94.

grants, and mortmain. Excommunication has proven to be historically the most effective tool in the papal bag of tricks. But Wyclif's doctrine that every man is a priest defuses it. "It is not possible for anyone to be excommunicated unless first and foremost they excommunicate themselves."[46] The ground for the infliction of this penalty is the transgression of Christ's law, which is a sin before God, and since no man can read another's soul, no one can accurately judge sin. Thus, no man can truly excommunicate another. The threat of excommunication in retaliation for material divestment flies in the face of the apostolic purity of the early church; Wyclif believes it to be unmistakably clear that the king's God-given duty is to relieve the church of her temporal burden.

Do heretics excommunicate themselves? This is not for men to know; clerical refusal to accept royal divestment would likely be heretical through its rejection of the poverty enjoined by *lex Christi*, but it would not be for the king to treat the obstinate clerics as excommunicates, for this would usurp divine authority. Forcible divestment accompanied by de-frocking would presumably be enough for Wyclif, for he never advocates stricter measures than these. "Since excommunication is a spiritual cauterization preceding ejection from the community of the faithful, it seems obvious that this should not be done when other medicines are available."[47]

The doctrine of papal *plenitudo potestatis*, founded primarily on the Petrine commission, had caused papalists to assume that the teaching "whatsoever you bind on earth shall be bound in heaven" implies, "if you bind a thing on earth, it shall be bound in heaven." Rather, says Wyclif, we should understand it as "if you bind a thing on earth, your having bound it is a result of it having been bound in heaven." This interpretation's determinism does not deter Wyclif, for he has already said that it is not what God knows that is necessary, but rather that He knows it.[48] The "rock" on which Christ founded His church is not a person, but a promise that He will act through Grace through Peter and his heirs in faith. The true holder of the keys of the kingdom has always been the divine Lord:

[N]evertheless ecclesiastical prelates have committed to themselves an instrumental power which enables judgment in two ways, namely in the power of arbitrating over the understanding, and in the power of judgment of action. The

---

[46] DCD, I, 38, 275.3: "Ergo nemo potest excommunicari, nisi primo et principaliter excommunicetur a se ipso."

[47] DOR, 7, 167.6–9: "Cum igitur excommunicacio sit cauterium spirituale precidens excommunicatum a communione fidelium, manifestum videtur quod hoc non debet fieri dum suppetit alia medicina."

[48] See *Tractatus de Universalibus*, ed. Ivan J. Mueller (Oxford, 1985), 14.

first of these is called the key of conscience in matters of penitence, and leads to the latter. No one has the power of definitive sentencing, unless first they have the power of understanding the cause . . . so the earlier key is not the act or possession of knowledge, but a power of antecedent understanding.[49]

That is, true fullness of power lies in Christ-like understanding, to which no man can aspire; indeed, any human claims to fullness of power contradict monotheism. Given Wyclif's Grace-*dominium* doctrine, wherein all earthly power justly held is on loan from God, the rejection of *plenitudo potestatis* is inevitable.

The impossibility of grants in perpetuity also follows. Although the papacy has used perpetual grants to hold onto property despite the rise and fall of secular governments, one can only grant that which is in one's power. No man can grant that another receive Grace, so nobody can grant a *dominium*-relation to another, much less one that stretches endlessly into the future. A just grant of *dominium*, or one of its feudal sub-types, in perpetuity to the family of B by the family of C would make possible one of B's descendants having just *dominium* over one of C's descendants, when the B descendant is damned, and the C descendant among the elect, which would be impossible.[50] Wyclif allows for the possibility of perpetual grants which, in accord with Christ's law, are "beneficiary, contractual, economic, and contribute to [social] stability."[51] He has in mind grants of alms here, which must be commensurate in spirit with evangelical law to be valid.

That the church cannot lay claim to any instance of civil *dominium*, whether in perpetuity or not, is clear. The church must be absolutely free of all material holdings, relying only on the civil lord for alms, so the practice of mortmain, whereby the lands of knights pass into ecclesiastical possession, is abhorrent to God and deleterious to the kingdom.[52] Not only does it allow priests to own property, but the practice would ultimately lead to the entire kingdom being in their hands. One might wonder what would be the matter with there being nothing for secular lords to

---

[49] *DCD*, I, 38, 282.12–24: "[T]amen prelati ecclesie habent sibi commissam potestatem instrumentalem, que est potestas iudiciaria consistens principaliter in duobus, scilicet, in potestate arbitrarie cognoscendi et in potestate incidentaliter iudicandi. Et prior istorum vocatur in foro penitencie clavis consciencie, et est dispositiva ad secundam principaliorem; cum nemo habet potestatem diffinitive sentenciandi, nisi prius habeat potestatem cognoscendi in causa qua dicitur arbitrari sentenciam: unde prior clavis non est actus vel habitus sciendi, sed potestas sic antecedenter cognoscendi."

[50] See my "Toleration in the Theology and Social Thought of John Wyclif," in *Difference and Dissent: Theories of Tolerance in Medieval and Early Modern Europe*, ed. Cary J. Nederman and John C. Laursen (Lanham, MD, 1996), pp. 39–66.

[51] *DCD*, I, 36, 255.14–16.   [52] *DOR*, 5, 97.28–98.28.

own. In general, this would be good, so long as nobody in the church, or anywhere else, held property either; then, all would enjoy communal ownership, which is the ideal state. But this is the only condition Wyclif could foresee in which the abolition of civil lordship was feasible, if not desirable.

THE PROBLEMS OF ROYAL SUCCESSION AND DEGENERATION

Two issues pertaining to the basic nature of kingship receive Wyclif's special attention: where to find a just, Grace-favored king, and what to do when kingship degenerates into tyranny. The first issue is an obvious problem for a philosopher believing private ownership to be sinful, for the three most familiar means of attaining kingship in human society involve a just Christian willfully acquiring private property. Hereditary succession appears to involve the passing-on of private ownership from holder to heir, thereby fostering the despicable institution of property. Conquest requires the conqueror to threaten, if not use violence, in attaining private ownership.

The popular appointment of a king is inadmissible, because, "it does not follow [that] 'all people want Peter to be their civil lord, therefore it is just'; indeed, the first consensus of the people for their civil lord, who would be pure of sin, cannot be just unless the person in lordship is accepted by God for that duty."[53] Since Grace is necessary for just civil *dominium*, and it cannot be discerned by others in the individual, popular election of a monarch would only be just by happenstance. One might imagine that Wyclif would advocate a king's being appointed by some holy advocate, as with Samuel and Saul, but he would never countenance any sacerdotal lord doing so, at the risk of ecclesiastical participation in civil *dominium*.

Might not the institution of hereditary succession indicate a God-ordained order, since God would only allow someone worthy of king-ship to be born as an heir? If God wills that a just king sire a child in a society the laws of which revolve around private ownership, is not God implicitly condoning hereditary succession? Indeed, God allows that certain diseases be passed genetically; does it not seem more likely that God would allow the passing of the parent's goods as well? Also, since children inherit original sin from their parents, is it not reasonable to assume that

---

[53] *DCD*, I, 18, 130.6–14: "Nam non sequitur, 'Totus populus vult Petrum dominari civiliter; ergo iuste': ymo primus consensus populi ad aliquem civiliter dominandum, qui tamen fuit a peccato purior, non fuit iustus nisi presupposita racione, scilicet quod persona dominans sit a Deo accepta ad illud officium."

God ordains that they inherit an institution consequent on original sin? Lordship is only just, Wyclif answers, if it is principally from God, and inheritance makes it altogether too likely that the king rule for himself and his heirs, rather than as God's steward.[54] Further, were inheritance natural, what was inherited would have to be something natural as well, yet civil *dominium* is in opposition to Natural *dominium*, and so must be unnatural. Yet Wyclif has doubts about these responses, for inheritance might well spur a prince to good government through love of his heir. But again, he reflects, popular election could as easily be a divine instrument as inheritance might be. Just at the point that one feels that Wyclif is casting about for any plausible alternative, he reminds us of the force of his Grace-*dominium* doctrine: "[T]hus since acquiring the title itself does not suffice, but clearly needs a title of *caritas* superadded, it is clear also that neither hereditary succession nor popular election suffices in itself either."[55]

Wyclif recognizes several sorts of filiation, of which the most relevant is "sonship through instruction." Through this, filial bonds arise as understanding passes from one to another, "which is analogously similar to natural sonship, for the seed, the Word of God, is sewn in an instructed soul."[56] This allows Wyclif to call spiritual sons any who have received Christ's laws in the Gospels, making the Grace-instilled obedient a "son through instruction by the divine Lord." "The title of *dominium* by law of heirship in Christ is naturally more prior and essentially more requisite after the Fall than any other mode of *dominium*."[57] Just as the postlapsarian institution of civil *dominium* is as nothing next to true Natural *dominium*, the earthly traditions governing the transmission of private ownership pale before spiritual filiation.[58]

---

[54] *Ibid.*, I, 29, 208.26–32.

[55] *Ibid.*, I, 30, 212.20–3: "unde, sicut titulus acquirendi non per se sufficit (ex xxi. capitulo); sed oportet precipue superaddere titulum caritatis, sic indubie nec successio hereditaria nec popularis eleccio per se sufficit." Until Wyclif returns to his Grace-*dominium* doctrine, his assessment of hereditary succession is similar to Marsilius of Padua's skepticism: Marsilius, too, addresses the prospect that a prince might be prone to good government in the interests of his heir in *Defensor Pacis*, ed. Richard Scholz (Hannover, 1932), I, 16, 1, and his rejection of that rationale relies too much on the prince's virtue, which Marsilius thinks is not the way to justify a secular government. Marsilius is arguing for a consensual government, and in *Defensor Pacis*, I, 16, 14 suggests that a prospective heir be subjected to election if inheritance of rule must be countenanced. See also Nederman, *Community and Consent: The Secular Political Theory of Marsiglio of Padua's Defensor Pacis* (London, 1995), pp. 109–15.

[56] *DCD*, I, 30, 215.10–12: "et est similitudo analoga ad filium naturalem; nam semen, verbum Dei, seminatum est in animam informati, Deo dante formam gracie."

[57] *Ibid.*, I, 30, 216.12–16: "sic titulus dominandi ex iure hereditario Christi per graciam est prius naturaliter et essencialiter requisitum post lapsum ad hoc quod quis quomodolibet dominetur."

[58] *Ibid.*, I, 21, 218.29–219.2.

Has Wyclif finessed his way out of the problem by invoking the need for Grace as the chief prerequisite for rulership? Are we back where we began, with no clear means by which rulership is passed from one just king to the next? This is probably Wyclif's aim; no human mechanism can function without God's assistance, and if material inheritance is really no better or worse than popular election, why rely on any established procedure? Wyclif is doing far more than playing a theological trump in a tight spot, for he is again showing just how he means civil *dominium* to be understood. Wyclif is not writing a handbook for rule, but rather a mirror of true perspective: God will provide the just ruler if given the chance, and any attempts to second guess the divine will must be doomed. If pressed, one is given to suppose that Wyclif would use instructional filiation as the most reliable means of just succession, in a relation grounded in *lex Christi* in which the just king would adopt and instruct a potential heir, reliant on God's Grace for illumination of the eligibility of the candidate.

As to how to initiate a tradition of just monarchy Wyclif is reticent, though unmistakably opposed to a Marsilian consent-based government. Here we should imagine him advocating something akin to William the Conqueror's approach. The English crown is founded on the Norman invasion, which Wyclif could not repudiate easily, for he sees much good to have come of it. A *caritas*-founded conquest must be legitimate, he explains, "and this is confirmed in the kingdom of England's conquest by the Britons, the Saxons, and the Normans, whose conquests are not ambiguously just, since from them have proceeded many holy and canonised kings."[59] The grounds for conquest must not be proprietary, but must be towards the betterment of the conquered. As an instance of this, Wyclif cites William having relieved the English church of excessive wealth, arguing that these actions show the Conqueror's actions were not tyrannical but meant to revive English Christianity.[60]

The other problem inherent to monarchy to which Wyclif devotes attention is the specter of its degeneration. Wyclif is known for his advice that tyrants should be obeyed and suffered, and not overthrown, but we should not suppose him to advocate absolutism because of this, for he does not advise complete acquiescence in tyranny. There are two species of obedience to temporal power, Wyclif explains:

[59] *Ibid.*, I, 21, 148.14: "Et confirmacio illius est de regno Anglie conquesto per Britones, Saxones, Normannos, quos conquestus non licet iustos ambigere cum in illo iure multi gloriosi sancti et canonizati reges processerant: et simile contingit de regnis aliis." This particular passage is from an argument Wyclif presents contrary to his position, but the passage is largely in line with Wyclif's sentiments; he is arguing against the legitimacy of a conquest founded in greed. See also *DOR*, 11, 248.18.

[60] *DCD*, II, 6, 47–9.

[E]ither passively, pursuing *caritas*, which cannot be evil, or actively giving material and bodily service, preserving all possible *caritas*, is without doubt a good. So since secular power does many good things which profit the church in many ways, and so please God, why should we not freely and obediently serve as Christians the fiscal requirements of secular princes?... Nevertheless, if through the absence of temporal cooperation [one] could destroy the power and abuse of the tyrant, we should withdraw our cooperation from him.[61]

This is not advocacy of Gandhi-like passive resistance, because Wyclif suggests that Christ, the Ideal of human behavior, though capable of resistance to Pilate or Herod, forbore for a higher purpose, which was subjection to God's will.[62] Wyclif is saying that passive obedience with a charitable will is commensurate with an absence of temporal cooperation, but that we should follow Christ's example and avoid active resistance to the tyrant. Is this contradictory?

Two options are open to the just subjected to a tyrant: one could either actively obey the tyrant, or one could maintain a charitable will while not providing active cooperation. This latter alternative is feasible only when it will result in the tyrant's downfall, and seems viable only for those with sufficient temporal power to topple a king by refraining from acting on his behalf. This is quite different from refraining to pay one's taxes, or participating in a popular campaign of passive resistance; it seems more like the sort of thing that led to the overthrow of Edward II. This leads us to what Wyclif believes to be the most important issue in secular tyranny, which is not the suffering it may involve, but who should concern themselves with it.

Wyclif suggests that the individual wholly adhering to Christ's law, one who lives in apostolic poverty and eschews the *vita activa* as much as possible, should pay no attention to the tyrant. Specifically, sacerdotal lords must never resist any form of temporal power. Still, Wyclif recognizes that a tyrant degrades his realm through his sin, which could well result in widespread sinning.[63] Could his advice to Christians entail collusion with the spread of sin? The individual Christian should look to his own spiritual purity in these cases.[64] In a well-structured state, effective theological counselors are the best prophylaxis against such an evil.[65] Secular

---

[61] *Ibid.*, I, 28, 201.15–33: "[V]el pure paciendo, servata caritate, quod non poterit esse malum; vel active ministrando in bonis fortune aut ministerio corporali, quod indubie, servata de possibili caritate, foret bonum. Unde, cum potentatus seculi faciunt multa bona de genere, que (ex secundo capitulo) multipliciter proficiunt ecclesie et per consequens placet Deo; quare ergo non gracia illius obedienter ministrarent Christiani stipendia mundi principibus?... Verumtamen, si esset verisimile homini per subtracciones temporalis iuvaminis destruere potentatus tyrannidem vel abusum, debet ea intencione subtrahere."

[62] *Ibid.*, I, 28, 199.9–14.   [63] *DOR*, 3, 48.18–52.20.

[64] *DCD*, I, 28, 201.15.   [65] *DOR*, 3, 48–9.

tyranny is to be borne by the Christian as a divine instrument, which God uses as a punishment for sins and as a means of discipline of the righteous to prepare them for future glory.[66] Thus Wyclif's attitude towards tyranny is that, from the point of view of the humble, it is God's scourge; only in rare cases does he recognize resistance to it as feasible.[67]

So Wyclif appears to temporize about how subjects ought to respond to tyranny, for on the one hand he says that it is to be borne with humility, while on the other, he seems to advocate rebellion against it. This ambiguity could come from a nebulous idea of what tyranny involves. If a king were to be tyrannical about temporal goods, unlawfully seizing property or crops, suspending trial by jury, and so forth, he might be acting in the best interests of the realm, despite his subjects' views to the contrary. Presumably this is the species of tyranny that Wyclif believes must be borne with humility. But if a king were to persecute the church in a spiritually deleterious fashion, say in withholding alms, impeding ministry, or legislating against *lex Christi*, as did Domitian, Wyclif would certainly advocate rebellion on the part of the Natural lords. Temporal tyranny is one thing, and spiritual tyranny is quite another.[68] In any given instance of tyranny regarding the material wealth of the realm, it is conceivable that the just civil lord is acting on behalf of God in his capacity as chief steward, but in instances of religious persecution of the apostolic community's spiritual welfare, such divine license is inconceivable.

Instances wherein a tyrant flouts *lex Christi* to further material gains, as with unjust conquest or pogroms, are examples of spiritual tyranny.[69] But what of cases in which a king uses deadly force to impede heresy or priestly tyranny? What of ostensibly just conquest, initiated on supposedly righteous spiritual grounds, but really carried out for material ends? What did Wyclif make of the historical reality of the Crusades? A king might well fool himself into believing he is acting on spiritually acceptable grounds for reasons that are, at base, avaricious. Here presumably Wyclif would rely on his class of theologian advisors to prune royal hubris, for they would surely be equipped to combat the lure of material gain.[70]

---

[66] *DCD*, I, 28, 199.29–33; I, 6, 43.15–35.

[67] *DOR*, 8, 201.14–18: "Et quantum ad illud in fine additum patet quod non oportet legium serviendo tyrano favere sibi in moribus. Favet autem homo nature hominis non solum resistendo sed eciam occidendo et sic stat eundem sine duplicitate favere proficiendo duobus contrariis dominis in causa et modo dispari."

[68] *Ibid.*, 1, 8.10–17: "Vel illata est iniuria quo ad causam propriam vel pure quo ad causam dei. In primo casu post exhortacionem evangelicam paciencia est optima medicina. si pure in causa dei cristianus debet, post correpcionem evangelicam, preposito suo usque ad mortem, si oportet, confidenter et obedienter resistere."

[69] See *DCD*, I, 21.   [70] *DOR*, 4, 72.15–25.

What of a civil lord who allows the church to continue cultivating private ownership and its accompanying spiritual poison?[71] What of the possibility of a king who, upon reading Wyclif's *dominium* treatises, dismisses them as so much wool gathering? Here the civil lord would be abrogating his primary responsibility, the well-being of the church, analogously to a physician permitting gangrene to develop unhindered. It is conceivable that Wyclif would believe that a civil lord, apprised of these arguments, who turns his back on this duty, would warrant the rebellion of his subjects more than any other sort of tyranny.

The secular tyrant embodies all that is imperfect in a society founded in private ownership, and Wyclif seems almost to expect the postlapsarian world to produce him. The church must expect better from its lords, though, and it is against spiritual tyranny that Wyclif believes attention should be directed; a priest who is draconian in his enforcement of Christ's law may be Christ's scourge, but one who is so depraved as to tyrannize in temporal affairs is intolerable.[72] Temporal sins in priestly offices are more onerous than spiritual sins in the royal office, because the former is a pollution of a higher office. Secular tyranny is certainly bad, but spiritual tyranny is far more monstrous, desecrating Christ's ideal.

What exactly is spiritual tyranny? Wyclif is not particularly careful to provide an exhaustive list of the possibilities. Priests who teach heretical ideas are certainly guilty of using their office for base tyrannical purposes.[73] Wyclif defines heresy as a persistently maintained concept founded in the false or sinful, or that which is contrary to Scripture.[74] The primary instance he presents is priests desiring to participate in civil *dominium*, which he explains is the most dangerous kind of heresy.[75] While Wyclif believes that the clergy are more bound to lead exemplary lives than civil lords, his interest in clerical morality is focused on the tendency of priests to desire private ownership.[76] He notes that excommunication has frequently been used to keep civil lords from trying to address this, and frequently refers to it as a tyrannical weapon used to defend priestly ownership.[77] Wyclif's further prescriptions for priestly morality, beyond

---

[71] Wyclif does suggest that the value of a king's reign is measurable in terms of how the clergy are freed of private ownership in *DOR*, 3, 59.32–62.12.

[72] *Ibid.*, 1, 22.5–9.   [73] *Ibid.*, 8, 215.15–20.

[74] *DCD*, II, 6, 59.3–18; also *DCD*, I, 43, 392.23–393.15, for Wyclif's reference to Grosseteste's definition.

[75] *Ibid.*, II, 6, 59.35ff: "[H]eresis periculosissima sequatur ex avaricia sacerdotum. Potest enim esse quod pars sacerdotum Christi mundo potencior sit tantum dedita avaricie ac civili dominio, quod doceat tam pertinaciter tam verbo quam opere quod licet illis secundum legem Christi."

[76] *DCD*, I, 14.18–30; *DOR*, 2, 42.4–9.

[77] *DOR*, 2, 22.5–9; *DOR*, 7, 166.5–176.30; *DOR*, 10, 231.1ff.; *DCD*, I, 38, 274–85.

the problem of property-ownership, are more in evidence in later works, including *De Ecclesia* and *De Potestate Pape*.[78]

It is not difficult to see where Wyclif's discussion will lead. In instances of priestly tyranny, it is the duty of the civil lord to correct priests by removing the means whereby tyranny is possible, the source of temporal power, or private property.[79] Later Wyclif would comment sadly that the tumultuous 1381 uprising and the death of Archbishop Sudbury would never have occurred had temporal lords been appropriately vigilant in rooting out priestly corruption.[80]

Several other elements of Wyclif's views on kingship are interesting, although less likely to clarify his picture of *dominium* as a theological and political term. These crop up throughout the two works, but most especially towards the end of *De Officio Regis*. Here Wyclif makes some effort to discuss just war, but, after making some fairly innocuous remarks about wars to stamp out heresies, and those of just conquest, he breaks off by dismissing the propriety of priests holding opinions on such matters. At this point Wyclif veers off into the familiar excoriation of priests who do concern themselves with war and temporal concerns, suggesting that a renunciation of Constantine's Donation would improve things markedly.[81] Priests should be freed of materialist greed, the temptation of simony, and so on, sufficiently to maintain a more balanced view of the world, possibly to provide worthwhile advice to the king regarding warfare. Such a theologian, Wyclif says, would be able to (1) show that a just war may be possible, but is very difficult; (2) point out the dangers as well as the legitimacy of such a war; (3) say how war is more dangerous now than it was when the Old Testament was written; and (4) advise that it is more in conformity with Christ's law to avoid war.[82]

Wyclif's belief in the superiority of the English system of government is also worth mentioning. Although all human law is defective, English law is less so than the Roman variety, not only for its tendency to be

---

[78] See *De Ecclesia*, 21, 513.6–524.18.   [79] *DOR*, 2, 38–46.

[80] *De Blasphemia*, ed. M. H. Dzwiecki (London, 1893), 13, 190–1; 17, 266–9 (*c.* August 1381).

[81] *DOR*, 12, 261.12–15; 276.7–10.

[82] *Ibid.*, 12, 17–31: "Theologus autem examinatus in isto per modum consilii posset dicere quod possible sed difficile est gwerrare. Secundo diceret plane talis gwerre licenciam et aliunde periculum. Tercio diceret quod bellum est hodie periculosius quam fuit in veteri testamento. Tunc enim bellarunt ex revelacione domini contra infideles propter hereditatem quam deus illis donaverat, sed hodie deficiente isto habent superaddita Cristi consilia ad que amplius obligantur quam ad precepta neutra terreni principis vel spiritalis prepositi. Quarto consulerent cum sit sanius securius et legi Cristi conformius quod seculares cessent a gwerris, licet quo ad civilitatem perdiderint terrenum dominium. Stultus enim foret qui inniteretur ore lacus labilis et profundi dum posset per medium strate regie faciliter munde et secure incedere." These are the benefits of having such a theologian relevant to this exposition; Wyclif presents several others of less import.

freer of hereditary servitude, but also because of its special utility for the English people.[83] "I do not believe Roman civil law to be more subtly rational or just than English civil law, and when it is said [that it is] by virtue of its language, Latin, or Greek, or some other, since reason comes before language, no cleric or philosopher is stronger for being a doctor of Roman civil law than a justiciar practising English law."[84] Those who would argue in favor of an empire over a kingdom miss the drawbacks that will ultimately nullify an empire. In general, the larger an empire becomes, the more prone it will be to factions, corruption, and the breakdown of the rule of law.[85] The Roman empire as it stands now is in a pitiable state, for "the Emperor allows his satraps to ravage his holdings and . . . to range like wolves [elsewhere]."[86] While a perfect empire would function as a kind of world-state on the civil *dominium* model,

If it were asked what would be the best form of government, I hold that . . . it is what would preserve the state of innocence throughout with exactions [on the governed] laid aside. This God ordained for the human race, and will be perfected after judgment day. Given the sinful nature of man and the rudeness of the rational abilities of the people, it is better now for the church that kings extend their jurisdiction [only] as far as it suffices for their rule. So it appears to me that since the king should desire to reign for the sake of doing meritorious work, he should not seek to conquer a second kingdom.[87]

It is clear that Wyclif believes the king has the final say in ecclesiastical affairs as well as in civil affairs. In fact, the king functions as the head of the realm's church, although Wyclif does not say this in so many words.[88]

---

[83] *DCD*, I, 34.

[84] *DOR*, 7, 193.31–194.1: "Sed non credo quod plus viget in romana civilitate subtilitas racionis sive iusticia quam in civilitate anglicana, et cum sit per se notum quod quecumque lingua, latina greca vel alia, sit impertinens clerimonie vel racioni, cum racio sit ante linguam, patet quod non pocius est homo clericus sive philosophus in quantum est doctor civilitatis romane quam in quantum est iusticiarius iuris Anglie."

[85] *Ibid.*, 12, 261.15–25.

[86] *Ibid.*, 11, 250.9–14: "imperator nedum permittit suos satrapas spoliare proprium et peculiare eius dominium, de quo oportet eum non obstante donacione quacunque habere capitale dominium, sed et permittit lupos suos ebulire ad insulas et terras exteras bona et personas simulacione maxime proditoria rapiendo."

[87] *Ibid.*, 12, 261.29–262.6: "Et si queratur quid foret optimum, dico quod optimum regimen humani generis foret quod servaret ex integro statum innocencie cum exaccione deposita. Sic enim deus instituit regimen humani generis et perficietur post diem iudicii. Supposito autem peccato viancium et ruditate plebis racionis expertis est melius pro nunc ecclesie quod sint reges extendentes iurisdiccionem suam ad tantum regnum quantum sufficiunt modo suo. Unde videtur mihi, cum rex debet per se regnum appetere propter opus meritorium, quod non debet duo regna appetere conquirendo."

[88] *Ibid.*, 1, 18.3–19.5; *DOR*, 3, 58.19–65.30; *DOR*, 4, 66.7–12; *DCD*, I, 26, 185.14–192.20; *DCD*, I, 37.

While it is true that the king is the ultimate mundane authority regarding excommunication, Wyclif believes that the individual warranting such a punishment has been excommunicated in God's eyes ever since first willing to sin mortally.[89] Grace enables the king only to carry out what God has already willed regarding the sinner. Insofar as the king strives to make human law conform to *lex Christi*, he is legally bound to cast Christ's enemies from the realm. What sort of legal obligation is this? Both the just laws of the realm and God's law compel the king to excommunicate the mortal sinner. Wyclif is silent regarding the specifics of this obligation. That is, if someone willfully murders, he has presumably sinned mortally; is he to be excommunicated, or do other more physically awful punishments await? Wyclif neither addresses the possibility of the mortal sinner repenting, nor the finer points of the civil law; we have no word on his opinion on use of capital punishment or imprisonment. Regarding repentance, Wyclif only suggests that Christians should pity malicious behavior, and that judges should be particularly circumspect in their reliance upon eye-witness accounts.[90] His chief concern in depicting civil *dominium*/kingship is to describe the king's primary duties before God, namely the reform of the church in the realm; he gives little to no attention to elements that he believes to be extraneous to that concern.

CONCLUSION

Our discussion of Wyclif's views on the jurisdictively orientated duties of the civil lord, which has served to outline a general version of Wycliffite kingship, has shown his reliance on his theological and realist ontology in *De Civili Dominio* and *De Officio Regis*. The concept of Natural *dominium* is inextricably linked to Wyclif's doctrine of civil *dominium*; his account of the civil lord's duties makes sense only in light of the notion that the church consists of redeemed Natural lords for whose material welfare the civil lord is obliged to provide. This responsibility becomes clearer with an understanding that just civil law is in harmony with God's law. Wyclif's underlying motive is to insure that the civil lord provides for the members of the church, the Natural lords, so that they may live in apostolic purity. To do this, the civil lord must legislate sufficiently for non-Christian subjects to live peacefully while Christians are free

---

[89] *DOR*, 9, 229.16; *DCD*, I, 38, 276.16–21: "Nam hoc est certum, quod omnis peccans mortaliter, ut sic, excommunicat se ipsum, id est ponit se extra communionem fidelium; et ad secundum sensum minister ecclesie excommunicat publicum peccatorem, id est, excommunicatum denuncciat [sic] et aliis communicacionem eius in nomine Domini vetat."

[90] *DCD*, II, 17, 234.31–235.30; *DCD*, II, 16, 218.22–233.22.

to pursue the *via contemplativa*. If sacrifices are necessary on the secular political plane for this latter good, they must be made by the civil lord through his legislation.

The reciprocity of Natural *dominium*, to which the civil lord is privy by virtue of his Grace-favored status, allows for the civil lord to recognize that his position is that of a divine steward rather than a sovereign lord. If we view civil *dominium* as that aspect of just human *dominium* facilitating the restoration of Natural *dominium* among the Grace-favored, we will be able to recognize that his jurisdictive authority is a means to a higher end, *lex Christi*. Just secular *dominium* is a participation in God's *dominium*, providing for the overcoming of original sin; all of Wyclif's discussions of the specific duties of the civil lord are predicated upon this. So the overriding emphasis on the civil lord's responsibilities for church reform makes sense, for if the civil lord neglects his chief charge towards the Natural lords, the possibility of just secular rule vanishes.

As chief property holder of the realm, the civil lord or king can have the final say in all temporal matters. Wyclif believes that the greatest moral threat to the kingdom is the Natural lords' subjection to the temptations of private ownership. If they are freed of this temptation the general moral tenor of the realm will be improved, allowing for more effective administration. He envisions the Natural lords serving as moral exemplars to their subjects, and the king, as Grace-favored Natural lord, has the responsibility not only to serve as chief moral exemplar, but also to ensure that all other Natural lords can serve in this capacity. The king is, in every sense, the steward of the morality of the realm by being the steward of the church. He is duty-bound to stamp out heresy, which frequently consists of clergy lusting for *temporalia*, and to that end he employs his bishops and theological advisors to police the kingdom.

It is likely that Wyclif felt the best means of selecting a just civil lord was to leave it to God, given his reticence to come to a conclusion regarding hereditary succession. Perhaps he felt the royal theological advisors would play an important part in all of this, in educating the king or in providing counsel when making such a decision. Wyclif's lack of practical prescription indicates a belief that this matter was of lesser import than a more temporally minded theorist might suppose it to be. The specter of tyranny is a matter requiring understanding of Wyclif's theological aims as well. An over-strict king is not necessarily evidence of unsuitability to rule; as a Grace-favored lord, depredations in the short run may lead to the moral betterment of the realm. But spiritual tyranny, of which the chief example is negligence regarding the state of the church, is a different matter, and is a case where the subjects serve the lord by rebelling.

In sum, the king is the temporal and spiritual steward of his realm, and must use his material means to provide for the realm's spiritual welfare. The chief means for this is the divestment of clerical private property, which will allow the body of Natural lords to serve as moral exemplars for the rest of the realm. Thus the king is truly a steward, enabling God's *dominium* to proceed as God wills through his jurisdictive action.

CONCLUSION

So far we have explained Wyclif's thought on divine and human *dominium* to show both how the two are connected with one another and how they are founded in his realism. The metaphysics of the *Tractatus de Universalibus* form the basis for the cosmological, social, and ecclesiastical arguments of the first books of the *Summa Theologie*. Earlier interpretations of Wyclif's thought have either denied connections between Wyclif's realism and his political thought or suggested that the tenor of the political thought indicates a likely abandonment of his realism. It will help, however, if we explore several possible alternative readings aside from the earlier interpretations, to be more certain that our reading is a viable alternative to the earlier approaches.

In place of interpretations of the universal–particular account of civil *dominium*, Wyclif might have had the theocratic model of kingship in mind, in which the secular lord is the sole rightful holder of all temporal authority, acting as God's intermediary on earth. But on most versions of this model, the king's sovereignty is absolute; in Wyclif's thought, the depiction of *dominium* as a reciprocal relation with the lord's subjects forestalls such relatively complete authority.[1] Such a theme is not as immediately evident in the theocratic model. We might also think that Wyclif's theory was patterned on a secular hierocratic scheme, in which the king replaces the pope at the summit of an earthly hierarchy of power imitative of the celestial hierarchy. This would be feasible only if Wyclif did not think that Natural *dominium* could be restored through apostolic poverty. Fitzralph, for example, did not believe that such a restoration was possible, and his thought is only slightly less hierocratic than was Giles of Rome's. But because Wyclif believed that Natural *dominium* was reattainable through apostolic poverty, and that civil *dominium* is less pure than just spiritual *dominium*, the king is only at a summit of temporal

---

[1] For a survey of the theocratic kingship model, see Janet Nelson, "Kingship and Empire", in *The Cambridge History of Medieval Political Thought*, ed. J. Burns (Cambridge, 1988), pp. 211–51; Walter Ullmann, *A History of Political Thought: The Middle Ages* (Baltimore, 1965), pp. 130–58.

authority. Further, Wyclif's contempt for hierarchical models was considerable. Why, he argued, should God's *dominium* need intermediaries? Divine lordship is unmediated and complete in every aspect, because God alone created every aspect. His *dominium* over universals prior to particulars does not suggest an ontological hierarchy, only that God's knowledge descends from the general to the particular.

Leaving aside the unlikely possibility that Wyclif's model is fundamentally Aristotelian, we are left with the possibility that Wyclif just did not have a model of any determinate kind. This is a valid approach, and of our three alternatives probably the most tenable, having been endorsed by Leff, McFarlane, Daly, and Workman. After all, he appears to wander digressively, riding his hobby-horse of ecclesiastical reform with boundless energy. But while arguable, it does not explain the consistencies apparent in the *Tractatus de Universalibus, De Dominio Divino, De Civili Dominio*, and *De Officio Regis* which the universal–particular model does.

What are the benefits of a theory of *dominium* founded on the universal–particular relation, in which all instances of just human *dominium* participate in divine *dominium*? If Wyclif's chief goal were simply to divest the church of its material holdings, he could have done at least as much with the theocratic model, or even with a variation of the Aristotelian model. The civil lord's Grace-favored nature and *caritas* need not enter into either account. If his real aim was to write a "mirror of princes," a universal–particular model is cumbersome at best. How to use it to explain the best way to deal with parliament, or to organize a taxation system, or devise a judicial program in such language? Why not just make political prescriptions in the plain language of men of action? The benefits of such a model were not payable in political coin because Wyclif was not interested in describing political power *per se*. His intention was to characterize all just human authoritative relations as phenomena in God's Creation. That the arguments of *De Civili Dominio* and *De Officio Regis* are directed towards secular *dominium* only shows what Wyclif believed to be the best way to address postlapsarian human society. Civil *dominium* is important insofar as it bears on Christ's restoration of Natural *dominium* in the church. Presumably, if a nation existed on some unapproachable island that consisted solely of the Grace-favored, civil *dominium* would not be in evidence; certainly there will be no such office in Paradise.

The universal–particular structure makes the best sense for Wyclif's aims by allowing him to show how a civil lord is a just material steward in Creation without giving the lord undue pre-eminence in his overall theological structure. The other species of just human *dominium* – natural and spiritual – shine through as obviously superior, and the connections between all of the species are plain and solid. Wyclif effectively describes civil, spiritual, and Natural *dominium* as being different tokens of one type (*dominium*). Through this he can show how man's fallen state, rectifiable through Christ's redemption, is not anything outside the type, namely divine *dominium*.

Using this approach has other benefits. First, it shows that Wyclif's philosophy is consistent. A justly famous scholastic metaphysician turned his attention to social concerns, producing philosophically complex arguments comprehensible in terms he had already defined. Comparatively few political theorists in the fourteenth century were prepared to defend definitions of such crucial terms as "relation," "having," and "power" with the ontological specificity that Wyclif used. This approach allows us to extend Wyclif's philosophical corpus through *De Civili Dominio* at least, rather than stopping with the *Tractatus de Universalibus*, as Robson's account does.[2]

Second, this approach disproves the contention that Grace-favored *dominium* was a red herring in Books 2 and 3 of *De Civili Dominio*, and in *De Officio Regis*. Wyclif viewed Grace as the primary factor allowing the civil lord to divest the church in the manner prescribed in these treatises. It also explains why *De Officio Regis* says little about the daily mechanics of rule. That Wyclif does not dwell on Grace-favored *dominium* there does not suggest that he had stopped believing in its import, only that he felt that the treatise's consistency with the first book of *De Civili Dominio* was obvious to anyone who had read *De Dominio Divino*.

Third, we can now begin looking seriously at the arguments presented in *De Ecclesia*, *De Potestate Pape*, and other later works to see if Wyclif diverges from the universal–particular model in his examination of spiritual *dominium*. By the end of his life, Wyclif was responsible for some less-than-philosophical polemics. This model of a coherent social philosophy consistent with a realist metaphysic allows us to determine when polemics began to outweigh dialectics. This model also shows new directions for further analysis of the *Summa de Ente*. For example, how does Wyclif's realism direct his contention that the church is the body of the Predestinate? D. P. Henry has argued that Wyclif's realism regarding relations between objects, and between people, necessitates the existence of aggregate universals: for any grouping of members into an aggregate whole, there exists a supervening aggregate being by which the group has reality. This suggests a strong tie between Wyclif's ontological interpretation of the Aristotelian categories and the identity of any being

---

[2] See Robson, *Wyclif and the Oxford Schools* (Cambridge, 1961), p. 17: "Though he remained the schoolman in technique and temperament, he had in reality abandoned the study of philosophy for that of political theory; and, if he employed scholastic forms of argument, he had by the mid-1370s ceased to think creatively in the field of scholastic studies."

explicable in terms of parts and whole, whether it be an individual human being, the Holy Trinity, the church, or Scripture.[3] If the church is the body of the Predestinate, then that body has an ontological reality supervening on the being of its members. Following Wyclif's contention that God knows universals before particulars, it follows that God knows the church as a universal aggregate being prior to knowing its individual members. Now that we have an appreciation for the pervasive nature of metaphysics in Wyclif's social thought, we have a standard with which to approach problems like that briefly described here.

Finally, the universal–particular model disproves the contemptible claim that Wyclif did little more than crib from *De Pauperie Salvatoris*.[4] As we have noted, Fitzralph said little to nothing about metaphysics, and what we can abstract reveals a moderate realist position more consonant with Giles of Rome than with Wyclif's realism. Fitzralph's picture of Natural *dominium* certainly influenced Wyclif, as did his notion that Grace is the only possible foundation for just human *dominium* after the Fall, but Fitzralph never put it in such ontologically complex language. Nor, of course, did he use the doctrine as Wyclif did. In this vein, the universal–particular explanation gives a solid foundation upon which to dismiss the charge that Wyclif wrote the *dominium* works primarily to serve John of Gaunt's needs.

EPILOGUE: LATIN WYCLIFFISM AND VERNACULAR TEXTS

Over the past three decades, Anne Hudson and two academic generations of her students have done much to explain the origins, development, and nature of the Lollard movement by editing and publishing many of the documents expressing Lollard beliefs and goals, and assessing their relation to Wyclif's thought.[5] In the interest of furthering Hudson's enterprise,

---

[3] See Desmond P. Henry, "Wyclif's Deviant Mereology," in his *Medieval Mereology* (Amsterdam, 1991), for an outline of Wyclif's conception of the reality of aggregate universals.

[4] K. B. McFarlane, *John Wycliffe and the Beginnings of English Nonconformity* (Aylesbury, 1952), pp. 58–89. A variation on this argument is that Wyclif meant his theology of apostolic poverty to serve as a stimulus for followers of Wat Tyler. Recently, Steven Justice has argued that Wyclif emphasized apostolic poverty to give rebels the idea that his writings had populist implications, all the while cynically using this as a ruse to overthrow ecclesiastical power in the service of the Duke of Lancaster. See Steven Justice, *Writing and Rebellion: England in 1381* (Berkeley, 1994), pp. 81–101.

[5] The list of Lollard texts edited over the past three decades is long; foremost are Anne Hudson and Pamela Gradon, eds., *English Wycliffite Sermons*, 5 vols. (Oxford, 1983–96); Anne Hudson, ed., *Selections from English Wycliffite Writings* (Cambridge, 1978); Anne Hudson, ed., *Two Wycliffite Texts*, EETS OS 301 (Oxford, 1993); Gloria Cigman, ed., *Lollard Sermons*, EETS OS 294 (Oxford, 1989). For a clearer picture of the many scholars who have contributed to the body of Lollard writings, see Fiona Somerset, *Clerical Discourse and Lay Audience in Late Medieval England* (Cambridge, 1998); also, the on-line bibliography of The Lollard Society, at http://home.att.net/~lollard/

it will be useful to see if our analyses of Wyclif's thought can shed light on the developing picture of Lollardy. Lollardy was a complex social phenomenon importantly connected to Wyclif at its inception, which connection became increasingly unimportant as the movement evolved. Hudson has argued that the critical phase for intellectual Wycliffism in the Lollard movement was 1381–1413; after the rebellion of the Lancastrian knights.[6]

Lollardy did not begin with Wyclif deciding that something "had to be done" and organizing a band of devoted followers to realize his dream. The first Lollards were scholars and students associated with Wyclif in Oxford, among them individuals, like Nicholas Hereford, who were instrumental in translating the Bible into Middle English, Philip Repington, an Austin canon in Leicester known to have preached Wyclif's ideas in Northamptonshire in 1382, and lay preachers like William Smith and William Swinderby, also of Leicester.[7] Their association with Wyclif began shortly after he finished *De Civili Dominio*, in 1378, when he was in the midst of articulating his position on ecclesiastical reform in *De Ecclesia*.[8] The movement grew slowly in its first five years, only when these men had the opportunity to preach in small churches in Melton Mowbray, Hallaton, Market Harborough, and Loughborough.[9]

When William Courtenay, who had long been opposed to Wyclif's social ideas, was made Archbishop of Canterbury in the spring of 1382, one of the first things he did was to begin persecuting his old enemy. The infamous "Earthquake Council" of May 17, 1382, was the beginning of a concentrated effort to silence Wyclif, which effort lasted until December 31, 1384, when Wyclif died.[10] The policy of the English

---

[6] The chief scholarly authority for this period is Anne Hudson: see her *Selections from English Wycliffite Writings* (Cambridge, 1978); *The Premature Reformation* (Oxford, 1988); *Two Wycliffite Texts* (Oxford, 1993). See also McFarlane, *John Wycliffe and the Beginnings of English Nonconformity*; Gordon Leff, *Heresy in the Later Middle Ages* (New York, 1967), pp. 559–606; Christina von Nolcken, "Another Kind of Saint: A Lollard Perception of John Wyclif," in *From Ockham to Wyclif*, ed. A. Hudson and M. Wilks, *SCH* Subsidia 5 (London, 1987), pp. 429–44; A. K. McHardy, "The Dissemination of Wyclif's Ideas," in *From Ockham to Wyclif*, pp. 361–3.

[7] It is unlikely that this band of preachers thought of themselves as "Lollards," for the word had been used to refer to grumblers and mumblers against the *status quo*. It is hard to imagine preachers taking pride in being referred to as mumblers. Indeed, not all of those associated with the Bible translation were necessarily allied with Wyclif; see David C. Fowler, *The Life and Times of John Trevisa, Medieval Scholar* (Seattle, 1995), pp. 225–34.

[8] See Thomson, *The Latin Writings of John Wyclyf*, pp. 58–9.

[9] See H. B. Workman, *John Wyclif: A Study of the English Medieval Church* (Oxford, 1926), vol. 2, pp. 201–20; McFarlane, *John Wycliffe and the Beginnings of English Nonconformity*, pp. 100–05.

[10] For a detailed account of the Council held at the Black Friars house that ended in an earthquake which both Wyclif and his persecutors interpreted as evidence of divine favor for their side, see Workman, *John Wyclif*, vol. 2, pp. 246–93; Dahmus, *The Prosecution of John Wyclyf* (New Haven, 1952), pp. 74–129. See also Thomas Walsingham, *Historia Anglicana* ed. H. T. Riley, Rerum Britannicarum Medii Aevi Scriptores 20 (London, 1862), vol. 1, pp. 50–61.

church was to make known which of Wyclif's beliefs were specifically detestable, but this, along with Wyclif's appeal to Parliament for support for the specifically anti-clerical and pro-secular elements of his thought, contributed to a swift widespread familiarity with the general tenets of Wyclif's political and ecclesiastical ideology.[11] Familiarity with the opinions of Wyclif that had been officially condemned did not mean universal condemnation, though; it also helped to gain him support among other scholars at Oxford.

Courtenay used all the powers at his disposal to attack Wyclif. Shortly after the Blackfriars Council in late June of 1382, he used his influence to get Richard II to agree to a blanket condemnation of preachers who were found expounding Wyclif's ideas. Parliament had just ended, and Courtenay, who knew that the Commons would not support such a condemnation, acted throughout the summer to be sure that he would be in a position to withstand legislative opposition when Parliament convened again. He had an ally in Richard Baybroke, who had been bishop of London during the Peasant's Revolt the year earlier; Baybroke was now royal chancellor, and was eager to promulgate Courtenay's condemnation through all the dioceses of England. At this point, although Wyclif's ideas were roundly condemned, his person was in no danger, for Courtenay had avoided actually using the name "Wyclif" in the blanket condemnation.[12] By the time the Commons was in session in October, their protestations had little effect.

In late May Courtenay condemned the tenets of Wycliffism that were being espoused in the teachings of Philip Repington, who was then prominent in Oxford. Oxford's chancellor, Robert Rigg, would have none of Courtenay's interference in university affairs, responding that "neither bishop nor archbishop had any power over the university, even in matters of heresy."[13] Rigg was strongly supported by the laity in Oxford, academics and townsfolk, and Repington continued his preaching and recruiting of other preachers. Opposition to Rigg, and to Wyclif, came from the friars at Oxford. It is certainly noteworthy that in their defense of

[11] Walsingham provides several lists of the general tenets of Wyclif's political and ecclesiastical program in the section referred to in n. 10. Dahmus provides an explanation of these tenets and a careful explication of which list Walsingham gives correlates to which party among Wyclif's persecutors constructed the list. For a more complete compilation of the documents of Wyclif's persecution, see Thomas Netter *Fasciculi Zizaniorum Magistri Johannis Wyclif*, ed. W. W. Shirley, Rerum Britannicarum Medii Aevi Scriptores 5 (London, 1858). Wyclif's own list of his tenets appears *ibid.*, pp. 115–33.

[12] See Workman, *John Wyclif*, vol. 2, pp. 269–73; Dahmus, *The Prosecution of John Wyclyf*, pp. 85–9; *Fasciculi Zizaniorum*, pp. 272–86; Thomas Walsingham, *Historia Anglicana*, pp. 57–8: "Archiepiscopus rem agit cum Coepiscopis de Conclusionibus Wycliff." For Courtenay's tenure as Archbishop, see Joseph Dahmus, *William Courtenay Archbishop of Canterbury 1381–1396* (University Park, 1966).

[13] Workman, *John Wyclif*, vol. 2, p. 275; Workman does not provide a source for this quotation.

Wyclif, secular "town and gown" were united. This indicates how quickly the basic tenets of Wyclif's thought on church reform were accepted, and suggests that the itinerant preachers who were increasingly to be found throughout England would be received favorably by the laity.

On June 12, 1382, Rigg was formally called before a second council at Blackfriars in London, where he was commanded to carry out Courtenay's wishes. Rigg backed down, and acceded to the archbishop, thereby inflaming mounting tensions between seculars and friars at Oxford. Repington and his associate John Aston were called before the council at Blackfriars during the next week for reprimand. They refused to cease their support of Wyclif's tenets, and were excommunicated in the last week of June. This only increased their currency among the common people. By August, most of the major figures of the newborn movement were only nominally associated with heresy, and were preaching and re-cruiting throughout the land. As Courtenay continued to exert pressure through the dioceses, some of these figures, including Repington, were caught and recanted. Wyclif was still left alone, thanks in no small part to his protection by John of Gaunt.

In October Courtenay moved to stamp out the heresy at Oxford in a far more serious manner; he took the final step and personally vis-ited the university to formally condemn Wycliffism as it had come to be understood. Several of the remaining Wycliffite figures, including John Aston, recanted at this point, but Rigg and some other secular scholars maintained a concerted opposition at the university level. Rigg was eventually to admit defeat for lack of support; too many seculars had joined the friars in support of the Archbishop. Still, Wycliffism re-mained a significant movement in Oxford for six years thereafter, for all of Wyclif's writings were formally condemned there in 1388. It appears that while the major figures were forced to bend to powerful ecclesiastical pressure, many anonymous individuals continued in their support.

By the late 1380s, academic support of Wycliffism and of the now so-called Lollardy had dwindled, but the movement had taken root among the common laity. When Courtenay finally died in 1396, Thomas Arundel, his successor, continued policing Oxford for any hint of a re-currence of Wycliffism. In his recounting of the history of Wycliffism at Oxford, Herbert Workman intimates that Courtenay's visit in 1382 heralded the end of philosophical innovation at Oxford.[14] More reli-able is William J. Courtenay, whose *Schools and Scholars in Fourteenth*

---

[14] See Workman, *John Wyclif*, vol. 2, p. 376.

Century England provides a less partisan interpretation of the atmosphere at Oxford in the 1370s and 1380s, suggesting that the innovatory spirit that had characterized English scholasticism since the time of Grosseteste did not leave the island, but shifted from the philosophy of the schools to a less formal venue in the court and among the literati.[15]

From the 1390s through the beginning of 1414, Lollardy grew markedly throughout England, but K. B. McFarlane notes that it was but tenuously connected to Wyclif's philosophical thought.[16] Townspeople and laborers, farmers and wayfarers, priests and lesser nobles came to align themselves with the growing popular movement that was founded in Wyclif's circle in Oxford, and in all the literature they produced, there is scant reference to the formal elements of Wyclif's arguments discussed in this study. In many cases, vernacular translations of Wyclif's sermons served as the staple diet for Lollards of the period, and the explosion of vernacular Lollard literature suggests Wyclif's belief in the need for devotional literature and Scripture to be available in the language of the people.

Given our enhanced understanding of Wyclif's philosophical program, particularly of the important part his realist metaphysics plays in his doctrine of Grace-founded *dominium*, it makes sense to ask what came of it all with respect to the Lollard literature. K. B. McFarlane notes that no one would give him a second glance had Wyclif not fathered this movement.[17] Does our explication of his pre-1379 *dominium* thought help us to understand the Lollard heresy better?[18] If so, can one argue that it is impossible to understand Lollardy without reading *De Civili Dominio* or the *Tractatus*

---

[15] William J. Courtenay, *Schools and Scholars in Late Fourteenth Century England* (Princeton, 1987), pp. 356–80. Courtenay mentions neither Archbishop Courtenay nor Arundel in his discussion of the gradual decline of Oxford's scholarly fortunes. He refers to the earlier Courtenay only to discuss the increasing influence aristocratic families had over policy at the university, see *ibid.*, pp. 144–6.

[16] See McFarlane, *John Wycliffe and the Beginnings of English Nonconformity*, p. 148.

[17] "Had his death occurred in 1374 or even as much as a year or two later Wycliffe would be remembered only by specialist historians as one of the lesser ornaments of medieval Oxford. They would know him as the author of a number of philosophical works of no particular brilliance through of sustained competence... It was only when this middle-aged doctor of divinity abandoned his crowded lecture-room for the royal service that there began that period of frenzied agitation upon which his later fame depends." *Ibid.*, p. 12.

[18] I have not selected 1379 arbitrarily; while Wyclif wrote the latter two books of *De Civili Dominio* in response to criticism from William Wodeford and others prior to that year, we can detect enough of the original thought from Book 1 of *DCD* in *De Officio Regis* to argue for a continuity in the two works. The dividing line is not perfect in a temporal sense, for he wrote *De Ecclesia* and *De Veritate Sacre Scripture* shortly before writing *DOR*, but little that he wrote afterwards carries the *dominium* theory as philosophically importantly. The *Trialogus*, for example, written in late 1382–early 1383, makes mention of civil *dominium* rarely, and then only in service of its anticlerical arguments.

de Universalibus? Is Lollardy Wyclif's *dominium* put into practice?[19] That Lollardy was a heresy in the fourteenth-century church is certainly true; is the realist metaphysics of the *Tractatus de Universalibus* heretical, given its place as the basis for the first books of the *Summa Theologie*? Is it Lollardy to argue for realism about relations? Some of Wyclif's near contemporaries certainly suspected that it might. The *Fasciculi Zizaniorum* lists seven metaphysical positions of Wyclif's that were generally regarded as heretical, each of which can conceivably be tied to his theory of relation. Further, Thomas Netter carefully argued against Wyclif's philosophical program in his *Doctrinale antiquitatum fidei ecclesiae catholicae* of 1421, the analysis of which will likely provide a much more complete picture of late fourteenth-century, post-Wyclif Oxford discourse.[20] If so, this could have import on the history of late medieval philosophy as a whole, for Wyclif's metaphysics represent an important Oxonian alternative to the conceptualism of the *Via Moderna*, and Ockhamism has been held to have been the philosophical foundation of the Protestant Reformation.[21] If the realism of fourteenth-century Oxford, an attempt to regain pure Augustinian philosophy, and the conceptualism of the Ockhamist *Moderni* both lead to heresy of some sort or other, what was left for the church to hold onto aside from the "moderate realist" compromise initiated by Aquinas and Scotus? I do not wish to argue that fifteenth-century philosophers likely saw that the two "extreme" positions were untenable, and so turned to enhancing the metaphysics of the Dominicans and conventional Franciscans. This would be simplistic, and it would ignore the influence of extra-philosophical forces on the development of late medieval thought. Further, too little scholarship exists at present to afford any conclusions about scholastic philosophy in that period. We should stay in the better charted waters of late fourteenth-century discourse by understanding how the philosophical program that Wyclif expounded through 1379 figures in Lollard doctrine. Is it the essence of this heresy, is it a significant part among other parts, or is it of little importance in defining the heresy?

How can an argument as to how a substance has properties, or how a relation is founded in some universal apart from the two *relata* involved, be heretical? There are no references to proscribed ideas about the divine nature, or about the proper organization of the church, or about the

---

[19] See Hudson, *The Premature Reformation*, p. 360: "Though Wyclif's theory of dominion was couched first in general terms, he used it almost exclusively as a rod with which to beat the church." Is this the theory's only use? Is it what Wyclif constructed it to do?

[20] *Fasciculi Zizaniorum*, pp. 3–4; see Robson, *Wyclif and the Oxford Schools*, pp. 219–40.

[21] Heiko Oberman, *The Harvest of Late Medieval Theology: Gabriel Biel and Late Medieval Nominalism* (Cambridge, MA, 1963).

clergy, in such talk; the discourse is as general and as abstract as can be. But Wyclif says that if one is the sort of realist that he is, then his position on *dominium* follows; if one has his position on *dominium*, then one has the raw materials for one of the main components of Lollardy and one can easily be branded a heretic.[22] I am not arguing that if one is a Lollard, then one must be a metaphysical realist of Wyclif's stamp; this would involve an argument moving from what I use as consequent to what I believe to be antecedent, which is certainly fallacious. One might become a Lollard for any number of reasons, and not care a fig about metaphysics. But if one is a disciple of Wyclif's brand of realism, can one avoid Lollardy? Wyclif's philosophical works were used as texts long after his later works had been condemned. Hudson notes, "Wyclif remained, it seems, a part of the ordinary academic inheritance of the late fourteenth-century Oxford, at least for those parts of his writings which did not concern obvious questions of heresy."[23] Indeed, several of his earliest writings on logic and terms were in use on the Continent well into the fifteenth century.[24] Historical evidence suggests that, at least in post-Wyclif Oxford, being a philosophical realist did not automatically lead to either defending against, nor to embracing, nor even to addressing Lollardy at all. Given Archbishop William Courtenay's vigorous persecution of Wyclif and his followers in 1382 and thereafter, the prospect of any scholar pursuing Wyclif's ontological position into ecclesiology, sacramental theology, or other sensitive areas was nonexistent. Jeremy Catto describes post-Wyclif Oxford's atmosphere as philosophically active, in which viewpoints such as those of William Woodford and other opponents of Wyclif modified ontological discourse sufficiently diverse as to allow consideration of Wyclif's realism possible. Hence, the fact seems to have been that being a philosophical realist did not lead one to Lollardy, despite the concerns of anti-Wycliffites like Netter.[25]

Is Wyclif's position on *dominium* important to Lollardy? Until recently, scholars have tended either to make no reference to Wyclif's philosophical

---

[22] Recall that, for Wyclif, God's *dominium* was the only relation now obtaining between God and Creation, and so one can only describe the divine relation to Creation in its terms. Thus, when he discussed the theological implications of his ontology, one could not escape framing it in terms of divine *dominium*.

[23] Hudson, *The Premature Reformation*, p. 86 and p. 87, n. 165.

[24] For example, The Seminar in the Auxiliary Disciplines of Medieval Studies, Department of History, Harvard University, "A New Work By John Wyclif?" in *The Marks in the Fields: Essays on the Uses of Manuscripts*, ed. Rodney G. Dennis and Elizabeth Falsey (Cambridge, MA, 1992), pp. 31–7; also Massimo Mugnai, "La 'Expositio Reduplicativarum' chez Walter Burleigh et Paulus Venetus," in *English Logic in Italy in the 14th and 15th Centuries*, ed. Alfonso Maiera (Naples, 1982), pp. 317–20. See also Courtenay, *Schools and Scholars in Late Medieval England*, pp. 357–65.

[25] J. I. Catto, "Wyclif and Wycliffism at Oxford 1356–1430," in *The History of the University of Oxford*, ed. (Oxford, 1992), vol. 2, pp. 218–61.

writings when discussing the heresy, or they have dismissed its relevance. Gordon Leff's assessment has been influential. In explaining the relation of *dominium* theory to Lollardy, he says, "Wyclif's doctrine of dominion and Grace, for all its seeming inexorability, was singularly devoid of immediacy."[26] It was an interesting position for a scholar to hold at one point in his development, Leff argues, but it mattered little to the thought that would influence Lollardy. Similarly, Malcolm Lambert believes the doctrine of Grace-founded *dominium* to be of little consequence in understanding the heresy.[27]

Not all scholars have accepted these conclusions about the place of Grace-founded *dominium* in Wyclif's thought. The foremost contemporary scholar of Lollardy has been Anne Hudson, who has published a collection of Wycliffite writings central to the late fourteenth-century version of the heresy, as well as the fullest historical account of its nature.[28] She warns that the argument at the heart of *De Civili Dominio* and *De Dominio Divino* should not be discounted in understanding the political aspects of Lollardy. Leff had argued that the impossibility of figuring out who was Grace-favored made the doctrine practically unworkable. Hudson suspects that it might not be as impractical as it seems. "[A]s has been seen in dealing with the nature of the church, even if only God could *know* the state of Grace, man could make a pretty shrewd guess in cases of outrageous behaviour; even if certainty was impossible of access, enough doubt was cast upon the legitimacy of actions, and more importantly on the legitimacy of laws, to render their force questionable."[29] So the *dominium* doctrine might be an important aspect of the ideas that lie at the center of Lollardy. Hudson's approach has been to define it in the terms used by Wyclif's earliest disciples, instead of relying on contemporary episcopal or secular court records. Texts that have direct links to Wyclif's works, including passages from them, or even those in praise of Wyclif's writings, are reliable sources, as are later texts that are themselves reliant on these earlier ones. While they are not perfectly definitive, we can gain an accurate picture of the body of belief of the heresy from such sources.[30] There are three generally recognized inter-connective headings under which Lollard belief can be categorized: beliefs about Scripture,

---

[26] Leff, *Heresy in the Later Middle Ages*, p. 549; cf. pp. 546–9.

[27] Malcolm Lambert, *Medieval Heresy: Popular Movements from the Gregorian Reform to the Reformation* (London, 1992), p. 237.

[28] Hudson, *Selections from English Wycliffite Writings*.

[29] Hudson, *The Premature Reformation*, p. 360.

[30] Problems of transmission of these texts include their being lost, damaged, or purposefully destroyed, their being used for extemporaneous proselytizing in which anything might have been added to the text being used, and the possibility of including among them texts not written by Lollards.

beliefs about the Sacraments, and beliefs about ecclesiastical and political matters.[31]

We need not devote much attention to the first two headings, for the Lollard positions on these topics, though of considerable importance for understanding the heresy, are not as directly rooted in *De Civili Dominio* and in *De Officio Regis* as is the third category. Wyclif's position on the proper attitude towards Scripture is certainly founded in *De Mandatis Divinis*, wherein he makes it clear that the only body of law founded in God's will is that taught in Scriptures, most importantly the *lex Christi*. And there can be little doubt that Wyclif's later, dramatic rejection of transubstantiation in the works on the Eucharist is securely grounded in the atomism he outlined in the *Summa de Ente* and in *De Materia et Forma*. Our aim, though, is to show that Wyclif's position on divine and human *dominium* is responsible for the Lollard beliefs on ecclesiastical and political matters. If it is, the thought of *De Civili Dominio*, *De Dominio Divino*, and *De Officio Regis* takes on a new relevance as the base of one third of the heresy.

There are six important points that define Lollard attitudes towards matters of church and state, each of which is founded in the arguments of Wyclif's works on *dominium*. These include (1) the belief that the predestined Elect make up the true church; (2) the rejection of the extant ecclesiastical hierarchy; (3) the denial of private ownership for the priesthood; (4) the hostility to "private religions," or religious orders; (5) the rejection of holy war in the absence of special revelation; and (6) the belief that secular lords have temporal authority over the church.[32] Not all Lollards in the period accepted all six of these positions, but the frequency of their appearance coupled with the justifications given for accepting them suggest that most were partial to most of these positions.[33] An instance

---

[31] Hudson organizes it somewhat differently in *The Premature Reformation*; her structure is Theology, Ecclesiology, and Politics, collapsing my first two distinctions into one and enlarging my third into two separate headings. In this discussion, I will pay little attention to the Theology (i.e. to scriptural and sacramental matters), concentrating upon Lollard attitudes towards the clergy, the church, and towards secular power. I argue that these three are of a piece, and that the theoretical justifications for the attitudes towards the clergy and the church lie in Wyclif's two tractates about secular power. Hence it makes better sense to include these three subjects under one heading; there is little in *De Civili Dominio* or in any of the works discussed in this study that indicates Wyclif's fully formed attitudes towards Scripture or towards the Sacraments.

[32] These are roughly based on the tenets of Wycliffism that Archbishop William Courtenay condemned in the summer of 1382. See Thomas Walsingham, *Historia Anglicana*, vol. 2, pp. 58–9; also Dahmus, *The Prosecution of John Wyclyf*, pp. 80–2, and Hudson, *The Premature Reformation*, pp. 67–73.

[33] I follow Anne Hudson's line of reasoning in *The Premature Reformation*, "A Lollard Creed?" pp. 382–9. See also McFarlane, *John Wycliffe and the Beginnings of English Nonconformity*, pp. 121–59; for a picture of the early influential Lollards' opinions regarding church and state matters, see McFarlane, "Employments, Rewards, and Landed Wealth," *Lancastrian Kings and Lollard Knights*

of this is the well-known "Twelve Conclusions of the Lollards" of 1395, in which five of these six points are featured.[34]

The first point, that the predestined Elect make up the true church, would be familiar to any reader of *De Civili Dominio*. The best example of this doctrine in Lollard writings is in *The Lanterne of Liȝt*, one of the best-known sources of Lollard doctrine. This work, written before 1413, was the evidence for which John Claydon, a currier of London, was burned under the orders of Henry Chichele, Archbishop of Canterbury. In Chapters 6–9 of this work, the church is described in its three modes of being, as it is truly known by God, as a material building, and as the individuals who congregate in the material building.[35] The first mode is identical with the body of the Elect, foreknown by God to be worthy of Christ's salvation.

þe firste is clepid a litil flok, as Crist seiþ [in *Luc.xii*] "Nile þe drede my litil flok, it plesiþ ȝoure fadir to ȝiue ȝou a kyngdom." And þis chirche is clepid e chosun noumbre of hem þat schullen be saued as it is writen [*Ecci.iii*] "þe sones of wisdam ben þe chirche of riȝtwise men, and þe nacioun of hem is buxumnesse to God and loue to her euenecristen" . . .[36]

The writer of the *Lanterne* is fairly expansive in describing this church, likening it to Christ's spouse, to a clean, chaste maiden, or a woman with child. One cannot define it in terms of earthly office. "þe chirche is not in men bi weye of powere or dignitie spiritual or temperal/for manye princis & hiȝe bischopis & oþir or lowere degree, state or dignite are founden to be apostataas, or haue gon abak from þe bileue/wherfore þe chirch stondiþ in þoo persoones in whom is knowyng &verri confessioun of feiþ & trouþe."[37]

Indeed, the members of the church are equal to one another before God, but differ in function; some may be laborers who fear God and walk

---

(Oxford, 1972), pp. 186–96; for similar appraisals of the importance of ecclesiastical reform in Lollardy, see W. H. Summers, "The Early Days of Lollardy," *The Lollards of the Chiltern Hills* (London, 1906), pp. 41–8; Lambert, *Medieval Heresy*, pp. 255–60; Leff, *Heresy in the Later Middle Ages*, pp. 559–86.

[34] Hudson, *English Wycliffite Writings*, pp. 24–9, 150–5. The missing point is the belief in the church comprising the foreknown Elect.

[35] There is no reference to the church as the living Body of Christ in this definition; that the writer immediately jumps to the church as the body of the Elect as the true, "formal" definition of the church suggests a Wyclif-influenced tendency to define mundane beings in their truest form in terms of God's knowing relation of them, as in *De Dominio Divino*. Cf. *DCD*, I, 39, 287.9–288.26, wherein Wyclif makes virtually the same definition of the church as the writer of *The Lanterne*. For further Lollard definition of the church, see Pamela Gradon and Anne Hudson, *English Wycliffite Sermons*, vol. 4 (Oxford, 1983), pp. 89–93.

[36] Hudson, *English Wycliffite Writings*, Text 22, p. 116; cf. *The Lanterne of Liȝt*, ed. Lilian M. Swinburn, EETS 05 151 (London, 1917), no. 151.

[37] *The Lanterne of Liȝt*, 5, 22.20–5.

in His ways, while others may be bearers of the material sword, "made mynystris of Cristis godhed/hauyng powere & drede in to wraþþe & veniaunce of hem þat don yuel/and preising of hem þat don wel."[38] Others again might be priests, whose duty it is to awaken people to the way of truth. The relation between the priests and the bearers of the secular swords, referred to as knights in this text, is important enough to mention even before describing the duties of the priests:

For þus seiþ seint Austin in de quest. veteris & nove legis. ca.xxxv, & ca.iii(xx)xi, 'rex est vicarius deitatis. & sacerdos est vicarius christi humanatatis. Knyȝhthod representing þe myȝht & þe powere of þe fadere is þe viker of þe godhed and presthod representing þe wisedam of þe sone is þe viker of Goddis right-wisenes . . .[39]

This division of secular lords and priests into vicars of God and Christ respectively is described in *De Officio Regis* as the reason for the civil lord/king's control of the material aspects of the church.[40] That the discussion in *De Officio Regis* is immediately preceded by a discussion of the aristocracy of the Elect, the true church, as being equal in God's eyes to one another and more truly lords than any merely temporal lord cannot be coincidental. It is at the least a strong possibility that the writer of the *Lanterne* had the argument of *De Officio Regis* fresh in mind while describing the nature of the true church, either directly from the Latin text, or from a translation like *Tractatus de Regibus*, which I will discuss below.

This definition of the church suggested the Donatist heresy; the Carmelite Thomas Netter angrily denounced Wyclif's position as being worse than Donatism, "quia Donatus solis justis et sanctis qui saltem essent secundum famem sancti, Wicleffus solis justis veris et praedestinatis ad vitam."[41] Hudson notes that the next logical step, the doctrine of the universal priesthood of believers, developed gradually.[42] For our purposes, the connection made between the *Lanterne* and *De Officio Regis* is a good start. We need only turn to the first book of *De Civili Dominio* to see how important Wyclif believes this definition of the true church to be. In the second chapter, in which he explains how true *dominium* can only come from God, and be given to those who merit it, he explains that it is the church alone who receives from God, for they alone are known to be worthy.[43] As we have seen, this idea that only the Elect can hold just human *dominium* is central to his arguments for relieving the

---

[38] *Ibid.*, 5, 33.22–4.   [39] *Ibid.*, 5, 34.11–18.
[40] *DOR*, 6, 137.20–3.   [41] Quoted in Hudson, *The Premature Reformation*, p. 316, n. 12.
[42] *Ibid.*, pp. 314–27.   [43] *DCD*, I, ii, 11.16–31.

clergy of material ownership and that just civil lords must tend to the material well-being of the church.

The second tenet, regarding the rejection of the sacerdotal hierarchy, follows closely on the logic of the first; if all of the foreknown are equal in the eyes of God, how to justify a ranking system in priests? Given the Donatist tendencies already evident in Lollardy, antipathy for the papacy and curial machinery would follow as a matter of course. How did the Lollards counter the Petrine commission? In the same way that Wyclif had, namely by shifting the weight of the question away from temporal power and towards the exemplary duties of Peter's official descendants.[44] Hudson quotes a ringing statement by Thomas Cole in 1460 in this vein. " 'God ʒave power to Petir beyng a good man and an holy man to bynde and to lose, and to his successoures beyng as good as he was–and els not.' "[45] Further, what in Scriptures leads us to suppose that Peter had more power to bind or loosen than any of the other Apostles? Is it not as easy to interpret Peter as having spoken on behalf of his companions when he identified Christ as Messiah? And to read Christ's response as directed to the group through Peter, not simply to Peter?

To suppose the pope in Rome to be the head of the church is to displace Christ from His rightful place. The author of *The Thirty Seven Conclusions of the Lollards* presents an argument flowing directly from Wyclif's reasoning; the evidence of a lack of suitability for spiritual lordship is a presumption to know whether or not one deserves Grace. For any priest in the church to suppose that he knows his moral worth to be greater than any other is blasphemously to pretend to divine knowledge; this is the true offence of most occupants of the papal office. No matter what a pope might say or believe about himself, his actions will out, and no amount of priestly casuistry can get around this. "Wheþer þe vicious and vnkunnynge colegie of fleishly cardynals shal ʒeue more grace and holynesse to a wordly prest, chosen of hem by fleisly eiþer wordly affecioun, þan Crist, God almʒytti, ʒaf to Iudas, chosen of hym by souereyn wisdam and goodnesse and loue to al holy chirche, his spouse?"[46]

It follows that if so unworthy a priest were to imagine himself worthy of such authority, his commands would be like those of Satan. Any commandment made by someone aspiring to spiritual authority must be commensurate with Christ's law, which is only possible when the commander's will is voluntarily subordinated to God's will.[47] Thus Christ's

[44] For example, *DCD*, II, 3, 17.16–19.8; I, 38, 281.3–285.5.
[45] Hudson, *The Premature Reformation*, p. 329, cf. n. 85. See also Gradon and Hudson, *English Wycliffite Sermons*, vol. 4, pp. 93–101.
[46] Hudson, *English Wycliffite Writings*, 123.28–32.
[47] *Ibid.*, Article 26, pp. 125.124–127.181. See also *DCD*, I, 38, 283.1–20.

vicar can only be recognized by having echoed what Christ had already willed. Why should one person alone lay claim to such an honor? Is it not equally likely that some might serve Christ in one way, while others do otherwise? "As seint Poule hadde more power þanne Petre as to many þingis to edifie holy chirche, so anoþer cristen bishope may haue more power grauntide of þe Lord þanne haþ þe bishop of Rome to edifie holy chirche in feiþ and vertues by excellence of holy conuersacioun and of more spedful techinge."[48]

As has been mentioned, this second point is little more than a development of the Donatist aspect of the first point. Its basis, like that of the first, is securely in *De Civili Dominio*, though Wyclif was to develop the sentiment into a fully anti-hierocratic argument in *De Potestate Pape*. He wrote that work directly upon finishing *De Officio Regis*, in fall 1379. J. Loserth, the work's editor, regarded it as being central to Wyclif's ecclesiology; it was likely as important to Wyclif's later work as *De Dominio Divino* was to the works that immediately followed it. Hudson argues that *De Potestate Pape* is at the core of Lollard anti-hierocratic tendencies, but only because it brought to fruition tendencies already evident in the *dominium* treatises.[49]

By the time *The Lanterne of Liȝt* was written, the belief had elided from the impossibility of a just act outside of *lex Christi* to the position that all actions against Christ's law are those of Antichrist. Antichrist does not figure very importantly in the *dominium* treatises, but became important in Wyclif's later writings, and especially in Wycliffite literature.[50] One element that runs through the Wycliffite literature and the *dominium* treatises is the excoriation of legal tools used for ill. In *De Civili Dominio* and in *De Officio Regis*, Wyclif devotes substantial attention to showing how papal excommunication is invalidly used as a means of maintaining papal power.[51] The author of *The Lanterne* lists five "assaults" which Antichrist uses to enforce his will, of which the first is the semblance of secular rule, which includes excommunication among its misappropriated tools:

---

[48] Hudson, *English Wycliffite Writings*, 125.109–13.

[49] Hudson, *The Premature Reformation*, pp. 327–34; for Wyclif's revision of the relation of the celestial to the ecclesiastical hierarchy, see *De Potestate Pape*, 2, 35.17–43.9, and Luscombe, "Wyclif and Hierarchy," in *From Ockham to Wyclif*, ed. A. Hudson and M. Wilks, *SCH* Subsidia 5 (London, 1987), 233–44.

[50] Relevant to this discussion is Wyclif's contention that priests have abandoned *lex Christi* to study *lex antichristi*; see, for example, *Trialogus*, IV, 7; *De Potestate Pape*, 12, 355; and esp. *De Antichristo*, I, 10, 38.27–36. While Wyclif frequently identifies the Pope with Antichrist, his definition of Antichrist is anyone or any group who is against Christ according to the scriptural sense, see *De Antichristo*, I, 29, 107.20.

[51] *DCD*, I, 38, 275.3–278.4; *DOR*, 9 and 10.

Anticrist vseþ fals lucratif or wynnyng lawis as ben absoluciouns. indulgence. pardouns. priuelegis. & alle oþir heuenli tresour. þat is brouȝt in to sale for to spoile þe peple of her worldli goodis/& principali þise newe constitutciouns.bi whos strengþe anticrist enterditiþ chirchis. soumneþ prechours.suspendiþ resceyououours. & priueþ hem þer bennefice . . .[52]

The author does not mention excommunication in his catalogue, but his condemnation of papal legal tactics is similar to Wyclif's. The other four "assaults" include tribulation, inquisition, persecution, and execution, all instruments of the secular law misappropriated by the papacy. Wyclif's advice that priests be kept from studying the civil law arises precisely from his outrage at this misappropriation.[53]

Probably the most dramatic of the Lollard tenets explicitly directed towards the priesthood is the call for the absolute surrender of all private ownership in the church. It is certainly one of the guiding elements of *De Civili Dominio*, for not only is all of the third book devoted to the need for this surrender, it is also the first thing the civil lord must accomplish in the reform Wyclif outlined in the first two books. One would expect Lollard writings on this topic to be plentiful, and they are. The first of the *Twelve Conclusions* sets the tone for the Lollard indictment of the state of the priesthood:

Qwan þe chirche of Yngelond began to dote in temperalte aftir hir stepmodir þe grete chirche of Rome, and chirchis were slayne be apropriacion to diuerse placys, feyth, hope and charite begunne for to fle out of oure chirche; for pride with this sori genealogie of dedly synnes chalingith it be title of heritage.þis conclusiun is general and prouid be experience, sustum and manere, as þu schalt herin aftir.[54]

In the sixth conclusion, the argument is against holding spiritual and temporal power in one position. "Us thinkith þat hermofrodrita or ambidexter wer a god name to sich manere of men of duble astate."[55]

The Lollards were not alone in this line of attack; throughout the period many had viewed the temporal wealth of the church as antithetical to its fundamental values and most used the same New Testament verses, such as Matthew 19:20–5, in their arguments. The *Sermon of William Taylor* serves as a useful vehicle for the typical Lollard condemnation of the priesthood regarding *temporalia*. A Master of Arts in Oxford, Taylor delivered this sermon on November 21, 1406, in London. He was one of

---

[52] *The Lanterne of Liȝt*, 5, 17.23–9.
[53] *DOR*, 10, 238. See also Hudson, *English Wycliffite Writings*, pp. 75–83, for selections from a sermon with anti-hierocratic arguments similar to those mentioned here.
[54] Hudson, *English Wycliffite Writings*, Text 3, *Twelve Conclusions of the Lollards*, 24.7–12.
[55] *Ibid.*, 26.67–9.

the Oxford Wycliffites, although he probably had never met Wyclif, and was burned on March 1, 1422. Taylor argues much the way Wyclif had in *De Civili Dominio* Book 3, that Christ's exemplary life and leadership of the apostolic community was characterized by *pauperitas et caritas*, and is the model for the contemporary church. When Christ was tempted by Satan to take mastery of the world, His refusal was exemplary for all who would follow in His spiritual leadership:

Neþeles for þis temporal lordship þat Crist, in ensaumple of þo þat shulden be hise foleweris, fully refuside, sum men, pretendinge or shewinge hemsilf to ocupie Cristis stide and his apostlis, goen ful lowe not oonly tobut also falliþ doun by symonye to þe deuel bi usurie, flateringe and leysynge and oþere hidouse synnes...So ferforþ þei ben bisottid bi vnordynat loue to þe world þat þei reioycen hem to be callid lordis and kingis in her owne. And certeyn in þis þei ben ful contrarious to Crist...[56]

Taylor's opinion of the consequences of Christ's refusal of temporal lordship is interesting; he explains that Christ's injunction to render to Caesar what was Caesar's implicitly confirmed the justice of civil *dominium* through His own refusal to take it on Himself. "Lo! Crist, notwiþstondynge þat Cesar was no riȝtful man but a mawmetrer, con-fermyde to him his seculer lordship raþer þan he wolde receȝue it himsilf."[57] This is not Wyclif's line of argument; nowhere does he say that Christ implicitly made Caesar's civil *dominium* just through His own refusal to its claim. Caesar would have had to be Grace-favored for Wyclif to acknowledge that his civil *dominium* was just, which possibility seems dim at best.

Still, Taylor's attack on clerical temporal power is consonant with Wyclif's. He argues forcefully for the responsibility priests bear towards their flock; if the spiritual leaders are unable to steer away from the mundane pleasures of postlapsarian life, how can their sheep hope to avoid sin? "And if þe clergie, þat shulde be þe spiritual part of þe chirche, quykenynge þe body of þe chirche as þe soule doiþ mannys body, be turned into deeþ no wondir þouy þe body of þe chirche ligge deed."[58]

The Lanterne provides similar reasoning, arguing that the priests' desire to be temporal lords precludes any claim they might have upon spiritual leadership:

It is pleyn to þe apostlis þis lordschip is enterdiȝtid/hou darst þou þanne take þis lordschip...? pleynli þou art forboden þe tone/for if þou wilt haue boþe þou

---

[56] *The Sermon of William Taylor*, in *Two Wycliffite Texts*, ed. Hudson, 5.98–6.113.
[57] *Ibid.*, 6.118–20.   [58] *Ibid.*, 11.304–7.

schalt leese boþe/þat is to sei. þi presthod & þi lordschip/or ellis þou schalt not be except of þis noumbre of þe whiche God pleyneþ him.[59]

Also useful is a Lollard commentary on John 10:11–16, "Y am a good schepparde. A good schepparde ȝyueþ his soule (þat is his liyf) for his scheep." The glossator argues that the priests, in their greed for the accumulation of temporal goods, have robbed their flock of the necessities of survival. "þe goodis of þe chirche ben patrymonyes of pore men, and by cursid cruelte it is takun fro hem whateuere þing þe mynystris and sispenderis (treuly not lordis or welderis) taken ouer liflode and cloþing."[60]

The solution for this sorry state is the secular disendowment of the temporal possessions of the spiritual offices, as is clear in Wyclif's writings. This aspect of the third point blends in with the sixth, that secular lords ought have temporal authority over the church. If they did not have temporal authority, how to justify their disendowment of the priesthood? A Lollard text articulating the argument of *De Officio Regis* says, "[C]risten men schulden be suget in mekenes to alle maner of men, to kyngus as passynge bifore oþer men, and to dukus as next vnder kyngis; and þese bene in statis to perfoureme þese offices, to take vengeaunce on yuell men and to prayse gode men."[61] As in *De Officio Regis*, the threat of universal papal temporal *dominium* makes disendowment an eminent necessity:[62]

As, if alle þo freris of Yngelonde hadden howses and godes in þo rewme of Yngelonde, and maden þo pope lord of hem, þo popis lordschipe were to myche and regale were lessid; and þus, by processe of tyme, myȝt þo londe be conquerid al into þo popis honde as oþer rewmys bene . . . Summe men sayne þat, if þo pope were lorde of al þinge in þis londe þat is in þo dede honde of prestys, he were more lorde þan oure kynge: þus forsakynge of Gods lawe, and florȝschyd wordys of anticriste destroyed rewmes in cristendame and pes and gode religioun.[63]

In another text, a dialogue between a priest and a knight of England, the absolute temporal authority of the king is put this way. "But in all þinge þat longeþ to temperalte þai schuld be suggetes to þe kinge and to oþer lordes temperales, and, ȝeue þai wiþstonde þe temperale power, þe kinge and þe lordes temperals schuld chastise hem and constreyne hem, for þereto þai bereþ þe swerd, as it es said tofore be authorite of saynte Poule."[64]

[59] *The Lanterne of Liȝt*, 12, 97.8–14.   [60] Hudson, *English Wycliffite Writings*, Text 12, 62.103–6.
[61] *Ibid.*, Text 25, 128.46–9. See also Gradon and Hudson, eds., *English Wycliffite Writings*, vol. 4, pp. 152–60.
[62] DOR, 7, 163.7ff.   [63] Hudson, *English Wycliffite Writings*, 131.127–43.
[64] *Ibid.*, Text 26, 134.94–8.

Conclusion

William Taylor cites the vision of Hildegard of Bingen as his authority for the temporal disendowment of the church, for which the priests had better be ready:

And to þat sowneþ þe profecie of Hildegar þat temporal lordis wiþ þe comuntee, þe whiche lȝuen actiifly and sumtyme weren but as erþe in comparisoun of þe clergie, whos lȝuyng or conversacioun shulde be in heuene (as þe Apostle seiþ), of wilful, free and meek delyueraunce of þe clergie shal take in greet partie þis flood fro þe clergie, and shal helpe it þat it be not drawun of þe flood of temporaltees fro his office, but þat it may freely flee into desert of contemplacioun and take entent to preestly ocupacioun. And to þis shulde þe be redy and wel willid.[65]

We need not produce more selections in this vein; this sampling is sufficient evidence for the continuation of Wyclif's call for the disendowment of priests by secular lords.[66] Hudson notes that Lollards were not much interested in the restoration of Natural *dominium* and the concomitant elimination of private property as a social goal.[67] Whether this is evidence of widespread ignorance of, or antipathy, or even apathy towards Wyclif's social vision is difficult to say. While this aspect of Wyclif's thought is indeed central to his *dominium* theory, we should not conclude that his Grace-founded *dominium* thought does not lead to Lollardy, but should recognize that this aspect did not figure importantly in the heresy.

Rather than devote attention to the fourth and fifth points, regarding the indictment of "private religions" and the rejection of the validity of holy wars which are not central issues in the *dominium* treatises, we should explore Lollard beliefs on temporal *dominium*.[68] Is there evidence for the most crucial aspect of Wyclif's *dominium* doctrine, the notion of Grace-founded *dominium*? There is certainly evidence that Lollards used Grace as an ultimate authority for their interpretation of Scripture.[69] Do Lollards believe that God alone justifies secular lords in their offices, that secular office without Grace cannot be just? If so, we shall have assembled enough of the consequences of Wyclif's version of that theory to show that Wyclif's *dominium* thought as it appears in *De Dominio Divino*, *De Civili Dominio*, and *De Officio Regis* is consistent with Lollardy.

[65] *The Sermon of William Taylor*, Hudson, *Two Wycliffite Texts*, p. 9.221–9.
[66] See Hudson, *The Premature Reformation*, pp. 334–47 for a fuller historical discussion of the topic.
[67] *Ibid.*, pp. 374–5.
[68] For "private religions" see Hudson, *The Premature Reformation*, pp. 347–51; Hudson, *English Wycliffite Writings*, Text 18, 93–6; *The Lanterne of Liȝt*, 7 ff.; Gradon and Hudson, eds., *English Wycliffite Writings*, vol. 4, pp. 121–45; for the validity of holy wars, see Hudson, *The Premature Reformation*, pp. 367–70; Gradon and Hudson, eds., *English Wycliffite Sermons*, vol. 4, pp. 159–60.
[69] See Fiona Somerset's discussion of William Thorpe's impassioned *Testimony* in *Clerical Discourse and Lay Audience in Late Medieval England* (Cambridge, 1998), pp. 179–215, both for evidence of Thorpe's reliance on the authority of Grace and for evidence of his familiarity with the formal discourse of *sophismata*.

We have noted William Taylor's relative lack of attention to the Grace-founded *dominium* doctrine in referring to his assumption that Christ implicitly authorized Caesar's authority through His own refusal to take civil office. But this is not evidence of outright rejection of the *dominium* doctrine. Nicholas Radcliffe, a Benedictine of St. Albans and an important anti-Lollard polemicist (*d.* 1396–1401), apparently believed the doctrine to be an important aspect of Lollard belief, for he directed considerable attention to combating Wyclif's theories of *dominium* and the papacy, and his rejection of clerical property-ownership. Radcliffe's writings were considered so well formulated and pertinent to anti-Lollard goals as to be included in John Mabulthorp's mid-fifteenth-century anti-Wycliffite polemics. Radcliffe's aim was to counter Wyclif's arguments, one by one, and his summation of Wyclif's *dominium* position is certainly both all-encompassing and succinct: "Nobody in mortal sin has true justice from any gift of God. All human law presupposes divine law, thus all just human *dominium* presupposes God's just *dominium*."[70]

This position appears to have been widespread enough to warrant its inclusion among the general beliefs of Lollardy. When the Franciscan Thomas Richmond was pressed to recant his Lollard statements in 1426, rather than be allowed to deny the simpler Donatist position that a priest in mortal sin was incapable of fulfilling his duties, he was forced to admit that, "þe auctorite or power of pope, archebisshop, bisshop, prest, kyng, duke, erle, iustice, maire, or oþer þat standes in office, ordir or state, spirituall or tenperall, comes noght nor growes noght of þe personne in hymself, nor of þe merits or demeritis of hym, or of his awne propir levyng or gouvernance of hymself, bot of God þat gifes all pwer."[71] The sense of this admission is that God may be the source of all human authority, but Grace need not underlie it.

Further, John Beket of Essex was accused in 1400 of teaching that secular power was authorized to persecute spiritual and lesser secular authority for all misdoings, temporal and spiritual alike. This exceeds even Wyclif's ideals. In a presently undated Lollard sermon on Luke 19:12–27, Wyclif's doctrine appears again, this time consonant with the thought of *De Civili Dominio*:

For þis is trew sentence of seyntus, þat iuste men þat han heuene han alle worldly þingus by resoun of þer Lord; and so alle vniuste men, þat God yyue ȝhelle for

---

[70] "Nemo dum est in mortali peccato habet iusticiam simpliciter ad aliquod donum Dei. Omne ius humanum presupponit ius diuinum, ergo omne iustum dominium quo ad homines presupponit dominium quo ad Deum." Nicholas Radcliffe, quoted in Hudson, *The Premature Reformation*, p. 359, n. 1; compare *DCD*, I, 1, 1.1–2: "Ius divinum presupponitur iuri civili/Dominium naturale presupponitur dominio civili."

[71] Quoted in Hudson, *The Premature Reformation*, p. 360, n. 10.

þer seruyse, han nouȝt iustli, al ȝif þei semon to haue myche ... And ȝif worldly men semon to haue muche goodus, yet þis is a false hauyng, for it is yniuste to God; and siþ God is cheef lord, þat iugeþ men þus to haue and þus to want by hys lawe, no man schulde aȝenseȝe þis.[72]

This familiar sentiment, that God's *dominium* is the sole foundation of all human *dominium*, is the basis for the Grace-founded *dominium*. This connection of divine and human *dominium* appears throughout the Lollard literature as well. William Taylor makes mention of it in his arguments against the friars, holding that begging goes against Christ's example:

And lete us not paciently heere so greete a blasfemye falsly put upon Crist, þat is to sei þat he, as þe bigylid puple weeneþ, hadde beggide, for þat myyte not he do for þe causis. First for Crist is God, wherfore he hadde ful lordship uppon alle craturis bi title of creacioun. Bi title also of innocense he hadde as Adam ful lordship of alle þingis þat nediden to mannys vse. And þe þirdde skile is for he was a trewe preest and bisshop to þe Iewis, doynge duly his office to þe puple, þerfore he myȝte, ad he dide bi title of þe gospel, receȝue þat þat was needeful to hym in execucioun of his office.[73]

Taylor here relies upon Wyclif's thought on the relation of human Natural *dominium* to God's own *dominium* as it appears in *De Dominio Divino* and in *De Mandatis Divinis*, and so affirms the notion that Christ's restored Natural *dominium* is only possible under the stewardship of a just civil lord. This is Wyclif's Grace-founded *dominium* theory made practical, for it takes so much of the *dominium* treatises as axiomatic in the course of the argument. Had Taylor been more careful in his assessment of the justice of Caesar's secular authority, we might be able to argue that he was familiar with Wyclif's own writings.

In F. D. Matthew's 1880 edition of Lollard texts attributed to Wyclif himself, the reliance of just human *dominium* on God's *dominium* appears frequently. While the likelihood that Wyclif himself actually wrote any of these tracts is questionable, they evoke the sentiments underlying *De Dominio Divino* III and *De Civili Dominio* I:

But here we schal suppose as Cristen mennes bileue, þat god is cheef lord of eche þing in þis world. And so, al ȝif kyngis & oþere han free lordschipe, neþeles god is more free lord of þat same þing, ne it is nouȝt leeful to seculere lordis, to alyenen his lordschipe wiþouten leeue of god; as in mannes lordschipe a litil

---

[72] Pamela Gradon, *English Wycliffite Sermons*, vol. 2 (Oxford, 1988), Sermon 78, 133.99–108.

[73] *The Sermon of William Taylor*, 21.698–22.707. Note Taylor's assumption that the just civil lord, presumably Caesar or perhaps Herod, provides the clergy with alms. This is Wyclif's goal, as we have noted, though Wyclif would probably have denied Taylor's assertion because of the lack of Grace in Caesar's or Herod's rule.

lord haþ no leeue to alienen his heritage but bi leue of þe chief lord, & þis lawe
haþ more resoun in þe lordschipe of god . . . Ne grucche noȝt herfore þat god is
cheif lord, for it falliþ to his godhed to be lord of eche þing . . .[74]

The argument that no one may be lord on earth unless God has eternally
ordained it is common as well. A selection from "The Clergy May Not
Hold Property" is illustrative, "And welle I wote þat þer is no lorde here
of þe erþe, but if he hold of hym as chefe lord, & haue his lordeschipe &
hold it by autorite of þis lorde god."[75]

Some Lollard texts evince more evidence of familiarity with Wyclif's
Latin writings than others. While Matthews sees direct evidence of
knowledge of the *Summa Theologie* in several of the tracts that he has
edited, it is possible that the author(s) of these texts had only a passing acquaintance with *De Civili Dominio* and other treatises. After all,
one can easily articulate the Grace-founded *dominium* concept without
taking into account each of the arguments Wyclif presents. But other
texts suggest direct reliance on Wyclif's Latin works, most notable is the
Tractatus de Regibus, (c. 1382) the unknown author of which appropriates
arguments directly from Wyclif's own pen. *De Regibus* opens with an un-
equivocal statement of the king's chief duty, to ensure that "goddis lawe
be better knowen and defendid, for þerinne is mannys helþe, boþe of
body and soule, þat evermore schal last."[76] Wyclif's distinction between
the power of Christ the divine and Christ the man in *De Officio Regis*
Chapter 1 appears clearly in *De Regibus*, suggesting that its author had a
well-schooled ear, attuned to elements of political theory more familiar
to university than to lay discourse:

And þus by mony resouns schulden men worschip kyngus and do open worschip
to hem by reson of þer state, and specially if þai do þer office þat God haþ lymytid
hem. For as Austeyn techis by wittenes of Gods lawe, kynge is vicar of God,
and preste vicar of Criste, for God wil þat kynges by pouste and by vengeaunce
defende Goddis riȝt and so doþe þo god hed, but popis and byschopis by mekenes
and pacience.[77]

Further, Wyclif's dictum that the lord acts through each action of his
subject, reliant on the universal–particular model of *dominium*, is echoed
in *De Regibus*. "Also, iche lege man of þo kynge þat doþ a werke in

---

[74] "Of Dominion," in *The English Works of Wyclif*, ed. F. D. Matthew, EETS OS 74 (London, 1880),
p. 284. See also "De Papa," in *ibid.*, pp. 469–70.
[75] "The Clergy May Not Hold Property," *Ibid.*, p. 373.
[76] "*Tractatus de Regibus*": *Four English Political Tracts of the Later Middle Ages*, ed. Jean-Philippe Genet
(London, 1977), p. 5. Genet suspects this tract to be either a summary of *De Officio Regis* or an
epitome of several treatises of the *Summa Theologie*.
[77] *Ibid.*, p. 8.

hys vertue is servaunt to þo kynge, and þo kynge in þat manere doþ that werke, but prestis ben hired to purge þo rewme of suche synnes þat fallen þerinne, and so þo kynge by his prestys purgiþ þo rewme of suchen synnes."[78]

The ideal of stewardship is present as well in Lollard texts. Some devote considerable attention to the analogy of the just human lord to the good shepherd. One might suppose that such discussions are exclusively related to the pastoral mission of spiritual lords, but the generality with which several writers refer to pastoral mission certainly leaves open the possibility that all human lords, spiritual and secular, are being considered. In a Lollard sermon on John 10:11–18, the discussion of the shepherd applies to all who have responsibility for the well-being of others. "[A] good heerde [i.e. shepherd], as Crist seiþ, puttiþ his lijf for hise scheep, for more charite mai noon haue þan to putt his lijf for his freendis, and, if he worchiþ wijsli, for to brynge þese scheepe to heuene, for þus þe heerde haþ moost peyne and þe scheep moost profit."[79] The sermon writer has portrayed the most important, or definitive quality of such a shepherd as "charite," a willingness to put the needs of those for whom one is responsible before one's own. This is commensurate with Wyclif's *caritas*, the hallmark characteristic of the Grace-favored civil lord. Shepherds lacking this quality lack a just claim on the name. "And, siþ þis properte of heerde groundiþ charite in men, ech man schulde haue herof algatis more-or lesse, as he is ferþer fro þis maner þat wole not ȝyue hise worldlii goodis to hise scheep or his briþeren, whanne þei han greet nede þerto, for such ben worse þan mannes lijf."[80] Not only does this refer to the exemplary duties a lord has, to instruct his subjects in caritative action, but it also points to the notion that all that a lord has is to be used for the upkeep of his charges. This comes from Wyclif's instrumentalist conception of human *dominium*, that just human lords are means for God's ends, and so are stewards of Creation rather than sovereign lords. The idea that the only source of human nurture is God's *dominium*, and that the only law whereby we can live justly is God's law, is directly connected to this:

It falliþ to a good heerd to lede hise scheepe in hool pasturis, and whane hise scheepe ben hirt or scabbid to hele hem and to grese hem, and whanne oþir yuel beestis assailen hem þanne helpe hem. And herto schulde he putt his lijf to saue hise scheep fro suche beestis. þe pasture is goddis lawe þat euermor is grene in truþe, and rotun pasture ben oþir lawis and oþir fables wiþoute ground. And cowardise of suche heerdis þat dar not defende Goddis lawe witnessiþ þat

---

[78] *Ibid.*, p. 11.   [79] Hudson, *English Wycliffite Writings*, Text 13, 64.13–16.
[80] *Ibid.*, p. 65.20–4.

þei failen . . . for he þat dar not for worldis dreed defendeþ lawe of his God, hou schulde defende hise scheepe for loue þat haþ to hem?[81]

The shepherd and the human lord's obligation to God's law above any human law or desire is very clear here, and from this the reformative duty of the civil lord towards the church described in *De Civili Dominio* and *De Officio Regis* flows quite naturally. Also clear is the impossibility of just human leadership without allegiance to God's law. The writer suggests that Grace alone makes this possible, for he next says that only Christ enables men to live by God's law, and that the shepherds have a responsibility to go out among the unbelievers and bring them into a life under God's law. What of cases when the temporal lord fails to put God's law before his own? In Wyclif's Latin works, a tyrant could not be overthrown justly save in extreme cases in which his tyranny is so laden with heresy as to threaten the well-being of the church. Hudson notes that most Wycliffite texts are more likely to countenance rebellion against priestly tyranny than against secular abuse of power, observing that few texts give evidence of having provided support for Oldcastle's rebellion.[82]

Thus we have strong evidence in vernacular Wycliffite texts for Wyclif's doctrine that human lords can only claim just *dominium* through Grace. That so much of our evidence either is reliant upon, or refers to other aspects of Wyclif's thought in the *dominium* treatises strongly suggests their influence, either direct or indirect. We can now affirm that if one holds Wyclif's Grace-founded *dominium* doctrine as true, then conclusions follow which are identifiably Lollard, and heretical, in nature, and that if one is a realist of Wyclif's stamp, then Wyclif's doctrine of Grace-founded *dominium* would appeal. One does not need to be a realist of Wyclif's stamp, nor need to have read the *dominium* treatises to be a Lollard, but the ontological position certainly overflows into more practical affairs.

---

[81] *Ibid.*, 66.77–87.
[82] Hudson, *The Premature Reformation*, pp. 366–7; see also Margaret Aston, "Lollardy and Sedition," in her *Lollards and Reformers* (London, 1984), p. 4. For instances of enjoinders to obey secular authority, see "Of Servants and Lords," in *The English Works of Wyclif*, ed. Matthew, p. 229; *Tractatus de Regibus*, 6–7.

BIBLIOGRAPHY

PRIMARY SOURCES

Thomas Aquinas, *An Apology for the Religious Orders*, trans. John Proctor (London, 1902)
    Contra Impugnantes Dei Cultum et Religionem, in *Parma*, vol. 15
    In Libros Politicorum Expositio, in *Parma*, vol. 21
    On Kingship, trans. Gerald Phelan (Toronto, 1982)
    Quaestiones Disputatae de Potentia, in *Parma*, vol. 8
    Quodlibetal Quaestiones, in *Parma*, vols. 8–9
    Scriptum super Libros Sententiarum, in *Parma*, vols. 6–7
    Summa Theologiae, Leonine ed. (Rome, 1948)
    Summa Theologiae, Blackfriars (London, 1964) translation
Augustinus Aurelius, *De Civitate Dei*, CCSL, vol. 48 (Turnhout, 1955)
    De Genesi ad Litteram, PL, vol. 35
    De Moribus Ecclesiae Catholicae, PL, vol. 32
    Ennaratio in Psalmum, PL, vol. 36
    Epistola, PL, vol. 33
Bradwardine, Thomas, *De Causa Dei contra Pelagium et De Virtute Causarum*, ed. H. Saville (London, 1618)
Fitzralph, Richard, *De Pauperie Salvatoris* in John Wyclif, *De Dominio Divino*, ed. R. L. Poole (London, 1890), pp. 257–476
Giles of Rome, *On Ecclesiastical Power: The De Ecclesiastica Potestate of Aegidius Romanus*, ed. and trans. R. W. Dyson (Drew, NH, 1986)
John XXII, *Quia vir reprobus*, *Bullarium Franciscanum*, vol. 6 (Rome, 1902)
Marsilius of Padua, *Defensor Pacis*, trans. Alan Gewirth (Columbia, OH, 1956)
Netter, Thomas, *Fasciculi Zizaniorum magistri Johannis Wyclif*, Rerum Britannicarum Medii Aevi Scriptores, RS 5, ed. W. W. Shirley (London, 1858)
The Lanterne of Liȝt, ed. Lilian M. Swinburn, EETS OS 151 (London, 1917)
William of Ockham, *A Letter to the Friars Minor and Other Writings*, ed. A. S. McGrade, trans. J. Kilcullen (Cambridge, 1995)
    Opus Nonaginta Dierum, in *Guillelmi de Ockham: Opera Politica*, vol. 1, ed. H. S. Offler (Manchester, 1940)
Walsingham, Thomas, *Chronicon Angliae*, ed. E. M. Thompson, Rolls Series 64 (London, 1874)
    Historia Anglicana, ed. H. T. Riley, Rerum Britannicarum Medii Aevi Scriptores 20, RS 28 (London, 1862, 1864)

Bibliography

John Wyclif, *De Civili Dominio Liber Primus*, ed. R. L. Poole (London, 1885)
   De Civili Dominio Liber Secundus, ed. J. Loserth (London, 1900)
   De Civili Dominio Liber Tertius, ed. J. Loserth, 2 vols. (London, 1903–04)
   De Composicione Hominis, ed. R. Beer (London, 1884)
   De Dominio Divino, ed. R. L. Poole (London, 1890)
   De Ente: librorum duorum excerpta, ed. M. H. Dziewicki (London, 1909)
   Dialogus sive Speculum Ecclesie Militantis, ed. A. W. Pollard (London, 1886)
   Miscellanea Philosophica, ed. M. H. Dziewicki, 2 vols. (London, 1901–02)
   On Simony, trans. T. A. McVeigh (New York, 1992)
   On Universals, trans. A. Kenny, with introduction by P. V. Spade (Oxford, 1985)
   Opera minora, ed. J. Loserth (London, 1913)
   Summa de Ente Libri Primi Tractatus Primus et Secundus, ed. S. H. Thomson (Oxford, 1930)
   The English Works of Wyclif Hitherto Unprinted, ed. F. D. Matthew, EETS OS 74 (London, 1880)
   Tractatus de Benedicta Incarnacione, ed. E. Harris (London, 1886)
   Tractatus de Ecclesia, ed. J. Loserth (London, 1886)
   Tractatus de Logica, ed. M. H. Dziewicki, 3 vols. (London, 1893)
   Tractatus de Mandatis Divinis accedit Tractatus de Statu Innocencie, ed., J. Loserth and F. D. Matthew (London, 1922)
   Tractatus de Officio Regis, ed. A. W. Pollard and C. Sayle (London, 1887)
   Tractatus de Potestate Pape, ed. J. Loserth (London, 1907)
   Tractatus de Universalibus, ed. Ivan J. Mueller (Oxford, 1985)
   Trialogus, ed. G. V. Lechler (Oxford, 1869)

SECONDARY SOURCES

Adams, Marilyn McCord, "Universals in the Fourteenth Century," *The Cambridge History of Later Medieval Philosophy*, ed. Anthony Kenny, Norman Kretzman and Jan Pinborg (Cambridge, 1982), pp. 411–39

Ashworth, E. Jennifer, and Spade, P. V., "Logic in Late Medieval Oxford," in *The History of the University of Oxford*, ed., J. I. Catto and R. Evans (Oxford, 1992), vol. 2, pp. 35–64

Aston, Margaret, "Lollardy and Sedition," in *Lollards and Reformers* (London, 1984), pp. 1–48

   "Wyclif and the Vernacular," in *From Ockham to Wyclif*, ed. A. Hudson and M. Wilks, *SCH* Subsidia 5 (London, 1987), pp. 281–330

Baker, Derek (ed.), *Schism, Heresy and Religious Protest*, *SCH*, 9 (Cambridge, 1972)

Blythe, James, *Ideal Government and the Mixed Constitution in the Middle Ages* (Princeton, 1992)

Brett, Annabel S., *Liberty, Right and Nature* (Cambridge, 1997)

Brown, Peter, "St. Augustine's Attitude to Religious Coercion," *Journal of Roman Studies*, 54 (1964), pp. 107–16

Burns, James, *Lordship, Kingship, and Empire* (Oxford, 1992)

Burns, James (ed.), *The Cambridge History of Medieval Political Thought 350–1450* (Cambridge, 1988)

Bibliography

Burr, David, *Olivi and Franciscan Poverty: The Origins of the Usus Pauper Controversy* (Philadelphia, 1989)

The Persecution of Peter Olivi, Transactions of the American Philosophical Society, 66, 5 (1976)

Canning, Joseph, *A History of Medieval Political Thought 300–1450* (New York, 1996)

Catto, J. I., "Wyclif and Wycliffism at Oxford 1356–1430," in *The History of the University of Oxford*, ed. J. I. Catto and R. Evans (Oxford, 1992), vol. 2, pp. 175–261

Cigman, Gloria (ed.), *Lollard Sermons*, EETS OS 294 (Oxford, 1989)

Coleman, Janet, "Fitzralph's Antimendicant 'proposicio' (1350) and the Politics of the Papal Court at Avignon," *JEH*, 35 (1984), pp. 376–90

"Property and Power" in *The Cambridge History of Medieval Political Thought*, ed. James Burns (Cambridge, 1988), pp. 607–48

Piers Plowman and the Moderni (Rome, 1981)

Conti, Alessandro, "Ontology in Walter Burley's Last Commentary on the *Ars Vetus*," *Franciscan Studies*, 50 (1990), pp. 121–76

"Logica intensionale et metafisica dell'essenza in John Wyclif," *Bullettino dell'Istituto Storico Italiano per il Medio Evo e Archivio Muratoriano*, 99 (1993), pp. 159–219

"Analogy and the Formal Distinction: The Logical Basis of Wyclif's Metaphysics," *Medieval Philosophy and Theology*, 6 (1997), pp. 133–65

Cook, William R., "John Wyclif and Hussite Theology," *Church History*, 42 (1973), pp. 335–49

Courtenay, William, *Capacity and Volition* (Bergamo, 1990)

"The Dialectic of Divine Omnipotence," in *Covenant and Causality* (London, 1984), pp. 1–37

"Force of Words and Figures of Speech: The Crisis over *Virtus Sermonis* in the Fourteenth Century," *Franciscan Studies*, 44 (1984), pp. 107–28

"The Reception of Ockham's Thought in Fourteenth-Century England," in *From Ockham to Wyclif*, ed. A. Hudson and M. Wilks, *SCH* Subsidia 5 (London, 1987), pp. 89–108

Schools and Scholars in Late Fourteenth Century England (Princeton, 1987)

"Theology and Theologians from Ockham to Wyclif," *The History of the University of Oxford*, ed., J. I. Catto and R. Evans (Oxford, 1992), vol. 2, pp. 1–34

Dahmus, Joseph, *The Prosecution of John Wyclyf* (New Haven, 1952)

"John Wyclif and the English Government," *Speculum*, 35 (1960), pp. 51–68

William Courtenay, Archbishop of Canterbury 1381–1396 (University Park, 1966)

Daly, Lowrie J., S. J., *The Political Theory of John Wyclif* (Chicago, 1962)

"Wyclif's Political Theory: A Century of Study," *Medievalia et Humanistica*, 4 (1973) pp. 177–87

Dawson, James Doyne, "Richard Fitzralph and the Fourteenth Century Poverty Controversies," *JEH*, 34, 3 (1983), pp. 315–44

De La Torre, Bartholomew, O. P., *Thomas Buckingham and the Contingency of Futures* (Notre Dame, 1987)

Dickens, A. G., *Lollards and Protestants in the Diocese of York 1509–1558* (Oxford, 1959)

Dipple, Geoffrey, "Uthred and the Friars: Apostolic Poverty and Clerical Dominion Between Fitzralph and Wyclif," *Traditio*, 49 (1994), pp. 235–58

Bibliography

Dolnikowski, Edith Wilks, *Thomas Bradwardine: A View of Time and a Vision of Eternity in Fourteenth-Century Thought* (Leiden, 1995)

Doyle, Eric, O.F.M., "William Woodford, O.F.M. and John Wyclif's *De Religione*," *Speculum*, 52 (1977), pp. 329–36

"William Woodford, O.F.M., His Life and Works," *Franciscan Studies*, 43 (1983), pp. 17–187

"William Woodford's *De Dominio Civili Clericorum* against John Wyclif," *Archivum Franciscanum Historicum*, 66 (1973), pp. 49–109

Evans, G. R., "Wyclif's *Logic* and Wyclif's Exegesis: The Context," in *The Bible in the Medieval World*, ed. Katherine Walsh and Diana Wood (London, 1985), pp. 287–300

"Wyclif on Literal and Metaphorical," in *From Ockham to Wyclif*, ed. A. Hudson and M. Wilks, *SCH* Subsidia 5 (London, 1987), pp. 259–66

Farr, William, *John Wyclif as Legal Reformer* (Leiden, 1974)

Fowler, David, *The Life and Times of John Trevisa, Medieval Scholar* (Seattle, 1995)

Gellrich, Jesse, *Discourse and Dominion in the Fourteenth Century* (Princeton, 1995)

Genet, Jean-Phillipe, *Four English Political Tracts of the Later Middle Ages* (London, 1977)

Genest, Jean-François, "Le *De futuris contingentibus* de Thomas Bradwardine," *Recherches Augustinienne*, 14 (1979), pp. 249–336

Gewirth, Alan, "Philosophy and Political Thought in the Fourteenth Century," in *The Forward Movement of the Fourteenth Century*, ed. F. L. Utley (Columbus, OH, 1961) pp. 125–64

Gilbert, Neil Ward, "Ockham, Wyclif, and the 'Via Moderna'," in *Antiqui et Moderni*, ed. Albert Zimmerman Miscellanea Mediaevalia 9 (Berlin, 1974), pp. 85–125

Grabmann, Martin, *Studien über den Einfluss der aristotelischen Philosophie auf die mittelalterlichen Theorien über das Verhältnis von Kirche und Staat*, Sitzungsberichte der Bayrischen Akademie der Wissenschaften, Phil.-Hist. Abteilung 2 (Munich, 1934)

Gradon, Pamela, *English Wycliffite Sermons*, vol. 2 (Oxford, 1988)

"Langland and the Ideology of Dissent," *Proceedings of the British Academy*, 66 (1980), pp. 179–205

Gwynn, Aubrey, *The English Austin Friars in the Time of Wyclif* (Oxford, 1940)

Hammerich, L. L. "The Beginning of the Strife Between Richard Fitzralph and the Mendicants," *Det Kgl.Danske Videnskabernes Selskab., Historisk-filologiske Meddelelser*, 36.3 (1938)

Harvey, Margaret, "Adam Easton and the Condemnation of John Wyclif, 1377," *English Historical Review*, 113 (April 1998), pp. 321–34

The English in Rome, 1362–1420 (Cambridge, 1999)

Heath, Peter, "Between Reform and Reformation: The English Church in the Fourteenth and Fifteenth Centuries," *JEH*, 41 (1990), pp. 649–78

Henry, Desmond P., "Wyclif's Deviant Mereology," in *Medieval Mereology* (Amsterdam, 1991)

Hudson, Anne, "Poor Preachers, Poor Men: Views of Poverty in Wyclif and His Followers," *Häresie und vorzeitige Reformation im Spätmittelalter*, 39 (Oldenbourg, 1998), pp. 41–53

The Premature Reformation (Oxford, 1988)

Bibliography

Selections from English Wycliffite Writings (Cambridge, 1978)

"Some Aspects of Lollard Book Production," in *Schism, Heresy and Religious Protest*, ed. Derek Baker (Cambridge, 1972), pp. 147–58

Two Wycliffite Texts (Oxford, 1993)

"Wyclif and the English Language," in *Wyclif in his Times*, ed. Anthony Kenny (Oxford 1986), pp. 85–104

"Wycliffism in Oxford 1381–1411," in *Wyclif in his Times*, ed. Anthony Kenny (Oxford, 1986), pp. 67–84

Hudson, Anne, and Gradon, Pamela, *English Wycliffite Writings*, vol. 4 (Oxford 1983)

Hudson, Anne, and Wilks, Michael (eds.), *From Ockham to Wyclif*, SCH Subsidia 5 (London, 1987)

Justice, Steven, *Writing and Rebellion: England in 1381* (Berkeley, 1994)

Kaminsky, Howard, "Wycliffism as Ideology of Revolution," *Church History*, 32 (1963), pp. 57–74

Kantorowicz, Ernst H., *The King's Two Bodies: A Study in Medieval Political Theology* (Princeton, 1957)

Karger, Elizabeth, "Walter Burley's Realism," *Vivarium*, 37 (1999), pp. 24–40

Keen, Maurice, "The Influence of Wyclif," in *Wyclif in his Times*, ed. Anthony Kenny (Oxford, 1986), pp. 127–46

"Wyclif, the Bible, and Transubstantiation," in *Wyclif in his Times*, ed. Anthony Kenny (Oxford, 1986), pp. 1–16

Kenny, Anthony, "Realism and Determinism in the early Wyclif," in *From Ockham to Wyclif*, ed. A. Hudson and M. Wilks, SCH Subsidia 5 (London, 1987), pp. 165–78

"The Realism of the *De Universalibus*," in *Wyclif in his Times*, ed. Kenny (Oxford, 1985), pp. 17–30

Wyclif (Oxford, 1986)

Kenny, Anthony (ed.), *Wyclif in his Times* (Oxford, 1986)

Knowles, David, "The Censured Opinions of Uthred of Boldon," in *The Historian and Character and Other Essays* (Cambridge, 1963), pp. 129–70

The Religious Orders in England, vol. 2 (Cambridge, 1953)

Kretzman, Norman, "Continua, Indivisibles, and Change in Wyclif's Logic of Scripture," in *Wyclif in his Times*, ed. Anthony Kenny (Oxford, 1986), pp. 31–67

Lahey, Stephen, "Toleration in the Theology and Social Thought of John Wyclif," in *Difference and Dissent: Theories of Tolerance in Medieval and Early Modern Europe*, ed. Cary J. Nederman and John C. Laursen (Lanham, MD, 1996), pp. 39–66

"Wyclif and Rights," *Journal of the History of Ideas*, 58 (1997), pp. 1–20

Lambert, M. D., *Franciscan Poverty* (St. Bonaventure, NY, 1998)

Lambert, Malcolm, *Medieval Heresy: Popular Movements from the Gregorian Reform to the Reformation* (London, 1992)

Lechler, G. V., *Johann Wiclif und die Vorgeschichte der Reformation* (Leipzig, 1873)

Leff, Gordon, *Bradwardine and the Pelagians* (Cambridge, 1957)

Heresy in the Later Middle Ages (New York, 1967)

"The Place of Metaphysics in Wyclif's Theology," in *From Ockham to Wyclif*, ed. A. Hudson and M. Wilks, SCH Subsidia 5 (London, 1987), pp. 217–32

Richard Fitzralph, Commentator of the Sentences (Manchester, 1963)

Bibliography

"Wyclif and Hus: A Doctrinal Comparison," in *Wyclif in his Times*, ed. Anthony Kenny (Oxford, 1986), pp. 105–26

Levy, Ian, "John Wyclif and Augustinian Realism," *Augustiniana*, 48 (1998), pp. 87–106

"Was John Wyclif's Theology of the Eucharist Donatistic?" *Scottish Journal of Theology*, 53, 2 (2000), pp. 137–53

"The Wyclif–Kenningham Debate Reconsidered," unpublished paper presented at the 33rd International Congress on Medieval Studies (Kalamazoo, 1998)

Lewis, Ewart, *Medieval Political Ideas 1* (New York, 1954)

Lewis, John, *The History of the Life and Sufferings of the Reverend and Learned John Wiclif, D.D.* (Oxford, 1820)

Loserth, Johann, "The Beginnings of Wyclif's Activity in Ecclesiastical Politics," *English Historical Review*, 9 (1896), pp. 319–28

Luscombe, David, "Wyclif and Hierarchy," *From Ockham to Wyclif*, ed. A. Hudson and M. Wilks, *SCH* Subsidia 5 (London, 1987), pp. 233–44

Markus, R. A., *Saeculum: History and Society in the Theology of St. Augustine* (Cambridge, 1970)

Martin, C., "Walter Burley," in *Oxford Studies Presented to Daniel Callus*, ed. R. W. Southern (Oxford, 1964), pp. 193–230

McEvoy, James, *The Philosophy of Robert Grosseteste* (Oxford, 1982)

McFarlane, K. B., *John Wycliffe and the Beginnings of English Nonconformity* (Aylesbury, 1952)

Lancastrian Kings and Lollard Knights (Oxford, 1972)

McGrade, A. S., *The Political Thought of William of Ockham* (Cambridge, 1974)

"Right, Natural Rights, and the Philosophy of Law," in *The Cambridge History of Later Medieval Philosophy*, ed. A. Kenny, N. Kretzman, and J. Pinborg (Cambridge, 1982), pp. 738–56

"Somersaulting Sovereignty: A Note on Reciprocal Lordship and Servitude in Wyclif," in *The Church and Sovereignty c. 590–1918 SCH* Subsidia 11 (London, 1991), pp. 261–8

McHardy, A. K., "The Dissemination of Wyclif's Ideas," in *From Ockham to Wyclif*, ed. A. Hudson and M. Wilks, *SCH* Subsidia 5 (London, 1987), pp. 361–3

McKeon, Richard, "The Development of the Concept of Property in Political Philosophy," *Ethics*, 48 (1938), pp. 297–366

Monahan, Arthur P., *John of Paris on Royal and Papal Power* (New York, 1974)

Mueller, Ivan J., "A 'Lost' *Summa* of John Wyclif," in *From Ockham to Wyclif*, ed. A. Hudson and M. Wilks, *SCH* Subsidia 5 (London, 1987), pp. 179–84

Muldoon, James, "John Wyclif and the Rights of Infidels," *Americas*, 3 (1980), pp. 301–16

Nederman, Cary J., "Bracton on Kingship Revisited," *History of Political Thought*, 5 (1984), pp. 61–78

Community and Consent: The Secular Political Theory of Marsiglio of Padua's Defensor Pacis (London, 1995)

Nelson, Janet, "Kingship and Empire," in *The Cambridge History of Medieval Political Thought*, ed. James Burns (Cambridge, 1988) pp. 239–42

Nineham, Ruth, "The So-called Norman Anonymous," *JEH*, 14 (1963), pp. 31–45

Bibliography

Oberman, Heiko, "*Via Antiqui* and *Via Moderna*: Late Medieval Prolegomena to Early Reformation Thought," in *From Ockham to Wyclif*, ed. A. Hudson and M. Wilks, *SCH* Subsidia 5 (London, 1987), pp. 445–64
  The Harvest of Medieval Theology (Cambridge, MA, 1963)
  Thomas Bradwardine: A Fourteenth-Century Augustinian (Utrecht, 1957)
Pantin, W. A., *The English Church in the Fourteenth Century* (Cambridge, 1955)
Phillips, Heather, "John Wyclif and the Optics of the Eucharist," *From Ockham to Wyclif*, ed. A. Hudson and M. Wilks, *SCH* Subsidia 5 (London, 1987), pp. 245–58
Poole, R. L., *Wycliffe and Movements for Reform* (London, 1902)
Pyper, Rachel, "An Abridgement of Wyclif's *De Mandatis Divinis*," *Medium Aevum*, 52 (1983), pp. 306–9
Robson, J. A., *Wyclif and the Oxford Schools* (Cambridge, 1961)
Scase, Wendy, *Piers Plowman and the New Anticlericalism* (Cambridge, 1989)
Skinner, Quentin, *The Foundations of Modern Political Thought*, vol. 2 (Cambridge, 1978), pp. 135–73
Smalley, Beryl, "Wyclif's *Postilla* on the Old Testament and his *Principium*," in *Oxford Studies Presented to Daniel Callus*, ed. R. W. Southern (Oxford, 1964), pp. 253–96
Somerset, Fiona, *Clerical Discourse and Lay Audience in Late Medieval England* (Cambridge, 1998)
Southern, R. W., *Robert Grosseteste: The Growth of an English Mind in Medieval Europe* (Oxford, 1986)
Strohm, Paul, *England's Empty Throne* (New Haven, 1998)
Summers, W. H., *The Lollards of the Chiltern Hills* (London, 1906)
Szittya, Penn, *The Antifraternal Tradition in Medieval Literature* (Princeton, 1986)
Tachau, Katherine, *Vision and Certitude in the Age of Ockham* (Leiden, 1988)
Tatnall, Edith C., "Church and State According to John Wyclif', Ph.D. diss., University of Colorado (1966)
  "John Wyclif and *Ecclesia Anglicana*," *Journal of Theological History*, 20 (1969), pp. 19–43
Thompson, A. Hamilton, *The English Clergy and their Organization in the Later Middle Ages* (Oxford, 1966)
Thomson, John, *The Later Lollards 1414–1520* (Oxford, 1955)
Thomson, S. Harrison, "A Gonville and Caius Wyclif Manuscript," *Speculum*, 8 (1933), pp. 197–204
  "A 'Lost' Chapter of Wyclif's *Summa de Ente*," *Speculum*, 4 (1929), pp. 339–46
  "The Philosophical Basis of Wyclif's Theology," *Journal of Religion*, 9 (1931), pp. 86–116
  "Some Latin Works Erroneously Attributed to Wyclif," *Speculum*, 3 (1928), pp. 382–91
  "Three Unprinted Opuscula of John Wyclif," *Speculum*, 3 (1928), pp. 248–53
Thomson, Williel, *The Latin Writings of John Wyclyf* (Toronto, 1983)
Tierney, Brian, *The Idea of Natural Rights* (Atlanta, 1997)
  Religion, Law, and the Growth of Constitutional Thought 1150–1650 (Cambridge, 1982)
Trapp, Damasus O. P., "Augustinian Theology of the 14th Century," *Augustiniana*, 6 (1956), pp. 146–274

Bibliography

Tuck, Richard, *Natural Rights Theories: Their Origin and Development* (Cambridge, 1979)

Ullmann, Walter, *The Growth of Papal Government in the Middle Ages* (London, 1955)

Vaughan, R. V., *Tracts and Treatises of John De Wycliffe, D.D.* (London, 1845)

Von Nolcken, Christina, "Another Kind of Saint: A Lollard Perception of John Wyclif," in *From Ockham to Wyclif*, ed. A. Hudson and M. Wilks, *SCH* Subsidia 5 (London, 1987), pp. 429–44

Walker, Simon, *The Lancastrian Affinity 1361–1399* (Oxford, 1990)

Walsh, Katherine, *A Fourteenth-Century Scholar and Primate: Richard Fitzralph at Oxford, Avignon and Armagh* (Oxford, 1981)

Wilks, Michael, "The Early Oxford Wyclif: Papalist or Nominalist?" *SCH*, 5 (London, 1969), pp. 69–98

"Predestination, Property and Power: Wyclif's Theory of Dominion and Grace," *SCH*, 2 (London, 1965), pp. 220–36

The Problem of Sovereignty in the Later Middle Ages (Cambridge, 1963)

"*Reformatio Regni*: Wyclif and Hus as Leaders of Religious Protest Movements," in *Schism, Heresy, and Religious Protest*, ed. Derek Baker (London, 1972), pp. 109–30

"Royal Patronage and Anti-Papalism," in *From Ockham to Wyclif*, ed. A. Hudson and Wilks *SCH* Subsidia 5 (London, 1987), pp. 135–63

"Royal Priesthood: The Origins of Lollardy," in *The Church in a Changing Society, CIHEC Conference in Uppsala 1977* (Uppsala, 1978), 135–63

"Wyclif and the Great Persecution," in *Prophecy and Eschatology*, ed. Wilks, *SCH* Subsidia 10 (London, 1994), pp. 39–63

"Wyclif and the Wheel of Time," *SCH*, 33 (London, 1997), pp. 177–93

"Wyclif (Jean)," in *Dictionnaire de Spiritualité*, vols. 106–7 (Paris, 1994), pp. 1501–1512, reprinted in translation in Wilks (2000), pp. 1–15.

Wyclif: Political Ideas and Practice (Oxbow, 2000)

Williams, George, *The Norman Anonymous of 1100 A.D.* (Cambridge, MA, 1951)

Wood, Rega, and Gideon, G., "Richard Brinkley and his *Summa Logica*," *Franciscan Studies*, 40 (1980), pp. 59–102

Workman, Herbert, *John Wyclif: A Study of the English Medieval Church* (Oxford, 1926)

Zuckerman, Charles, "The Relationship of Theories of Universals to Theories of Church Government in the Middle Ages: A Critique of Previous Views," *Journal of the History of Ideas*, 35 (1975), pp. 575–94

INDEX

Index

Index

Index

Cambridge Studies in Medieval Life and Thought
Fourth series

Titles in series

Also published as a paperback